To Nigel
Very best wishes for
your 50th Birthday

from

Graham

THE FORD IN BRITAIN FILE

AN ERIC DYMOCK MOTOR BOOK

THE FORD IN BRITAIN FILE

MODEL BY MODEL

AN ERIC DYMOCK MOTOR BOOK

DOVE PUBLISHING

First published in Great Britain in 2002

by

DOVE PUBLISHING
Old West Church Manse, 31 Argyle Terrace, Rothesay, Bute PA20 0BD

Text copyright © Eric Dymock 2002

Designed by Ruth Dymock
Jacket design Andrew Barron

ISBN 0 9534142 6 4

British Library Cataloguing-in-Publication Data A catalogue record
for this book is available from the British Library

Colour separation by Colourwise, Burgess Hill, West Sussex

Printed and bound in China by Midas Printing International Ltd

Contents

Foreword

In 1903, the same year Henry Ford founded Ford Motor Company in the United States, two Ford Model A cars were shipped from Detroit to the United Kingdom – the very first Ford cars to arrive on our shores. I doubt whether even the great visionary Henry Ford could have imagined what the next hundred years would bring for his company, or just how far reaching its impact would be on the social, cultural and economic framework of the UK.

As we fast approach Ford's centenary in the UK, it is only right we should reflect on the relationship between the company and the country over the past hundred years – and what better way to do this than by focusing on the cars, both on the street and on the race track, and the commercial vehicles that have played such an important role in the Ford story in the UK.

Eric Dymock's *Ford File* is the essential reference work on Ford's vehicle heritage in our country. It traces the history of Ford from its earliest days in the UK right up to the present, and gives the most comprehensive overview yet provided to the public of the numerous Ford cars and commercial vehicles that have meant so much to many of us over the years. Whether your interest is in the Ford Model T or the Ford Model Y, the London-Mexico Rally-winning Ford Escort, or the mighty Ford Transit, all are discussed in detail in this outstanding book.

Roger Putnam, Chairman, Ford Motor Company Limited

A hundred years of Ford

Throughout its hundred years in Britain, Ford did not so much climb a social ladder as ascend a long gradient. For half of the twentieth century it was the pre-eminent source of motoring for the masses. By the beginning of the twenty-first it was flourishing, making some of the best luxury cars in the world. It began by importing Fords from America. By the 1990s it was bringing them to Britain from all over Europe. Its manufacturing base began by assembling cars in Manchester, and it carried on making the best-selling cars in the country, through industrialized component-making, to becoming a workshop for Ford throughout the world.

When it was profitable to make cars in large numbers, Ford did so. The Model T in America and in Britain was unsurpassed in one-design terms with over 15 million, unlike other claimants for the title of the most-produced model on the planet. Twenty-first century Volkswagens were far removed from the 1938 prototype, yet the Model T Ford of 1925 was much the same as it had been in 1909, with the same straight-sided frame, the

Left: **Henry's masterpiece, the Model T, the most produced car in the world. 1912 Town Car.**

same three point transverse leaf springs, the same lusty 4-cylinder side valve engine and quirky planetary transmission, the same torque tube drive to the rear axle. The only real difference lay in how it was made.

Ford did not invent the moving production line. It combined two well-established American technologies, the interchangeable componentry of the gun-making industry, and the conveyor belts used in Chicago's meat trade warehouses. Hitherto cars had been assembled on the shop floor; components brought to the raw chassis and bolted on. Putting the chassis on a conveyor and taking it to the components, rather than the other way round, reduced the time it took to build a car from twelve and a half hours to one and a half. It was ten times as fast. It demanded components machined to close tolerances, as nearly identical as possible, so that they fitted together perfectly. This was a huge step forward from making parts roughly to size, then filing and fettling them to work together in some sort of harmony. It meant that spare parts could be supplied when originals broke or wore out, and they would always fit, something far from routine in early twentieth century engineering.

But making cars quickly was not without its problems. Green or red paint took too long to dry, so to speed things up the cars

THE FORD CAR.

MODEL F. 14 Brake Horse Power.

Price as Illustrated with Side Entrance Tonneau,

£275.

Price as Illustrated with Side Entrance Tonneau,

£275.

SPECIFICATION.

Weight	1,400 pounds.
Motor	Ford 2 Cylinder, horizontal opposed 4½×4.
Wheelbase	84 inches.
Wheels	30 inches.
Tyres	3¾ inch Continental.
Maximum Speed	35 miles an hour.
Petrol Tank Capacity	9 gallons.

Colour: Dark Green, Yellow Running Gear.
Upholstering: Black Leather.

Reliable & Stylish.   **Simple & Economical.**

FORD
SHOWROOMS.

The Central Motor Car Company, Ltd.,
117, LONG ACRE, W.C.

Telegrams:
"AMMOTICAR," LONDON.

Nat. Telephones:
5011 GERRARD.
3137 do.

were sprayed with black japan enamel, leading to Henry Ford's famous aphorism that customers could have any colour they liked, so long as they liked black. Nobody can be sure that he ever actually said it. Ford accumulated a lexicon of legend and folklore like no other company on earth. The Model T and the Fordson tractor effectively replaced the horse, which had been serving mankind for generations, so by the middle of the century a car could be as familiar to a family as its sitting room. Ford cars, Ford vans, trucks and buses, and Ford military vehicles made Ford a feature of Western culture.

In Britain Ford established itself almost immediately after the creation, in 1903, of Ford in the United States. Britain was its second biggest market after the US, and ironically Ford turned out to be more stable and consistent in the United Kingdom than the indigenous motor industry. It became integrated so completely into the domestic industrial and manufacturing scene, that it was often regarded (sometimes even by Detroit),

Left: **Early days.** Before the Model T, the Central Motor Car Company imported the Model F of 1905-1906.

Far right: **The former** tramcar factory at Trafford Park assembled Model Ts from 1911 to 1913 before the installation of a moving assembly line.

A hundred years of Ford

as quintessentially British. In 1903 the nascent Ford of America had been ready to sell cars anywhere, and before the end of the year two Model As were shipped to Britain. It is not clear how or by whom, but in the prosperous post-Victorian era the motorcar was emerging as something more than a sport and pastime for the well off. The market was on the rise. The 1903 Motor Car Act raised the speed limit to 20mph, cars had to have number plates and drivers licences (but not yet tests of competence), roads improved, and London forsook the Hansom cab and embraced cars, as what were still called Hackney Carriages. In 1906 the Model N Ford at the Olympia motor show cost £165, the cheapest 4-cylinder on the British market.

Bristol-born Percival L D Perry saw an opportunity. He had been raised in Birmingham, gained a scholarship to King Edward's School, and then went to work for Harry Lawson in London. Lawson planned a motor industry monopoly, buying up patents for car designs in the fond hope of rich rewards in royalties, but by the turn of the century his schemes had collapsed. Disillusioned Perry went back to a family business in Hull, but soon returned to London and partnership with an entrepreneur who had bought the Ford franchise for Europe

for £500. Business was steady rather than brisk, sales were barely a car a month but, undaunted, Perry Thornton & Schreiber took premises in Long Acre. There was an improvement in 1905 when the more powerful Ford Model B came out, and Perry negotiated the rights for the United Kingdom, reorganising the firm in 1906 as the Central Motor Car Company.

A hundred years of Ford

Results were encouraging. American-made cars sold well in Britain; Central retailed 400 of them a year, so by 1909 Ford decided it needed a formal base in Britain. Perry was given the job of running the Ford Motor Company (England) Ltd, established March 1911, from a showroom at 55 Shaftesbury Avenue selling Models C and F. There never was a D or E. But in 1910 Lloyd George's so-called Peoples' Budget raised car tax disproportionately on large cars. A 60HP went up from £5 to £42 (£2000 in modern money), a move Henry Ford claimed was discriminatory and aimed at his principal product.

Fords were practical and solidly made and, with the Model T intended to sell throughout the world, plans were laid for assembly in Britain. Henry Ford decreed that his factories should be accessible by sea so, following a visit he made in 1912, chose Cork in the south of Ireland. It was then still part of the United

Right: **The substantial premises of 55-59 Shaftesbury Avenue from which 400 Fords were sold in the first year. The cars were unloaded from America and wheels, hood, and windscreen screwed on at nearby Vauxhall.**

Far right: **The intrepid Henry Alexander on rocky scree during his assault on Ben Nevis with a Model T.**

Kingdom and the nearest European port to America. A plant was set up with the intention of making tractors to help Britain's war effort but production did not get under way until 1919. There was an emotional connection with Ireland; Henry Ford's father emigrated from County Cork following the failure of the potato crop in 1847. For the next factory Percival Perry preferred Southampton, but settled for Manchester, and spent £2,000 leasing a 5½ acre site on a new industrial estate at Trafford Park. Model Ts were made there from 1911.

Components reached Trafford Park through the 40-mile Manchester Ship Canal. Steep port and rail charges had threatened cotton-spinning Manchester's prosperity, and until Queen Victoria opened the canal in 1894, it cost almost as much to send goods and raw materials there from Liverpool as it had to send them across the Atlantic. The Ship Canal made inland Manchester the fourth largest port in Britain after London, Liverpool, and Hull. An engineering wonder of the age, it followed the River Irwell along the north side of Sir Humphrey de Trafford's country estate. To the south, two sections of the 1761 Bridgewater Canal rendered the deer park a picturesque island, but at length Sir Humphrey grew tired of large ships passing his window, and in 1896 disposed of the entire 1200 acres for development as expensive villas or a racecourse. The canal manager had other ideas, building factories serviced by ships and new railways.

The factory Ford took over had belonged to the British Electric Car Company (BECC), builders of tramcars for towns from Ayr to Weston-super-Mare, exporters to Egypt and Argentina. BECC was bought and wound up by the rival United Electric Car Company of Preston, leaving its buildings on the corner of Westinghouse Road and First Avenue to become one of the best equipped and most productive car factories in the

A HAZARDOUS RIDGE, 4,000 FEET ABOVE SEA LEVEL

A hundred years of Ford

country. A neighbour on the canal side was a crane manufacturer, Frederick Henry Royce, (born, like Henry Ford, in 1863) who later went into cars and aero engines.

Each factory had its own railway siding and, since Trafford Park was at the hub of Britain's rail network, by 1914 Ford was distributing vehicles in covered wagons to 1,000 dealers. Sir Percival Perry said Manchester was, "The very best geographical and economic centre for our business." The workforce welcomed Ford with enthusiasm; it paid the best rates in the district, 10d to 1s 3d (4p to 6.25p) an hour although under their terms of employment, every employee had to be able to shift from trade to trade on demand.

Henry Ford had a high regard for Perry's business acumen, while laying down strict rules, such as making Ford England pay for its cars, as they were loaded on board ship in New York. No loose credit arrangements there. Freight charges for imported bodies were high, (bodywork was light but bulky) so Perry bought Trafford Park Woodworkers Ltd to make them. From 1914 Model Ts were made on moving assembly lines, just like Detroit, and local content increased until they were wholly British, which was just as well on the eve of the Great War. Morris Motors suffered badly when American-made

A hundred years of Ford

Continental engines for the 11.9HP Cowley were sunk in the Atlantic. The new McKenna Duties on imports made those that did get through uneconomic. Ford production in 1912 had reached 3,000, prices were cut, production doubled, and only 1914 frustrated an increase to 10,000. In 1925 the plant made its 250,000th vehicle and was working to capacity.

The stricture about black paintwork did not at first affect British Fords. Applying paint kept in a tank in the roof was an unskilled job at Trafford Park; each of the three coats was dried in a large gas oven and British Fords up to 1913 were blue. Then they became green with black wings. For 1914 they were to have been a rich brown but, following an edict from Detroit and the introduction of the Manchester assembly line, they were obediently black. The line was a chain conveyor 114ft (34.75metres) long that could move at 15in (38.1cm) per minute, so the production cycle for seven cars an hour was 90 minutes. At 21in (53.3cm) per minute 14 cars could be made, or faster still at 27in (68.6cm) per minute 21 cars an hour. Bodies were spray-painted in three minutes, wheels were dipped into a paint vat, then spun at high speed to throw off the excess.

Perry worked for the government during the war as Deputy Controller of Mechanical Warfare at the Ministry of Munitions,

15

A hundred years of Ford

and was knighted in 1917. Following the Armistice however he resigned from Ford over dealer policy, and encouraged by what he had seen at Trafford Park, joined the consortium setting up Slough Trading Estates. Greatly enriched in 1922 he retired to the Channel Islands.

Perry's departure was serious. Competition after the war was intense, and from being market leader Ford, now making left hand drive Model Ts following a bizarre edict from Henry Ford, dropped to fourth behind Austin, Morris, and Singer. In 1922, the Austin Seven and the reduction of import levies made the challenge even stiffer. A succession of American chief executives came and went. Following establishment of the Irish Free State, castings from the Cork plant suffered a 22 per cent duty. More production was essential to make up lost ground, but there was no room to expand the factory. Britain was explored for somewhere by the sea to build a modern car plant.

This was to be no piecemeal assembly operation. Ford wanted to build cars from scratch, from raw materials to the finished product, so every operation had to take place on site. As much as possible had to be under one roof, so in 1924 the company committed to 295acres (119.4hectares) of Essex marshland, alongside the Thames near Dagenham. A self

contained plant with services, including suppliers feeding components straight on to the assembly line, was drawn up, setting an example car manufacturers the world over would follow well into the twenty-first century.

But who was to run Dagenham? In 1928, with plans well advanced, Henry Ford was advised to take Sir Herbert Austin into partnership, but decided instead to approach his trusted friend Sir Percival Perry. Perry met him on board ship at Southampton, accepted his offer, and recruited as closest advisor, general manager, and eventual successor a former Humber apprentice A Rowland Smith.

Smith had worked with Ford's distributor in Calcutta, but was disappointed in a bid to become assistant manager at Trafford Park. He became works manager at Standard Motor Company in 1928-1929, but went back to Ford as Perry led the build-up to production at Dagenham, scheduled for the summer of 1932. Another newcomer was a young Irish purchasing manager from the Cork tractor plant, Patrick Hennessy, who in 1928 had saved a major tractor order from Russia from cancellation. Perry had installed a dynasty of senior management that would carry Ford of Britain through four decades.

Commercial vehicles were part of Ford's production plans

from the Model T and its lorry derivatives. In 1929 production of tractors was moved from Cork, where they had been made since 1919, to Dagenham. British trucks were much the same as the American ones until 1932 when a 1-ton lorry, with a 3-speed gearbox and a 3.3-litre 4-cylinder side-valve engine was introduced, built alongside the 10cwt van on a derivative of a car chassis.

Dagenham was Ford's most ambitious expansion outside America. It was four years in the planning, before Edsel Ford cut the first sod (with a silver spade that bent and had to be hammered straight again) for construction to begin on 17 May 1929, and took two and a half years to build. Ford was in no hurry. The timing could scarcely have been worse. When the decision to expand in Britain had been taken, America was on the crest of a wave. In 1927 it had nine million cars, one for every six Americans. In England the ratio was still 1 to 57, in

Germany 1 to 289. In May, as Charles Lindbergh flew the Atlantic, the 15 millionth Model T rolled off the line in Detroit. In November General Motors declared the biggest profit in American corporate history, and Ford's new Model A went on display at the Waldorf Hotel in New York, with an instant order book for 50,000 cars. Secretary of Commerce, Herbert Hoover, asserted in his annual report that American workers' wages were

Right: **100 years of Ford in motor sport. Glen Miller, development engineer at Ford Special Vehicle engineering, and Edsel B. Ford II in the Ford 1901 Sweepstakes Replica.**

A hundred years of Ford

"higher than anywhere else in the world, or than at any other time in history".

But in April 1928, within months of Hoover's up-beat assessment, share prices on Wall Street faltered. The market value of General Motors that had soared in the wake of its record profits fell just as swiftly. So did Chrysler's. In May the aircraft industry was hit by a wave of selling, Dodge and Chrysler were forced into a merger. Yet accepting the Republican Party's nomination for President, the ever-optimistic Hoover was looking forward to, "A chicken in every pot, a car in every garage." In December 1928 Ford of Britain was refloated, its £7 million capital furnished by still-confident investors.

In October 1929 Wall Street finally crashed. The domestic market collapsed and Ford's overseas investments acquired a new urgency even though the money to pay for them became scarce. Still, Maurice Sampson in *The Autocar* greeted Dagenham enthusiastically: "In a period of difficulty and world wide depression (it) is an example of heroic pluck. It lifts the beckoning hand of faith in a time when many men are losing courage. It is not being built in a period of boom when goods almost sell themselves; it is being erected in a time of depression, its purpose and mission to create international trade."

Above: **Ford in the Second World War. WOT3C 30cwt general service truck with V8 engine, 143.5in (364.49cm) wheelbase, 10.50 x 16 cross country tyres (single rears) and demountable canvas tilt.**

Right: **Sir Patrick Hennessey, 1898-1981, masterminded rebuilding Ford in Britain after the war. Chairman 1956-1968.**

Too true. Dagenham was a daring act of faith. Its capacity of 1,000 to 1,500 vehicles a day meant it replaced Detroit as supplier of Fords to Europe. It cost American jobs. Yet Dagenham was an Essex job creation scheme on a grand scale. Ford's inward investment was £5,000,000, a lot of money in 1930, for a new complex on the London Tilbury and Southend Southern Railway (SR) lines, with a London Midland and Scottish (LMS) branch connection. The completed factory covered 600acres (242.8hectares).

A 2,000ft (610m) jetty capable of berthing 12,000 ton (12,192 metric tonne) ships provided facilities for incoming raw materials and outgoing vehicles. Ford had the only blast furnace with its own coke ovens in the south of England, so made its own iron and steel. Iron ore unloaded at the jetty duly left again as manufactured goods.

Reclaiming the marshes involved one of the biggest pile-driving operations ever. Some 22,000 concrete piles between 40ft (12.2metres) and 75ft (22.9metres) were driven into the soggy ground before it was possible to erect buildings, their floors laid with eight million wood blocks. Production stopped at Trafford Park on a Friday, with the 301,980th Model T, a van, and recommenced albeit haltingly, at Dagenham the following Tuesday. Special trains took 2,000 employees and their families from Manchester to Essex over the weekend. Trains took production machinery from Trafford Park straight into Dagenham's new railway sidings, where it was unloaded into the factory, and bolted into prepared places ready to restart after the weekend. A ready-made supply of labour came from the London County Council's imaginative rehousing programme focussed on still rural Dagenham. Perry had not forgotten his trading estate principles; independent suppliers Briggs Motor Bodies and the Kelsey-Hayes Wheel Company set up facilities within the Dagenham complex.

The new plant's first product was a 30cwt (1524kg) AA truck. Car sales were still so depressed that only five came off the line in the first three months, and Percival Perry went to Henry Ford with bad news. Ford of Britain would be insolvent unless there was a new small car, unburdened by the big bore American engines that attracted British Treasury Rating horsepower tax. Work began almost at once in Dearborn, on a car coded Model 19 that would reach the market as the Model Y. By the end of the year Rowland Smith, Dagenham's general manager, was in America to see the prototype. Henry Ford, now 68, joined in to lend urgency to the project, and by the beginning of February,

A hundred years of Ford

14 prototypes were on test. It was one of the shortest gestation periods ever for any major Ford model, barely ten months elapsing from drawing board to production.

It was just in time. Ford UK lost £681,000 in 1932. The Model Y was also built in Germany in the new Ford plant at Cologne, also in Barcelona Spain, and Asnières, France but Dagenham did not get it free. Dearborn sent a design bill for $535,360 (£160,287). Following protests it was reduced to $210,000 (£62,874) but still Dagenham was not out of danger, Ford Holland had to help with £1million of ready cash, until production built up from 8260 in 1932 to 33,958 in 1933. Model Y also appeared as a 5cwt van, and Ford of Britain's fortunes were turned round to a profit of £388,170, then in 1934 to over half a million pounds. The Y was also the basis for the Fordson Tug, a curious 3-wheeler only 10ft long with a coil-sprung single front wheel.

In 1933 Fordson, previously applied to tractors, appeared on a new truck, and the commercial sector covered payloads from 5cwt to 2 tons. It extended to 6x2 Surrey and 6x4 Sussex variations on the 2-tonner, while the new V8 was still only available for a Ford 20-seat coach, and was only offered on a truck in 1936. The V8 became the regular commercial engine from then until the outbreak of war, just as the medium and heavy Fordsons were renamed Thames, a name that continued until 1965.

By 1936 the factory was making 75,000 cars a year and rising, and the style of small British Fords looked set to continue even though some features of the Model Y, like the transverse leaf springs, were handed down from the Model T. The Y and its progenitors the Anglia and Popular stuck with them for another 25 years, giving rise to a conviction that Ford technology was laggardly, as indeed it was, but in the 1930s it scarcely mattered. Price mattered more and Ford was already ahead of most of the industry with its careful attention to cost control. Design often evolved according to what could be made on existing machinery. A change of engine was only countenanced if it could be machined with the same bore centres as before. Quality was maintained by keeping change to a minimum. Ford was able to introduce the first full-sized £100 car in 1935 and still show a profit. It was also demonstrating mastery of marketing and advertising as the disconsolate family at the bus stop showed. In a famous advertisement, the son pointed enviously at the £100 Ford, small tired daughter rested on a suitcase, wife stooped under the weight of baby, husband looked

Top: **8 March 1963.**
First car produced from
Halewood, an Anglia.

"deferred payment" schemes. Ford's moves into hire purchase finance would make it as much of a bank as a car manufacturer.

Yet no car manufacturer could get by on a lacklustre range, no matter how worthy. The Model Y and its successor the Model C brought style to a sector of the market from which it had been largely absent. Themes were borrowed from the new trend-setting car of the 1930s, the Ford V8, its heart-shaped radiator and curving front bumper evoking a racier sleeker appearance that Hollywood was making familiar throughout the world.

The V8 itself was what a later era would call aspirational; that is, not many could afford it but lots of people admired it. It was too big and used too much petrol to be agreeable to large numbers of British drivers, but it lent glamour to the small Fords in a way that would become marketing strategy throughout the automotive industry. The first V8s sold in Britain were made by Ford Canada, the Empire-made label tangible evidence of Ford's United Kingdom credentials.

Still, there was no gainsaying Ford's core market, and at its annual motor shows held in the Albert Hall it introduced sturdy 8HP and 10HP saloons that became the Anglia and Prefect, together with upright vans and small trucks. They were always amongst the cheapest on the market, and although their price

uncomfortable, almost shifty. The message was inescapable. The only way the breadwinner could restore his self-respect was with a £100 cheque for a Model Y, or by taking up one of the new

A hundred years of Ford

was no reflection on their quality (that was the achievement of the most cost-conscious regime in the industry), they were nevertheless widely regarded as utilitarian, while Morris and Singer responded with homegrown rivals.

Above: **Racing driver Frank Gardner with Chitty Chitty Bang Bang made for the film on Ford Transit underpinnings.**

Far right: **Brands Hatch Formula Ford "Star of Tomorrow" race, Gerry Birrell leads Ian Ashley and Tony Trimmer.**

Dagenham persevered with civilian production as long as it could until, when war broke out in 1939 it felt itself, not without cause, in the firing line. The factory was exposed, a landmark on the flat Essex coast to enemy bombers from the Low Countries of occupied Europe, and suffered attacks and casualties. It retaliated by making 347,371 trucks, tractors, Bren Gun Carriers and numerous associated products including V8 engines used in coastal patrol boats and landing craft. At a new factory at Urmston in Manchester, not far from Trafford Park, intended for peacetime truck production, Ford made 30,000 Rolls-Royce Merlin aero engines.

As a multi-national company during the war Ford suffered some discomfort. The German factory was effectively taken over by the Third Reich so technically Ford international could have been liable for paying company tax twice in different countries. To avoid this Perry set up a temporary holding company, first in Lichtenstein, then in Luxembourg, and finally in German-occupied Channel Islands. Up to the time of Pearl Harbor, executives in Ford Germany and Ford UK could in theory remain in touch with one another through Dearborn. Most bizarrely the jig-boring machinery used for the manufacture of the crucial Merlin aero engines, had to be

Henry Ford's early days had been dogged by American interest groups, so he discouraged Perry from joining the British Society of Motor Manufacturers and Traders. Ford's discomfiture was small; it had to stage its annual motor shows away from the main exhibition hall, but by the end of the 1930s it was such an integral part of the British industry that it joined, to take part in the first post-war industry-wide motor show in 1948.

Almost as soon as the guns stopped firing in Europe in May

obtained from Switzerland. Scrupulously neutral, the Swiss maintained trade with both sides in the conflict. Each acknowledged the consequences of refusal or impediment, accordingly the huge borers had to be shipped through Vichy France, then by ostensibly neutral but avowedly Fascist Spain, en route to Britain.

Above: **19 March 1960, Goodwood. Jim Clark drives a Lotus 18 to victory in a Formula Junior race, first win for a Ford Cosworth engine.**

A hundred years of Ford

1945, car production recommenced, with much the same small models as before. It was 1947 before the V8 was reintroduced into a market desperate for cars, but fraught with difficulties over steel supplies and government restrictions. They were austere times, with Britain obliged to pay off its war debts by exporting all it could, and the demand for cars to be sold abroad (mostly from the Dominions and the near Continent) led to the abolition of the restrictive horsepower tax. This had led to a generation of unsuitable long-stroke engines, and its removal encouraged radical new designs, pre-eminent among which was the Consul and Zephyr, introduced at the London Motor Show in 1950. Technical triumphs, these were the first Fords with a unitary, monocoque bodyshell; the first car in the world to feature Macpherson strut independent front suspension, named after Ford's engineering vice-president Earle MacPherson, and the first Fords with an ohv petrol engine.

Fatigued by ten years of wartime and post-war hardship, Britain took the flush-sided American-styled cars to its heart as symbols of a return to peace and prosperity. They became as much part of the national revival as the Festival of Britain, although their design credentials lasted rather better than the tacky exhibitionism on London's South Bank. They were well

Left: **Lotus Cortina.**

Above: **World Champions.** Jackie Stewart, on the right, was associated with Ford throughout his racing career. He and Emerson Fittipaldi, left, took the title on alternate years between 1971 and 1974.

A hundred years of Ford

Above: **In 1969 Ford took to the high seas with a team of power boats using 6.0-litre turbocharged Ford marine diesel engines. This 28-foot Fairey Huntsman "Seaspray" won 16 major awards.**

Far right: **Formula Ford for two. Sports 2000 racing with Duratec HE engines.**

proportioned and, when the Zephyr Zodiac appeared two years later resplendent in its "two-tone" colour scheme, Ford went up another rung on the social ladder. "Planned obsolescence", the culture that led to annual model facelifts, was being gradually discredited as needlessly wasteful, but Ford knew it was profitable to raise the profile of a car, lift it into a new market segment by adding value, or even simply by making it bigger. Following the cars' success, employment at Dagenham peaked in 1953 at 40,000.

Ford applied its new technique often, introducing cars at bargain, so-called entry-level prices, then enhancing them, making them better equipped or faster, so that a greater proportion could be sold at premium prices. The introduction of the 100E Anglia in 1953 was at an entry-level basic price before tax of £360. By the time of the final version, long after the initial investment had been paid off by close on three quarters of a million cars, the 107E Prefect of 1961 (much the same car with four doors and an overhead valve engine) still cost only £438.

Ford's mastery of advertising was matched by its creativity in public relations. Fordspeak, a slang expression for industry jargon, later elevated the science to Public Affairs.

A hundred years of Ford

Accompanying Percival Perry on a 1930s visit to Ford's European factories had been a talented young linguist fresh from Eton, Maurice Buckmaster. Perry had been trying to create a Ford Europe, with Dagenham as its hub, but found most plants wanted to preserve their autonomy; the time for international co-operation aided by ease of travel and modern communications had not arrived, and the war would see its

postponement. During the conflict Buckmaster's fluency in languages brought him to the attention of the Special Operations Executive (SOE) and he returned to Ford afterwards as head of Public Affairs. His successors included such luminaries as Walter Hayes, a former Fleet Street editor, whose influence on Ford in Europe and the United States went well beyond the customary boundaries of motor industry PR.

In 1955 commercial vehicle production passed 50,000, and although vans and light trucks still had side-valve engines, they now enjoyed the comfort of independent front suspension and hydraulic brakes as well as the economy of Ford's first diesel. Tractors and commercial vehicles had been offered with a Perkins P6, but now there was a 3.6-litre ohv compression ignition engine of 70bhp. The 1957 Thames Trader range had synchromesh gearboxes, hypoid back axles, with all its engines Ford-made, the 4-cylinder joined by a petrol 4.9-litre 115bhp and a 5.4-litre diesel of 108bhp.

In 1960 commercial vehicle operations were transferred to Langley, west of London, and by 1965 it was making over 85,000 units including buses. From 1971 the hugely successful Transit was made in Southampton, and the D-series of forward control trucks with tilt cabs and inclined engines covered the 2 to 9-ton

Below: **Ford produced a range of light vans from the 1930s. This Mark I Escort saw service with the AA in 1971.**

Far right: **Based on a shortened 2-litre Cortina, Megastar II was a dramatic silver and black wedge-shaped car with a contrasting orange tape-stripe.**

Above: **Mark I Escort**
leapt to success.

market. In 1966, with 113,623 units, Ford was Britain's leading producer of commercial vehicles.

Landmark cars came and went. The Cortina of 1962, created under the steady hand of talented executive Terry (later Sir Terence) Beckett, as a straight-panelled middle market family saloon, grew in size and speed from the fleet "repmobile" to a

A hundred years of Ford

sophisticated car of the 1970s and 1980s. The Capri became a social icon, proof that a sporty car was no longer the exclusive property of a privileged class. Anybody could have one. And in the face of opposition from Ferrari, Ford won the Le Mans 24 Hours race, perhaps the most prestigious event on the world motor sporting calendar. The secure prestige of the classic makes of car would never be the same again. Formula 1 came to be dominated by Ford. Those in the know could see that the Cosworth-Ford evolved through the genius of Cosworth Engineering, and was paid for by Ford, but it said FORD on the cam covers and Walter Hayes's astute management of Public Affairs ensured the connection was strongly made. There were

Right: **In 1986 Ford merged New Holland with its tractor operations, its range encompassing 4wd tractors like this TW35 made in America being tested rather tentatively by the author. In 1991 Ford New Holland was acquired by Fiat, renamed NH Geotech, and relinquished its title to the Ford name in 2001.**

Left: **1971 Bristol Street Motors Mark I Escort with the RAF Red Arrows aerobatic team.**

A hundred years of Ford

Lotus Cortinas and Sierra Cosworths, and Ford cars won rallies. Ford was in the performance league; the youth market belonged to Ford, the Capri was not a flash in the pan with a long bonnet and a tiny engine. It was part of a well-constructed policy that refuted the picture of Ford as mass-market or down-market.

No self-respecting car manufacturer could do without its own research and development centre if it was to gain any sort of autonomy. Ford in Britain had been self sufficient in almost every way since the turn of the century but from time to time had had to turn to Detroit for new model design. The Mark II Zephyr and Zodiac were designed in Dagenham on the platform of the Mark I designed in America. Under Sir Patrick Hennessey, who succeeded Sir Rowland Smith in 1956, The Three Graces, as they were known established a British style and character in contrast to a less distinctive strain that was being developed in Cologne. Ford soon outgrew its existing research and development facilities and a new one was laid down close to Dagenham, at Dunton in Essex. But under government direction Ford had to expand in the provinces and Anglia production was transferred to a new plant on Merseyside at Halewood. In 1960 Ford USA bought all privately-held Ford of Britain shares, paying £7.25 for each £1 ordinary share, an estimated total of £128.5 million, as Ford-Britain engineers engaged in styling, designing and building prototypes of future models moved into a purpose-built location at Aveley (Essex).

Over the years Fords became bigger and faster. In 1967 the convergence of Ford Britain and Ford Germany was formalised in the creation of Ford Europe. Common resourcing took years. The Cortina and Taunus programmes gradually found common ground, so did the Escort and Granada, finding success throughout the 1970s and 1980s. By then the big Fords could get no bigger and by the 1990s Ford's Premier Automotive Group embraced Jaguar, Land Rover, Volvo, and for a time Lincoln. This was not to be like Ford's takeover of Ghia in

Right: **Ford's research into hybrid drives was exemplified by this 1993 1.2-litre 60kW (80.5bhp) 3-cylinder 2-stroke with an asynchronous 40kW (53.6bhp) electric motor. The hybrid Escort estate reached 65kph (40.5mph) with zero emissions before the combustion engine took over.**

A hundred years of Ford

A hundred years of Ford

1973. The great Italian coachbuilding house had been devalued as no more than a label for luxury interiors and shiny embellishments, a job that could

Left: **Ian McAllister CBE chairman and managing director Ford of Britain 1991-2002.**

easily have been done in-house. But Ford had paid £1.6 billion for Jaguar, and this time there would be no devaluing. Jaguars had to remain Jaguars notwithstanding that late Scorpio Cosworths of the 1960s could well have passed themselves off as Jaguars in almost every respect; speed, refinement, handling, ride, everything in fact except presence. They remained Fords, and with classic makes like BMW, Mercedes-Benz Volvo, and Alfa Romeo at the expensive end of the market, it was apparent that buyers demanded a prestige symbol. Yet Ford had at long last shaken off its blue-collar image.

By the 21st century Ford UK factories and offices extended well beyond Essex to Bristol, Croydon, Daventry, Edinburgh, Halewood, Leamington, Leeds, Southampton, and Trafford House in Manchester. The Dunton Technical Centre became the largest automotive design and engineering facility in Britain and one of the most advanced in the whole of Europe. It was home to over 5,000 engineers, designers, and support staff who, together with colleagues in Cologne, were responsible for design and development of all Ford's small and medium cars and vans, and commercial vehicles throughout the world. After 21 years, in 2001 the Bridgend engine plant made its ten millionth engine, investment of £225million created new jobs and doubled engine production to more than a million annually in 2004. There was investment of £345million for a new model at the Southampton

Transit factory. In 2001 Ford marked 25 years as Britain's best-selling car brand, 36 years as medium commercial vehicle market leader, 23 years as light commercial vehicle market leader.

At Dagenham, Ford's British home for over 70 years, vehicle production came to an end after 10,980,368 had been made. It remained London's largest industrial centre, and following a £375 million programme a new assembly hall increased diesel engine capacity from 650,000 to 900,000. Together with Bridgend production, one in four of all Fords world wide were being equipped with British made engines.

Right: **engines stretching to infinity. The Dagenham diesel production line.**

1908 Model T

Convinced of the Model T's worldwide appeal, Henry Ford shipped the first 8 for display at Olympia in London on 13 November 1908, then in Paris. Fords had been sold in Britain since 1903 yet the Model T represented a new approach. Among its radical features were cylinders cast in one block, and an integral engine, clutch, and gearbox. The easily handled epicyclic gear train drew inspiration from the works of Frederick Lanchester, and its principles would form the basis of the modern automatic transmission. There were 3 pedals, the middle one engaged reverse, the left one engaged low when pressed, high when released, and the right operated the transmission brake. A steering column throttle controlled engine speed, and mounting springs transversely meant only 2 were required, not 4. Transverse springs offered less resistance to side-roll and twisting on corners. American carmakers had followed European practice and put the steering wheel on the right. Henry Ford decided it was more logical, where the rule of the road was keep right, to have it on the left. He was a passionate advocate of vanadium steel, which he believed would make cars stronger and lighter, so used it for the Model T's frail looking but sturdy drop forged front axle, spindly crankshaft, and transmission parts. Henry's confidence was well placed.

INTRODUCTION 27 September 1908, produced until 26 May 1927.
BODY Various body styles; 2 or 4-seats; weight 1200lb (544kg).
ENGINE 4-cylinders, in-line; front; 3.75in (95.25mm) x 4in (101.6mm), 2896cc (176.7cu in); compr 4.5:1; 20bhp (14.9kW) @ 1800rpm; 6.9bhp/l (5.1kW/l).
ENGINE STRUCTURE L-head side valve; gear-driven camshaft; non-adjustable tappets; detachable cast iron cylinder head and block; Holley or Kingston updraught single jet carburettor, mixture adjustable by driver; low-tension flywheel magneto, low tension distributor and separate trembler coil for each cyl, standby battery for starting; splash lubrication; gravity fuel feed; 3-bearing crankshaft; cooling by multi-tube radiator (brass shell in UK until 1916 thereafter black), thermo-syphon, and fan.
TRANSMISSION rwd; epicyclic 2-speed and reverse gearbox, steel disc clutches for low speed and reverse by contracting bands on epicyclic drums; multi-disc clutch for direct drive top; propeller shaft enclosed in torque tube;

final drive passenger cars and light vans straight-tooth bevel gears; 1-ton truck overhead worm and wheel; ratio 3.64:1 high 10:1 low.
CHASSIS straight steel channel-section chassis; transverse leaf springs front and rear with radius rods; mechanical brakes, foot: contracting band on direct-drive clutch, hand: expanding shoes in rear wheel drums; steering: epicycle reduction gear in steering wheel boss, drop arm on end of steering column, transverse drag link, 1.25 turns lock to lock; 10 gal (45.5l) (12 US gal) fuel tank; 30 x 3in front, 30 x 3.5in rear, variations on balloon and straight-sided tyres; hickory-spoked artillery wheels, non-detachable, fixed rims; detachable rims after 1919.
DIMENSIONS wheelbase 100in (254cm); track 56in (142.2cm) later 60in (152.4cm); length 134in (340.4cm); width 66in (167.6cm); gd clearance 10.5in (76.2cm).
EQUIPMENT 1909-1915 no electrical system; 1915-1919 8v headlamps and horn from flywheel magneto; 1919-1927 dynamo and battery for 6v starting and lighting.

PERFORMANCE maximum speed
45mph (72.2kph) approx, claim by Ford,
15mph (24kph) in low; 27.2kg/bhp
(36.fkg/kW); fuel consumption 28mpg
(10.1l/100km).
PRICE in the US $850, reduced to $600
in 1913, $360 by 1918. UK price 1910
£220.
PRODUCTION 15,007,033 in US and
Canada, total from all sources about
16,500,00.

**Model T coachwork came
in a variety of styles. This
1909 example** (right) **could
be described as minimalist
with no doors, a tall
windscreen braced with
leather straps, and not much
weather protection except
a sketchy folding hood.**

1911 Trafford Park Model T

The success of the Model T was overwhelming; all other Fords were discontinued; yet the company was unable to meet demand. Car assembly was still a stationary affair, and with axles and chassis laid out on the floor, building one took 12 hours. Moving assembly tracks had been used in other industries, but Ford had to wait until components could be made accurately enough to be interchangeable from car to car, before adopting them. By 1914 the build-up time was cut to an hour and a half. A quarter of a million Model Ts came off the line at the new plant in Detroit's Highland Park. Ford sales in the United Kingdom flourished, but even 500 cars a year was still good business, so Ford Motor Company (England) Ltd was established at Trafford Park Manchester. The first British Ford assembled from imported parts was produced on 23 October 1911, and by the 1920s Trafford Park was making them from home grown components. Ford's Irish factory supplied chassis parts until Joseph Sankey of Hadley Shropshire could take over. Trafford Park progressed from shop floor assembly to a moving production line in September 1914. The following year the flywheel magneto was made to operate an electric lighting set, not altogether satisfactorily, since being dependent on engine speed the lights became dim when going slowly.

INTRODUCTION 27 September 1908, produced until 26 May 1927. BODY Various styles; 2 or 4-seats; weight 1200lb (544kg). ENGINE 4-cylinders, in-line; front; 3.75in (95.25mm) x 4in (101.6mm), 2896cc (176.7 cu in); compr 4.5:1; 20bhp (14.9kW) @ 1800rpm; 6.9bhp/l (5.1kW/l). ENGINE STRUCTURE L-head side valve; gear-driven camshaft; non-adjustable tappets; detachable cast iron cylinder head and block; Holley or Kingston single jet updraught carburettor, mixture adjustable by driver; low-tension flywheel magneto, low tension distributor and separate trembler coil for each cylinder, standby battery for starting; splash lubrication; gravity fuel feed; 3-bearing crankshaft; cooling by multi-tube radiator (brass shell in UK until 1916 thereafter black), thermo-syphon, and fan. TRANSMISSION rear wheel drive; epicyclic two-speed and reverse gearbox, steel disc clutches for low speed and reverse by contracting bands on epicyclic drums; multi-disc clutch for direct drive top; propeller shaft enclosed in torque tube; final drive passenger cars and light vans straight-tooth bevel gears; 1-ton truck overhead worm and wheel; ratio 3.64:1 high 10:1 low. CHASSIS straight steel channel-section chassis; transverse leaf springs front and rear with radius rods; mechanical brakes, foot : contracting band on direct-drive clutch, hand : expanding shoes in rear wheel drums; steering: epicycle reduction gear in steering wheel boss, drop arm on end of steering column, transverse drag link, 1.25 turns lock to lock; 10gal (45.46l) (12US gal) fuel tank; 30 x 3in front, 30 x 3.5in rear, variations on balloon and straight-sided tyres; hickory-spoked artillery wheels, non-detachable, fixed rims; detachable rims after 1919; wire-spoked wheels 1925. DIMENSIONS wheelbase 100in (254cm); track 56in (142.2cm) later 60in (152.4cm); length 134in (340.4cm); width 66in (167.6cm) ground clearance 10.5in (76.2cm). EQUIPMENT from 1909-1915 no electrical system; 1915-1919 8v headlamps and horn from flywheel magneto; 1919-1927 dynamo and battery for 6v starting and lighting.

PERFORMANCE maximum
speed 45mph (72.2kph)
approx, claim by Ford, 15mph
(24kph) in low; 27.2kg/bhp
(36.5kg/bhp); fuel
consumption 28mpg (10.1l/
100km).
PRICE various models,
roadster, tourer, 2-door,
4-door saloons, and town car,
chassis 1919 £170, 1921 £250,
1924 2-seater £110.
PRODUCTION 300,000.

1916 Military Model T

Almost as soon as the assembly line was installed at Trafford Park, the factory went over to war production, supplying the government with 30,000 vehicles during the hostilities. The Model T served on the Western Front, and was one of only two vehicles endorsed by Lawrence of Arabia during his campaign in Mesopotamia. The other was his armoured Rolls-Royce Silver Ghost. Blakes of Liverpool was appointed a Ford dealer in 1910, and made bodies for Model T ambulances, of which 2645 were produced between 1915 and 1920. The army devised a more aggressive role, mounting a Vickers machine-gun on the scuttle, and using the Model T as a reconnaissance patrol car. Others were fitted with flanged wheels to act as railway trolleys on narrow-gauge lines, and after the war M Kègresse evolved one into a half-track all-terrain vehicle, but it failed to find favour with the forces. The Royal Flying Corps developed a model T chemical fire engine with extinguisher canisters in the rear. Also RFC Captain Benny Hucks, a test pilot for the Airco company of Hendon, designed a mechanism to start aircraft engines off the Model T's epicyclic transmission. A chain drive from the rear of the gearbox to an overhead shaft spun the propeller, which was a good deal safer than having it swung by a hapless aircraftsman.

INTRODUCTION 1916-1918.
BODY 2-seat panel van with C-cab or open truck; weight approx 1540lb (698.5kg).
ENGINE 4-cylinders, in-line; front; 3.75in (95.25mm) x 4in (101.6mm), 2896cc (176.7 cu in); compr 4.5:1; 20bhp (14.9kW) @ 1800rpm; 6.9bhp/l (5.1kW/l).
ENGINE STRUCTURE L-head side valve; gear-driven cam; non-adjustable tappets; detachable cast iron cyl head and block; Holley or Kingston single jet updraught carburettor, mixture adjustable by driver; low-tension flywheel magneto, low tension distributor and separate trembler coil for each cyl, standby battery for starting; splash lubrication; gravity fuel feed; 3-bearing crankshaft; cooling by multi-tube radiator, thermo-syphon, and fan.
TRANSMISSION rear wheel drive; epicyclic 2-speed and reverse gearbox, steel disc clutches for low speed and reverse by contracting bands on epicyclic drums; multi-disc clutch for direct drive top; propeller shaft enclosed in torque tube; final drive light van straight-tooth bevel gears; 1-ton truck overhead worm and wheel; ratio 3.64:1 high 10:1 low.
CHASSIS straight steel channel-section chassis; transverse leaf springs front and rear with radius rods; mechanical brakes, foot: contracting band on direct-drive clutch, hand: expanding shoes in rear wheel drums; steering: epicycle reduction gear in steering wheel boss, drop arm on end of steering column, transverse drag link, 1.25 turns lock to lock; 10 gal (45.5l) (12 US gal); 30 x 3in front, 30 x 3.5in rear, variations on balloon and straight-sided tyres; hickory-spoked artillery wheels, non-detachable, fixed rims.
DIMENSIONS wheelbase 100in (254cm); track 56in (142.2cm), later 60in; length 134in (340.4cm); width 66in (167.6cm) ground clearance 10.5in (76.2cm).
EQUIPMENT 1915-1918 8v headlamps and horn from flywheel magneto.
PERFORMANCE maximum 45mph (72.2kph) approx, 15mph (24kph) in low; 34.9kg/bhp (46.9kg/kW); fuel consumption 28mpg (10.1l/100km)
PRODUCTION approximately 30,000.

1918 Model T 1-Ton

Ford's first British-built commercial vehicle was a delivery van introduced in 1912, which could carry loads up to 7cwt (356kg), and became the basis of Model T commercials that by 1924 were outstripping production of cars. The delivery van often replaced horse-drawn carts, and was adequate for light loads such as bakeries driving door-to-door, but it was too short for a proper truck. Proprietary conversions were offered from 1914 that took a chain drive to a second axle on half-elliptic springs. Payload increased to 1 ton (1016kg) and the conversion cost £92. In 1919 Ford introduced its own Model TT truck with the frame extended by 24in (61cm), a stronger back axle on the familiar transverse spring, and the choice of solid rear tyres or smaller-diameter pneumatics. Trafford Park sold complete Ton Vans as they were known, as well as the TT chassis for proprietary bodywork. Over 1,000 were bought as Post Office vans, with the chassis also used for charabancs, furniture vans, and even petrol tankers. The British American Import Company (BAICO), which carried out extended-chassis conversions, produced the Extendatonna with a 1.5-ton (1512kg) capacity, and the Supertonna capable of taking 2.5-tons (2540kg). The feeble power unit needed all the help it could get to move such a load, so an extra 3-speed gearbox provided even lower gearing.

INTRODUCTION 1918, produced until 1927.
BODY 2-seat panel van with C-cab or all-steel cab after 1924; weight approx 1540lb (698.5kg).
ENGINE 4-cylinders, in-line; front; 3.75in (95.25mm) x 4in (101.6mm), 2896cc (176.7 cu in); compr 4.5:1; 20bhp (14.9kW) @ 1800rpm; 6.9bhp/l (5.1kW/l).
ENGINE STRUCTURE L-head side valve; gear-driven camshaft; non-adjustable tappets; detachable cast iron cylinder head and block; Holley or Kingston single jet updraught carburettor, mixture adjustable by driver; low-tension flywheel magneto, low tension distributor and separate trembler coil for each cylinder, standby battery for starting; splash lubrication; gravity fuel feed; 3-bearing crank; cooling by multi-tube radiator, thermo-syphon, and fan.
TRANSMISSION rear wheel drive; epicyclic two-speed and reverse gearbox, steel disc clutches for low speed and reverse by contracting bands on epicyclic drums; multi-disc clutch for direct drive top; propeller shaft enclosed in torque tube; final drive light van straight-tooth bevel gears; 1-ton truck overhead worm and wheel; ratio 3.64:1 high 10:1 low.
CHASSIS straight steel channel-section frame; transverse leaf springs front and rear with radius rods; mechanical brakes, foot: contracting band on direct-drive clutch, hand: expanding shoes in rear wheel drums; steering: epicyclic reduction gear in steering wheel boss, drop arm on end of steering column, transverse drag link, 1.25 turns lock to lock; 10 gal (45.5l) (12 US gal) fuel tank; 30 x 3in front, 30 x 3.5in rear, variations on balloon and straight-sided tyres; hickory-spoked artillery wheels, non-detachable, fixed rims; detachable rims after 1919.
DIMENSIONS wheelbase 100in (254cm), TT 124in (314.9cm); track 56in (142.2cm) later 60in (152.4cm); length 134in (340.4cm); width 66in (167.6cm); ground clearance 10.5in (76.2cm).
EQUIPMENT 1915-1919 8v headlamps and horn from flywheel magneto; 1919-1927 dynamo and battery for 6v starting and lighting.

PERFORMANCE maximum speed
45mph (72.2kph) approx, claim by Ford,
15mph (24kph) in low; 34.9kg/bhp
(46.9kg/kW); fuel consumption 28mpg
(10.1l/100km).
PRICE various, chassis only 1919 £170,
1921 £250.
PRODUCTION 37,556 Trucks; 11,307
Ton Vans, 56,301 chassis.

**Ten years after its
introduction the price
of a 1-ton truck had
dropped to £137.**

1918 Fordson tractor and Model T racer

Fordson was the telegraphic address of Henry Ford & Son, a new company established in America to make Ford's first tractor. It had a bigger engine than the Model T and a conventional 3-speed gearbox in the back axle. The structure was a combined engine block, transmission, and rear axle, the inspiration of Ford's Hungarian-born engineer Eugene Farkas. Percival Perry was on the British Board of Agriculture, under pressure to increase food production during the war, so once the prototype Fordson was demonstrated to the board, it was immediately put into production in Cork. Henry Ford made a gift of the drawings and patent rights to Britain for the duration of the war. The fierce clutch and short wheelbase made starting off alarming and it had a tendency to rear over backwards if its plough encountered an obstruction. Cork was unable to meet the demand so the Ministry of Munitions ordered a further 6,000 from Detroit for British farms.

A Model T racer such as Frank Kulick's could average 107.8mph (173kph) on the frozen surface of Lake St Clair in the winter of 1912. His Super T was not much more than a chassis, with the engine in a box, and a pointed radiator. This was a popular feature of T Torpedo Runabouts, and the 1912 Speedster looked every inch a sportsman's car.

INTRODUCTION production 1918-1927 and 1933-1946.
BODY open; 0-doors, 1-seat; weight 2710lb (1229.3kg) 1920; 3175lb (1440.2kg) 1926 with ballast. Specification material based on Nebraska tractor test laws 1920 and 1926.
ENGINE 4-cylinders, in-line; front; 4in (101.6mm) x 5in (127mm), 251cu in (4118cc); 18.2bhp (13.6kW) gross at power take-off @ 1100rpm 1920; 22.3bhp (16.6kW) 1926; 4.41bhp/l (3.3kW/l).
ENGINE STRUCTURE L-head side valve; gear-driven camshaft; non-adjustable tappets; detachable cast iron cylinder head and block; Ford brass single jet carburettor, kerosene mixture adjustable by driver, with gasoline for starting; low-tension flywheel magneto, low tension distributor and separate trembler coil for each cylinder, standby battery for starting; splash lubrication; gravity fuel feed; 3-bearing crankshaft; cooling by multi-tube 11gal (50litre) radiator, thermo-syphon, and fan.
TRANSMISSION Rear wheel drive; 3-speed manual gearbox; worm and wheel final drive.
CHASSIS unitary bolted and cast structure of engine, transmission and axle; no suspension; drop arm on end of steering column to drag link, 1.25 turns lock to lock; steel wheels by Whitehead & Kales and Kelsey; solid rubber optional.
PERFORMANCE 64.6kg/bhp (86.6kg/kW) 1926; fuel consumption 7.32hp/hour per gallon 1920, 9.63 hp/hour per gallon 1926 (Nebraska test).
PRICE
PRODUCTION Cork, from July 4 1919: 63,001-63,200 and 65,001-65,103. 1920: 65,104 - 65,500 and 105,001-108,229. 1921: 108,230 -109,672. 1922: 109,673-110,000 and 170,958-172,000 and 250,001-250,300 and 253,001-253,552.

Right: **steel wheels with cleats on the back, the Fordson F was the world's first mass produced tractor.**

1923 Model T

Model Ts were mostly blue, green, or grey. Black was not an option until the production line created Henry Ford's aphorism about customers having cars any colour they liked provided they liked black. Speed of production was essential to meet demand and the quickest-drying paint was black japan enamel. Body-painting was done 24 hours ahead of assembly with coats of colour varnish and finishers.

Trafford Park was obliged to become self-sufficient, particularly in wartime, and radiators and wings were made on the premises, although chassis and engines were shipped from the US until 1921, when they came from Cork. The following year, after the foundation of the Irish Free State, new import duties were imposed and Manchester was encouraged once again to be autonomous. On 17 April 1925 it made its 250,000th Model T, advertised as a British car made of British parts by British labour.

By the time production ended in 1927 the Model T was more sophisticated, with a rounded nickel-plated radiator, and lower, more comfortable bodywork. Problems with the electrical system persisted, and in winter the clutch tended to seize, so cranking the engine produced unwanted creep that could run an unwary owner over.

INTRODUCTION 27 September 1908, produced until 26 May 1927. BODY various styles; 2-door; 2 or 4-seats; weight 1540lb (698.5kg). ENGINE 4-cylinders, in-line; front; 3.75in (95.25mm) x 4in (101.6mm), 2896cc (176.7 cu in); compr 4.5:1; 20bhp (14.9kW) @ 1800rpm; 6.9bhp/l (5.1kW/l).
ENGINE STRUCTURE L-head side valve; gear-driven camshaft; non-adjustable tappets; detachable cast iron cylinder head and block; Holley or Kingston single jet updraught carburettor, mixture adjustable by driver; low-tension flywheel magneto, low tension distributor and separate trembler coil for each cylinder, standby battery for starting; splash lubrication; gravity fuel feed; 3-bearing crankshaft; cooling by black-painted multi-tube radiator, thermo-syphon, and fan.
TRANSMISSION rear wheel drive; epicyclic two-speed and reverse gearbox, steel disc clutches for low speed and reverse by contracting bands on epicyclic drums; multi-disc clutch for direct drive top; propeller shaft enclosed in torque tube; final drive passenger cars and light vans straight-tooth bevel gears; 1-ton truck overhead worm and wheel; ratio 3.64:1 high 10:1 low.
CHASSIS straight steel channel-section frame; transverse leaf springs front and rear with radius rods; mechanical brakes, foot: contracting band on direct-drive clutch, hand: expanding shoes in rear wheel drums, 8in later 11in with asbestos linings; steering: epicyclic reduction gear in steering wheel boss, drop arm on end of steering column, transverse drag link, 1.25 turns lock to lock; 10 gal (45.5l) (12 US gal) fuel tank; 30 x 3in front, 30 x 3.5in rear, 4.40 x 21 balloon in 1927 tyres; wire-spoked wheels 1926.
DIMENSIONS wheelbase 100in (254cm); track 56in (142.2cm) later 60in (152.4cm); length 134in (340.4cm); width 66in (167.6cm); ground clearance 10.5in (76.2cm).
EQUIPMENT Fordor body added 1923; 8v headlamps and horn from flywheel magneto; 1919-1927 dynamo and battery for 6v starting and lighting.

PERFORMANCE maximum speed
45mph (72.2kph) approx, claim by
Ford, 15mph (24kph) in low;
34.9kg/bhp (46.9kg/kW); fuel
consumption 28mpg (10.1l/100km).
PRICE various models, roadster, tourer,
2-door, 4-door saloons, and town car,
chassis 1919 £170, 1921 £250,
1924 2-seater £110.
PRODUCTION 300,000.

Accessory firms sold
Model T-specific items
such as cradles and supports
to strengthen the notoriously
weak engine bearers. Colour
options returned in 1926.

1927 Model A 3285cc 22hp

If the Model T was a motor industry Holy Grail, a single design sold the world over, the Model A that came next showed that such universalism was no longer tenable. In Europe cars were taxed by engine size, petrol was becoming expensive, roads were small, narrow and congested, and no sooner had Ford introduced the Model A than market differences became obvious. In the United States a big 3-litre engine was fine for open roads and fuel was cheap even in the wake of the Depression. However once production got under way at Cork in Southern Ireland, and at Trafford Park Manchester, a smaller-engine option the AF (for A Foreign) had to be introduced in response to a cautious market. Model A innovations included abandonment of the epicyclic gearbox, but the transverse leaf springs, torque tube transmission, and stout channel-section chassis of the Model T remained. The body shape was not unlike the Model T although a bigger radiator and engine cowling made it seem larger. Enclosure of all rotating parts from the starting handle to the back axle was a strong sales point, in an era when whirring chains and shafts, and exposed oscillating valves were not uncommon. Top gear pulling power was robust but when shifts did need to be made *The Autocar's* testers marvelled at "a gear control simply made for caressing."

INTRODUCTION 1927 produced until 1932.
BODY 2-seat 2-door, 4-seat tourer, 2-door 4-seat Tudor saloon or coupe; 2-door 4-seat sports coupe and 4-door 4-seat saloon Fordor; weight 22.75cwt (1156kg) (2548lb).
ENGINE 4-cylinders, in-line; front; 98mm (3.875in) x 108mm (4.25in), 3285cc; compr 5.2:1; 40bhp (29.8kW) @ 2200rpm; 12.2bhp/l (9.1kW/l).
ENGINE STRUCTURE side valves; gear-driven camshaft; cast iron detachable cylinder head and block; coil ignition; gravity fuel supply; automatic multi-jet needle valve carburettor; 3-bearing crankshaft; cooling by thermo-syphon later with centrifugal water impeller.
TRANSMISSION rear wheel drive; multi-disc clutch at first, later single dry plate; 3-speed manual gearbox, synchromesh later; freewheel later; torque tube; spiral bevel final drive 4.66:1.
CHASSIS pressed steel channel frame; front and rear suspension transverse leaf spring; Houdaille hydraulic dampers; radius rods front and rear; mechanical 4-wheel drum brakes; worm and sector steering 11.25:1; 8 gal (36.4l) (9.6 US gal) fuel tank; 30 x 4.5in tyres, 21in, later 19in wire wheels.
DIMENSIONS wheelbase 103.5in (263cm); length 151.5in (385cm); width 66in (167.6cm); ground clearance 9in (22.9cm); turning circle 34ft (10.4m).
EQUIPMENT stop-lamp, hand throttle, hand ignition control, Triplex glass standard, theft-proof ignition cable, 6 volt electrical system.
PERFORMANCE maximum speed 65mph (105kph); 28.9kg/bhp (38.8kg/kW); fuel consumption 19.4mpg (14.5l/100km).
PRICE chassis £120, 2-seater £145, tourer £150, Tudor saloon or coupe £185, sports coupe and Fordor £215.
PRODUCTION in Britain 14,516; total 4,320,466.

With production under Edsel Ford's direction the "Little Lincoln" came in a variety of styles. The millionth was made within 14 months.

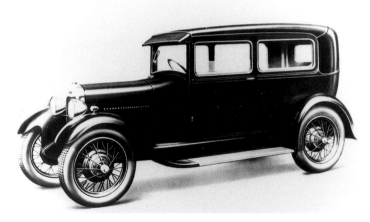

1928 Model AF

The AF engine had a smaller 3.05in (77.47mm) bore but the same stroke as the regular A, yet in a world of small long-stroke treasury-rated horsepower (HP) Eights and Tens, a 2038cc of 14.9HP was still too much of a good thing. Despite the anomalous £5 premium on the price however, it outsold the full-size 3295cc 23.8 HP Model A. Only a handful was made in the months after inauguration of the new Dagenham plant in October 1931. The number of leaves in the chrome alloy steel transverse leaf springs depended on what body it was going to have. There was no independent braking system at first; a Model A's footbrake and handbrake actuated the same mechanism, slots on the ends of the connecting rods enabling one to be applied without the other. Authorities in Britain, France, and Germany objected on safety grounds and the system was redesigned with an independent handbrake. Another early modification was the adoption of 3 instead of 4 engine mounts to reduce vibration, but the steel body remained obstinately noisy. The interior was plain with an unwinding ribbon speedometer and a central throttle pedal. Transverse leaf springing was all very well on the lightweight Model T but Ford's continued dedication to it in the heavier A (it saved money on springs) invited body roll on corners.

INTRODUCTION 1927 produced until 1932.
BODY saloon; 4-doors, 5-seats; weight 22cwt (1118kg) (2464lb).
ENGINE 4-cylinders, in-line; front; 77.5mm x 108mm, 2038cc; compr 5.2:1; 28bhp (20.9kW) @ 2600rpm; 13.7bhp/l (10.2kW/l).
ENGINE STRUCTURE side valves; gear-driven camshaft; cast iron detachable cylinder head and block; coil ignition; gravity fuel supply; automatic multi-jet needle valve carburettor; 3-bearing carbon manganese steel crankshaft, cooling by thermo-syphon, later with centrifugal water impeller.
TRANSMISSION rear wheel drive; multi-disc clutch at first, later single dry plate; 3-speed manual gearbox, synchromesh later; freewheel later; torque tube; spiral bevel final drive 4.66:1.
CHASSIS pressed steel channel frame; front and rear suspension transverse leaf spring; Houdaille double acting hydraulic dampers; radius rods front and rear; mechanical 4-wheel drum brakes; worm and sector steering

11.25:1; 8 gal (36.4l) (9.6US gal) fuel tank; 30 x 4.5in tyres, 21in later 19in wire wheels.
DIMENSIONS wheelbase 103.5in (262.9cm); track 56in (142.2cm); length 151.5in (384.8cm); width 66in (167.6cm); ground clearance 9in (22.9cm); turning circle 34ft (10.4m).
EQUIPMENT stop-lamp, hand throttle, hand ignition control, Triplex glass standard, theft-proof ignition cable, 6-volt electrical system.
PERFORMANCE maximum speed AF 54mph (87kph) *The Autocar;* 39.9kg/kW (53.5kg/bhp); 39.9kg/bhp (53.5kg/kW); fuel consumption 27.4mpg (10.3l/100km).
PRICE £185 2-door saloon; £135 chassis.
PRODUCTION in Britain 14,516; total 4,320,466.

Right: **indistinguishable from the AF, production of Model As like this 1932 example got under way slowly at Dagenham.**

1931 Fordson 30-40cwt AA truck

First to roll off the production line at the new Dagenham plant was AA4791110, a one-and-a-half ton truck. There were no major differences between British and American Ford trucks until the 1932 3-speed 1-tonner 3.3-litre 4-cylinder. The AA was based on the Model A car with a number of important differences including longitudinal rear springs (stronger for different applications) and 4-speed gearbox. The torque tube transmission introduced complications; with a fixed length connection to the back axle the spring seating had to move on bump and rebound. The A's worm drive was replaced by a crown wheel and pinion. Pressed steel wheels gave a sturdy appearance with a roomy cab, and drop-sides and tailboard that lowered, as the brochure put it, "in a trice". Payloads went up to 40cwt, and among the body options was the "Luton" van, "…of a type originally laid down for the service of the hat-makers after whose metropolis it is named." Twin rear wheels were an option on the short or long chassis to "facilitate the operation of the truck on soft yielding surfaces (such, for example, as those of a newly-opened building estate) and also reduce very considerably any possibility of skidding, or side-slip, on greasy, wet, or frost-rimed roads." All 6 wheels were interchangeable so that only one spare wheel had to be carried.

INTRODUCTION 1931, produced until 1935.
BODY flatbed truck and cab; 2-doors, 2-seats; chassis weight 27cwt (1371.6kg), vehicle 3370lb (1528.6kg) to 33.5cwt (1701.8kg); hydraulic tipper 42.5cwt (2159kg).
ENGINE 4-cylinders, in-line; front; 98mm (3.875in) x 108mm (4.25in), 3285cc; compr 5.2:1; 52bhp (38.8kW) @ 2600rpm; 11.8bhp (15.8kW)/l.
ENGINE STRUCTURE side valves; Bakelised fabric gear-driven cam; cast iron detachable cyl head and upper block; automatic ign; fuel supply cam-driven pump for tank beneath driver's seat; auto multi-jet needle valve carb; 3-bearing crank; cooling by thermo-syphon with centrifugal water impeller.
TRANSMISSION rear wheel drive; single plate clutch; 4-speed manual gearbox; torque tube; spiral bevel final drive 8.7:1; low ratio 11.13:1.
CHASSIS pressed steel 6in (15.2cm) side-member, 7in (17.8cm) with 3in (7.6cm) flanges on 2-tonner, channel frame; front suspension transverse leaf spring; rear cantilever half-elliptic graduated-thickness springs; radius

rods front and rear; mechanical 4-wheel 14in (35.6cm) drum brakes; worm and sector steering 11.25:1; 12 gal (54.6l) (14.4 US gal) fuel tank; wired-on cord 20 x 6in front tyres, 32 x 6in rear (6 x 20 all round with twin rear wheels); perforated steel wheels.
DIMENSIONS wheelbase 131.5in (334cm) or 157in (398.8cm); track 55.1in (139.9cm) front, 68.8in (174.75cm) rear; length 206.5in (524.5cm), Luton van 228in (579.1cm); width 73.5in (186.7cm); height 71in (180.3cm), Luton van 122in (309.9cm); ground clearance 8in (20.3cm); turning circle 47ft (14.3m).
EQUIPMENT 6-volt electric system; safety glass windscreen; windscreen wiper; petrol gauge, speedometer, toolkit, electrical lighting and starting.
PERFORMANCE legal max 20mph (32.1kph); 26.4kg/bhp (35.4kg/kW).
PRICE chassis only £174 swb, £181.10s (£181.50p) with twin rear wheels, to £190 lwb; truck £210 ex-works Manchester; Luton van £260, hand-tipping truck £227, hydraulic tipper £277.10s (277.50p), farm utility truck £238.

1932 Model B 2043cc and 3285cc

Still quite a big car by British standards, the Model B shared its chassis with the new V8, which also had a 106in (269.2cm) wheelbase, and had more powerful versions of the two engine options of the Model A. Chassis improvements were scant, retaining the transverse springing familiar since the Model T, but the body sheet metal was consciously designed in an appealing style, with a more rounded grille, and although not as sleek as its American counterpart acknowledged the growing importance of keeping up appearances. The petrol tank was now at the back instead of in the scuttle, and by 1934 the wings were curvier and skirted, with streamlined sidelight housings, and the instruments were placed in the driver's line of sight. The headlamp tie-bar was straight instead of curved, fatter tyres gave a smoother quieter ride, and all the improvements incorporated in later Model As such as synchromesh gears were passed on. Ford's official chassis-plate designations were Model AB for the larger engined car, and Model ABF for the smaller, titles generally discarded in favour of plain Model B. Success did not attend it in Britain where taxation and the economic depression conspired in favour of smaller cars. It was just as well that the truck side was flourishing and new small Fords were on their way.

INTRODUCTION 1932, production to 1935.
BODY roadster, cabriolet, tourer, Tudor, Fordor; 2/4-doors, 2/4-seats; weight approx 1464lb (1118kg).
ENGINE Model AB 4-cylinders, in-line; front; 98mm (3.875in) x 108mm (4.25in), 3285cc; compr 5.2:1; 48bhp (35.8kW) @ 2400rpm; 14.6bhp/l (10.9kW/l).
Model BF: 77.5mm x 108mm, 2038cc; compr 5.2:1; 41bhp (30.6kW) @ 3000rpm; 20.1bhp/l (15kW/l).
ENGINE STRUCTURE side valves; gear-driven camshaft; cast iron detachable cylinder head and block; automatic ignition; mechanical fuel pump; automatic multi-jet needle valve carburettor; 3-bearing crankshaft; cooling by thermo-syphon and centrifugal water impeller.
TRANSMISSION rear wheel drive; multi-disc clutch at first, later single dry plate; 3-speed manual gearbox, synchromesh; torque tube; spiral bevel final drive 4.66:1.
CHASSIS pressed steel channel frame; front and rear suspension transverse leaf spring; Houdaille hydraulic

dampers; radius rods front and rear; mechanical 4-wheel drum brakes; worm and sector steering 11.25:1; 8 gal (36.4l) (9.6 US gal) fuel tank; 5.25 x 18 tyres, big-hub wire wheels.
DIMENSIONS wheelbase 106in (269.2cm); track 56in (142.2cm); length 142in (360.7cm); width 67.5in (171.4cm).
EQUIPMENT 6 volt electrical system.
PERFORMANCE maximum speed ABF 57mph (91.5kph), AB 65mph (104.3kph); 23.3kg/bhp (31.2kg/kW), BF 27.3kg/bhp (36.5kg/kW); fuel consumption ABF 32mpg (8.8l/100km), AB 19.4mpg (14.6l/100km).
PRICE ABF Tudor £180; Fordor £210; deluxe £225; AB £Tudor £190, Fordor £220, deluxe £235.
PRODUCTION 8784.

Right: **extra lights, a robust-looking horn, and an AA badge on the radiator equip this Model B for long distance touring.**

1932 V8 18 30HP

Ford did not invent the V8 engine, although it may have felt like it at the time. That distinction belonged to Clément Ader, whose Societé Industrielle des Téléphones-Voitures Automobiles systèm Ader evolved the first (really two V4s coupled together), for the 1903 Paris-Madrid race. De Dion Bouton, Cadillac, Lincoln, and NAG followed, then in the 1930s Cord, Riley, and Horch made the V8 engine trustworthy. Ford's V8 was so overwhelmingly successful that the two became synonymous, and casual references to "the V8" habitually meant, "the Ford". It was generic as Hoover or Mini or Beetle, and although demand in Britain for large engines during the depressed 1930s was sluggish, show business stars welcomed the V8 along with racing drivers (Richard Seaman among them), who wanted a turn of speed together with the security of Ford's service network. A new generation of pan-European travellers found that when their other classic makes broke down (as they did), spares were problematical. A Ford V8 could be fixed as easily in Nice as in Nottingham, its reliability was exemplary, and it could negotiate Alpine passes, although the flexible chassis of the V8-18 had to be beefed up before sportsmen could enter it in the Monte Carlo Rally with confidence. Pretty racy, its engine was used in several reputable sports cars.

INTRODUCTION October 1932, production to October 1933, Treasury rating 30HP.
BODY Coupe, Victoria, Tudor, Fordor, Convertible; 2/4-doors, 2/4-seats; weight 23cwt (1168kg) (2576lb).
ENGINE 8-cylinders in 90deg Vee; front; 77.8mm x 95mm, 3622cc; compr 5.5:1; 65bhp (48.5kW) @ 3400rpm; 17.9bhp/l (13.4kW/l); 130 lbft (176Nm) @ 1250rpm.
ENGINE STRUCTURE side valves; centre gear-driven 3-bearing camshaft; cast iron detachable cylinder heads, blocks and upper crankcase unitary cast iron; engine wt 581lb (263.5kg); 1.25in (3.175cm) downdraught carburettor, coil ignition, camshaft-driven distributor; AC fuel pump; 3-bearing cast steel crankshaft; thermosyphon cooling, two belt-driven pumps, pressure lubrication by camshaft pump.
TRANSMISSION rear wheel drive; 9in (22.9cm) sdp clutch; 3-speed manual gearbox, synchromesh on 2 gears; helical bevel final drive 4.11:1, 3.78 optional.
CHASSIS steel frame with 4 cross-members; suspension by transverse leaf springs; 4 hydraulic lever arm dampers; mechanical drum brakes; worm and sector steering; 11.5 gal (52.3l) (13.8 US gal) rear-mounted fuel tank; 5.25-18 tyres.
DIMENSIONS wheelbase 106in (269.2cm); track 56in (142.2cm); length 165in (419.1cm); width 67.5in (171.45cm).
PERFORMANCE maximum speed 76mph (122kph); 0-60mph (96kph) 17.0sec; 18kg/bhp (24.1kg/kW); fuel consumption 16mpg (17.6l/100km).
PRICE Tudor saloon £230; Coupe £295; Victoria Coupe £285; Fordor saloon £260; Cabriolet £295; Fordor with sunroof £275; leather upholstery £7 10s (£7.50) extra.
PRODUCTION 911 including V8-40.

1932 Model Y

A member of the longest-running model dynasty in motoring history, the Model Y inherited features from the Model T, and passed them on to small Fords for the next quarter of a century. Except during the Second World War, Ford made a car with transverse leaf springs, a side valve 4-cylinder engine, torque tube transmission and mechanical brakes, until 1959. Yet the Y was introduced in desperate circumstances. The £5 million investment in Dagenham was not bearing fruit, Model A sales were collapsing, and although the factory was in theory up and running, it produced only 5 vehicles between its first AA truck on 1 October, and the end of 1931. Hurriedly built prototypes of the Model Y were introduced at the Royal Albert Hall London on 18 February 1932, and in 6 months the car was in production. Its heart-shaped radiator grille, windscreen sloped at 10 degrees, and curvy lines looked rakish against the angular small cars of the time. Before long it accounted for two out of every five 8HP cars sold in Britain. The production Y was given 2in (5.1cm) more elbow room, the fuel tank was located aft, fuel filler and radiator filler caps were concealed, and a fine moulded coachline was introduced to increase the effect of length. To Dagenham's relief the engine was rated at 7.9HP, making the annual road tax £8.

INTRODUCTION August 1932 production to August 1937.
BODY saloon; 4-doors, 2-doors, 4-seats; weight 1630lb (739.4kg); Tudor, 1660lb (753kg) Fordor.
ENGINE 4-cylinders, in-line; front; 56.6mm x 92.5mm, 933cc; compr 6.2 x:1; 23.4bhp (17.5kW) @ 4000rpm; 25.1bhp/l (18.7kW/l); 36.5 lbft (49.5 Nm) @ 2300rpm.
ENGINE STRUCTURE side valve; gear-driven camshaft; cast iron detachable cylinder head and block; cast aluminium sump; aluminium pistons; Zenith downdraught carburettor; coil ignition, and mechanical fuel pump; 3-bearing crankshaft; thermo-syphon cooling; splash and pressure lubrication.
TRANSMISSION rear wheel drive; 7.4in (18.73cm) sdp clutch; 3-speed manual gearbox, later synchromesh on 2 and 3; torque tube; spiral bevel final drive 5.43:1 to Sep 1933, later 5.5:1.
CHASSIS pressed steel channel-section frame with three crossmembers; suspension, transverse leaf springs front and rear with triangulated radius arms; dampers round Luvax hydraulic to 1933, pear-shaped Luvax to 1937; rod actuated 10in (25.4cm) drum brakes; planetary steering gearbox to November 1932, then Burman worm and nut; 6.5 gal (29.5l) (7.8US gal) rear fuel tank; 4.50-17 Firestone tyres; steel spoke welded wheels
DIMENSIONS wheelbase 90in (228.6cm); track 45in (114.3cm); length 143in (363.2cm); width 57in (144.8cm); height 63in (160cm); ground clearance 8.25in (21cm); turning circle 31ft (9.45m).
EQUIPMENT 6 volt electrical system; 7 optional colours; Rexine or leather upholstery.
PERFORMANCE maximum speed 59mph (94.7kph); 0-50mph (80.3kph) 34sec; 31.6kg/bhp (42.4kg/kW); fuel consumption 35-45mpg (8-6.3l/100km) at normal speeds.
PRICE Tudor £120, Fordor £135, 5cwt van £115.
PRODUCTION 135,244 all Model Ys.

14 prototypes were shipped to Europe as well as body dies, jigs, and fittings to equip Dagenham and the adjacent Briggs Motor Bodies factory for production. Transatlantic sea borne traffic included sending 3 British cars, an Austin 7, Standard 9, and Morris Minor to Dearborn for comparison with what was known as Model 19. It was changed to Model Y as part of Sir Percival Perry's plans to sell cars in Europe. Prototype engines had 2-bearing cranks, quickly changed to 3-bearing after tests.

It can be yours -

THE £100 FORD SALOON

1933 Fordson tractor

There was little change in the Fordson tractor between its introduction in 1917 and 1928, and not much after production moved to Dagenham in 1933. Built in the United States to meet the British government's needs in wartime, it was the world's first mass produced tractor, using assembly techniques learned with the Model T.

Identifiable by the perforated ladder-type radiator sides, early Model Fs, as they became known, were sold off cheaply in the 1920s to the discomfiture of the indigenous tractor industry. Production continued at Cork as the model N from 1919 until 1923, restarted in 1929 but was then moved out of the Irish Free State when production had fallen to 50-60 tractors a week. UK improvements included discarding the troublesome trembler coil ignition, increasing the cylinder bore and the size of the bearings, and the provision of a water pump. Dust was cleaned from the carburettor intake by bubbling it through water.

Dagenham tractors had a ribbed pattern on the radiator header tank and Fordson cast into the side panels. Among wartime production for the Royal Air Force, which used them for towing aircraft, were several hundred Roadless half-tracks with rubber jointed tracklaying at the back. Some even had full-length tracks round the front wheels as well.

INTRODUCTION Dagenham production February 19 1933-1945. BODY open; 0-doors, 1-seat; weight 3000lb (1360.8kg), on front wheels 1300lb (589.7kg) on rear 1850lb (839.2kg). ENGINE 4-cylinders, in-line; front; 4.125in (104.78mm) x 5in (127mm), 4380cc; Model F 20.2bhp (15.1kW); Model N 23.2bhp (17.3kW) @ 1000rpm on kerosene; 29.1bhp (21.7kW) on petrol; Model F 4.6bhp (3.4kW)/l, Model N 5.3bhp/l (3.9kW/l) on kerosene, 6.6bhp (5kW)/l. ENGINE STRUCTURE side valves; side camshaft gear-driven from crankshaft; iron cylinder head, block; Holley model 234 vaporiser for kerosene, Zenith carburettor for petrol, ignition by low-tension flywheel magneto and trembler coils, later Bosch FU4 magneto; gravity fuel feed; 3-bearing crankshaft; cooling by thermo-syphon, fan, and (later) impeller; flat-type air-washer; oilbath air cleaner from 1938. TRANSMISSION rear wheel drive; multi-plate clutch; constant-mesh; 3-speed manual gearbox; low, intermediate, and high; transmission brake; underslung worm final drive; four pinion differential. CHASSIS integral engine clutch, gearbox, final drive; front axle buffer; mechanical brakes, front & rear drums; worm and sector steering; 16 gal (72.7l) (19.2 US gal) fuel tank; wheels standard agricultural; rear spoked with cleats or spade lugs, Land Utility with cast centres for Dunlop, Firestone, Goodyear or French & Hecht tyres; cast front wheels; Rowcrop Vee formation optional, with independent pedal-operated brakes. DIMENSIONS wheelbase 63in (160cm); length 102in (259.1cm); width 62.75in (159.4cm); height 54.5in (138.4cm); ground clearance 11.6in (29.5cm); turning circle 21ft (6.4m). EQUIPMENT Dearborn grey, red oxide wheels, Cork grey or blue, Dagenham darker blue with red wheels; orange from December 1938 then green in October 1940. PRICE £130 lowest in 1920s, 1933 £155, Rowcrop £187, Land Utility £175. PRODUCTION 750,000 1917-1928.

Roadless Fordsons
sold off as war surplus
carried instructions on
dismantling the 1-ton
hand-operated crane
mounted over the front
wheels, employed for
bomb loading.

Right: Around half
of 1930s Land utility
Fordson tractors were
on fourteen spoke steel
wheels with spade lugs.

1933 V8 40 30HP

As a result of a bargain struck by Henry Ford in 1904, Ford of Canada supplied the V8-18s that introduced British drivers to the delights of 8-cylinder motoring. The V8-40 that replaced it in 1933 was assembled in Cork and Cologne, and although with better handling thanks to a stronger X-braced chassis, it sold in small numbers only. The stiff British horsepower tax and heavy fuel consumption produced the anomaly of a car that was cheap to buy but costly to run.

Specialist coachbuilders such as Jensen could make it costly to buy as well, and a team of 3 was run in the 1934 Ards TT but without much success. Jensen's links with Ford, which began with the Mistral Model Y for Bristol Street Motors, flourished with around 30 Jensen V8s made over 3 years. One was ordered, although not actually bought, by screen star Clark Gable. From there it was but a step to fully fledged Jensen cars on modified V8 chassis, of which 50 were sold at between £645 and £765 in the years up to 1941.

The V8-40's heart-shaped radiator and flared wings were reproduced in the Model Y. Available as a roadster, saloon, or 3-window coupe it may have looked as though Ford was getting above itself; not the last time this accusation would be levelled at a company making its way up in the world.

INTRODUCTION October 1932 production to October 1933, Treasury rating 30HP.
BODY Coupe, Victoria, Tudor, Fordor, Convertible; 2/4-doors, 2/4-seats; weight 23cwt (1169kg) (2576lb).
ENGINE 8-cylinders in 90deg Vee; front; 77.8mm x 95mm, 3622cc; compr 6.3:1; 75bhp (55.9kW) @ 3800 rpm; later 85bhp (63.4kW); 20.5bhp/l (15.4kW/l), later 20.7bhp/l (17.5kW/l); 145 lbft (197Nm) @ 1500rpm.
ENGINE STRUCTURE side valves; centre gear-driven 3-bearing camshaft; aluminium detachable cylinder heads, blocks and upper crankcase unitary cast iron; engine weight 581lb (263.5kg) Stromberg 48 twin choke downdraught carburettor, coil ignition, camshaft-driven distributor; AC fuel pump; 3-bearing cast steel crankshaft; thermosyphon cooling, two belt-driven pumps, pressure lubrication by camshaft pump.
TRANSMISSION rear wheel drive; 9in (229mm) sdp clutch; 3-speed manual gearbox, synchromesh on 2 gears; final drive 4.11:1, 3.78 optional.
CHASSIS steel X-braced with 4 cross-members; suspension by transverse leaf springs; 4 hydraulic lever arm dampers; mechanical drum brakes; worm and sector steering; 11.5 gal (52.3l) (13.8 US gal) rear-mounted fuel tank; 5.25-18 tyres.
DIMENSIONS wheelbase 112in (284.5cm); track 56in (142.2cm); length 176in (447cm); width 67.5in (171.45cm).
PERFORMANCE maximum speed 81mph (130kph); 15.6kg/bhp (20.9kg/kW), later 13.8kg/bhp (18.4kg/kW); fuel consumption 16mpg (17.6l/100km).
PRICE Tudor saloon £230, Coupe £295; Victoria Coupe £285; Fordor saloon £260, Cabriolet £295; Fordor with sunroof £275; leather upholstery £7 10s (£7.50) extra.
PRODUCTION 911 including V8-18.

1934 Model C and CX 10HP

Designed, like the Model Y, in America the Model C made progress in styling. This was the era of Art Deco, the Bauhaus, Chrysler Airflow, streamlined trains and a new design consciousness, so the Model C was made to resemble the successful and emblematic V8. Dagenham called it the 10HP De Luxe to distinguish it from the £100 Popular, and although the chassis had cross members and was plated to form a sort of platform, it sustained the familiar small Ford formula. There was talk of a small V8 but it never materialised. Similarity to the Model Y enabled the C to be built on the same Dagenham track. The cylinder block had the same stroke, and could be machined on the same tools, yet the De Luxe made something of a fashion statement, especially with racy 2-colour paint. After a season the CX came in, with a small but astute styling change; horizontal bars on the radiator grille made it look more like a mini-V8 than ever. Henry Ford's determined opposition to adjustable tappets remained, despite the production difficulties it imposed, throughout the life of the engine. Another persistent problem was suction operated screen wipers that almost ceased working when needed most, accelerating or climbing hills. Not exactly a failure, the Model C nevertheless failed to match Ford's ambitious sales expectations.

INTRODUCTION Model C October 1934 to 31 October 1935, CX to March 1937.
BODY Fordor, Tudor, and 4-seat Tourer; weight Tudor 1828lb (829kg).
ENGINE 4-cylinders, in-line; front; 63.5mm x 92.5mm, 1172cc; compr 6.16:1; 30bhp (22.4kW) @ 4000rpm; 25.6bhp/l (19kW/l).
ENGINE STRUCTURE side valves; gear-driven side camshaft; cast iron cylinder head and block; aluminium pistons; Ford downdraught carburettor; coil ignition; mechanical fuel pump; 3-bearing crankshaft; thermo-syphon cooling; splash and pressure lubrication.
TRANSMISSION rear wheel drive; sdp clutch; 3-speed manual gearbox, synchromesh on 2 and 3; torque tube; spiral bevel final drive 5.5:1.
CHASSIS pressed steel channel-section frame with 7 x-braced crossmembers; suspension, transverse leaf springs front and rear with triangulated radius arms; Luvax hydraulic dampers; rod actuated 10in (254mm) drum brakes; worm and nut steering; 6.5 gal (29.5l) (7.8 US gal) fuel tank; 4.50-17 Firestone tyres; steel spoke bolt-on welded wheels.

DIMENSIONS wheelbase 90in (228.6cm); track 45in (114.3cm); length 147in (373.4cm); width 57in (144.8cm); height 63in (160cm); ground clearance 8.25in (20.9cm); turning circle 33ft (10.06m).
EQUIPMENT 6 volt electrics; rear window blind, clock, driver's sun visor, roof net, interior roof light; optional leather upholstery, sliding roof, both £5.
PERFORMANCE maximum speed 65.5mph (105.1kph) Autocar; 0-60mph (96kph) 39sec; 27.6kg/bhp (37kg/kW); fuel consumption 32-35mpg (8.8-8.1l/100km).
PRICE 1936 Tudor £135, Fordor £155.
PRODUCTION 21,340 including 3699 CKD.

Right: **Body tumble-home and slatted grille gave a premium appearance to the cleverly styled Model C and CX.**

1935 Model Y

The first production Model Y had a straight bumper and short radiator, but from 1933 it took on some of the new V8's character, with a longer radiator and gracefully bent bumper. Planetary gearbox steering was abandoned; the speedometer read up to 80mph instead of 70mph, and there was an electric fuel gauge. It had better brakes and, following the introduction of the 10HP Model C, in October 1935 the price was reduced to £100. The specification was not downgraded and it became known as the Popular. There was nothing to match it. Morris had taken the lead with a £100 car in 1932, but that was a 2-seat tourer. The 1934 Austin Opal of 1934 was also a 2-seater and the closest 4-seater was the Austin Ruby at £118.

Among the optional extras offered for the Ford were a sliding roof, a luggage rack, and with customary Ford whimsy that named 4-door cars Fordor and 2-doors Tudors, a radio set called the Lissen. The £100 price came about following pressure on suppliers. Sir Percival Perry proposed that Briggs, which made the body, should reduce its price by £2 with a view to doubling Model Y sales. In the event the target was not reached, but the Popular increased Ford's share of the 8HP market from 22 per cent to 41 per cent.

INTRODUCTION October 1935, production until August 1937.
BODY saloon; 4-doors, 2-doors, 4-seats; weight 1630lb (739.4kg) Tudor, 1660lb (753kg) Fordor.
ENGINE 4-cylinders, in-line; front; 56.6mm x 92.5mm, 933cc; compr 6.2 x:1; 23.4bhp (17.5kW) @ 4000rpm; 25.1bhp/l (18.7kW/l); 36.5 lbft (49.5Nm) @ 2300rpm.
ENGINE STRUCTURE side valve; gear-driven camshaft; cast iron detachable cylinder head and block; aluminium pistons; Zenith downdraught carburettor; coil ignition, and mechanical fuel pump; 3-bearing crankshaft later counterbalanced; thermo-syphon cooling; splash and pressure lubrication.
TRANSMISSION rwd; 7.375in (18.73cm) sdp clutch; 3-speed manual gearbox, synchromesh on 2; torque tube; spiral bevel final drive 5.5:1.
CHASSIS pressed steel channel-section frame with three crossmembers; suspension, transverse leaf springs front and rear with triangulated radius arms; pear-shaped Luvax; rod actuated 10in (254mm) drum brakes; Burman

worm and nut steering; 6.5 gal (29.5l) (7.8 US gal) rear tank; 4.50-17 Firestone tyres; steel spoke welded wheels.
DIMENSIONS wheelbase 90in (228.6cm); track 45in (114.3cm); length 143in (363.2cm); width 57in (144.9cm); height 63in (160cm); ground clearance 8.25in (20.95cm); turning circle 31ft (9.45m).
EQUIPMENT 6v electrics; 2 optional colours; Rexine or leather upholstery, Lissen radio £10, sliding roof, luggage rack.
PERFORMANCE maximum 59mph (94.7kph); 0-50mph (80.3kph) 34sec; 31.6kg/bhp (42.4kg/kW); 35-45mpg (8-6.3l/100km) at normal speeds.
PRICE Tudor £100, Fordor £112.10s (£112.50), 5cwt van £115. In July 1937 the Tudor price went up to £105.
PRODUCTION 135,244 all Model Ys.

Top right: post 1933 cranked bumper for the Model Y. The mechanically identical German-built Köln had the hood irons obligatory for a market dominated by large classic touring cars.

Road test reports of
the £100 Ford were almost
all eulogistic, the only critical
note struck by The Light Car :
"It would be too much
to expect an electric screen
wiper on a car of such low
price, but more than once
during heavy rain we had
occasion to wish that this
were a £101 Ford…"

1935 Model Y Fordson 5cwt van and Tug 3-wheeler

The Model Y made a good van with 50 cu ft (1416l) of space within a floor 51.2in (130cm) long and 43.5in (110.5cm) wide. Objects 42.5in (108cm) wide x 36.5in (92.7cm) tall could be loaded through the back doors. There was no passenger seat, making access to the load space easier during door to door deliveries, but these early models were criticised for no rearward-facing windows or (a production economy measure) driver's door. Horse haulage was by no means a thing of the past in the 1930s, so mechanical varieties that could be harnessed to different vans and carts for short-haul deliveries, from railway goods-yards or docksides, were logical. A mechanical horse could make a journey with one trailer while its next cargo was being loaded-up (or unloaded). The Ford Tug was based on a design by County Commercial Cars, with a heavy-duty chassis, and the engine and front half cab from the Model Y. Made first as a Ford then a Fordson, with a single fat sprung front wheel, it had a reduction gearbox behind the 8HP engine and the steering drop-arm mounted in the stout chassis side member behind a bulge on the side of the bodywork, effectively a Model Y shorn of its wings. The Tug made its debut at the Royal Albert Hall on October 17 1935 as, "an entirely new transport unit."

INTRODUCTION August 1932 production to August 1937, Tug September 1935 to September 1937. BODY van; 1 (later 2)-doors, 1-seat (passenger seat optional); weight 1316lb (596.9kg), Tug 14cwt (711kg). ENGINE 4-cylinders, in-line; front; 56.6mm x 92.5mm, 933cc; compr 6.2 x:1; 23.4bhp (17.5kW) @ 4000rpm; 25.1bhp/l (18.8kW/l); 36.5 lbft (49.5 Nm) @ 2300rpm. ENGINE STRUCTURE side valve; gear-driven cam; cast iron detachable cyl head and block; cast aluminium sump; aluminium pistons; Zenith downdraught carburettor; coil ign, and mechanical fuel pump; 3-bearing crank; thermo-syphon cooling; splash and pressure lubrication. TRANSMISSION rwd; 7.38in (187mm) sdp clutch; 3-speed manual gearbox, later synchromesh on 2 and 3; torque tube, roller bearings; spiral bevel final drive; 5.5:1. Tug reduction gearbox behind engine and final drive 4.11:1. CHASSIS pressed steel channel-section frame with three crossmembers; Tug heavy duty A-frame; suspension, transverse 8-leaf springs front, 12-leaf rear with triangulated radius arms; dampers Ford-made; rod actuated 10in (25.4cm) drum brakes (Tug rear wheels only 12in (30.5cm) drums); Burman worm and nut steering; 6.5 gal (29.5l) (7.8 US gal) rear fuel tank; tyres 4.50-17, Tug front 18in x 7in oval section; steel spoke welded wheels. DIMENSIONS wheelbase 90in (228.6cm); track 45in (114.3cm); length 135.8in (344.8cm); width 54in (137.2cm); height 65in (165.1cm); ground clearance 8.4in (21cm); turning circle 31ft (9.5m), Tug 21ft (6.4m), with trailer 16ft (4.9m). EQUIPMENT 6v electrics; 7 colours, Rexine upholstery; Tug vineyard green; front bumper semi-circular spring steel. Optional standard 2-wheel trailer, 131in (332.7cm) Fordson truck dropside body. PERFORMANCE maximum 59mph (94.7kph), Tug maximum legal 20mph (32.1kph), design top speed 24mph (38.5kph); 0-30mph (48.2kph) 10.5sec; 24.4kg/bhp (34.1kg/kW); 40mpg (7.1l/100km) *Commercial Motor*, 18mpg (15.7l/100km) *Modern Transport*. PRICE 5cwt van £115, Tug £185. PRODUCTION 135,244 all Model Ys, 111 Tugs.

1935-1937 van, truck, and bus

By the mid 1930s Ford's commercial range went from 5cwt to 3 tons and soon to 5 tons. There were 4-cylinder (or 4-cylindered as brochures said), and V8s of 2 sizes, 3.6-litre for power, 2.2-litre for economy. The 4-cylinder Model A was straight out of the car with 40bhp (29.8kW) @ 2200rpm, installed in vans and trucks without modification, the only concession to its new role being a 4-speed gearbox. From 1933 6 rear wheels were an option on the 131.5in (334cm) and 157in (398.8cm) wheelbases. These were developed jointly with County Commercial Cars Ltd of Fleet, with the drive to one axle or both with double spiral bevel drives, continuing as Surrey or Sussex models up to the war. The commercials' straight-sided chassis frame, inherited from the American designs with which Ford started the 1930s, was used for any number of applications, tall vans, dropside trucks, tippers, or from 1932 as a 20-seat coach, which was the first commercial application of the V8 engine. The 6in (15.2cm) side-members were increased to 7in (17.8cm) with 3in (7.6cm) flanges on the 2-tonner and went up to 17in (43.2cm) in places on the heaviest 6-wheelers. Forward-control trucks had been available as proprietary conversions for operators wanting more space for payload, until in 1934 the first production forward control Ford entered service as the BBE 2-tonner.

Dagenham commercial vehicles 1928-1939

1928-1932 A van 3.2-litre 4-cyl 10cwt
1928-1932 AF van 2.0-litre 4-cyl 10cwt
1928-1935 AA and AAF 3.2-litre 4-cyl 1ton & 30cwt trucks, vans, chassis
1932-1935 B van 3.2-litre 4-cyl 10-12cwt
1932-1935 BF van 2.0-litre 4-cyl 10-12cwt
1932-1936 BB and BBF 3.2-litre 4-cyl; 3.6-litre V8 2-tonner
1933-1935 BB Sussex 3.2-litre 4-cyl and 3.6-litre V8 6-wheeler double drive
1933-1935 BB Surrey 3.2-litre 4-cyl and 3.6-litre V8 6-wheeler single drive
1934-1938 BBE 3.6-litre V8 2-ton forward control
1933-1937 Model Y van 933cc 4-cyl 5cwt
1935 Model 50 3.6-litre V8 15cwt van
1935 Model 60E 2.2-litre V8 15cwt van
1936 Model 51 3.6-litre V8 2- and 3-tonners
1936 Model 51 Sussex 3.6-litre V8 6-wheeler double drive
1936 Model 51 Surrey 3.6-litre V8 6-wheeler single drive
1936-1939 Model 61 2.2-litre V8 25cwt forward control
1936 Model 67 V8 15cwt van
1936-1937 Tug 933cc 4-cylinder 3-wheeler mechanical horse
1937-1939 933cc 4-cyl 5cwt van
1937 Model 73 2.2-litre V8 15cwt van
1937 Model 77 3.6-litre V8 15cwt van
1937 Model 79 3.2-litre 4-cy, 3.6-litre V8 2- and 4-tonner
1937 Model 79 Sussex 3.2-litre 4-cyl & 3.6-litre V8 6-wheeler double drive
1937 Model 79 Surrey 3.2-litre 4-cyl & 3.6-litre V8 6-wheeler single drive
1937-1946 Model 7V 3.2-litre 4-cyl & 3.6 V8 2- 3- 5-ton forward control
1937-1939 Model 7V Sussex 3.2-litre 4-cyl & 3.6 V8 6-wheel double drive
1937-1939 Model 7V Sussex 6-wheeler forward control.

Dagenham commercial vehicles model year 1936-1937

Details and prices

4-cyl 5cwt light van 90in wb £112 road tax £10
V8 15cwt light van 112in wb £220 road tax £20 (also with 2.2-litre V8)
V8 25cwt truck 106in wb £200 road tax £20
V8 25cwt van 106in wb dual rear wheels £240 road tax £20
4-cyl or V8 2-ton truck 131.5in wb dual rear wheels £236 road tax £25
4-cyl or V8 hand tipper 131.5in wb dual rear wheels £246 road tax £30
4-cyl or V8 hydraulic 3-way 2ton tipper 131.5in wb dual rears £294 tax £30
Forward control V8 2ton truck 118in wb £250 road tax £25
Forward control V8 2ton van 118in wb £286 road tax £25
4-cyl or V8 3-ton truck 131.5in wb dual rear wheels £271 road tax £30
4-cyl or V8 3-ton hydraulic 3-way tipper 131.5in wb dual rears £345 tax £30
4-cyl or V8 3-ton hydraulic end tipper 131.5in dual rears £325 road tax £30
4-cyl or V8 3-ton truck 143.5in wb dual rear wheels £295 road tax £30
Fordson-Surrey-Sussex V8 118in wb forward control 131.5in normal control,
    6-wheeled specially built to order.

Right: **The BBE forward
control 2-ton truck was
the first to dispense with
the transverse front spring.
Shackles for the front springs**
(bottom right) **were at the
front of the chassis. 1936
models had the V8** (bottom
far right) **with 4-speed
crash change gearbox.**

1935 V8 48 30HP

A short-lived model introduced 7 months behind Detroit, the first V8 made at Dagenham was also the first to have an all-purpose van-like body, known as Shooting Brake or Utility depending on what part of the market it was aiming at. The good-looking varnished wood body demonstrated Ford's ambition to go for quality clientele, to counterbalance its established reputation for low-cost economical cars. With a family resemblance to the Model C and CX with its broad radiator grille with horizontal bars, the V8-48 had the engine up close to the front wheel centre line, increasing room inside and bringing the occupants within the wheelbase. This was an innovation Ford described as "centrepoise riding". The sweeping wings and rounded lines "strike a very modern note without being blatant," according to *The Motor*, and the seat cushions were softer, "to damp out road shocks". An all-synchromesh gearbox was a welcome improvement, and touring saloons de luxe had additional built-in luggage containers, against the ordinary saloons' sweeping tail with externally mounted spare wheel. Special-bodied V8s for 1935 included Dagenham Motors' special saloon at £395 and a 2-door sports saloon with fat tyres, extravagant bonnet louvres, spotlights and ornate bonnet mascot at £425.

INTRODUCTION March to November 1935.
BODY Tudor and Fordor saloons 5-6-seat, cabriolet 2-seat, coupe 2-seat, utility 4-door 5-6-seat; coupe weight 23cwt (1168kg) (2576lb).
ENGINE 8-cylinders in 90deg Vee; front; 77.8mm x 95mm, 3622cc; compr 6.3:1; 80bhp (59.6kW) @ 3500 rpm; 22.1bhp/l (16.5 kW/l); 140 lbft (190Nm) @ 1500rpm.
ENGINE STRUCTURE side valves; centre gear-driven 3-bearing camshaft; aluminium detachable cylinder heads, blocks and upper crankcase unitary cast iron; engine weight 581lb (263.5kg); Stromberg 48 twin choke downdraught carburettor, coil ignition, camshaft-driven distributor; mechanical fuel pump; 3-bearing cast steel crankshaft; thermosyphon cooling, 2 belt-driven pumps, pressure lubrication by camshaft pump.
TRANSMISSION rear wheel drive; 9in (229mm) sdp clutch; 3-speed manual all-synchromesh gearbox; final drive 4.11:1.
CHASSIS steel X-braced frame with 4 cross-members; suspension by transverse leaf springs; 4 hydraulic lever arm dampers; mechanical drum (non-scoring alloy) brakes; worm and sector steering; 11.5 gal (52.3l) (13.8 US gal) rear-mounted fuel tank; 6.00-16 tyres.
DIMENSIONS wheelbase 112in (284.5cm); track 56in (142.2cm); length 183in (464.8cm); width 67.5in (171.45cm).
EQUIPMENT 6-volt electrics, cigar lighter, smokers' companion, self-cancelling trafficators, leather upholstery £7 10s (£7.50) extra, twin horns.
PERFORMANCE maximum speed 86mph (138kph); 0-60mph (96kph) 17sec; 14.6kg/bhp (19.6kg/kW); fuel consumption 16mpg (17.6l/100km).
PRICE Touring Tudor £235, Touring Fordor £250, Cabriolet £240, Coupe £230, Utility £245. Rated at 30HP, the 3622cc V8 attracted an annual tax of £22.10s (£22.50), almost 10 per cent of its purchase price.
PRODUCTION 616.

Henry Ford called his
V8 "My last mechanical
triumph," so Ford Germany
equipped this 1935 V8 48
with suitably spectacular
bodywork. British V8s
on show at Ford's Albert
Hall exhibitions were
similarly equipped.

1935 V8 60 22HP

Ford's traditional antipathy to trade associations persisted into the 1930s, preventing it joining the Society of Motor Manufacturers and Traders (SMMT), which organised the London Motor Show. As a result, from 1928 to 1938 Ford held its own motor exhibition in the autumn, coinciding with the SMMT show, usually in the Royal Albert Hall on Kensington Gore. At the 1935 event, in acknowledgment of the dire economic circumstances the country faced, Ford introduced the £100 Model Y and a new 22HP V8 with the annual Road Fund tax cut to £16 10s (£16.50). The V8-60 was outwardly identical to the V8-48 but the crucial cylinder bore, on which the Treasury RAC horsepower was calculated, was reduced from 77.8mm to 66mm. The stroke was shorter as well bringing the capacity to 2227cc. The engine had been designed for the French market but it was pressed into service with some success in Britain, with lower gearing, so the resulting car was by no means slow. The transverse springs were now rubber-mounted, the rear one behind the back axle. Coupes and Cabriolets were 2-seaters with dickey seats in the sweeping tail. For 1936 Jensen had a stylish 4-seat open sports, with deeply cutaway doors, on a shortened 22HP chassis sold through Bristol Street Motors. The Harris V8 special saloon with hide upholstery was £575.

INTRODUCTION September 1935, produced until June 1936.
BODY saloons Tudor and Fordor 5-6-seat, cabriolet 2-seat, roadster 2-seat, coupe 2-seat, utility 4-door 5-6-seat; coupe weight 23cwt (1168kg) (2576lb).
ENGINE 8-cylinders in 90deg Vee; front; 66mm x 81.28mm, 2227cc; compr 6.3:1; 60bhp (44.7kW) @ 3500 rpm; 26.9bhp/l (20.1kW/l).
ENGINE STRUCTURE side valves; centre gear-driven 3-bearing camshaft; aluminium detachable cylinder heads, 17-stud blocks and upper crankcase unitary cast iron; engine weight 581lb (263.5kg); Stromberg 48 twin choke downdraught carburettor, coil ignition, camshaft-driven distributor; electric fuel pump; 3-bearing cast steel crankshaft; thermosyphon cooling, two belt-driven pumps, pressure lubrication by camshaft pump.
TRANSMISSION rear wheel drive; 9in (229mm) sdp clutch; 3-speed manual all-synchromesh gearbox; final drive 4.77:1.
CHASSIS steel X-braced frame with 4 cross-members; suspension by transverse leaf springs; 4 hydraulic lever arm dampers; mechanical drum (non-scoring alloy) brakes; worm and sector steering; 11.5 gal (52.3l) (13.8 US gal) rear-mounted fuel tank; 6.00-16 tyres.
DIMENSIONS wheelbase 112in (284.5cm); track 56in (142.2cm); length 183in (464.8cm); width 67.5in (171.45cm).
EQUIPMENT 6-volt electrics, cigar lighter, smokers' companion, self-cancelling trafficators, leather upholstery £7 10s (£7.50) extra, twin horns.
PERFORMANCE maximum 76mph (122kph); 19.5kg/bhp (26.1kg/kW); 20-25mpg (14.1-11.3l/100km).
PRICE saloon 2-door £215, 4-door £230, Touring saloon £235, Coupe, Roadster £215, Tourer £225, Utility £230.
PRODUCTION 2807.

Right: **A small-bore engine and all-up weight well over a ton did not provide much in the way of speed, but the big Ford had plenty of room inside.**

1936 V8 68 30HP

In America most marketing plans of the 1930s set off the ritual of annual facelifts. The V8 68 was not much more than a well-groomed V8 60, yet it was the most successful of the entire pre-war series of 30HP cars.

One determinedly US feature was the progressive fall in the steering ratios of all the V8s between 1932 and 1939. The Model 18 of 1932 had been quick and responsive but, as the demand for lighter steering grew, 5 turns from lock to lock, as with this car, became commonplace. Its great virtue of engine flexibility remained however, and *The Autocar* of 3 July 1936 enthused that it was: "…almost fantastically fast and lively for its price … (yet) figures alone do not convey the whole meaning. A V8 … is virtually a unique motoring experience. It suits the laziest driving mood with its … top gear running abilities."

Drivers in the 1930s did not enjoy changing gear and the lusty torque of the V8 engine enabled first and second to be engaged for the first few yards, "…and then the engine will at once pick up and pull away smoothly on the quite high top gear ratio. It runs thereafter, even in slow-moving traffic and on right-angle corners, without the slightest need for a change down to be made." Praise indeed.

INTRODUCTION Nov 1935, produced until December 1936.
BODY saloons Tudor and Fordor 5-6-seat, cabriolet 2-seat, coupe 2-seat, utility 4-door 5-6-seat; coupe weight 23cwt (1168kg) (2575.9lb), 4 door touring saloon 28cwt (1422.4kg) (3135.8lb).
ENGINE 8-cylinders in 90deg Vee; front; 77.8mm x 95mm, 3622cc; compr 6.3:1; 80bhp (59.6kW) @ 3500 rpm; 22.1bhp/l (16.5kW/l); 140 lbft (190Nm) @ 1500rpm.
ENGINE STRUCTURE side valves; centre gear-driven 3-bearing camshaft; aluminium detachable cylinder heads, blocks and upper crankcase unitary cast iron; engine weight 581lb (263.5kg); Stromberg 48 twin choke downdraught carburettor, coil ignition, camshaft-driven distributor; mechanical fuel pump; 3-bearing cast steel crankshaft; thermosyphon cooling, two belt-driven pumps, pressure lubrication by camshaft pump.
TRANSMISSION rear wheel drive; 9in (229mm) sdp clutch; 3-speed manual gearbox with synchromesh 2 and 3; final drive 4.11:1.

CHASSIS steel X-braced frame with 4 cross-members; suspension by transverse leaf springs; 4 hydraulic lever arm dampers; mechanical drum (non-scoring alloy) brakes; worm and sector steering; 11.5 gal (52.3l) (13.8 US gal) rear-mounted fuel tank; 6.00-16 tyres.
DIMENSIONS wheelbase 112in (284.5cm); track 55in (139.7cm); length 185in (470cm); width 67.5in (171.5cm); height 68in (172.77cm) touring saloon; ground clearance 8.5in (21.6cm); turning circle 40ft (12.2m).
EQUIPMENT 6-volt electrics, cigar lighter, smokers' companion, self-cancelling trafficators, leather upholstery £6 extra, twin horns.
PERFORMANCE maximum speed 83.9mph (134.7kph) *The Autocar*; 0-60mph (96kph) 17.5sec; 14.6kg/bhp (19.6g/kW); fuel consumption 18mpg (15.7l/100km).
PRICE Chassis £195, Touring Tudor £235, Touring Fordor £250, Cabriolet £240, Coupe £230, Utility £245.
PRODUCTION 4527.

1937 7Y Eight

First British Ford with a British-designed body, the Model Y replacement defined the entry level to the range for the next 20 years. The 7Y was rated at 8HP, the closely related 7W announced 4 months earlier 10HP. The 7Y was on the shorter wheelbase of the original Model Y, with a one-piece grille, instead of the 7W's three vertical slats.

"Completely new" was a relative term at Ford, and while steel slotted wheels and bodywork with a crease in the front door to make it look longer were new, much of the specification was familiar. The chassis was stronger, with steel panelling under the rear seat and floor, and the springs were longer for a more resilient ride. It was still firm however, and the car had put on weight, 105lb (47.6kg), so it was less lively. A 5cwt (25kg) van had the front of the saloon, with the rear in sheet steel on a wooden frame, with a wooden floor. It weighed under 12cwt (609.6kg) and had 52cu.ft (1473 litres) of load space.

The GPO was a big customer, and among the special bodies built on the 7W chassis was one by Bonallack & Son of East London. First displayed at the Smithfield Show, its Utilecon was an ancestor of many years' small Ford estate cars and camper vans.

INTRODUCTION August 1937 production to September 1939.
BODY saloon; 2-doors, 4-seats; weight 1735lb (787kg).
ENGINE 4-cylinders, in-line; front; 56.6mm x 92.5mm, 933cc; compr 6.2:1; 23.4bhp (17.5kW) @ 4000rpm; 25.1bhp/l (18.7kW/l); 36.5 lbft (49.5Nm) @ 2300rpm.
ENGINE STRUCTURE side valve; gear-driven camshaft; cast iron detachable cylinder head and block; aluminium pistons; Zenith downdraught carburettor; coil ignition, and mechanical fuel pump; 3-bearing counterbalanced crankshaft; thermo-syphon cooling; splash and pressure lubrication.
TRANSMISSION rear wheel drive; 7.375in (18.73cm) sdp clutch; 3-speed manual gearbox, synchromesh on 2; torque tube; spiral bevel final drive 5.5:1.
CHASSIS pressed steel channel-section frame with three crossmembers and central box-section; suspension, transverse leaf springs front and rear with triangulated radius arms; pear-shaped Luvax dampers; rod actuated 8in (203mm) front 7in (178mm) rear drum brakes; Burman worm and nut steering; 6.5 gal (29.5l) (7.8 US gal) rear fuel tank; 4.50-17 Firestone tyres; steel spoke welded wheels.
DIMENSIONS wheelbase 90in (228.6cm);track 45in (114.3cm); length 148in (375.9cm);width 57in (144.8cm); height 63in (160cm); ground clearance 6.25in (15.9cm); turning circle 36ft (11m).
EQUIPMENT 6volt electrical system; fixed-rate charging; 10amps at 30mph; leathercloth upholstery, leather trim and sliding roof optional.
PERFORMANCE maximum speed 59mph (94.7kph); 0-50mph (80.3kph) 35sec; 33.6kg/bhp (45kg/kW); fuel consumption 35-45mpg (8-6.3l/100km) at normal speeds.
PRICE standard 2-door £117.10s (£117.50), de luxe £127.10s (£127.50).
PRODUCTION 59,598 plus 5,500CKD.

1937 7W Ten

The new Ten announced in April 1937, replacing the Model C, had the same stiffer frame as the Eight. The middle was braced by a strong welded and riveted box-section that included the propeller shaft tunnel, and there was an extra 4in (10.2cm) of wheelbase to provide for a 4-door body. The robust frame also encouraged the introduction of an open 4-seat Tourer with cutaway doors. A roadster had been planned for the Model Y back in 1932, and some were built by outside coachbuilders, but this Tourer, *The Motor* thought, would "appeal to open car enthusiasts (to be) used with a measure of success in trials and competitions." Innovations included front-hinged doors, which had hitherto been difficult to hang on raked windscreen pillars, but were safer and gave better access to the back on 2-door cars.

In August the 7W Ten was joined by a de luxe version of the Eight. Both had 2 windscreen wipers, a facia clock, metal spare wheel cover, interior light, map pocket, chrome hubcaps and windscreen frame, trafficators, glovebox lid, and opening windscreen. Running boards, which were a sort of step under the door dating from an era of taller cars, ran from the trailing edge of the front wing to the leading edge of the rear wing, and were done away with in 1938 for non-de luxe cars.

INTRODUCTION August 1937 production to September 1939. BODY saloon, 2-doors, 4-doors, 4-seats; Tourer, 2-door 4-seats; weight (2-door) 1735lb (787kg). ENGINE 4-cylinders, in-line; front; 63.5mm x 92.5mm, 1172cc; compr 6.6 x:1; 30bhp (22.4kW) @ 4000 rpm; 25.6bhp/l (19.1kW/l); 60 lbft (81Nm) @ 2000rpm. ENGINE STRUCTURE side valve; gear-driven camshaft; cast iron detachable cylinder head and block; aluminium pistons; Zenith downdraught carburettor; coil ignition, mechanical fuel pump; 3-bearing counterbalanced crankshaft; thermo-syphon cooling; splash and pressure lubrication. TRANSMISSION rear wheel drive; 7.37in (18.73cm) sdp clutch; 3-speed manual gearbox, synchromesh on 2; torque tube; spiral bevel final drive 5.5:1. CHASSIS pressed steel channel-section frame with three crossmembers and central box-section; suspension, transverse leaf springs front and rear with triangulated radius arms; pear-shaped Luvax dampers; rod actuated 10in (254mm) drum brakes; Burman worm and nut steering; 6.5 gal (29.5l) (7.8 US gal) rear fuel tank; 4.50-17 Firestone tyres; steel spoke welded wheels. DIMENSIONS wheelbase 94in (238.8cm); track 45in (114.3cm); length 156in (396.24cm); width 57in (144.8cm); height 63in (160cm); ground clearance 6.25in (15.9cm); turning circle 36ft (10.97m). EQUIPMENT 6volt electrical system; fixed-rate charging; 10amps at 30mph; leathercloth upholstery, leather trim and sliding roof optional. PERFORMANCE maximum 59mph (94.7kph); 0-50mph (80.26kph) 35sec; 26.2kg/bhp (35.1kg/bhp); 35-45mpg (8-6.3l/100km) at normal speeds. PRICE 2-door £150, 4-door and Tourer £162 10s (£162.50). PRODUCTION 59,598 plus 5,500CKD all 7Y and 7W.

Right: Enduring shape. The silhouette of the small Ford of the late 1930s was to last so long it came to be known as Early English Perpendicular.

1937 V8 78 30HP

By 1937 it looked as though the Ford V8 was going to emulate the Lincoln Zephyr V12 in appearance. Perhaps the classiest-looking of all the pre-war V8s, the Model 78's front strongly resembled the Zephyr, with sloping headlamps sunk in the wings either side of a stylish "fencer's mask" radiator grille. It conformed to a fashionable trend that was making American cars much admired in Europe, and the home grown Ford competed with imported Hudson Terraplane (from £299), Dodge (£345), Oldsmobile, Chrysler, Packard, Pontiac, Buick and the Lincoln itself from within the Ford orbit. The Zephyr with a V12 engine, essentially a Ford V8 with 4 more cylinders, started at £475 under the handicap of a Treasury rating of 37HP and annual tax of £22 10s (£22.50). A 6-cylinder Nash cost £445 and a 4-cylinder Willys Coupe £252. The V8 78 was regarded as vaguely mid-Atlantic, British made perhaps, but by an American company in an American idiom. It was profitable, for while import duty was responsible for a large part of the price difference between home and imported cars, a V8 could cost as little as $500 (£100) in America and $1300 (£260) in Britain. Henry Ford still would not sanction a change to hydraulic brakes, but with the 78 rod operation gave way to cable, without much effect on comfort or efficiency.

INTRODUCTION January 1937, produced until June 1938.
BODY saloons Tudor and Fordor 5-6-seat, cabriolet 2-seat, coupe 2-seat, utility 4-door 5-6-seat; coupe weight 23cwt (1168kg) (2575.9lb), 4 door touring saloon 28cwt (1422.4kg) (3135.8lb).
ENGINE 8-cylinders in 90deg Vee; front; 77.8mm x 95mm, 3622cc; compr 6.3:1; 80bhp (59.6kW) @ 3500 rpm; 22.1bhp/l (16.5kW/l); 140 lbft (190Nm) @ 1500rpm.
ENGINE STRUCTURE side valves; centre gear-driven 3-bearing camshaft; aluminium detachable cylinder heads, blocks and upper crankcase unitary cast iron; engine weight 581lb (263.5kg); Stromberg 48 twin choke downdraught carburettor, coil ignition, camshaft-driven distributor; mechanical fuel pump; 3-bearing cast steel crankshaft; thermosyphon cooling, two belt-driven pumps, pressure lubrication by camshaft pump.
TRANSMISSION rear wheel drive; 9in (229mm) sdp clutch; 3-speed manual gearbox with synchromesh 2 and 3; final drive 4.11:1.
CHASSIS steel X-braced frame with 4 cross-members; suspension by transverse leaf springs; 4 hydraulic lever arm dampers; mechanical drum (non-scoring alloy) brakes; worm and sector steering; 11.5 gal (52.3l) (13.8 US gal) rear-mounted fuel tank; 6.00-16 tyres.
DIMENSIONS wheelbase 112in (284.5cm); track 55in (139.7cm); length 185in (470cm); width 67.5in (171.45cm); height 68in (172.7cm) touring saloon; ground clearance 8.5in (21.6cm); turning circle 40ft (12.2m).
EQUIPMENT 6-volt electrics, cigar lighter, smokers' companion, self-cancelling trafficators, leather upholstery £6 extra, twin horns.
PERFORMANCE maximum speed 87mph (139.7kph); 0-60mph (96kph) 17sec; 14.6kg/bhp (19.6kg/kW); fuel consumption 16mpg (17.6l/100km).
PRICE October 1937: Chassis £195, Touring Tudor £245, Touring Fordor £260, Club Cabriolet £255, Coupe £235, Club Coupe £250, Utility £280.
PRODUCTION 4331.

1937 V8 62 22HP 2227cc

Most prolific of the pre-war V8s, the 62 reinforced the French connection created by putting the Alsace engine of the Matford in the V8 60, adopting the Matford body as well but with rear-hinged doors. The Model 62 had a revised chassis frame, it was 10in (25.4cm) shorter than before and the roofline was 2.5in (6.4cm) lower. The definitive British-made V8 of the years leading up to the war, a few were even made in 1941, and many were impressed into service as WOA staff cars for the military. Early cars had the spare wheel on the sloping tail, with luggage space access from the back seat. After 1938 there was a projecting luggage boot, with the spare wheel under a metal cover in a recess on the external downwards-folding lid and access from the outside. The engine was carried even further forward, on top of the front wheels, to provide more room inside. Free-standing headlamps, horn grilles, and V8 insignia everywhere, made this essentially mid-sized Ford easily identifiable, and its lively acceleration established it as a firm favourite with keen drivers wanting as much punch per £ as they could. Among the attractions at Ford's 1937 exhibition at the Royal Albert Hall was the spectacle of 2 mechanics dismantling a V8 engine in 6 minutes, and reassembling it in 9 minutes.

INTRODUCTION June 1936, production until February 1941.
BODY saloons Tudor and Fordor 5-6-seat, cabriolet 2-seat, roadster 2-seat, coupe 2-seat, utility 4-door 5-6-seat; coupe weight 23cwt (1168kg) (2575lb).
ENGINE 8-cylinders in 90deg Vee; front; 66mm x 81.28mm, 2227cc; compr 6.3:1; 60bhp (44.7kW) @ 3500 rpm; 26.9bhp/l (20.1kW/l); Treasury rating 21.63HP, annual tax £16 10s (£16.50).
ENGINE STRUCTURE side valves; centre Celeron helical-cut gear-driven 3-bearing camshaft; aluminium detachable cyl heads, blocks and upper crankcase cast iron; Stromberg 48 twin choke downdraught carburettor, coil ignition, camshaft-driven distributor; electric fuel pump; 3-bearing cast steel crankshaft; thermosyphon cooling, two belt-driven pumps, pressure lubrication by camshaft pump.
TRANSMISSION rear wheel drive; 9in (229mm) sdp cushioned clutch; 3-speed manual all-synchromesh gearbox; spiral bevel final drive 4.55:1.
CHASSIS steel X-braced frame with 4 cross-members; suspension by transverse leaf springs; 4 hydraulic lever arm dampers; mechanical drum (non-scoring alloy) brakes; worm and sector steering; 12.5 gal (56.8l) (15 US gal) rear-mounted fuel tank; 5.75-16 tyres; electrically welded steel disc wheels.
DIMENSIONS wheelbase 108.25in (275cm); track 55.25in (140.3cm) front, 58in (147.3cm) rear; length 173.25in (440cm); width 69.5in (176.5cm); ground clearance 8.25in (20.9cm).
EQUIPMENT 6-volt electrics; combined ignition and steering column lock; body colours Black, Cordoba Tan, Gunmetal Grey, Vineyard Green.
PERFORMANCE maximum 76mph (122kph); 19.5kg/bhp (26.1kg/kW); 20-25mpg (14.1-11.3l/100km).
PRICE 1936 introduction Saloon 4-door £210 (1937 £240), Chassis £180.
PRODUCTION 9239.

Archetypal V8. The middle portion of the 22HP survived the war as the V8 Pilot.

1938 V8 81A 30HP

It was perhaps just as well that the V8 81A was relatively short-lived. It tried to catch up with Dearborn on style, sinking the headlamps downwards and inwards, extending the bulge of the front wings rearwards giving the grille the appearance of a liner's bow-wave, but the result was compromised. Among the UK-specific items found necessary were semaphore direction indicators on the windscreen pillars and wing-mounted sidelamps. A basic no-frills model was sold in America but only the de luxe was available in the United Kingdom. The saloons were straight-backed, a retrograde step following the Model 78's external-booted body bulge, but Dagenham acknowledged the growing popularity of wood-framed estate car-style bodies by making the 30HP V8s available on a chassis-only basis. A number of these utilitarian multi-purpose vehicles were supplied to the British army with wide-section tyres. A talented carpenter could construct one cheaply, and with a third row of seats and fibre-board lining inside, the Woodie (a title not adopted until much later) became fashionable on the grouse moor as well as practical as an urban people carrier. Coachbuilders Corsica, better known for lightweight low-slung sports bodies on Daimler Double-Six, Triumph Dolomite, Squire, and Bugatti chassis did build a 7-seat limousine on one V8 81A.

INTRODUCTION April-November 1938.
BODY saloons Tudor and Fordor 5-6-seat, cabriolet 2-seat, coupe 2-seat, utility 4-door 5-6-seat; coupe weight 23cwt (1168kg) (2575.9lb), 4 door touring saloon 28cwt (1422kg) (3135.8lb).
ENGINE 8-cylinders in 90deg Vee; front; 77.8mm x 95mm, 3622cc; compr 6.3:1; 80bhp (59.6kW) @ 3500 rpm; 21.8bhp/l (16.5kW/l); 140 lbft (190Nm) @ 1500rpm.
ENGINE STRUCTURE side valves; centre gear-driven 3-bearing camshaft; aluminium detachable cylinder heads, blocks and upper crankcase unitary cast iron; engine weight 581lb (263.5kg); Stromberg 48 twin choke downdraught carburettor, coil ignition, camshaft-driven distributor; mechanical fuel pump; 3-bearing cast steel crankshaft; thermosyphon cooling, two belt-driven pumps, pressure lubrication by camshaft pump.
TRANSMISSION rear wheel drive; 9in (229mm) sdp clutch; 3-speed manual gearbox with synchromesh 2 and 3; final drive 4.11:1.

CHASSIS steel X-braced frame with 4 cross-members; suspension by transverse leaf springs; 4 hydraulic lever arm dampers; mechanical drum (non-scoring alloy) brakes; worm and sector steering; 11.5 gal (52.3l) (13.8 US gal) rear-mounted fuel tank; 6.00-16 tyres, 9.00-13 on Station Wagons.
DIMENSIONS wheelbase 112in (284.5cm); track 55in (139.7cm); length 185in (470cm); width 67.5in (171.5cm); height 68in (172.7cm) touring saloon; ground clearance 8.5in (21.6cm); turning circle 40ft (12.2m).
EQUIPMENT 6-volt electrics.
PERFORMANCE maximum speed 87mph (139.7kph); 0-60mph (96kph) 17sec; 14.6kg/bhp (19.8kg/kW); fuel consumption 16mpg (17.6l/100km).
PRICE Chassis £195, Touring Tudor £245, Touring Fordor £260, Club Cabriolet £255, Coupe £235, Club Coupe £250, Utility £280.
PRODUCTION 1200.

1938 Fordson or Thames E83W 10cwt

A versatile Ford commercial vehicle was based on the 10HP Prefect, traced its ancestry to the Model T, and remained in production for 20 years. The E38W had the Prefect's 1172cc engine, torque tube transmission, and transverse springing. Available as a roomy panel van, it was obtainable as a chassis-cab for specialist bodywork, and put to any number of uses including hand-operated tipper refuse collector and dropside truck. During the war it served as an ambulance, Auxiliary Fire Service (AFS) tender, and in utility roles for all three services. Yet it became best known as the Ford Emergency Food Van, 450 of which were paid for personally by Henry and Edsel Ford, equipped with tall bodywork so that occupants could stand upright in the back. Here they cooked food, and served it through a hatch in the side. The vans were operated by the YMCA, the Salvation Army, the Church Army, and the Society of Friends and were on hand at air raids, or acting as mobile canteens for outlying service sites such as anti-aircraft or barrage balloon posts, docks, workshops, farms, schools, and aerodromes. It was calculated that these vans served nearly 82 million meals. Ford dealers up and down the country maintained them free of charge. The E83W was only replaced by the Consul-engined 400E, a forerunner of the modern Transit.

INTRODUCTION March 1938, production to September 1957.
BODY semi forward control van; 2-doors, 2-seats.
ENGINE 4-cylinders, in-line; front; 63.5mm x 92.56mm, 1172cc; compr 6.6:1; 32.5bhp (24.2kW) @ 4000rpm; 27.7bhp (20.7kW)/l; 52.6lbft (71.3Nm) @ 2350rpm.
ENGINE STRUCTURE side valve; gear-driven camshaft; cast iron detachable cylinder head and block; aluminium pistons; Zenith downdraught carburettor; coil ignition, mechanical fuel pump; 3-bearing counterbalanced crankshaft; thermo-syphon cooling; splash and pressure lubrication.
TRANSMISSION rear wheel drive; sdp clutch; 3-speed synchromesh gearbox; torque tube; final drive spiral bevel; three-quarter floating axle.
CHASSIS pressed steel channel-section frame with three crossmembers and central box-section; separate composite wood and metal cab and panel van by Briggs Motor Bodies; suspension, transverse leaf springs front and rear with triangulated radius arms; lever arm dampers; I-beam front axle, live rear

axle; differential offset to left side; mechanical brakes, 11in (279mm) dia drums.
DIMENSIONS wheelbase 90in (228.6cm); track 50.5in (128.3cm); load length 80in (203.2cm), capacity 110cuft.
EQUIPMENT 6 volt electrical system 63amp battery.
PRICE £168.
PRODUCTION 188,577.

Right: **As versatile in its day as the Transit would be in years to come, the 10cwt was sold as both van and chassis-cab or even chassis-scuttle for all kinds of specialist bodywork.**

1939 V8 91A 30HP

The last V8 before the Second World War was more Dearborn than ever. With the grille abbreviated and the headlamps at the outer edges of the wings, it was based on the 1939 Mercury. Its major technical novelty represented a break with tradition. It was provided at last with hydraulic brakes. Henry Ford's distrust of hydraulics was well known and he clung to rod or cable-operated systems for as long as his slogan, "the safety of steel from toe to wheel," would last, but in the end the market demanded change. There were changes too in the flathead V8. After nearly a decade it still used too much oil, and relocating the water pumps had not altogether cured its tendency to overheat. The petrol pump was moved away from the warmth, the distributor away from the wet, and the 21 studs holding down the cylinder heads increased to 24.

Less than 2,000 91As were made. The September 5 1939 issue of *The Motor* advertised used V8s at bargain levels. A one-owner 30HP Club Cabriolet with brown leather and 6,000 miles on the clock, was "almost as new" for £165. A 1939 22HP saloon only a month old was £195, a new unregistered one £240. A 1936 V8 Cabriolet could be picked up for £30, a 1937 22HP for £5 deposit or 45Gns (£47.25p) cash.

INTRODUCTION December 1938, production to January 1940. BODY saloons Fordor 5-6-seat, convertible 2-seat, utility 4-door 5-6-seat; 4 door touring saloon 28cwt (1422kg) (3135.8lb). ENGINE 8-cylinders in 90deg Vee; front; 77.8mm x 95mm, 3622cc; compr 6.3:1; 80bhp (59.6kW) @ 3500 rpm; 21.8bhp/l (16.5kW/l); 140 lbft (190Nm) @ 1500rpm. ENGINE STRUCTURE side valves; centre gear-driven 3-bearing camshaft; aluminium detachable cylinder heads, 24-stud blocks and upper crankcase unitary cast iron; engine weight 581lb (263.5kg); Stromberg 48 twin choke downdraught carburettor, coil ignition, camshaft-driven spiral bevel gear to distributor; mechanical fuel pump; 3-bearing nodular iron crankshaft; thermosyphon cooling, two belt-driven pumps, pressure lubrication by camshaft pump. TRANSMISSION rear wheel drive; 9in (229mm) sdp clutch; 3-speed manual gearbox with synchromesh 2 and 3; final drive 4.11:1. CHASSIS steel X-braced frame with 4 cross-members; suspension by transverse leaf springs; 4 hydraulic lever arm dampers; hydraulic drum (non-scoring alloy) brakes; worm and sector steering; 11.5 gal (52.3l) (13.8 US gal) rear-mounted fuel tank; 6.00-16 tyres, 9.00-13 on Station Wagons.

DIMENSIONS wheelbase 112in (284.5cm); track 55in (139.7cm); length 185in (470cm); width 67.5in (171.45cm);height 68in (172.7cm) touring saloon;ground clearance 8.5in (21.6cm); turning circle 40ft (12.2m). EQUIPMENT 6-volt electrics. PERFORMANCE maximum speed 87mph (139.7kph); 0-60mph (96kph) 17sec; 17.8kg/bhp (23.9kg/kW); fuel consumption 16mpg (17.6l/100km). PRICE September 1939: Touring Fordor £280, Convertible Coupe £300, Estate Car £325, Commercial Utility Car £325. PRODUCTION 1878.

Right: **firmly transatlantic, the 91A was a US Mercury lookalike.**

1938 Prefect E 93 A

The first Ford with a name, not a letter or number, could still claim Model T pedigree with transverse leaf springs, side valve engine, and torque tube transmission. Despite prodigious advances in production techniques, enabling Fords to be made at prices the rest of industry could only envy, the model that (owing to the war) was to span the family car market for 10 years was still made to roughly the specification of the Model Y. Stretched to accommodate 4 doors, its chassis was less Model Y than Model C, with a dip in the middle, and the floor and rear seat wells reinforced by steel panelling. The engine casting was wider than the Y, to accommodate larger bore cylinders, and it could still be machined on the same ingenious transfer equipment as its smaller counterparts. Non-adjustable tappets were a legacy of Henry Ford's stubbornness and it had 6-volt electrics. There were some innovations. The cheap vacuum-operated screen wipers acquired the luxury of a vacuum tank so that they did not stop quite so profoundly at inconvenient times such as overtaking. Unlike the Model C, the additional length was made good use of for an extra window in the rear quarters, running boards were reinstated, and there was a boot with a let-down door on leather straps providing a platform for holiday luggage.

INTRODUCTION October 1938, civilian production to July 1940, wartime until February 1942. Recommenced June 1945-Jan 1949. BODY saloon, 2-doors, 4-doors, 4-seats; Tourer 2-door, 4-seats; weight (4-door) 15cwt (762kg) (1680lb) *The Autocar*.
ENGINE 4-cylinders, in-line; front; 63.5mm x 92.5mm, 1172cc; compr 6.6 x:1; 30bhp (22.4kW) @ 4000 rpm; 25.6bhp/L (19.1kW/L); 60 lbft (81Nm) @ 2000rpm.
ENGINE STRUCTURE side valve; gear-driven camshaft; cast iron detachable cylinder head and block; aluminium pistons; Zenith downdraught carburettor; coil ignition, and mechanical fuel pump; 3-bearing counterbalanced crankshaft; thermo-syphon cooling; splash and pressure lubrication.
TRANSMISSION rear wheel drive; 7.4in (187mm) sdp clutch; 3-speed manual gearbox, synchromesh on 2; torque tube; spiral bevel final drive 5.5:1.
CHASSIS pressed steel channel-section frame with three crossmembers and central box-section; suspension, transverse leaf springs front and rear with triangulated radius arms; pear-shaped Luvax dampers; rod actuated 10in (25.4cm) drum brakes; Burman worm and nut steering; 6.5 gal (29.5l) (7.8 US gal) rear fuel tank; 4.50-17 Firestone tyres; steel spoke welded wheels.
DIMENSIONS wheelbase 94in (238.8cm); track 45in (114.3cm); length 155.5in (395cm); width 57in (144.8cm); height 63in (160cm); ground clearance 6.25in (15.9cm); turning circle 36ft (10.97m).
EQUIPMENT 6volt electrical system; fixed-rate charging; 10amps at 30mph; leathercloth upholstery, leather trim and sliding roof optional.
PERFORMANCE maximum speed 65mph (104.4kph); 0-50mph (80.3kph) 35sec; 56kg/bhp (75kg/kW); fuel consumption 35-45mpg (8-6.3l/100km) at normal speeds.
PRICE 2-door £150, 4-door and Tourer £162 10s (£162.50).
PRODUCTION 1938-1949 120,505, including 1028 tourers, 667 coupes, 10,163 Tudor, 37,502CKD.

1938 Bren Gun Carrier V8 3622cc, later Universal Carrier

Vickers' 1934 tracked gun-towing vehicle, the Light Dragon (from drag-gun) Tractor with first an Armstrong-Siddeley air-cooled V8, and later a Meadows 6-cylinder, was redeveloped in 1936 as an infantry carrier. It mounted a Vickers machine gun and then, following the introduction of the Bren light machine-gun, the superstructure was modified and in 1938 Carriers were issued on a basis of 10 per infantry battalion as "Carrier, Bren, No 2 Mark 1". In 1938 it came out as "Carrier, Scout" for mechanised cavalry regiments then "Carrier, Cavalry" with lighter armour and accommodation for six men under a canvas tilt. The "Carrier, Armoured, OP", for Royal Artillery forward observation officers, had a radio (with the ignition suitably suppressed) and a telephone cable wound off a drum at the back to report back the fall of shot to the gunners. In 1940 the design was developed as the Universal Carrier, with various option kits for different roles, and better armour. Steering was by a novel track warping arrangement, activated by steering wheel, enabling it to be driven on the road, like a wheeled vehicle. It also had a brake on the differential that allowed it to slew around in its own length. Experimental models carried 2-pdr, 6-pdr and 25-pdr guns and various multiple machine guns without seeing service.

INTRODUCTION 1936 production in small numbers as machine gun carrier, 1936 as Bren carrier, 1940 as Universal Carrier.
BODY open-topped; 0-doors, up to 6-seats; 8400lb (3810kg) payload 1212lb (550kg); weight of Universal 9520lb (4318kg); front armour .393in (10mm), side .275in (7mm).
ENGINE 8-cylinders, in 90deg V; mid; 77.79mm x 95.25mm, 3622cc; compr 5.5:1; 85bhp (63.4kW) @ 3500rpm; approx 130 lbft (176Nm) @ 1250rpm; 21.7bhp (16.2kW)/l. US engine 95bhp (70.8kW), UK 65bhp (48.5kW).
ENGINE STRUCTURE side valves; centre gear-driven 3-bearing cam; alumin detachable cyl heads, 24-stud blocks and upper crankcase unitary cast iron; twin choke downdraught carb, coil ignition, camshaft-driven spiral bevel gear to distributor; mechanical fuel pump; 3-bearing nodular iron crank thermosyphon cooling, 2 belt-driven pumps, pressure lubrication by camshaft pump.
TRANSMISSION rear drive sprockets; front idlers; single dry plate clutch; 4-speed and reverse manual gearbox;

final drive 5.883:1.
CHASSIS steel monocoque; 3 bogie wheels to tracks, leading and trailing arms, coil springs and hydraulic dampers; mechanical hydraulic servo drum brakes; steering by track braking; opt 120 gal (545.5l) fuel tank for flamethrower; steel linked track-laying.
DIMENSIONS track width to centres 62.5in (158.75cm); length 144in (365.8cm), Universal 148in (375.9cm); width 69in (175.3cm), Universal 71in (180.3cm); height 57in (144.8cm), Universal 63in (160cm); ground clearance 8.75in (22.2cm); turning circle own length using tracks.
EQUIPMENT opt OP sliding shutter in lieu of gun port, rifle racks, ammunition boxes, fire extinguishers, smoke canisters, starting handle, Verey pistol; Universal, mud deflectors, armour plating on engine compartment, rear steps for entry, optional flame-thrower or mortars, mountings for .55in Boys anti tank rifle, Wasp Mark 2 model with "Ronson" flamethrower.
PERFORMANCE maximum 30mph (48kph); range 110mls (177km) approx.
FORD PRODUCTION 13,942.

Universal Carriers were made by Thornycroft Basingstoke, Morris Cowley, Sentinel Steam Wagon Company Shrewsbury, Aveling Barford, and Ford. They had Canadian, UK or US V8s, and were also made at Windsor Ontario, by GM New Zealand, the New Zealand State Railways Workshop, and in Australia. America made 2,500 of a more powerful, but ultimately unsatisfactory version, the T16.

Right: The ten thousandth Universal Carrier made by Ford between 1940 and 1945 undergoes its pre-delivery field trials.

1940 Ford WOA1 saloon

Using the 4-light body of the 22HP Model 62, with an austere military-pattern grille, the WOA1 staff car with a 30HP engine saw service throughout WW2. Designated WOA1 and WOA1/A they were for the army, but were used by all 3 services together with 81 and 91 saloons and estate cars from a variety of sources including Canada. Allocation of staff cars to senior officers could be contentious, especially to those of field rank, sensitive about status turning up at conferences. Field Marshal Viscount Montgomery of Alamein made his open Humber Super Snipe "Old Faithful" famous in the desert campaign and later in Northern Europe, but preferred his Rolls-Royce Phantom III with unusual reverse-raked windscreen body by HJ Mulliner. Formerly Field Marshall Lord Gort's car, it passed to "Monty" and became his personal property. Fords were for middle-ranking officers although Field Marshal Earl Alexander of Tunis hung on to his Canadian-made Ford C11AD with US 3.9-litre 95bhp (70.8kW) V8. The bodywork was a combination of estate car framed doors and open top with reinforcements to compensate for the absence of the steel roof. Wartime regulations demanded headlight hoods for the black-out and white-painted bumpers, wings, and running boards to help pedestrians see them.

INTRODUCTION production 1941 to 1944.
BODY saloon Fordor; 5-6-seat; weight 25cwt (2800lb) (1279kg).
ENGINE 8-cylinders in 90deg Vee; front; 77.8mm x 95mm, 3622cc; compr 6.3:1; 80bhp (59.6kW) @ 3500 rpm; 22.1bhp/l (16.5kW/l); 140 lbft (190 Nm) @ 1500rpm.
ENGINE STRUCTURE side valves; centre gear-driven 3-bearing camshaft; aluminium detachable cylinder heads, blocks and upper crankcase unitary cast iron; engine weight 263.5kg (581lb); Stromberg 48 twin choke downdraught carburettor, coil ignition, camshaft-driven distributor; mechanical fuel pump; 3-bearing cast steel crankshaft; thermosyphon cooling, two belt-driven pumps, pressure lubrication by camshaft pump.
TRANSMISSION rear wheel drive; 9.0in (229mm) sdp cushioned clutch; 3-speed manual all-synchromesh gearbox; spiral bevel final drive 4.55:1.
CHASSIS steel X-braced frame with 4 cross-members; suspension by transverse leaf springs; 4 hydraulic lever arm dampers; mechanical drum (non-scoring alloy) brakes; worm and sector steering; 12.5 gal (56.8l) (15 US gal) rear-mounted fuel tank; 5.75-16 or 9.00-13 or 6.50-16 (Model WOA1/A) tyres; electrically welded steel disc wheels.
DIMENSIONS wheelbase 108.25in (275cm); track 55.25in (140.3cm) front, 58in (147.3cm) rear; length 173.25in (440cm); width 69.5in (176.5cm); turning circle 40ft (12.2m).
EQUIPMENT 6-volt electrics, body colours according to service
PERFORMANCE maximum speed 76mph (122kph); 0-62mph (100kph) 17sec; 16kg/bhp (21.5kg/kW); fuel consumption 20-25mpg (14.1-11.3l/100km).

Right: **Model 62 on war service with white painted bumpers and running boards to enhance visibility in the blackout. Regular headlights were out of use, replaced by small hooded ones above the front bumper.**

1940 WOA2 heavy utility

An upright rugged shooting brake style of body on a reinforced Model 62 chassis, again with an austere military-pattern grille, the WOA2 had a 30HP engine, and many survived to be used as commercial workhorses. Production continued after the war and, long before the introduction of leisure 4x4s, became general purpose vehicles for off-road use. The Post Office Telephones Home Counties Division bought them for essential line maintenance during the war and in 1946 added ex-military reconditioned examples to carry on the work. The body had a horizontally split tailgate and there were 2 rows of seats with 2 more tip-up seats in the rear. Equipment varied according to service demands. For use as a staff car a folding map table could be installed behind the front seats, and many were modified as open tourers for use in the desert. The WOA2 was adapted as a 15cwt GS truck known as the WOT2, using the same bonnet and radiator, with forward control that resulted in a narrow toe-board. As a result the accelerator pedal had to be mounted aft of the front wheel arch. The simplified cab had canvas top and doors, and individual small windscreens; later versions had fully enclosed cabs and evolved into proper trucks. A number of WOT2s were equipped as fire appliances and used by the National Fire Service.

INTRODUCTION production May 1941, production until 1947.
BODY saloon, 5-door, 7-seat.
ENGINE 8-cylinders in 90deg Vee; front; 77.8mm x 95mm, 3622cc; compr 6.3:1; 80bhp (59.6kW) @ 3500 rpm; 22.1bhp/l (16.5kW/l); 140 lbft (190Nm) @ 1500rpm.
ENGINE STRUCTURE side valves; centre gear-driven 3-bearing camshaft; aluminium detachable cylinder heads, blocks and upper crankcase unitary cast iron; engine weight 581lb (263.5kg); Stromberg 48 twin choke downdraught carburettor, coil ignition, camshaft-driven distributor; mechanical fuel pump; 3-bearing cast steel crankshaft; thermosyphon cooling, two belt-driven pumps, pressure lubrication by camshaft pump.
TRANSMISSION rear wheel drive; 9in (229mm) sdp cushioned clutch; 3-speed manual all-synchromesh gearbox; spiral bevel final drive 4.55:1.
CHASSIS steel X-braced frame with 4 cross-members; suspension by transverse leaf springs; 4 hydraulic lever arm dampers; mechanical drum (non-scoring alloy) brakes; worm and sector steering; 12.5 gal (56.8l) (15 US gal) rear-mounted fuel tank; 9.00-13 or 6.50-16 tyres; electrically welded steel disc wheels.
DIMENSIONS wheelbase 108.25in (275cm); track 55.25in (140.3cm) front, 58in (147.3cm) rear; length 173.25in (440cm); width 69.5in (176.5cm).
EQUIPMENT 6-volt electrics, body colours according to service.
PERFORMANCE fuel consumption 20mpg (14.1l/100km).
PRODUCTION 11,754.

Right: **still wearing its military camouflage and headlamp blackout masks, one of the Post Office's reconditioned ex-army WOA2 Heavy Utilities.**

1944 Ford Merlin V12

In 1933 the ailing Sir Henry Royce persevered with a V12 aero engine in the face of Air Ministry indifference and prevarication. The PV (for Private Venture) 12 was a straightforward upright V12 of a sort with which Rolls-Royce was already familiar. An inverted layout was considered, which would have given the pilots of the single seater monoplane fighters for which it was intended a better view, but there were difficulties with lubrication. Sir Henry Royce did not much like novelties, and the idea was dropped. The great engineer died on 22 April 1933 just as the final drawings were being completed. The first engine ran on 15 October 1933 and Royce's vision resulted in one of the most significant aircraft power units of the Second World War. Developed from the Kestrel and the R-type that had been successful in the Schneider Trophy Supermarine S6 racing seaplanes, the Merlin was not named after the legendary wizard, but was one of a series designated by birds of prey. It was used not only in the front-line fighters in the Battle of Britain, the Hawker Hurricane and Supermarine Spitfire, but also in celebrated aircraft including the Avro Lancaster and de Havilland Mosquito. Later ones were developed to produce substantial power increases at high altitude and by the end of the war specialist versions were turning out 2640bhp (1969kW).

Rolls-Royce did not have capacity in its factories at Derby, Crewe, and Hillington Glasgow to meet the demand. 4 times as many Merlins were needed to equip the new 4-engined bombers. Packard made them in America and Ford was invited to set up a plant at Urmston, Manchester, not far from Trafford Park. Rowland Smith guessed it would cost £7m, telling Rolls-Royce chairman Lord Hives that Ford could not build engines from the drawings supplied by Rolls-Royce. The tolerances were too wide. Ford production machinery would have to work to much closer limits than Rolls-Royce did with hand-finished engines.

ENGINE 12-cylinders, 60deg V; front; 5.4in (1371mm) x 6in (1524mm), 1649 cu in (27,021cc); compr 6.0:1; 1030bhp (768kW) @ 3000rpm @ 16,250ft (4940m) Merlin I, to 1480bhp (1104kW) @ 3000rpm @ 6000ft (91830m), to 12,250ft (3740m) from Merlin XX; weight 1385lb (629kg) Merlin I, 1450lb (647kg) Merlin XX, 1640lb (744kg) for 1565bhp (1167kW) Merlin 61 onwards.
ENGINE STRUCTURE 4 inclined 45deg KE965steel valves per cylinder (4 valves parallel from Merlin G); sodium-cooled exhaust valves; Stellited ends to inlet valves; double valve springs; Silchrome valve seats screwed into heads; one shaft bevel gear-driven 7-bearing overhead camshaft per bank; 2 2-piece cylinder blocks cast in RR50 aluminium alloy; detachable cylinder heads; wet high carbon steel cylinder liners; alumin crankcase split horizontally; twin choke updraught R-R/SU carb with anti-ice heating; gear-driven centrifugal supercharger,

2-spd from Mark X; liquid-cooled
intercooler; 2 mechanical fuel pumps
on quill shafts; 2 magnetos; one-piece
6-throw chrome molybdenum steel
7-bearing crank; dry sump lubrication;
70% water 30% ethylene glycol cooling;
centrifugal pump; electric starter;
air compressor take-off for aircraft
services.
TRANSMISSION single plain spur
0.477:1 or 0.42:1 reduction gears to
propeller from front of crankshaft.
PRODUCTION over 30,000.

Right: **Merlin production,
Manchester.** Engines were
assembled on trolleys on
a production line by fitters
seen here lowering one bank
of the V12's cylinders in
to place. The opposing
bank shows the 4-valve
heads already in position.

1939-1945 Anglia E04 A

Pool petrol, rationing, the end of car production for all but the military, shortages of many things hitherto regarded as essential, the onset of war changed everything except the specification of the smallest Ford. One innovation was a name, Anglia, unmistakably British even though Dagenham was more Essex than Anglian. War broke out on September 3 1939, yet until the real conflict began nobody knew what to do, and Ford went ahead and proceeded to introduce a new car. The upright square grille gave it good proportions, and although a coupe was proposed with independent front suspension, it never reached production. The return to peacetime manufacture was planned well in advance, and barely 3 weeks after the guns stopped firing in Europe, Dagenham was making cars for the biggest seller's market in history. Running boards were deleted, windscreens no longer opened, there were no indicators until 1948, but cars were once again in production and Ford was making the cheapest one. It was fairly nimble, with one and three quarter turns of the steering from lock to lock, so changes of direction were quite swift and, despite the high gearing, it was not heavy to drive. For the post-war export drive Anglias shipped to North America had the 1172cc 10HP engine and, astonishingly for such a narrow car, a bench front seat.

INTRODUCTION October 1939, production until November 1948 (chassis nos Y278543-Y369249, final wartime 1941 Anglia Y287241, first postwar May 25 1945 Y291482). BODY saloon; 2-doors, 4-seats; weight 1940 1735lb (787kg), 1945 1706lb (774kg). ENGINE 4-cylinders, in-line; front; 56.6mm x 92.5mm, 933cc; compr 6.2 x:1; 23.4bhp (17.5kW) @ 4000rpm; 25.1bhp/l (18.7kW/l); 36.5 lbft (49.5Nm) @ 2300rpm. ENGINE STRUCTURE side valve; gear-driven camshaft; cast iron detachable cylinder head and block; aluminium pistons; Zenith downdraught carburettor; coil ignition, and mechanical fuel pump; 3-bearing counterbalanced crankshaft; thermo-syphon cooling; splash and pressure lubrication. TRANSMISSION rear wheel drive; 7.4in (187mm) sdp clutch; 3-speed manual gearbox, synchromesh on 2; torque tube; spiral bevel final drive 5.5:1. CHASSIS pressed steel channel-section frame with three crossmembers and central box-section; suspension,

transverse leaf springs front and rear with triangulated radius arms; pear-shaped Luvax dampers; rod actuated 10in (254mm) drum brakes; Burman worm and nut steering; 6.5 gal (29.5l) (7.8 US gal) rear fuel tank; 4.50-17 Firestone tyres; steel spoke welded wheels. DIMENSIONS wheelbase 90in (228.6cm); track 45in (114.3cm); length 152in (386.1cm); width 57in (144.8cm); height 63in (160cm); ground clearance 6.25in (15.9cm); turning circle 36ft (11m). EQUIPMENT 6 volt electrical system; fixed-rate charging; 10amps at 30mph; leathercloth upholstery, leather trim optional, sliding roof optional for £3 in 1940; vacuum reservoir for wipers. PERFORMANCE maximum speed 59mph (94.7kph) (*The Autocar* 1940); 0-50mph (80.3kph) 35sec; 33.6kg/kW (45kg/kW) 1940, 33.1kg/bhp (44kg/kW) 1945; fuel con 35-45mpg (8-6.3l/100km) at normal speeds. PRICE 1940 de luxe £140; 1945 £293. PRODUCTION 46,745 plus 9062 CKD.

1945 Prefect E93A

Dagenham's millionth car was an E93A Prefect. The rounded grille and so-called "alligator" front-opening bonnet lent it a vaguely exotic air when it was relaunched only as a 4-door. Tourers were unwanted interruptions to the serious business of resuming car production. With rationing still in force economy was important, even though low-quality Pool petrol was only 2 shillings (10p) a gallon, but Purchase Tax at 33.3 per cent raised car prices against those of 1939. An annual road tax based on cubic capacity had been proposed but it was not invoked until 1946. The distorted market reversed the pre-war position in which the Anglia outsold the Prefect. Now the 10HP car outsold the 8 by almost two to one, although both were virtually unchanged from 1939. The Prefect had a bigger dynamo, and the seats tubular frames, which were not only cheaper to make but also conferred more comfort. There were minor differences in trim and colour but by 1948 *The Autocar* was finding the Prefect noisy and the handling indifferent. There was body roll on corners and a lot of pitching. "The system of suspension," it observed icily, "gives comfortable riding in the sense that it takes the shock out of poor surfaces, and allows the car to be driven over really bad surfaces, without causing one to feel it is being done any harm."

INTRODUCTION October 1938, production to January 1949.
BODY saloon; 4-doors, 4-seats; weight 15.7cwt (797.6kg) (1758lb).
ENGINE 4-cylinders, in-line; front; 63.5mm x 92.5mm, 1172cc; compr 6.6 x:1; 30bhp (22.4kW) @ 4000 rpm; 25.6bhp/l (19.1kW/l); 97.8 lbft (132.6Nm) @ 2400rpm.
ENGINE STRUCTURE side valve; gear-driven camshaft; cast iron detachable cylinder head and block; aluminium pistons; Zenith downdraught carburettor; coil ignition, and mechanical fuel pump; 3-bearing counterbalanced crankshaft; thermo-syphon cooling; splash and pressure lubrication.
TRANSMISSION rear wheel drive; 7.375in (18.73cm) sdp clutch; 3-speed manual gearbox, synchromesh on 2; torque tube; spiral bevel final drive 5.5:1.
CHASSIS pressed steel channel-section frame with three crossmembers and lowered central box-section; suspension, transverse leaf springs front and rear with triangulated radius arms; pear-shaped Luvax dampers; rod actuated 10in (25.4cm) drum brakes; Burman worm and nut steering; 7 gal (31.8l) (8.4 US gal) fuel tank; 5.00-16 tyres; steel spoke welded wheels.
DIMENSIONS wheelbase 94in (238.8cm); track 45in (114.3cm); length 155.5in (395cm); width 57in (144.8cm); height 63in (160cm); ground clearance 8.75in (22.2cm); turning circle 36ft (10.97m).
EQUIPMENT 6 volt electrical system; fixed-rate charging; 10amps at 30mph; rear window blind; cloth upholstery, leather trim £7 13s 4d (£7.67p).
PERFORMANCE maximum speed 59.7mph (95.8kph) *The Motor*; 0-50mph (80.3kph) 26.9sec; 26.6kg/bhp (35.6kg/kW); fuel consumption 33.8mpg (8.35l/100km).
PRICE 4-door £275 plus PT £77 2s 9d, £352 2s 9d (£352.77p).
PRODUCTION 1938-1949 120,505 including 1028 tourers, 667 coupes. 10,163 Tudors, 37,502CKD.

Right: **firmly sprung seats but quite a lot of leg room in the first post-war Prefect.**

1945 Fordson Major E27N

When tractor production restarted postwar, the Model N's replacement used the same engine and a new axle, later incorporated in the 1952 New Fordson Major. Modern farm machinery required a driving force and the W27N had an optional central Power Take Off (PTO), a hydraulic power lift, and sufficient ground clearance for rowcrop as well as general agriculture. Diesel tractors were still in a minority despite Ford's efforts to promote multi-fuel, until 1948 when the Perkins P6 TA became an option, its 45bhp (33.6kW) the greatest power of any tractor based on the 1917 design principles of Eugene Farkas, Ford's Hungarian-born chief engineer. Practical styling came in with a radiator cowl with vertical slats and lights and it was available with a wide range of attachments including a Roadless half-track kit and the County Full Track (CFT). Ford had been working on its own diesel engine since 1944 but farmers proved reluctant to endorse diesels owing to their reputation for difficult starting. Following the success of the Perkins however, Ford was encouraged to introduce the New Major in 1951 with curved styling and a 4-cylinder 3.6-litre with a compression ratio ranging between 4.35:1 to 16:1. It could thus be used with petrol, petrol-TVO, or diesel fuel. The diesel was also employed in the range of Thames Trader commercials.

INTRODUCTION March 19 1945, production to 1952.
BODY open; 0-doors, 1-seat; weight 4000lb (1814.4kg); 4500lb (2041.2kg) with Perkins P6.
ENGINE 4-cylinders, in-line; front; 4.125in (104.78mm) x 5in (127mm), 4380cc; 27bhp (20.1kW) @ 1200rpm; 6.2bhp/l (4.6kW/l). Perkins P6 6-cylinders; 3.5in (88.9mm) x 5in (127mm); 4730cc; 45bhp (33.6kW) @ 1500rpm; 9.5bhp/l (7.1kW/l).
ENGINE STRUCTURE side camshaft gear-driven from crankshaft; iron cyl head, block; vaporiser for TVO, Zenith carb for petrol, ignition Lucas high tension magneto; gravity fuel feed; 3-bearing crankshaft; cooling by pump and fan; flat-type air-washer. P6 valve in-head with high level camshaft; indirect injection by CAV in-line pump, with swirl pre-combustion chambers; starting by Ki-gas pump and heater plug.
TRANSMISSION rwd; wet single-plate clutch; constant-mesh; 3-speed manual gearbox; low, intermediate, and high; slewing brakes on bull pinion shafts; transmission brake; spiral bevel final drive; four pinion differential.

CHASSIS integral engine clutch, gearbox, final drive; front axle buffer; mechanical brakes, front drums; worm and sector steering, later worm and nut with PAS optional; 16 gal (72.7l) (19.2 US gal); standard agricultural wheels; rear, optional steel spoked with cleats or spade lugs, Land Utility with cast centres for Dunlop, Firestone, Goodyear or French & Hecht tyres; cast front wheels; Rowcrop Vee formation optional, with independent pedal-operated brakes.
DIMENSIONS wheelbase 63in (160cm); length 102in (259.1cm); width 62.75in (159.4cm); height 54.5in (138.4cm); ground clearance 11.6in (29.5cm); turning circle 21ft (6.4m).
EQUIPMENT optional electric starter; dark blue with orange wheels, later light blue. Cab optional from 1960.
PRICE Standard agricultural £237 on metal wheels; Land Utility on rubber tyres £281; Row Crop £255-£285.

Right: rudimentary enclosure of the driver, pneumatic tyres, power take-offs, and a fetching colour scheme were on offer to farmers by the 1950s.

1947 Pilot E71A

Ford's first new model after the war was derived from the 1937 22HP V8-62, with the addition of a distinctive radiator grille. It was announced with cylinder dimensions of 65mm x 95mm (the old 22HP was 66mm x 81mm) giving 2535cc, but with only 66bhp (49.22kW) it was too slow or, as Ford put it at the time, "after further research into overseas markets, it was decided not to proceed with a 2.5-litre". The 95mm stroke was retained, even though the 3.6-litre's fuel consumption was inappropriate for an era of austerity and shortages. Among the innovations was a Clayton Dewandre heater, with demisting and de-icing vents under the windscreen, as standard equipment. The Smith's Jackall four wheel jacking system had hydraulic rams that could be pumped down to raise the car for wheel-changing. The Pilot chassis-cab that continued into 1952 as the E71C commercial, encouraged the production of wood-panelled estate cars and even pick-ups. King George VI had a Pilot shooting brake, on a rare long wheelbase chassis, which was preserved at Sandringham. A 12-volt electrical system was produced for export police cars, and heavy-duty clutch and high capacity water pumps were optional. Several Pilots apeared in Monte Carlo Rallies in which V8s had done well before the war, and Ken Wharton used one to win the 1950 Tulip Rally.

INTRODUCTION August 1947, production to May 1951.
BODY saloon, 4-door, 5-6-seat, weight 29cwt (1473kg) (3248lb).
ENGINE 8-cylinders in 90deg Vee; front; 77.8mm x 95.3mm, 3622cc; compr 6.15:1; 85bhp (63.4kW)@ 3500 rpm; 23.5bhp/l (17.5kW/l); 140 lbft (190Nm) @ 1500rpm; Treasury rating 30.01HP.
ENGINE STRUCTURE side valves; centre Celeron helical-cut gear-driven 3-bearing camshaft; cast iron detachable cylinder heads, blocks and upper crankcase unitary cast iron; Solex twin choke downdraught carburettor, coil ignition, camshaft-driven distributor; electric fuel pump; 3-bearing cast steel crankshaft, separate bearings for each big-end; thermosyphon cooling, two belt-driven pumps, pressure lubrication by camshaft pump.
TRANSMISSION rear wheel drive; 9in (229mm) sdp cushioned clutch; 3-speed manual gearbox, synchromesh on 2 and 3; steering column change; torque tube; spiral bevel final drive 4.11.
CHASSIS steel X-braced frame with 4 cross-members; suspension by transverse leaf springs; front anti-roll bar; 4 hydraulic lever arm dampers; hydro-mechanical drum brakes; worm and sector steering; 12.5 gal (56.8l) (15 US gal) rear-mounted fuel tank; 6.00-16 tyres; bolt-on pierced steel wheels.
DIMENSIONS wheelbase 108.25in (275cm); track 55.25in (140.3cm) front, 58in (147.3cm) rear; length 174.75in (444cm); width 69.5in (176.5cm); height 66in (167.6cm); ground clearance 8.25in (21cm); turning circle 40ft (12.19m).
EQUIPMENT 6 volt electrics; automatic voltage control, cloth upholstery, leather £16 extra; interior heater; radio optional; combined ignition and steering column lock; floor carpets; hydraulic jacks; colours available black, dark blue, beige, or light green.
PERFORMANCE maximum speed 82.5mph (132.4kph) *The Autocar*; 0-60mph (96kph) 20.5 sec; 17.3kg/bhp (23.2kg/bhp); fuel consumption 17-20mpg (16.6-14.1l/100km).
PRICE £585 plus PT £163 5s, £748 5s (£748.25p).
PRODUCTION 21,487, 668CKD.

1948 Anglia E494A

The only British car with a basic price under £250, the Anglia gained only minor changes for 1949. The grille became an erect oval with a divider down the middle. But there was not much cheer for Ford in the first post-war motor show at Earl's Court following the introduction of the Morris Minor at only £358 10s 7d (£358.53). The Minor still had side-valves but it had full-width styling, a roomy interior, independent front suspension, rack and pinion steering, a 4-speed gearbox, generous luggage accommodation, and exemplary ride and handling. The writing was surely on the wall for Model T technology as Nuffield and Austin announced the "constant interchange of information and pooling of resources," that would lead to the formation of the British Motor Corporation. *The Autocar* found it increasingly difficult to write about the Anglia kindly: "(The Fords) have years of experience behind them and the resources of the great plant at Dagenham, which is synonymous with service. All 3 models are lively in their respective classes, as their construction is light, and their engines reliable and willing." Faint praise. Ford hoped to keep the price the same as the outgoing Anglia, £242 + PT £67 19s 5d making £309 19s 2d (£309.97p). By the motor show it was £255 + PT £71 11s 8d making £326 11s 8d, perilously close to the Morris.

INTRODUCTION November 1948, production to October 1953.
BODY saloon; 2-doors, 4-seats; weight 1940 1735lb (787kg), 1945 1706lb (774kg).
ENGINE 4-cylinders, in-line; front; 56.6mm x 92.5mm, 933cc; compr 6.2 x :1; 23.4bhp (17.5kW) @ 4000rpm; 25.1bhp/l (18.7kW/l); 36.5 lbft (49.5Nm) @ 2300rpm.
ENGINE STRUCTURE side valve; gear-driven camshaft; cast iron detachable cylinder head and block; aluminium pistons; Zenith downdraught carburettor; coil ignition, and mechanical fuel pump; 3-bearing counterbalanced crankshaft; thermo-syphon cooling; splash and pressure lubrication.
TRANSMISSION rear wheel drive; 7.375in (18.73cm) sdp clutch; 3-speed manual gearbox, synchromesh on 2; torque tube; spiral bevel final drive 5.5:1.
CHASSIS pressed steel channel-section frame with three crossmembers and central box-section; suspension, transverse leaf springs front and rear with triangulated radius arms;

pear-shaped Luvax dampers; rod actuated 10in (25.4cm) drum brakes; Burman worm and nut steering; 6.5 gal (29.5l) (7.8 US gal) rear fuel tank; 4.50-17 tyres; steel spoke welded wheels.
DIMENSIONS wheelbase 90in (229cm); track 45in (114.3cm); length 152in (386.1cm); width 57in (144.8cm); height 63in (160cm); ground clearance 6.25in (15.9cm); turning circle 36ft (10.97m).
EQUIPMENT 6 volt electrical system; fixed-rate charging; 10amps at 30mph; cloth upholstery, leather trim optional; vacuum reservoir for wipers.
PERFORMANCE maximum speed 59mph (94.7kph) (*The Autocar* 1940); 0-50mph (80.3kph) 35sec; 33.6kg/bhp (45kg/kW); fuel consumption 35-45mpg (8-6.3l/100km).
PRICE £255 plus PT £71 11s 8d, £326 11s 8d (£326.58p).
PRODUCTION 108,000.

1949 Prefect E493A

A hint that Ford was aware of the need for change came with the facelifted Prefect at the 1949 London Motor Show. A Pilot-style grille and headlamps faired into the wings was not much, in the light of what was to follow, but it was a start. The swage line in the front doors that had served little purpose but imitate a longer front wing was discarded. Style was becoming important as the post-war seller's market began to decay, and while cars were still in short supply and subject to a Covenant forbidding resale and profiteering, as the 1950s began so did competition grow.

The Prefect still did not have a heater, even as an option, but in 1948 it acquired swivelling instead of fixed scuttle vents so that the air inside the car, even if not heated, was at least fresh. Export Prefects were equipped with an optimistic bench-type 3-abreast seat. Yet no sooner was the new improved Prefect on the road than there was a 4-door Morris Minor, restyled with high-mounted headlamps, and as a result of the nascent BMC merger, with the overhead valve Austin A30 engine waiting in the wings. Its price went up to £429 including Purchase Tax but the pressure of competition was starting to tell. Only bargain hunters were now going for Fords.

INTRODUCTION December 1948, production to September 1953. BODY saloon; 4-doors, 4-seats; weight 1808lb (820.1kg). ENGINE 4-cylinders, in-line; front; 63.5mm x 92.5mm, 1172cc; compr 6.6 x:1; 30bhp (22.4kW) @ 4000 rpm; 25.6bhp/l (19.1kW/l); 97.8 lbft (133Nm) @ 2400rpm. ENGINE STRUCTURE side valve; gear-driven camshaft; cast iron detachable cylinder head and block; aluminium pistons; Zenith downdraught carburettor; coil ignition, and mechanical fuel pump; 3-bearing counterbalanced crankshaft; thermo-syphon cooling; splash and pressure lubrication. TRANSMISSION rear wheel drive; 7.375in (18.73cm) sdp clutch; 3-speed manual gearbox, synchromesh on 2; torque tube; spiral bevel final drive 5.5:1. CHASSIS pressed steel channel-section frame with three crossmembers and lowered central box-section; suspension, transverse leaf springs front and rear with triangulated radius arms; pear-shaped Luvax dampers; rod actuated 10in (25.4cm) drum brakes;

Burman worm and nut steering; 7 gal (31.8l) (8.4 US gal) fuel tank; 5.00-16 tyres; steel spoke welded wheels. DIMENSIONS wheelbase 94in (238.8cm); track 45in (114.3cm); length 155.5in (395cm); width 55.75in (141.6cm); height 63in (160cm); ground clearance 8.75in (22.2cm); turning circle 36ft (10.97m). EQUIPMENT 6 volt electrical system; fixed-rate charging; 10amps at 30mph; rear window blind; cloth upholstery; leather trim £7 13s 4d (£7.67p). PERFORMANCE maximum speed 59.7mph (95.8kph) *The Motor;* 0-50mph (80.3kph) 26.9sec; 27.3kg/bhp (36.7kg/kW); fuel consumption 33.8mpg (8.35l/100km). PRICE 4-door £310 plus PT £86 17s 3, £396 17s 3d (£396.86p). PRODUCTION 117,206, 75,023 CKD.

1950 Consul EOTA saloon and estate

Almost overnight in 1950 Ford was transformed from a manufacturer of small, black, cheap, working class cars into a design conscious, avant garde fashion house. The new Consul and Zephyr not only had the glamour and elegant proportions of the 1949 American Fords, they had innovative engineering as well. They were the first mass-market cars to make the most of the abolition of the old RAC Treasury rating for road tax; their new overhead valve engines were over-square, with a bore/stroke ratio of 0.96:1. They were the first Fords with unitary structures, 12volt electrics, 13in wheels, a hydraulic clutch, and independent front suspension employing a new layout that was the brainchild of engineering vice-president Earle Steele MacPherson. The ingenious and widely copied MacPherson strut distributed the suspension loads throughout the front of the monocoque, and the bottom link incorporated an anti-roll bar that bent as well as twisted. The design work was done in Detroit, bringing in new production techniques that made engines twice as quickly, by automatically transferring the cylinder blocks from one machining operation to another.

The cheaper 4-cylinder Consul was 4in (10.2cm) shorter than the 6-cylinder Zephyr with its longer bonnet and additional chrome.

INTRODUCTION Motor Show October 1950, production January 1951 until February 1956.
BODY saloon; 4-doors, 5-seats; weight 1080kg (2380lb).
ENGINE 4-cylinders, in-line; front; 79.37mm x 76.2mm, 1508cc; compr 6.8:1; 35kW (47bhp) @ 4400rpm; 23.2kW/l (31.2bhp/l); 98Nm (72 lbft) @ 2400rpm.
ENGINE STRUCTURE pushrod ohv chain-driven camshaft; cast iron cylinder head and block; 30mm downdraught carburettor, 12v coil ignition AC mechanical fuel pump; 3-bearing cast iron counterweighted crankshaft.
TRANSMISSION rear wheel drive; 203mm (8in) single plate hydraulic clutch; 3-speed manual synchromesh (on 2nd and top) gearbox; steering column shift; hypoid final drive 4.625:1.
CHASSIS steel monocoque structure; ifs by coil springs and hydraulic telescopic dampers integral with kingpins; single track control arms located by triangulated anti-roll bar; live rear axle with half-elliptic springs and piston dampers; Girling hydraulic 229mm (9in) drum brakes, 2 leading shoe at front; Burman worm and peg steering; 40.9l (9 gal) (10.8 US gal) fuel tank; steel disc wheels, 5.90 x 13in tyres.
DIMENSIONS wheelbase 254cm (100in); track front 127cm (50in), 124.5cm (49in) rear; length 412.8cm (162.5in); width 162.6cm (64in); height 164.3cm (60.75in); ground clearance 17.1cm (6.75in); turning circle right 12.5m (41ft), left 12m (39.5ft).
EQUIPMENT bench front seat, radio optional, heater optional £10.
PERFORMANCE maximum speed 120.4kph (75mph); 23.9kph (14.9mph) @ 1000rpm; 0-96kph (60mph) 31.1sec; 30.8kg/kW (23kg/bhp); fuel consumption 11.8-10.1 l/100km (24-28mpg).
PRICE £425 plus £118.16s 2d purchase tax, £543.16s 2d (£543.81).
PRODUCTION 231,481.

1950 Zephyr Six EOTTA saloon and estate

The first British Ford with 6 cylinders, the Zephyr had a longer bonnet than the Consul to accommodate the longer engine, and a distinctive front grille. Both cars had bench seats front and rear that could accommodate three occupants abreast. From the B-post rearwards the bodies were identical so with more weight in front, the Zephyr had a reputation for readiness to spin its rear wheels on loose surfaces. Unaccustomed to copious power from a smooth-revving engine, some drivers carried ballast in the boot to try and keep a grip on things. Proving the Zephyr had satisfactory ride and handling, Dutch driver Maurice Gatsonides won the 1953 Monte Carlo Rally in VHK194, standard except for an elaborate glare-shield over the battery of fog lights, and an adjustable jet carburettor. At the 1954 motor show ED Abbott, a small Farnham coach-building firm, brought out an estate car version of Consul and Zephyr. Abbott had made high-class coachwork for Daimlers and Lanchesters since the 1920s, and had a strong commercial line in bus bodies. Under the proprietorship of Gordon Sutherland, formerly of Aston Martin and owner of Friary Motors which did estate car conversions throughout the 1950s, the estate car roof extension was developed using concrete dies to form the roof pressing. The estate car with side-hinged tailgate cost only £145 extra.

INTRODUCTION Motor Show October 1950, production February 1951 to February 1956.
BODY saloon; 4-doors, 5-seats; weight 1187.5kg (2618lb).
ENGINE 6-cylinders, in-line; front; 79.37mm x 76.2mm, 2262cc; compr 6.8:1; 50.7kW (68bhp) @ 4000rpm; 22.4kW/l (30.1bhp/l); 152Nm (112 lbft) @ 2000rpm.
ENGINE STRUCTURE pushrod ohv chain-driven camshaft; cast iron cylinder head and block; 30mm downdraught carburettor, 12v coil ignition AC mechanical fuel pump; 4-bearing cast iron counterweighted crankshaft.
TRANSMISSION rwd; 203mm (8in) single plate hydraulic clutch; 3-speed manual synchromesh (on 2nd and top) gearbox; steering column shift; hypoid final drive 4.375:1.
CHASSIS steel monocoque structure; independent front suspension by coil springs and hydraulic telescopic dampers integral with kingpins; single track control arms located by triangulated anti-roll bar. Live rear axle with half-elliptic springs and piston dampers; Girling hydraulic 229mm (9in) drum brakes, 2 leading shoe at front; Burman worm and peg steering; 40.9l (9 gal) (10.8 US gal) fuel tank; steel disc wheels, 6.40 x 13in tyres.
DIMENSIONS wheelbase 104in (264.2cm); track front 50in (127cm), 49in (124.5cm) rear; length 431.8cm (170in); width 162.6cm (64in); height 154.3cm (60.75in); ground clearance 17.1cm (6.75in); turning circle right 12.5m (41ft), left 12m (39.5ft).
EQUIPMENT bench front seat, radio optional, heater optional £10.
PERFORMANCE maximum speed 130kph (81mph); 26.3kph (16.4mph) @ 1000rpm; 0-96kph (60mph) 21.1sec; 23.4kg/kW (17.5kg/bhp); fuel consumption 12.3-11.3l/100km (23-25mpg).
PRICE £475 plus £132.13s 11d purchase tax £607.13s 11d (£607.70). 1953 with pvc upholstery £667, £684 with leather.
PRODUCTION 152,677.

Right: **Maurice Gatsonides** (of the Gatso speed camera) removed his glare-shield from the front of his Zephyr for the final test on the Monte Carlo Rally. Engine cooling on the 21km (13mile) descent of the Col de Castillon was at a premium. So was brake cooling. Teams of helpers were placed on slow corners to throw buckets of water on the hot drums.

1951 Consul and Zephyr Convertibles

The prototype Convertibles were shown a year after the saloons' introduction, but they did not make it into production for a further two years while problems of reinforcing the monocoque structure were dealt with. This work was entrusted to one of the oldest contract coachworks in the industry, Carbodies of Coventry. As specialists in convertibles Carbodies was supplier to Alvis, MG, and Rover as well as making Hillman Minx dropheads from 1932. Post-war it made London taxis, worked for Singer and Standard, and bodied the Austin Somerset and Hereford convertibles, so it was a natural choice for the complex task of designing a cross-bracing underneath the Fords to stiffen them in the absence of a steel roof. The shells were modified with 2 instead of 4 doors, and trimmed by Carbodies, but final assembly took place at Dagenham. Like Carbodies' contemporary Daimler and Lanchester, the Ford Convertible top could be rolled back in the intermediate "de ville" position and both cars were catalogued with an electro-hydraulic power-operated roof, optional on the Consul. The rear seat back was repositioned to make way for the hood stowage, about an inch forwards, and the front seat backs hinged to give access to the rear. In 1954 as work on the Ford contract got under way the proprietors sold Carbodies to the BSA group.

Specification for Consul
INTRODUCTION Motor Show October 1951, production 1953 until February 1956.
BODY Convertible; 2-doors, 5-seats.
ENGINE 4-cylinders, in-line; front; 79.37mm x 76.2mm, 1508cc; compr 6.8:1; 35.1kW (47bhp) @ 4400rpm; 23.2kW/l (31.2bhp/l); 98Nm (72 lbft) @ 2400rpm.
ENGINE STRUCTURE pushrod ohv chain-driven camshaft; cast iron cylinder head and block; 30mm downdraught carburettor, 12v coil ignition AC mechanical fuel pump; 3-bearing cast iron counterweighted crankshaft.
TRANSMISSION rear wheel drive; 20.3cm (8in) single plate hydraulic clutch; 3-speed manual synchromesh (on 2nd and top) gearbox; steering column shift; hypoid final drive 4.625:1.
CHASSIS steel monocoque structure with additional X-bracing; ifs by coil springs and hydraulic telescopic dampers integral with kingpins; single track control arms located by triangulated anti-roll bar. Live rear axle with half-elliptic springs and piston dampers; Girling hydraulic 229mm (9in) drum brakes, 2 leading shoe at front; Burman worm and peg steering; 40.9l (9 gal) (10.8 US gal) fuel tank; steel disc wheels, 5.90 x 13in tyres.
DIMENSIONS wheelbase 254cm (100in); track front 127cm (50in), 124.5cm (49in) rear; length 412.75cm (162.5in); width 162.6cm (64in); height 154.3cm (60.75in); ground clearance 17.1cm (6.75in); turning circle right 12.5m (41ft), left 12.1m (39.5ft).
EQUIPMENT bench front seat, radio optional, heater optional £10.
PERFORMANCE maximum speed 120.4kph (75mph); 23.9kph (14.9mph) @ 1000rpm; 0-96kph (60mph) 31.1sec; fuel consumption 11.8-10.1 l/100km (24-28mpg).
PRICE 1953 Consul £809 with pvc and manual hood, £890 power hood and leather; Zephyr £960 pvc, £981 leather (including purchase tax).
PRODUCTION 3749 Consul 4048 Zephyr.

1953 Popular 103E

Last survivor of the 1932 Y-type, indeed the last of a lineage that could be traced to the Model T, the 1949 Anglia was relaunched as back-to-basics family transport with a solitary screen wiper without vacuum reservoir, three instrument dials in a plain body-coloured facia, undersized 24w headlamps, silver-painted wheels, bumpers without over-riders, and a choice of four colours. The only concession to decoration was a thin chrome strip round the radiator grille. The parcels shelf under the facia and the plywood boot floor were deleted and only the passenger seat tipped for access to the rear. Luggage was laid on top of the spare wheel or tied to the bootlid, which was opened by a carriage key, and let down on stout straps. There were no door map pockets, and winding windows allowed the driver hand signals in the absence of mechanical direction indicators. The 1172cc engine, hitherto available on export Anglias, was kept for the tough and reliable Popular, the last British car catalogued at a retail price of under £400. The newly imported Volkswagen was nearly twice the price at £739, the Series II Morris Minor £530, and the new Standard Eight £481. A heater and a second wiper, with vacuum reservoir to keep it working on hills, were amongst the options that could take the Popular's price over £400.

INTRODUCTION October 1953, produced until 1959.
BODY saloon; 2-doors, 4-seats; weight 737kg (1624lb).
ENGINE 4-cylinders, in-line; front; 63.5mm x 92.5mm, 1172cc; compr 6.16:1; 22.4kW (30.1bhp) @ 4000rpm; 19.1kW/l (25.7bhp/l); 63Nm (46.4 lbft) @ 3000rpm.
ENGINE STRUCTURE side valve; chain-driven camshaft; cast iron cylinder head and block; downdraught Zenith carburettor, coil ignition, AC mechanical fuel pump; 3-bearing crankshaft.
TRANSMISSION rear wheel drive; single dry plate 187.3mm (7.375in) clutch; 3-speed manual gearbox, synchromesh on 2nd and top; torque tube; spiral bevel final drive 5.5:1.
CHASSIS Pressed steel channel-section chassis; transverse semi-elliptic springs front and rear; double-acting lever arm damper; Girling mechanical 254mm (10in) drum brakes; worm and nut steering; 31.8l (7 gal) (8.4 US gal) fuel tank; 4.50-17 tyres; spoked disc wheels.
DIMENSIONS wheelbase 228.6cm (90in); track 114.3cm (45in) front and rear; length 384.8cm (151.5in); width 143.5cm (56.5in); height 163.2cm (64.25in); ground clearance 22.2cm (8.75in); turning circle 10.6m (34.75ft).
EQUIPMENT 6 volt electrical system, plastic-faced felt floor covering, no ashtrays, no interior light.
PERFORMANCE maximum speed 96kph (60mph); 22.3kph (13.9mph) @ 1000rpm; 0-80.3kph (50mph) 29.2sec; 32.9kg/kW (24.5kg/bhp); fuel consumption 8.1l/100km (35mpg).
PRICE 1954 £275 plus £115.14s 2d purchase tax, £390 14s 2d (£390.71p).
PRODUCTION 155,350.

1953 Anglia 100E

After the Consul and Zephyr of 1950, the next Ford milestone came with the redesigned Anglia and Prefect in 1953. The old reinforced chassis frame was discarded giving a lower build, out went transverse leaf springs, in came MacPherson strut independent front suspension, and although the cylinder dimensions of the side-valve engine remained the same it was a completely new smoother-running and more powerful unit with bigger valves and bearings, and at long last adjustable tappets. The dedication to 63.5mm x 92.5mm was only to enable the blocks to be machined on the same production plant. The styling replicated bigger Fords, the handling was transformed, and the accommodation enhanced.

There were 2 facelifts during the model's 6-year span. In 1955 the indirect gear ratios were lowered and the instrument panel enlarged. A new mesh grille and a bigger rear window came in 1957, together with NewtonDrive semi-automatic transmission, but only about 50 100Es were ever made with it. The Anglia was a nimble club rally car, and even won its class in the 1956 Safari Rally, although the brisk performance was bought at the expense of fuel consumption that was no better than average.

INTRODUCTION October 28 1953, produced until September 4 1959.
BODY saloon; 2-doors, 4-seats; weight 774.75kg (1708lb).
ENGINE 4-cylinders, in-line; front; 63.5mm x 92.5mm, 1172cc; compr 7.0:1; 26.8kW (36bhp) @ 4400rpm; 22.9kW/l (30.7bhp/l); 70.5Nm (52 lbft) @ 2500rpm.
ENGINE STRUCTURE side valve; chain-driven camshaft; cast iron cylinder head and block; downdraught Solex 26ZIC carburettor, 12volt coil ignition, AC mechanical fuel pump; 3-bearing crankshaft.
TRANSMISSION rear wheel drive; single dry plate 7.38in hydraulic clutch; 3-speed manual gearbox, synchromesh on 2nd and top; Hardy Spicer open prop shaft; spiral bevel final drive 4.429:1.
CHASSIS steel monocoque structure; independent front suspension by MacPherson struts; live rear axle with half-elliptic springs; telescopic dampers; Girling hydraulic 178mm (7in) drum brakes, 2LS at front; anti-roll bar; Burman worm and peg steering; 31.8l (7 gal) (8.4 US gal) fuel tank; 5.20 x 13in tyres steel disc wheels.
DIMENSIONS wheelbase 220.9cm (87in); track front 121.9cm (48in); rear 120.7cm (47.5in); length 384.2cm (151.25in); width 153.7cm (60.5in); height 150.5cm (59.25in); ground clearance 17.8cm (7in); turning circle 9.8m (32.25ft).
EQUIPMENT sun visor, screen wiper, 4 body colours, self-cancelling flashing indicators, pump, fan, and thermostat cooling, baulk-ring synchromesh, moulded rubber floor covering, heater extra.
PERFORMANCE maximum speed 109kph (68.3mph) (*The Autocar*); 23.9kph (14.9mph) @ 1000rpm; 0-96kph (60mph) 33.2sec; 28.9kg/kW (21.5kg/bhp); fuel consumption 29.7mpg (9.5 l/100km).
PRICE £360 plus £151 2s 6d purchase tax, £511 2s 6d (£511.12¹/₂p).
PRODUCTION 279,203 plus 66,638 as assembly kits.

1953 Prefect 100E

Essentially the same as the Anglia, with 4 doors and superior trim, the Prefect was some 50lb (22.7kg) heavier and identifiable by chrome headlight surrounds and a slatted grille. Among detail features welcomed by *The Autocar* in 1955 were its hydraulic clutch and pendant pedals. Most cars still had pedals sprouting through the toe-board with consequent problems of sealing from wind and water. Not so the new Fords with their hydraulic cylinder mounted on the clutch housing. The only sour note was struck by the vacuum operated wipers, which still "stopped in a most irritating fashion when the engine was pulling hard." The drive was taken up smoothly and firmly, although a rapid take-off from rest could spin the rear wheels, if the rear seat was not occupied. Yet for a small car the 100E's refinement was a revelation. Relatively narrow-section tyres did not set up much resonance through the monocoque structure, the engine was relatively small and quiet, there was not much wind noise at 60-odd mph, bulkhead sealing was quite good, and the three-box configuration absorbed vibrations well. There was a useful amount of luggage boot room with the spare wheel on the floor and the fuel tank to one side. The bonnet opened to a vertical position from the windscreen end so engine accessibility was excellent.

INTRODUCTION December 17 1953, produced until September 15 1959.
BODY saloon; 4-doors, 4-seats; weight 796kg (1755lb).
ENGINE 4-cylinders, in-line; front; 63.5mm x 92.5mm, 1172cc; compr 7.0:1; 26.8kW (36bhp) @ 4400rpm; 22.7kW/l (30.7bhp/l); 70.5Nm (52 lbft) @ 2500rpm.
ENGINE STRUCTURE side valve; chain-driven camshaft; cast iron cylinder head and block; downdraught Solex 26ZIC carb, 12volt coil ignition, AC mechanical fuel pump; 3-bearing crank.
TRANSMISSION rwd; single dry plate 7.38in hydraulic clutch; 3-speed manual gearbox, synchromesh on 2nd and top; Hardy Spicer open prop shaft; spiral bevel final drive 4.429:1.
CHASSIS steel monocoque; ifs by MacPherson struts; live rear axle with half-elliptic springs; telescopic dampers; Girling hydraulic 178mm (7in) drum brakes, 2LS at front; anti-roll bar; Burman worm and peg; 31.8l (7 gal) (8.4 US gal); 5.20 x 13in tyres, steel disc wheels.
DIMENSIONS wbase 220.9cm (87in); track 121.9cm (48in) front, 120.7cm

(47.5in) rear; length 384.2cm (151.25in); width 153.7cm (60.5in); height 150.5cm (59.25in); ground clearance 17.8cm (7in); turning circle 9.8m (32.25ft).
EQUIPMENT horn ring, interior light, 2 sun visors, 2 screen wipers, 5 colours, self-cancelling flashing indicators, pump, fan, thermostat cooling, baulk-ring synchromesh, heavy moulded rubber floor covering, heater extra.
PERFORMANCE maximum 108.9kph (67.7mph) (*The Autocar*); 23.9kph (14.9mph) @ 1000rpm; 0-96kph (60mph) 38.9sec; 29.7kg/kW (22.1kg/bhp); 8.3l/100km (33.8mpg).
PRICE £395, purchase tax £165 14s 2d, total £560 14s 2d (£560.71).
PRODUCTION 178,750 plus 76,905 as assembly kits.

Right: **As radical for small cars in 1953 as the Consul and Zephyr had been three years earlier, the 100E Anglia and Prefect were a runaway success. The Prefect was distinguished by four doors, chrome grille, and chrome headlamp surrounds.**

1954 Zodiac EOTTA

2-tone paintwork, white sidewall tyres, 9-carat gold-plated script, leather upholstery in 2 colours matching the exterior, chrome wing mirrors, Lucas "flamethrower" driving lamp and foglamp, all epitomised the 1950s. The Ford Zodiac was as compelling an automotive icon as the E-type Jaguar or the Mini. It was a flash of glamour in a new Elizabethan age, inspiring a host of really quite inappropriate accessories, such as a slatted blind for the big back window, and a sun visor over the windscreen more appropriate to Marbella than Marylebone. To a nation only just breaking the habit of buying cars in black, or for a showy fringe gunmetal grey, the 2-colour Zodiac was a revelation. It was symptomatic of the British discovering that they were not dull at all, and the nation relished the high-compression engine with its valve cover painted red, allegedly for identification but in reality to give the underbonnet a touch of class. Ferrari was thus not the first to think of a Testa Rossa.

By 1955 the axle ratio of the Zephyr had been raised slightly and the Zodiac's higher compression took advantage of the increasingly available premium-quality fuel. The reversing light was not turned on simply by engaging reverse, but by a separate switch with, as required by law, an illuminated tell-tale to prevent it being left alight inadvertently.

INTRODUCTION Motor Show October 1953, production November 1953 until February 1956.
BODY saloon; 4-doors, 5-seats; weight 1206.5kg (2660lb).
ENGINE 6-cylinders, in-line; front; 79.37mm x 76.2mm, 2262cc; compr 7.5:1; 52.9kW (71bhp) @ 4200rpm; 23.4kW/l (31.4bhp/l); 152Nm (112 lbft) @ 2000rpm.
ENGINE STRUCTURE pushrod ohv chain-driven camshaft; cast iron cylinder head and block; 30mm downdraught carburettor, 12v coil ignition AC mechanical fuel pump; 4-bearing cast iron counterweighted crankshaft.
TRANSMISSION rear wheel drive; 203mm (8in) single plate hydraulic clutch; 3-speed manual synchromesh (on 2nd and top) gearbox; steering column shift; hypoid final drive 4.44:1.
CHASSIS steel monocoque; ifs by coil springs and hydraulic telescopic dampers integral with kingpins; single track control arms located by triangulated anti-roll bar. Live rear axle with half-elliptic springs and piston dampers; Girling hydraulic 22.9cm (9in) drum brakes, 2 leading shoe at front;

Burman worm and peg steering; 40.9l (9 gal) (10.8 US gal) fuel tank; steel disc wheels, 6.40 x 13in tyres.
DIMENSIONS wheelbase 264.2cm (104in); track front 127cm (50in), rear 124.5cm (49in); length 431.8cm (170in); width 162.6cm (64in); height 154.3cm (60.75in); ground clearance 17.1cm (6.75in); turning circle right 12.5m (41ft), left 12m (39.5ft).
EQUIPMENT radio optional £47 17s 1d (£47.85°p); heater, screenwasher, whitewall tyres standard.
PERFORMANCE maximum speed 130kph (81mph); 25.9kph (16.2mph) @ 1000rpm; 0-96kph (60mph) 20.4sec; 22.8kg/kW (17kg/bhp); 11.91/100km (23.7mpg) (The Autocar).
PRICE £600 plus £251 2s 6d purchase tax 1955, £851 2s 6d (851.12½p).
PRODUCTION 22,634.

The Zodiac's two-tone paintwork and white sidewall tyres brought colour to 1950s motoring. Additional Lucas fog and spotlights were part of the package.

1954 Thames, 1950s Thames Trader

Thames was applied to Ford and Fordson medium and heavy trucks early in 1939. After the war, until 1965, it became the brand name for all Ford's commercial activities. The first post-war commercials were the established 5 and 10cwt vans, and forward control V8 2-5 tonners that were replaced in 1949 by Thames 4x2s, 6x4s, articulated units, and a Public Service Vehicle (PSV) chassis. Payloads ranged from 2-8tons, hydraulic brakes were introduced, with vacuum servos for heavy versions, there were semi-elliptic springs at the front, and the option of the Perkins P6 diesel. The petrol V8 continued until 1953, the advent of the 3.6-litre ohv 5-bearing 4-cylinder of 52.2kW (70bhp) that would also form the basis of Ford's first diesel in 1954. The heaviest range, 4 tons and over, retained the V8 until 1957 when the Thames Trader came in. This had a synchromesh gearbox and hypoid final drive, and was the first wholly British designed and developed British Ford commercial range, carrying the type number 508, suffixed E for England. The Trader's engines were all Ford-built, the 4-cylinder and 6-cylinder petrol 4.9-litre 85.8kW (115bhp), and a 5.4-litre 80.5kW (108bhp) diesel. The first 2 ton to 5 ton forward control range embraced tippers and an articulated tractor unit, and later extended to low frame models, 4x4 conversions by Vickers, and 6x2 and

6x4 reworkings by County Commercial Cars along the lines of the pre-war Surrey and Sussex models. There was also a 41-seater PSV chassis, one of which, equipped with a singular double-deck body, was used for taking cyclists through the Dartford-Purfleet Tunnel.

By the middle 1950s Ford had forward control vehicles from 2 to 7tons. The range was augmented by a series of normal control Traders with a cab from Germany, Cologne having ceased commercial vehicle production. From 1957 a new van, the 10/12cwt 400E, used a commercial version of the Consul 4-cylinder 1508cc following the withdrawal of the long-lasting 10cwt E83. The 400E had integral construction, forward control, side loading, 3-speed gearbox with steering column shift, independent front suspension, and hypoid final drive. It remained in production into the 1960s with the option of a Perkins diesel and, in 1964, a fourth gear. Commercial vehicle assembly moved to Langley, by what was still in 1960 the Cromwell Road Extension, the first part of the M4. The move marked an assault on the heavy end of the truck business that lasted well into the 1970s. By the time the M4 stretched to Wales in the west, and the link was established to the nearby M25 and the rest of the motorway network, it faced closure.

129

1955 Escort and Squire

Ford's first production estate car was no in-house saloon conversion but a stand-alone new model, with the underpinnings of the 100E Anglia and Prefect. It met a growing demand for carrying capacity for the hobbyist or small business. The rear doors were split horizontally, so there was no confusion with the Thames 5cwt van, and as a means of emphasising its saloon car credentials there were two models. Both were 3-door, the higher-priced Prefect-equivalent Squire denoting its place in the class structure by appliqué timber strips on the body sides. The less grand Escort had fewer frills (and certainly no wood), a cheaper model with mesh grille, less chrome, and less elaborate side windows. Testers complained that the bluff rear tended to suck along exhaust fumes, which had to be directed out again by the sliding side windows. The only mechanical difference from the saloons was stiffer rear springs, making the back axle hop a bit. The saloons' lower gearing was largely offset by the estates' larger-section tyres and economy was aided by the engines' ability to run on cheaper low-grade fuel, equivalent in cost to an extra 56.5l/100km (5mpg). The increase in weight resulted in some loss of performance. In October 1957 the Squire lost its much-derided wooden strips and the model was amalgamated with the Escort in 1959.

INTRODUCTION both models September 1955. Escort produced to April 1961, Squire discontinued September 1959.
BODY estate; 3-doors, 4-seats; weight 838.25kg (1848lb).
ENGINE 4-cylinders, in-line; front; 63.5mm x 92.5mm, 1172cc; compr 7.0:1; 26.8kW (36bhp) @ 4400rpm; 22.9kW/l (30.7bhp/l); 70.5Nm (52 lbft) @ 2500rpm.
ENGINE STRUCTURE side valve; chain-driven camshaft; cast iron cylinder head and block; downdraught Solex 26ZIC carburettor, 12volt coil ignition, AC mechanical fuel pump; 3-bearing crankshaft.
TRANSMISSION rear wheel drive; single dry plate 7.4in hydraulic clutch; 3-speed manual gearbox, synchromesh on 2nd and top; Hardy Spicer open prop shaft; spiral bevel final drive 4.429:1.
CHASSIS steel monocoque structure; independent front suspension by MacPherson struts; live rear axle with half-elliptic springs; telescopic dampers; Girling hydraulic 203mm (8in) drum brakes, 2LS at front; anti-roll bar; Burman worm and peg steering; 31.8l (7 gal) (8.4 US gal) fuel tank; 5.60 x 13in tyres steel disc wheels.
DIMENSIONS wheelbase 220.9cm (87in); track 121.9cm (48in) front, 120.7cm (47.5in) rear; length 361.3cm (142.25in); width 153.7cm (60.5in); height 160cm (63in); ground clearance 17.8cm (7in); turning circle 9.14m (30ft).
EQUIPMENT 8 body colours, pump, fan, and thermostat cooling, baulk-ring synchromesh, rubber floor covering, pvc plastic upholstery, leather extra, heater extra, Ecko radio extra.
PERFORMANCE maximum speed 112.2kph (69.9mph) *The Motor;* 24.2kph (15.1mph) @ 1000rpm; 0-96kph (60mph) 33.8sec; 31.3kg/kW (23.3kg/bhp); fuel consumption 7.9l/100km (35.7mpg).
PRICE 1956 Squire £445 plus purchase tax £223 16s, £668 16s (£668.80p). 1959 Escort £434, £615.96p.
PRODUCTION Escort 30,976, 2155 as assembly kits; Squire 15,952, 1860 as kits.

Top: when Squire still had
an upper class ring and an
estate car could well be
something used on an estate,
woodiness was an essential
ingredient of the trim even
though, as it this case,
it was pure trompe d'oeil.

Right: First use of Escort
as a Ford name, this was
the Anglia equivalent to
the Squire's Prefect.

1956 Consul Mark II 204E

Once the momentum of the first Consul and Zephyr was established it had to be maintained. Planned obsolescence was not yet discredited, new shapes and new fashions were brought in, so slightly hooded headlights and a hint of tail fins arrived with Mark II versions of cars that characterised the transformation of British motoring. Ford was repositioning itself in a market that in the 1930s was dominated by Morris, where it shared second place with Austin followed by Rootes and Standard, with Vauxhall a distant sixth. Imports were still negligible, as Ford overtook the combined Austin and Morris British Motor Corporation, progressively moving up from its bargain basement position by keeping cars like the Consul updated and re-skinned with eye-catching styles, colours, and trim. Price competition was maintained by manufacturing efficiency, which meant long production runs for engines and transmissions as well as, so far as possible, a car's basic platform and running gear. The Mark II Consul and Zephyr carried forward the Mark I's principle of a common central bodyshell with differences confined to front and back. Body stiffness was improved, they were roomier with wider track and longer wheelbases, and more deeply curved windscreen and rear windows.

INTRODUCTION February 1956, production until April 1962.
BODY saloon; 4-doors, 5-seats; weight 1143kg (2520lb).
ENGINE 4-cylinders, in-line; front; 82.55mm x 79.5mm, 1702cc; compr 7.8:1; 44kW (59bhp) @ 4200rpm; 25.8kW/l (34.7bhp/l); 124Nm (91 lbft) @ 4400rpm.
ENGINE STRUCTURE pushrod inclined ohv: chain-driven camshaft; cast iron cylinder head and block; Zenith 34WIA downdraught carburettor, centrifugal and vacuum ignition; mechanical fuel pump; 3-bearing hollow-cast counterweighted crankshaft.
TRANSMISSION rear wheel drive; 8in sdp clutch; 3-speed manual gearbox with steering column shift; synchromesh on 2nd and top; optional Borg Warner overdrive; Hardy Spicer open prop shaft; final drive 4.11:1.
CHASSIS steel monocoque structure; independent front suspension by MacPherson struts; anti-roll bar; live rear axle with half-elliptic springs and lever arm dampers; Girling hydraulic 9in drum brakes, 2LS at front;

worm and peg steering, recirculating ball after 1958; 50l (11 gal) (13.2 US gal) fuel tank; 5.90-13 tyres.
DIMENSIONS wheelbase 265.4cm (104.5in); track front 134.6cm (53in), rear 132.1cm (52in); length 438.2cm (172.5in); width 170.2cm (67in); height 151.1cm (59.5in); ground clearance 16.5cm (6.5in); turning circle 9.7m (32ft).
EQUIPMENT vacuum operated wipers; Optional fresh-air heater with demister, radio, screenwash, electric clock, cigar lighter, overdrive. Oct 1957: Consul de luxe 2-tone paintwork, cigar lighter, leather and nylon weave upholstery standard.
PERFORMANCE maximum speed 127.3kph (79.3mph) *The Motor*; 26.7kph (16.6mph) @ 1000rpm; 0-96kph (60mph) 23.2sec; 26kg/kW (19.4kg/bhp); fuel consumption 12.8l/100km (22.1mpg).
PRICE £520, purchase tax £261 7s 0d, total £781 7s 0d (£781.35) 1956. De luxe 1958 £871.35.
PRODUCTION: 290,951 saloons assembled 59,293 kits of parts.

Three years into
the model cycle the
roofline was lowered
by 1.5in (3.8cm) in
a comprehensive
facelift that kept
sales flourishing.

1956 Consul Convertible, Estate car

Soft-top versions of popular cars were always to represent a small proportion of production, yet they were important for Ford as range enhancements, in keeping with the abandonment of its old smokestack image. Again Carbodies was enlisted for their manufacture, strong flitch-plates reinforcing the sills and transmission tunnel, making them stiffer than the Mark I to ensure closer door shut-lines. The engineering used up some rear seat and boot space, and *The Motor* was disappointed with the power-operated hood on a Consul it tested in 1958. The switch-controlled electrical power system only moved the hood from the "de ville" position and the testers complained about the effort involved in rolling up or restoring the forward part. A fully manual hood, they concluded, would be lighter, better, and cheaper. Complete bodyshells were brought to Carbodies' works at Holyhead Road Coventry where the roof and doors were removed, new rear wings and doors manufactured, underbody reconstruction and reinforcement carried out, and the hood installed. The bodies were painted and trimmed, then taken back to Dagenham for wiring and assembly with the mechanical units. The estate car was once more entrusted to Abbott of Farnham with extended roof, new side panels with windows behind the rear doors, and a single piece tailgate.

INTRODUCTION October Motor Show 1956, production to Feb 1962.
BODY convertible; 2-doors, 5-seats; weight 1206.5kg (2660lb).
ENGINE 4-cylinders, in-line; front; 82.55mm x 79.5mm, 1702cc; compr 7.8:1; 44kW (59bhp) @ 4200rpm; 25.8kW/l (34.7bhp/l); 123Nm (91 lbft) @ 4400rpm.
ENGINE STRUCTURE pushrod inclined ohv; chain-driven camshaft; cast iron cylinder head and block; Zenith 34WIA downdraught carb, centrifugal and vacuum ignition; mechanical fuel pump; 3-bearing hollow-cast counterweighted crankshaft.
TRANSMISSION rwd; 8in sdp clutch; 3-speed gearbox with steering column shift; synchro on 2nd and top; optional Borg Warner overdrive; Hardy Spicer open prop shaft; final drive 4.11:1.
CHASSIS steel monocoque; ifs by MacPherson struts; anti-roll bar; live rear axle with half-elliptic springs and lever arm dampers; Girling hydraulic 9in drum brakes, 2LS at front; worm and peg steering, recirculating ball after 1958; 47.7l (10.5 gal) (12.6 US gal) fuel tank; 5.90-13 tubeless tyres.

DIMENSIONS wheelbase 265.4cm (104.5in); track front 134.6cm (53in), rear 132cm (52in); length 438.2cm (172.5in); width 170.2cm (67in); height 151.1cm (59.5in); ground clearance 16.5cm (6.5in); turning circle 9.7m (32ft).
EQUIPMENT vacuum operated wipers; pile carpet; 8 body colours. Optional fresh-air heater with demister, radio, screenwash, electric clock, cigar lighter, overdrive.
PERFORMANCE maximum speed 125.4kph (78.1mph) *The Motor*; 26.7kph (16.6mph) @ 1000rpm; 0-96kph (60mph) 24.2sec; 27.4kg/kW (20.4kg/bhp); 11.4l/100km (24.7mpg).
PRICE including power-operated roof £713, purchase tax £357 17s 0d, £1070 17s 0d (£1070.85) manual hood total £991.35).
PRODUCTION: 9398 convertibles, 5643 estates including Zephyrs.

Right: **Clean clipped uncluttered Consul. Stronger underpinnings compensated for absence of roof.**

1956 Zephyr Mark II 206E

Consul, Zephyr, and Zodiac underwent a number of changes over 6 years, besides the lowering of the roofline in 1959. The instrument panel was flattened out, interiors redesigned, and stainless steel was used for roof guttering and windscreen surrounds. Safety received more than lip service, with the scuttle topped off in soft padded plastic material, and sun visors with collapsing frames. In 1960 the entire range was given the option of disc front brakes after being used on works rally cars. By the following year discs were standard, together with sealed-beam headlamps. The bench front seat was retained despite some resentment over handling, and roadholding now so good that their occupants slid from side to side uncomfortably. Its accompanying steering column shift was one of the best of its kind, as well it ought, having only 3 forward speeds to select. Suspension tuning that induced understeer and curbed body roll subdued earlier models' tiresome rear wheel skittishness, and the change to recirculating ball restored feel to the steering. Engine changes from the Mark I included an extra 3.175mm (.125in) on the bore and stroke, and a new cylinder head with inclined valves in a wedge-shaped combustion chamber, giving much the same power output as before but at lower rpm, to the advantage of high-geared economy and refinement.

INTRODUCTION February 1956, production to April 1962.
BODY saloon; 4-doors, 5-seats; weight 1218kg (2695lb).
ENGINE 6-cylinders, in-line; front; 82.55mm x 79.5mm, 2553cc; compr 7.8:1; 64.1kW (86bhp) gross @ 4200rpm; 25.1kW/l (33.7bhp/l); 184Nm (136 lbft) @ 2000rpm.
ENGINE STRUCTURE pushrod inclined ohv; chain-driven camshaft; cast iron cylinder head and block; Zenith 36WIA downdraught carburettor, centrifugal and vacuum ignition; mechanical fuel pump; 4-bearing hollow-cast counterweighted crankshaft.
TRANSMISSION rear wheel drive; 8in sdp clutch; 3-speed manual gearbox with steering column shift; synchromesh on 2nd and top; optional Borg Warner overdrive on 2nd and top; Hardy Spicer open prop shaft; final drive 3.9:1, 2.83:1 overdrive; automatic optional.
CHASSIS steel monocoque structure; ifs by MacPherson struts; anti-roll bar; live rear axle with half-elliptic springs and lever arm dampers; Girling hydraulic 9in drum brakes, 2LS at front,

from 1960 servo-assisted disc brakes; worm and peg steering, recirculating ball after 1958; 50l (11 gal) (13.2 US gal); 6.40-13 tyres; 4¹/₂J rim steel wheels.
DIMENSIONS wheelbase 271.8cm (107in); track 134.6cm (53in) front, 132.1cm (52in) rear; length 453.4cm (178.5in); width 170.2cm (67in); height 151.8cm (59.75in); ground clearance 17.1cm (6.75in); turning circle 10.9m (36ft).
EQUIPMENT optional radio £30; heater £14; overdrive £64, automatic transmission, from 1960 disc brakes.
PERFORMANCE maximum 135.7kph (84.5mph) overdrive top *The Autocar*; 29.5kph (18.4mph) @ 1000rpm, 40.6kph (25.3mph) in overdrive; 0-96kph (60mph) 17.9sec; 19kg/kW (14.2kg/bhp); 11.7l/100km (24.1mpg).
PRICE £580, purchase tax £292, total £872.
PRODUCTION: 301,417 including Zodiac.

Right: **second thoughts on the Zephyr featured a mouth-organ grille and embryo tail fins.**

137

1956 Zephyr Mark II Estate car, Convertible, pick-up

Abbott-built Zephyr Estates had a wide but shallow tailgate aperture, as it was important not to dispense with the stiffening effect of the transverse panel between the tail-lights. Customers could specify a heavy wooden floor over the boot platform of the original saloon, with the spare wheel underneath. Access to it could be gained through a trapdoor. Alternatively, the existing boot floor could remain the basis of a large though uneven rear compartment, with the spare wheel upright at the side. The rear seat was liberated by draw-bolts and could be lifted out and placed vertically behind the front seat back or removed altogether. It was an unsophisticated arrangement but it worked, and the easily removable seat cushion was available for picnics or impromptu grandstand comfort at sporting events. The increasing popularity of the estate car as a fashion accessory was country-pursuit led. There was a small loss in performance from the saloon Zephyr through the addition of 68kg (150lb) in weight, and although there was more rearwards weight bias, the handling was not much affected. An unlikely variation on the Zephyr platform resulted from Dagenham building Knock-Down (KD) kits for assembly in Australia. This was a pick-up truck that proved popular among rural customers and of which 46 were exported as built-up vehicles.

INTRODUCTION February 1956, produced to April 1962.
BODY estate car, 5-doors, 5-seats; weight 1287kg (2838lb); convertible, 2-doors, 5-seats, 1270kg (2800lb).
ENGINE 6-cylinders, in-line; front, 82.55mm x 79.5mm, 2553cc; compr 7.8:1; 64.1kW (86bhp) gross @ 4200rpm; 25.1kW/l (33.7bhp/l); 184Nm (136 lbft) @ 2000rpm.
ENGINE STRUCTURE pushrod inclined ohv; chain-driven camshaft; cast iron cyl head and block; Zenith 36WIA downdraught carb, centrifugal and vacuum ign; mechanical fuel pump; 4-bearing hollow-cast counterweighted crankshaft.
TRANSMISSION rear wheel drive; 8in sdp clutch; 3-speed manual gearbox with steering column shift; synchromesh on 2nd and top; optional Borg Warner overdrive on 2nd and top; Hardy Spicer open prop shaft; final drive 3.9:1, 2.83:1 overdrive; automatic optional.
CHASSIS steel monocoque structure; ifs by MacPherson struts; anti-roll bar; live rear axle with half-elliptic springs and lever arm dampers; Girling hydraulic 9in drum brakes, 2LS at front,

from 1960 servo-assisted disc brakes; worm and peg steering, recirculating ball after 1958; 50l (11 gal) (13.2 US gal) fuel tank, Convertible 10.5 gal; 6.70-13 tyres; 4^1/$_2$J rim steel wheels.
DIMENSIONS wb 271.8cm (107in); track 134.6cm (53in) front, 132.1cm (52in) rear; length 453.4cm (178.5in); width 170.1cm (67in); height 151.8cm (59.75in); ground clearance 17.1cm (6.75in); turning circle 10.9m (36ft).
EQUIPMENT optional radio £30; heater £16; overdrive £64, automatic transmission, from 1960 disc brakes.
PERFORMANCE max 133.6kph (83mph) direct top *The Autocar*, 128.7kph (80mph) overdrive, Con 141.75kph (88.3mph) *The Motor*; 30.8kph (19.2mph) @ 1000rpm in top, 43.9kph (27.4mph) overdrive; 0-96kph (60mph) 18.7sec, Con 17sec; 20.1kg/kW (15kg/bhp), Con 19.8kg/kW (14.8kg/bhp); 11.3l/100km (25mpg).
PRICE £817 10s, purchase tax £410 2s, total £1227 12s (£1227.60); Convertible £841 10s plus purchase tax £351 15s, total £1193 5s (£1193.25p).
PRODUCTION 5643, including Consul estates.

Top right: the add-on element of the estate car bodywork was plain to see despite the disguising effect of two-colour paint and the distraction of chrome stripes.

Right: with the decks cleared the Zephyr had a wonderfully Transatlantic aspect. White sidewall tyres were much in vogue but not easy to keep clean.

1956 Zodiac Mark II 206E

Wide front-hinged doors, a generous boot, and all 4 extremities of the car visible from the driving seat, were among the practical aspects of the cleverly proportioned body. As bench seats and 3-speed gearboxes with steering column control became discredited, relief arrived with the development of a 3-speed automatic by Borg Warner, with small power losses suitable for a modest 2½-litre engine. Once manufacture started in the UK, the Borg Warner 35 found its way into an increasing number of British cars, among which were the 6-cylinder Fords. Automatic transmission matched their vaguely mid-Atlantic temperament perfectly and set new standards of refinement. It weighed an extra 63.5kg (140lb), absorbing more power than a conventional gearbox, so although fuel consumption was not much affected, acceleration suffered. An optional extra, around 15% of the purchase price on the Zephyr, automatic was eventually standard on the Zodiac. By the late 1950s heaters were usually fitted as standard, but it was not until the effects of Japanese imports were felt that radios followed suit. Ford's own-brand radio, the Enfo, had an amplifier behind the rear seats. If it was loud enough for the driver to hear, any rear-seat passengers were deafened. The Enfo set, even on the Zodiac, had manual tuning only.

INTRODUCTION February 1956, production until April 1962.
BODY saloon; 4-doors, 5-seats; weight 1311kg (2891lb).
ENGINE 6-cylinders, in-line; front; 82.55mm x 79.5mm, 2553cc; compr 7.8:1; 63.4kW (85bhp) net @ 4400rpm; 24.8kg/l (33.3bhp/l); 180Nm (133 lbft) @ 2000rpm.
ENGINE STRUCTURE pushrod inclined ohv; chain-driven camshaft; cast iron cylinder head and block; Zenith 36WIA downdraught carburettor, centrifugal and vacuum ignition; mechanical fuel pump; 4-bearing hollow-cast counterweighted crankshaft.
TRANSMISSION rear wheel drive; 3-speed automatic Borg Warner 35 gearbox; Hardy Spicer open prop shaft; final drive 3.9:1.
CHASSIS steel monocoque; ifs by MacPherson struts; anti-roll bar; live rear axle with half-elliptic springs and lever arm dampers; Girling hydraulic 9in drum brakes, 2LS at front, from 1960 servo-assisted disc brakes; worm and peg steering, recirculating ball after 1958; 47.7l (10.5 gal) (12.6 US gal);

6.70-13 tyres; 4.5J rim steel wheels.
DIMENSIONS wheelbase 271.8cm (107in); track 134.6cm (53in) front, 132.1cm (52in) rear; length 458.5cm (180.5in); width 170.2cm (67in); height 151.8cm (59.75in) (low roofline); ground clearance 17.1cm (6.75in); turning circle 10.9m (36ft).
EQUIPMENT from 1960 disc brakes.
PERFORMANCE maximum speed 133.2kph (83mph) *The Autocar*; 30.7kph (19.1mph) @ 1000rpm; 0-96kph (60mph) 20.9sec; 20.7kg/kW (15.4kg/bhp); 12.2l/100km (23.1mpg).
PRICE £790 plus purchase tax £396 7s, total £1186 7s (£1186.35).
PRODUCTION: 301,417 including Zephyr.

Two-tone paint and plenty of chrome were the ingredients of success in the 1950s.

1959 Popular 100E

Ford carried on making the cheapest car in Britain into the 1960s with a Popular version of the 100E Anglia. Just as the previous Popular had continued after a replacement Anglia came out, so the well-liked Anglia became the Popular by slightly de-trimming it and discarding the parcels shelf and opening quarter lights. It was no more than a gesture. The new Popular was an Anglia at a discount and owed nothing to the Model T heritage of the old Popular with its transverse leaf springing and rod-operated brakes. Road testers obediently compared it with this car rather than the 100E whose genes it really inherited. It was up to date, notwithstanding its side-valve engine and Hardura floorcloth. Vindication of continuing production after its Anglia years came with the extension of its lifespan to nearly a decade and the manufacture of nearly half as many examples again. While the long list of extras explains some of the cost-cutting to get the price not only under £500 but also below the new Mini (by barely £1), the Popular did have up to date equipment where appropriate. The brakes were enlarged and 4-ply tubeless tyres fitted to meet contemporary standards. Most buyers equipped Populars with the de luxe extras including no less than 3 ashtrays. Chief demerit was that by the 1960s much of the competition was smoother-riding and had 4 gears.

INTRODUCTION August 25 1959, produced until June 1962.
BODY saloon; 2-doors, 4-seats; weight 749kg (1652lb).
ENGINE 4-cylinders, in-line; front; 63.5mm x 92.5mm, 1172cc; compr 7.0:1; 26.8kW (36bhp) @ 4500rpm; 22.9kW/l (30.7bhp/l); 70.5Nm (52 lbft) @ 2500rpm.
ENGINE STRUCTURE side valve; chain-driven camshaft; cast iron cylinder head and block; downdraught Solex 26ZIC2 carburettor, 12 volt coil ignition, AC mechanical fuel pump; 3-bearing crankshaft.
TRANSMISSION rear wheel drive; single dry plate 7.4in hydraulic clutch; 3-speed manual gearbox, synchromesh on 2nd and top; Hardy Spicer open prop shaft; spiral bevel final drive 4.429:1.
CHASSIS steel monocoque structure; independent front structure by MacPherson struts; live rear axle with half-elliptic springs; telescopic dampers; Girling hydraulic 20.3cm (8in) drum brakes, 2LS at front; anti-roll bar; Burman worm and peg steering; 31.8l (7 gal) (8.4 US gal) fuel tank; 5.20 x 13in

4-ply tubeless tyres, steel disc wheels.
DIMENSIONS wheelbase 220.9cm (87in); track 121.9cm (48in) front, 120.7cm (47.5in) rear; length 384.2cm (151.25in); width 153.7cm (60.5in); height 150.5cm (59.25in); ground clearance 17.8cm (7in); turning circle 9.8m (32.25ft).
EQUIPMENT 8 exterior colours, 11 on de luxe, sun visor, 2 screen wipers, pump, fan, and thermostat cooling, baulk-ring synchromesh, moulded rubber floor covering. Heater, screenwashers, radio, roof rack, wheel trims, bumper overriders, interior light, cigar lighter, carburettor air cleaner, underbody spare wheel carrier, tool kit, reversing lamp, boot handle, extra.
PERFORMANCE maximum speed 109kph (68.3mph) *The Autocar*; 23.9kph (14.9mph) @ 1000rpm; 0-96kph (60mph) 33.2sec; 27.9kg/kW (20.8kg/bhp); fuel consumption 9.5 l/100km (29.7mpg).
PRICE £348 plus purchase tax £146 2s 6d, total £494 2s 6d (£494.12½p).
PRODUCTION 120,815, 5300279,203 plus 66,638 as assembly kits.

Right: the success of the **100E Anglia** was sustained by the same-design **Popular** with lusty side-valve engine and well-proportioned three-box body.

1959 Anglia 105E

Features like tailfins became part of the stylist's stock-in-trade, but the reverse-rake rear window was gimmicky from the start. Drawn up by peripatetic American designer Elmwood Engel, and advertised as providing a clear view behind on a bad day, it may have gone down well at design clinics but it got short shrift by customers who could see no rationale for it beyond a perverse desire to be different. The new Anglia was more notable for its overhead valve engine and long-legged high-geared performance than for a back window whose only real merits lay in a bigger luggage boot aperture, and more headroom in the back. An important feature was the 80-bore engine, more over-square in its cylinder dimensions (0.6:1) than anything hitherto, and high gearing anticipating the opening of Britain's new motorways.

The new Anglia may not have been as technically avant garde as the other 1959 Earls Court debutants, the Mini and the Triumph Herald, yet it transcended both in build quality. The result was a saloon, with estate car launched in 1961, that sold more than a million. Production was transferred in March 1963 to a new factory at Halewood on Merseyside. Yet the Anglia's significance lay well beyond its immediate lifespan; like the Model T it became the basis for Ford models several generations ahead.

INTRODUCTION September 3 1959, produced until November 1967.
BODY saloon; 2-doors, 4-seats; weight 737kg (1624.8lb), 5 door estate 786kg (1732.8lb).
ENGINE 4-cylinders, in-line; front; 80.96mm x 48.41mm, 996.6cc; compr 8.9:1; 29.1kW (39bhp) @ 5000rpm; 29.2kW/l (39.1bhp/l); 71Nm (52.5 lbft) @ 2700rpm.
ENGINE STRUCTURE pushrod ohv, chain-driven camshaft; cast iron cyl head and block; Solex downdraught 30ZIC2 carb, centrifugal and vacuum ignition; AC mechanical fuel pump; 3-bearing hollow-cast crankshaft.
TRANSMISSION rwd; 18.4cm (7.25in) sdp clutch; 4-speed manual gearbox, synchro on 3; Hardy Spicer open prop shaft; hypoid bevel final drive 4.12:1.
CHASSIS steel monocoque; ifs by MacPherson struts with Armstrong double-acting integral dampers and anti-roll bar; live rear axle with half-elliptic springs and Armstrong lever arm dampers; hydraulic 203mm (8in) drum brakes; Ford recirculating ball steering; 31.8l (7 gal) (8.4 US gal) fuel tank; 5.20-13 tubeless tyres; 5.60-13 estate.

DIMENSIONS wheelbase 229.2cm (90.25in); track 117.5cm (46.25in); length 390.5cm (153.75in), estate 392cm (154.3in); width 143.5cm (56.5in); height 142.2cm (56in); ground clearance 15.2cm (6in); turning circle 9.9m (32.4ft).
EQUIPMENT 8 exterior colours on standard spec, 12 single and 4 dual-tone on de luxe; heater £14.17; moulded rubber floor covering, 2-colour pvc upholstery on de luxe, one colour on standard; radio, screenwasher, leather upholstery optional extras.
PERFORMANCE maximum speed 123.3kph (76.8mph) *The Autocar*; 25.8kph (16.1mph) @ 1000rpm; 0-96kph (60mph) 29.4sec; 25.3kg/kW (18.9kg/bhp), estate 27kg/kW (20.2kg/bhp); 7.8l/100km (36.1mpg).
PRICE £430, purchase tax £180 5s 10d, total £610 5s 10d (£610.29).
PRODUCTION 1,083,960 including 129,528 estates.

First car off the Halewood production line was a 105E Anglia, presented to the Liverpool museum (see p21).

Right: **Anglia in rural setting shows off its reverse rake rear window. Publicity shots liked to suggest an up-market image.**

Top right: **Anglia interiors were carefully designed to be suitable for left and right hand drive without too much disruption.**

1959 Prefect 107E

Ford was good at ringing the changes in its model range, and while the new Anglia borrowed the 100E's MacPherson strut suspension and other running gear, the old Prefect 4-door bodyshell inherited the 107E overhead valve engine for a new lease of life than lasted 2 more years. The new Anglia was a 2-door only, the Classic was a relatively large car, and so the 107E was invoked to keep Ford in the small 4-door saloon market. Distinguishable from the old side-valve Prefect by means of chrome side strips and optional 2-colour paintwork, it was available only in de luxe form with more comfortable seats, carpets, and the Anglia's 4-speed gearbox. Its clientele remained faithful, and although the engine was of 15 per cent smaller displacement, its modern design and over-square cylinder dimensions gave it just as much torque and far more power. It was good value, and even if the body styling had begun to look a bit staid and upright, it was a practical 3-box shape, easy to get in and out of, with a useful boot and its performance and economy were ideal for the family motorist. *The Motor* found the ride a bit lively when there was little weight aboard and although there was "quite fair" insulation against shock was agreeably surprised to find no "exaggerated softness to make passengers queasy."

INTRODUCTION May 5 1959, produced until June 1961.
BODY saloon; 4-doors, 4-seats; weight 800kg (1764lb).
ENGINE 4-cylinders, in-line; front; 80.96mm x 48.41mm, 996.6cc; compr 8.9:1; 29.1kW (39bhp) net @ 5000rpm; 29.2kW/l (39.1bhp/l); 71Nm (52.5 lbft) @ 2700rpm.
ENGINE STRUCTURE pushrod overhead valve, chain-driven camshaft; cast iron cylinder head and block; Solex downdraught 30ZIC2 carburettor, centrifugal and vacuum ignition; AC mechanical fuel pump; 3-bearing hollow-cast crankshaft.
TRANSMISSION rwd; 18.4cm (7.25in) sdp clutch; 4-speed gearbox, synchro on 3; Hardy Spicer open prop shaft; hypoid bevel final drive 4.429:1.
CHASSIS steel monocoque structure; ifs by MacPherson struts; live rear axle with half-elliptic springs; telescopic dampers; Girling hydraulic 17.8cm (7in) drum brakes, 2LS at front; anti-roll bar; Burman worm and peg steering; 31.8l (7 gal) (8.4 US gal); 5.20 x 13in tubeless tyres, steel disc wheels.
DIMENSIONS wheelbase 220.9cm (87in); track 121.9cm (48in) front, 120.7cm (47.5in) rear; length 384.2cm (151.25in); width 153.7cm (60.5in); height 150.5cm (59.25in); gc 17.8cm (7in); turning circle 9.8m (32.25ft).
EQUIPMENT Heater extra £13 9s 2d, leather trim £14 3s 4d, 2-colour paint £7 1s 8d, whitewall tyres £5 13s 4d, also bumper overriders, wheel trims, hub cap medallions, exhaust deflector, seat covers, cigar lighter, vanity mirror, radiator blind, screenwashers Standard, carpets, 12 exterior colours, 4 2-colour.
PERFORMANCE maximum speed 117kph (72.9mph) *The Motor*; 23.9kph (14.9mph) @ 1000rpm; 0-96kph (60mph) 27.2sec; 27.5kg/kW (20.5kg/bhp); 9.4l/100km (30.1mpg).
PRICE £438, purchase tax £183 12s 6d, total £621 12s 6d (£621.62½).
PRODUCTION 38,154 including 10,840 in kit form.

Right: 1959 107E Prefect owned by Laurie Menear of Woodley, Berkshire took part, ironically enough, in a Ford Sidevalve Owners' Club cavalcade to Dagenham.

1961 Consul Classic 315 109E

The reverse-rake rear window of the Anglia was perpetuated on the Classic, arguably a good car condemned to mediocrity by this flight of fancy. Filling a vacancy between the Anglia and the now grown-up Consul, and essentially stop-gap in anticipation of the Cortina, the Classic was not expected to have a long life-span. In this respect Ford planners were not disappointed, the 1340cc lasting a year, and the 1500 only a year on from that. A production run for the combined Classic and Capri of less than 130,000 was hardly up to par, and the best that could be said was that the model had been used as a test-bed for innovation. It had the appearance, feel, and luggage capacity of a larger car, and it returned Ford gear levers firmly to the floor, although with true marketing caution the steering column change was retained as an option.

The engine was essentially Anglia with the same bore and longer stroke. Separate front seats, disc brakes, electric screen wipers, four headlamps, a choice of 2 or 4 doors, and a good standard of trim for only just over £800 (the 2-door was under £750) raised the stakes in the market. Even if the customers eventually turned down the radical styling, there was quite a lot to be said for the Classic as a wide-ranging brand in the evolution of Ford.

INTRODUCTION 4-door and de luxe 2-door April 1961-July/August 1962; standard 2-door June 1961-August 1962.
BODY saloon; 2 and 4-doors, 5-seats; weight 920kg (2025lb) 2-door, 945kg (2080 lb) 4-door.
ENGINE 4-cylinders, in-line; front; 80.96mm x 65.07mm, 1340cc; compr 8.5:1; 40.3kW (54bhp) @ 4900rpm; 30.1kW/l (40.3bhp/l); 100Nm (74 lbft) @ 2500rpm.
ENGINE STRUCTURE pushrod overhead valve, chain-driven camshaft; cast iron cylinder head and block; Zenith 32VN downdraught carburettor, centrifugal and vacuum ignition; AC mechanical fuel pump; 3-bearing hollow-cast crankshaft.
TRANSMISSION rear wheel drive; 18.4cm (7.25in) hydraulic sdp clutch; 4-speed manual gearbox, synchromesh on 3; hypoid bevel final drive 4.13:1.
CHASSIS steel monocoque structure; ifs by MacPherson struts and anti-roll bar; live rear axle with half-elliptic springs and lever arm dampers; Girling hydraulic non-servo 24.1cm (9.5in) disc front, 22.9cm (9in) drum rear brakes; recirculating ball steering; 4ll (9 gal) (10.8 US gal) fuel tank; 5.60-13 tyres.
DIMENSIONS wheelbase 252cm (99in); track 126cm (49.5in); length 434cm (170.8in) width 166cm (62.2in); height 142cm (56in); ground clearance 15cm (5.9in); turning circle 10.36m (34ft).
EQUIPMENT fresh-air heater, leather upholstery, push-button or manual control radio optional extras; screenwasher standard, pvc upholstery, carpet, 12 body colours, 7 2-colour choices.
PERFORMANCE maximum speed 125.8kph (78.4mph) *The Motor*; 26.4kph (16.45mph) @ 1000rpm; 0-96kph (60mph) 22.5sec; 22.8kg/kW (17.1kg/bhp) 2-door, 23.4kg/kW (17.5kg/bhp) 4-door; fuel consumption 9.9l/100km (28.6mpg).
PRICE 4-door £565, purchase tax £236 10s 10d, total £801 10s 10d (£801.54).
PRODUCTION 84,694.

Right: Inveraray, Argyll, Scotland is the tranquil setting for this Consul Classic 315 4-door de luxe saloon.

1961 Capri 109E

The voluptuous lines of the Capri were a surprise to a British market that regarded 2+2s as sports cars, and was unfamiliar even uncomfortable with the concept of a car in which appearance took precedence over passenger space. It was legitimate if space was sacrificed to speed, but a rear window raked at 40 degrees, and an enormously long rear deck just for appearances' sake was somehow too contrived. The name outlasted the model. It had been used on a Lincoln, and Ford now applied it to a version of the Classic intended for export, but to which the home market unexpectedly warmed. 5cm (2in) lower than the saloon, its small frontal area gave it an advantage in top speed, but it had no sporting pretensions. Rather thin cushions could be specified for the rear shelf, normally carpeted as an addition to the enormous boot, enabling it to serve as a back seat when absolutely necessary. Luggage room was even bigger than the Classic and the boot floor, which was of pick-up truck proportions, was rubber-covered. The front seats were better shaped than the saloon's and finished in 2 colours of pvc. Like the Classic however the Capri driver was still required to do a certain amount of home maintenance to ensure satisfactory running. 10 points required attention with a grease-gun every 1000 miles.

INTRODUCTION July 1961 - August 1962.
BODY coupe; 2-doors, 2+2-seats; weight 2055lb (932.1kg).
ENGINE 4-cylinders, in-line; front; 80.96mm x 65.07mm, 1340cc; compr 8.5:1; 40.3kW (54bhp) @ 4900rpm; 30.1kW/l (40.3bhp/l); 100Nm (74 lbft) @ 2500rpm.
ENGINE STRUCTURE pushrod overhead valve, chain-driven camshaft; cast iron cylinder head and block; Zenith 32VN downdraught carburettor, centrifugal and vacuum ignition; AC mechanical fuel pump; 3-bearing hollow-cast crankshaft.
TRANSMISSION rear wheel drive; 18.4cm (7.25in) hydraulic sdp clutch; 4-speed manual gearbox, synchromesh on 3; hypoid bevel final drive 4.13:1.
CHASSIS steel monocoque structure; ifs by MacPherson struts and anti-roll bar; live rear axle with half-elliptic springs and lever arm dampers; Girling hydraulic non-servo 24.1cm (9.5in) disc front, 22.9cm (9in) drum rear brakes; recirculating ball steering; 41l (9 gal) (10.8 US gal) fuel tank; 5.60-13 tubeless tyres.

DIMENSIONS wheelbase 252cm (99in); track 126cm (49.5in); length 434cm (170.8in); width 166cm (62.2in); height 137.2cm (54in); ground clearance 15cm (5.9in); turning circle 10.36m (34ft).
EQUIPMENT fresh-air heater, leather upholstery, push-button or manual control radio optional extras; screenwasher standard, pvc upholstery, carpet, 12 body colours, 7 2-colour choices.
PERFORMANCE maximum speed 130.35kph (81.2mph) *The Autocar;* 26.4kph (16.5mph) @ 1000rpm; 0-96kph (60mph) 21.3sec; 30.9kg/kW (17.3kg/bhp); 10.1l/100km (27.9mpg).
PRICE £627, purchase tax £288 12s, total £915 12s (£915.60).
PRODUCTION 11.143 including 1291 kits.

Right: **the five stars in the air intake were the visible embodiment of Ford's series of advertisements for "Five star motoring".**

1962 Classic 116E

Despite being the beneficiary of the new strain of Ford engines, the Classic's second year of production saw its decline. 5 main bearings made for smooth running, there was 10 per cent more pulling power and an increase in top speed, yet the Classic spent a shorter time in production than any Ford since the war. It was all very well to claim it was never meant to survive long and that the body dies were made of short-duration Kirksite and not case-hardened steel, its reception from the press was lukewarm and customers failed to materialise in their customary numbers. Ford had enjoyed unbroken success since the Consul and Zephyr of 1950, its transformation from working-class to middle-class was complete, but the Classic was a salutary reminder that sustained effort and good judgement were required to remain on top of the market. The engine was the third (105E, 109E and 116E) to use the same cylinder block, with the same bore of 1.187in, variations being attained by lengthening the stroke from 1.906in, to 2.562in and finally 2.86in. This last had the cylinder top face raised by .66in (16.76mm) and the change to 5 main bearings was accompanied by a change to a solid crankshaft rather than a nodular cored-out one. Cylinder heads were not interchangeable however and the combustion chambers were fully machined.

INTRODUCTION July 1962, production until September 1963.
BODY saloon; 2 and 4-doors, 5-seats; weight 2-door 935kg (2058lb), 4-door 955kg (2106 lb) 4-door.
ENGINE 4-cylinders, in-line; front; 80.96mm x 72.7mm, 1499cc; compr 8.3:1; 44.4kW (59.5bhp) @ 4600rpm; 29.6kW/l (39.7bhp/l); 110.5Nm (81.5 lbft) @ 2300rpm.
ENGINE STRUCTURE pushrod overhead valve, chain-driven camshaft; cast iron cylinder head and block; Zenith 33VN downdraught carburettor, centrifugal and vacuum ignition; AC mechanical fuel pump; 5-bearing crankshaft.
TRANSMISSION rear wheel drive; 18.4cm (7.25in) hydraulic sdp clutch; 4-speed manual gearbox, all-synchro; hypoid bevel final drive 4.13:1.
CHASSIS steel monocoque structure; ifs by MacPherson struts and anti-roll bar; live rear axle with half-elliptic springs and lever arm dampers; Girling hydraulic non-servo 24.1cm (9.5in) disc front, 22.9cm (9in) drum rear brakes; recirculating ball steering; 41l (9 gal) (10.8 US gal) fuel tank;

5.60-13 tubeless or tubed tyres.
DIMENSIONS wheelbase 252cm (99in); track 126cm (49.5in); length 434cm (170.8in); width 166cm (62.2in); height 142cm (56in); ground clearance 15cm (5.9in); turning circle 10.36m (34ft).
EQUIPMENT fresh-air heater, leather upholstery, push-button or manual control radio optional extras; screenwasher standard, pvc upholstery, carpet, 12 body colours, 7 2-colour choices.
PERFORMANCE maximum speed 129.6kph (80.7mph) *The Motor*; 26.4kph (16.5mph) @ 1000rpm; 0-96kph (60mph) 20.1sec; 21.1kg/kW (15.7kg/bhp) 2-door, 21.5kg/kW (16.1kg/bhp) 4-door; fuel consumption 11l/100km (25.8mpg).
PRICE £565, purchase tax £212 17s 9d, total £777 17s 9d (£777.89p) 4-door.
PRODUCTION 24,531, 2000KD. standard 4-door 1770; de luxe 2-door 6742; de luxe 4-door 17,179.

1962 Capri 116E, Capri GT

The Capri 335 inherited the Classic's 5-bearing engine and all-synchromesh gearbox and managed to outlast the saloons by almost a year. It was all part of Ford's repositioning of itself, the GT invoking what Ford liked to call a spirit of fun, which meant more speed and style, better handling, and just a whiff of sportiness.

The 105E engine was already the mainstay of Formula Ford, and the 5-bearing engine with its robust bottom end, encouraged tuners and special builders. The 116E for the GT was equipped with a twin-choke Weber carburettor, essential to any engine with competition aspirations in the 1960s, a 4-branch exhaust, and a high-lift camshaft designed by a new name in high performance engines, Keith Duckworth. The co-founder of Cosworth Engineering, Duckworth had a close relationship with Ford. "I hadn't designed many cams," he said later. "I had read all the books on cam design and believed them, but they only tended to mislead me. I decided it was better to work things out from first principles." His engineering genius was yet to reach full flower, and although the Capri GT was a lively performer with 30 per cent more power and 12 per cent more torque, it never really found favour as a sporty car and only 412 were sold in its final year.

INTRODUCTION July 1962, produced until September 1963; GT February 1963 until July 1964. BODY coupe; 2-doors, 2+2-seats; weight 946.7kg (2087lb). ENGINE 4-cylinders, in-line; front; 80.96mm x 72.7mm, 1499cc; compr 8.3:1; 44.4kW (59.5bhp) @ 4600rpm; 29.6kW/l (39.7bhp/l); 110.5Nm (81.5 lbft) @ 2300rpm. GT compr 9:1; 58.2kW (78bhp) @ 5200rpm; 38.8kW/l (52bhp/l); 123Nm (91 lbft) @ 3600rpm.
ENGINE STRUCTURE pushrod ohv, chain-driven camshaft; cast iron cyl head and block; Zenith 33VN downdraught carb, centrifugal and vacuum ignition; AC mechanical fuel pump; 5-bearing crank. GT Weber 28/36 DCD22 2-choke compound downdraught carb.
TRANSMISSION rear wheel drive; 18.4cm (7.25in) hydraulic sdp clutch; 4-speed manual gearbox, all-synchro; hypoid bevel final drive 4.13:1.
CHASSIS steel monocoque structure; ifs by MacPherson struts and anti-roll bar; live rear axle with half-elliptic springs and lever arm dampers; Girling hydraulic non-servo (GT Servo) 24.1cm (9.5in) disc front, 22.9cm (9in) drum rear brakes; recirculating ball steering; 41l (9 gal) (10.8 US gal) fuel tank; 5.60-13 tubeless tyres.
DIMENSIONS wheelbase 252cm (99in); track 126cm (49.5in); length 434cm (170.8in); width 166cm (62.2in); height 142cm (56in); ground clearance 15cm (5.9in); turning circle 10.36m (34ft).
EQUIPMENT fresh-air heater standard, Cirrus or leather/pvc upholstery, push-button (£33 3s 11d, £33.20) or manual control radio optional extras; screenwasher standard, pvc upholstery, carpet, safety belts £4 15s 0d (£4.75p), occasional seat cushion £9. 9s 0d (£9.45p).
PERFORMANCE max speed GT 149.8kph (93.3mph) *The Motor*, 26.4kph (16.5mph) @ 1000rpm; 0-96kph (60mph) 20sec, GT 14.1sec; 21.3kg/kW (15.9kg/bhp); fuel consumption GT 10.4l/100km (27.1mpg).
PRICE £864 total with purchase tax. GT £745, purchase tax £155 15s 5d, total £900 15s 5d (£955.77p).
PRODUCTION 6868 plus 705 in kits, 2002 total GTs.

One of the most glamorous
Fords of the decade. With the
side windows down, the Capri
had the aspect of what the
American industry of the time
called without a trace of irony,
"fixed head convertibles."

1962 Anglia Super 123E

The Anglia Super was presented as a high performance luxury version with a 1200cc engine. It was only 2 weeks later that its new place in the scheme of things was revealed, when the cheapest Cortina was announced at £639 a bare £40 dearer. Like the Cortina, the Anglia Super had synchromesh on all 4 gears, with the ratio of first raised to make the most of it. Wider brake drums were fitted, and it had the favourite distinguishing feature of the time, duo-tone paintwork. Wheel trims were included in the price, which was £60 over the standard Anglia. The result was a good deal livelier than the 105E but used more fuel. Customers, soon to be exposed to Oriental imports with radios, heaters, and suchlike included in the price, were expecting better equipment from domestic producers, although they had to wait until 1964 for a built-in radio and seat belt attachments. The Anglia Super had pleated pvc upholstery (whose silvery finish *The Motor's* road testers found slippery during cornering), woven-cord carpet, padded dashboard, screenwashers, and a cigarette lighter. Production was transferred to Halewood in March 1963, in 1965 the estate car gearing was standardised on saloons, and the Anglia went on to have an eight-year run of success. In 1966 Ford introduced an in-house carburettor to replace the original Solex downdraught.

INTRODUCTION September 1962, production until November 1967.
BODY saloon; 2-doors, 4-seats; weight 778kg (1715lb).
ENGINE 4-cylinders, in-line; front; 80.96mm x 58.17mm, 1198cc; compr 8.7:1; 36.5kW (49bhp) @ 4800rpm; 30.5kW/l (40.9bhp/l); 86Nm (63 lbft) @ 2700rpm.
ENGINE STRUCTURE pushrod overhead valve, chain-driven camshaft; cast iron cylinder head and block; Solex B30 PSEI-2 downdraught carburettor, centrifugal and vacuum ignition; AC mechanical fuel pump; 3-bearing hollow-cast crankshaft.
TRANSMISSION rear wheel drive; Borg & Beck 18.4cm (7.25in) clutch; 4-speed manual gearbox all-synchro; Hardy Spicer series 1140 prop shaft; hypoid bevel final drive 4.125:1.
CHASSIS steel monocoque structure; ifs by MacPherson struts and anti roll bar; live rear axle with half-elliptic springs, lever arm damper; Girling hydraulic 20.3cm (8in) drum brakes; Burman recirculating ball steering; 31.8l (7 gal) (8.4 US gal) fuel tank; 5.20-13 tubeless tyres.

DIMENSIONS wheelbase 229.2cm (90.25in); track 117.5cm (46.25in); length 390.5cm (153.75in), estate 392cm (154 3in); width 143.5cm (56.5in); height 142.2cm (56in); ground clearance 15.2cm (6in); turning circle 9.88m (32.4ft).
EQUIPMENT manual pump screenwashers, self-parking wipers, heater, carpets standard, Ford manual or push-button radio optional extra, eight duo-tone colours.
PERFORMANCE maximum speed 131.3kph (81.8mph) *The Motor*; 25.2kph (15.7mph) @ 1000rpm; 0-96kph (60mph) 21.6sec; 21.3kg/kW (15.9kg/bhp); fuel consumption 33mpg (8.56l/100km).
PRICE de luxe £495, purchase tax £103 13s 9d, total £598 13s 9d (£598.69p).
PRODUCTION 79,223.

Anglia 1964

Anglia 1965

Anglia 1964

1962 Cortina 113E 2-door, 4-door, Estate car

The Classic appeared first as a Consul Classic and the Cortina a Consul Cortina, meeting an obscure concern in the marketing department that nobody would know what it was. The Consul on the bonnet was soon dropped. The Cortina never needed spin-doctoring. It was one of the most successful Fords ever and outshone more technically adventurous competitors. It even outshone a front wheel drive that rival Ford Germany was developing jointly with Detroit, codenamed Cardinal.

The Cortina was developed in Britain under the codename Archbishop, and was straightforward front-engined rear-drive and 3-box. Its highest-tech feature was a monocoque shell designed to new heights of aerospace excellence, calculating stress requirements so precisely that surplus metal, and thus surplus weight, could be discarded. The process saved some 68kg (150lb), making the Cortina cheaper, faster, and more economical than anything in its class. It was claimed that the weight saved was equivalent to the weight of an adult occupant. Roy Brown was responsible for the shape (as he was for the Mk III Zephyr) and got the proportions right.

The Cortina was *Auto Universum's* car of the year. Priced at the level of many 1-litre cars, and as roomy as lots of 1.5-litre cars (it was analogous with the Classic), the 1.2 Cortina 2-door was a revelation. It could seat 6 with the optional bench seat and the ingenious cable-operated steering column gearshift, even though most buyers preferred this on the floor. Introduced with a rather severe interior of painted metal and rubber-covered floor it was not long before the Cortina moved up-market with better furnishings and a higher price.

INTRODUCTION 2-dr Nov 1962 followed by 4-door & estate; produced until Nov 1966.
BODY saloon 2-door, 4-door, estate 5-door, 5-seats; wt 4-door 809kg (1783.5lb), 2-door 794kg (1750.5lb), estate 912kg (2010.6lb).
ENGINE 4-cylinders, in-line; front; 80.96mm x 58.17mm, 1198cc; compr 8.7:1; 36.5kW (49bhp) @ 4800rpm; 30.5kW/l (40.9bhp/l); 85Nm (63 lbft) @ 2700rpm.
ENGINE STRUCTURE pushrod overhead valve, chain-driven camshaft; cast iron cylinder head and block; Solex B30 PSEI-2 downdraught carburettor, centrifugal and vacuum ignition; AC mechanical fuel pump; 3-bearing hollow-cast crankshaft.
TRANSMISSION rear wheel drive; Borg & Beck 18.4cm (7.25in) clutch; 4-speed manual gearbox all-synchro; Hardy Spicer series 1140 prop shaft; hypoid bevel final drive 4.125:1.
CHASSIS steel monocoque structure; ifs by MacPherson struts and anti roll bar; live rear axle with half-elliptic springs, telescopic dampers; Girling hydraulic 20.3cm (8in) drum brakes; Burman recirculating ball steering; 31.8l (7 gal) (8.4 US gal) fuel tank; 5.20-13 tubeless tyres.
DIMENSIONS wheelbase 249cm (98in); track 126cm (49.6in), estate front 127cm (50in); length 427.5cm (168.3in), estate 428cm (168.5in); width 159cm

(62.6in); height 144cm (56.7in),
estate 146cm (57.5in); ground
clearance 16cm (6.3in), estate 17cm
(6.7in); turning circle 9.6m (31.5ft).
EQUIPMENT 8 exterior colours,
6 duotone at extra cost; bench seat
with steering column gearchange,
heater, radio, whitewall tyres, leather
upholstery optional extras.
PERFORMANCE maximum speed
123.2kph (76.5mph) *The Autocar*;
25.8kph (16.1mph) @ 1000rpm;
0-96kph (60mph) 22.4sec; 22.2kg/kW
(16.5kg/bhp); fuel consumption
9.4l/100km (30.2mpg).
PRICE £484, purchase tax
£182 10s 3d, £666 10s 3d (£666.51p).
PRODUCTION 1,013,391 all Mark 1.

1962 Zephyr 4 Mark III 211E saloon, estate car

The Mark III Zephyr marked a further step into the premium-priced large car market, although at the entry level it was promoted as a Consul replacement (the name was at last abandoned) Zephyr 4. Stylist Canadian Roy Brown, whose predilection for ovoid shapes had helped fashion the ill-starred Edsel, took over after in-house and Frua designs were abandoned, designing a homely trio with sufficient tailfin and good balance to be in vogue. The Zephyr 4 was plainest, with a one-piece grille and less brightwork, even though it offered the same room inside and had the same boot and bonnet. Rear legroom was less than generous however, and had to be increased with a package of modifications within nine months of launch, when the interior was improved cosmetically with simulated wood like the 6. There were a few technical innovations such as a new sort of recirculating ball steering, with variable ratio to make it lighter at parking speeds. There was not much demand for technical novelty. Once again Farnham did the estate car conversions using Zodiac bodyshells, which had more appropriate rear window configuration, and adding a rear tailgate in glass reinforced plastic (grp). A floor gearshift was introduced for the 1964 model year, with better-class simulated wood interior in American walnut grain-effect.

INTRODUCTION January 1962, production until January 1966.
BODY saloon; 4-doors, 5-seats; weight 1163kg (2564lb).
ENGINE 4-cylinders, in-line; front; 82.55mm x 79.5mm, 1703cc; compr 8.3:1, 7.0:1 optional; 50.7kW (68bhp) @ 4800rpm; 29.8kW/l (39.9bhp/l); 94 lbft (127Nm) @ 2000rpm.
ENGINE STRUCTURE pushrod overhead valve, chain-driven camshaft; cast iron cylinder head and block; Zenith 36VN downdraught carburettor, centrifugal and vacuum ignition; AC mechanical fuel pump; 5-bearing crankshaft.
TRANSMISSION rear wheel drive; hydraulic sdp clutch; 4-speed manual synchromesh gearbox; overdrive and Borg Warner automatic optional; hypoid bevel final drive 3.9:1, 4.11:1 with overdrive; 3.545:1 with auto.
CHASSIS steel monocoque structure; ifs by Macpherson telescopic damper and coil spring strut, lower wishbone incorporating anti roll bar; rear half elliptic leaf springs with Armstrong lever arm dampers; Girling hydraulic servo disc front 24.8cm (9.75in) and drum rear 22.9cm (9in) brakes; Ford-Burman recirculating ball steering; 12.5 gal (56.8l) (15 US gal); 6.40-13 4-ply tubeless tyres.
DIMENSIONS wheelbase 271.8cm (107in); track 135.25cm (53.25in) front, 135.6cm (53.5in) rear, later 140.3cm (55.25in); length 458.5cm (180.5in); width 175.3cm (69in); height 146cm (57.5in); ground clearance 15.2cm (6in); turning circle 10.67m (35ft).
EQUIPMENT electric windscreen wipers, heater optional, radio optional pvc upholstery leather extra, rubber floor covering, 12 colour options.
PERFORMANCE maximum speed 126.7kph (78.9mph) automatic *The Motor*, 31.9kph (19.9mph) @ 1000rpm (auto); 0-96kph (60mph) 22.8sec (auto); 22.9kg/kW (17.1kg/bhp); fuel consumption 10.4l/100km (27.2mpg).
PRICE £695, PT £261 12s 9d, total £956 12s 9d (£956.64).
PRODUCTION 106,810 saloons, 13,628 estate cars.

Following the styling triumphs of the Zephyr and Zodiac I and II, Ford went to great lengths to get the shape right. After Frua was rejected except for some details, initiatives by Colin Neale who designed the Mark II, and Detroit's Elwood Engel were likewise discarded. Roy Brown won the day, and although the result was something less than a dazzling success, he did achieve a distinct identity for the three models, Zephyr 4, Zephyr 6 and Zodiac.

1962 Zephyr 6 Mark III 213E saloon, estate car

By the Mark III the Zephyr was losing some of its piquancy. The competition was catching up. Despite the stylists' best efforts, to say nothing of the long-running TV police series Z-Cars, the gaping grille was neither trend setting nor cute. It was even a bit late in the day for fins. Large overhangs made the Zephyr III seem bigger than it was, and although generously proportioned, space inside was at a premium owing to the steeply raked windscreen, big boot, and low roof. Curved side windows enhanced elbowroom, but it was not enough, and rear seat legroom became an issue. Marketing had decreed a boot of 6.2cu m (22cu ft), to catch the eye of the fleet business driver, still a major influence in the British market. The penalty was shortage of passenger space. The floor pan had to be urgently reworked, the rear bulkhead moved back to provide 5.1cm (2in) more legroom, the wheel arches were modified, and a new axle casing and half shafts resulted in an increase in rear track by 4.5cm (1.75in). It was a major undertaking only months after launch. Throughout its 5-year life the Mark III Zephyr needed constant promotion and the estate was probably the most successful with a torsion bar counterbalanced glass reinforced plastic tailgate, yet even it failed to sell in large numbers.

INTRODUCTION Jan 1962, production until Jan 1966.
BODY saloon; 4-doors, 5-seats; weight 1223kg (2696lb).
ENGINE 6-cylinders, in-line; front; 82.55mm x 79.5mm, 2553cc; compr 8.3:1 7:1 optional; 73.1kW (98bhp) @ 4750rpm; 28.6kW/l (38.4bhp/l); 182Nm (134 lbft) @ 2000rpm.
ENGINE STRUCTURE pushrod ohv, chain-driven camshaft; cast iron cylinder head and block; Zenith 36WIA-2 downdraught carb, centrifugal and vacuum ignition; AC Delco mechanical fuel pump; 7-bearing crankshaft.
TRANSMISSION rwd; hydraulic sdp clutch; 4-speed manual synchromesh gearbox; overdrive and Borg Warner 3-speed automatic optional; hypoid bevel final drive 3.545:1.
CHASSIS steel monocoque; ifs by Macpherson telescopic damper and coil spring strut, lower wishbone incorporating anti roll bar; rear half elliptic leaf springs with Armstrong lever arm dampers; Girling hydraulic servo disc front 24.8cm (9.75in) and drum rear 22.9cm (9in) drum brakes; Ford-Burman recirculating ball steering;

56.8l (12.5 gal) (15 US gal) fuel tank; 6.40-13 4-ply tubeless tyres.
DIMENSIONS wheelbase 271.8cm (107in); track front 135.25cm (53.25in), rear 135.6cm (53.5in), later 140.3cm (55.25in); length 458.5cm (180.5in); width 175.3cm (69in); height 146cm (57.5in); ground clearance 15.2cm (6in); turning circle 10.67m (35ft).
EQUIPMENT electric windscreen wipers, screen washers, heater optional, radio optional pvc upholstery leather extra, carpet, individual front seats optional, 12 colour options.
PERFORMANCE maximum 140.3kph (87.4mph) *The Motor*, automatic 31.9kph (19.9mph) @ 1000rpm; 0-96kph (60mph) 17.5sec; 16.7kg/kW (16.7kg/bhp); 17.6-14.9l/100km (16-19mpg).
PRICE £772 plus PT £161 7s 11d, total £933 7s 11d 9 (£933.58p).
PRODUCTION 107,380, estate 1632.

Far right: Ford re-enacted scenes from the popular television series for publicity shots, curiously with a non-Ford, although perhaps supposedly stolen van.

1962 Zodiac Mark III saloon, estate

2-colour paint may have become passé but the Zodiac still had allure. 4 headlamps, a shiny mouth-organ grille, a subtle change from the Zephyr's side elevation with 6 windows, and gold-plated badges could still command attention. With an extra 8.2kW (11bhp) available from the Zephyr engine Ford's first catalogued 100mph model still cost less than £1000, the gearshift was firmly back on the floor, and although the steering was a bit lifeless the handling was safe and predictable, and the ride smooth. The new gearshift did not earn universal praise. Marketing was still nervous about individual front seats, yet a floor change made a third occupant of a bench seat problematical, so the gear lever was angled towards the driver and its movement canted over uncomfortably. In January 1965 the Zodiac's prestige as a businessman's saloon was enhanced when a new name was coined for the top of the range. "Executive" as in washroom keys, desks, office suites, jet aircraft and airport lounges, carried cachet. The Zodiac Executive had a push-button Motorola radio, extra lights, seat belts, high-output dynamo, black crushed hide upholstery, and among the five colours were two acrylic metallics. Although in some respects it was a perfectly run-of-the-mill Zodiac, the Executive label remained in Ford model nomenclature for a generation.

INTRODUCTION December 1961, production until January 1966, estate car from November 1962.
BODY saloon; 4-doors, 5-seats; weight 1288kg (2839.5lb).
ENGINE 6-cylinders, in-line; front; 82.55mm x 79.5mm, 2553cc; compr 8.3:1 7:1 optional; 81.3kW (109bhp) @ 4800rpm; 31.8kW/l (42.7bhp/l); 191Nm (140.5 lbft) @ 2400rpm.
ENGINE STRUCTURE pushrod overhead valve, chain-driven camshaft; cast iron cylinder head and block; Zenith 42WIA-2 downdraught carburettor, centrifugal and vacuum ignition; AC Delco mechanical fuel pump; 7-bearing crankshaft.
TRANSMISSION rear wheel drive; Ford Borg & Beck hydraulic 20.9cm (8.25in) sdp clutch; 4-speed manual synchromesh gearbox; overdrive and Borg Warner 3-speed automatic optional; Hardy Spicer needle roller propeller shaft; hypoid bevel final drive 3.545:1.
CHASSIS steel monocoque structure; independent front suspension by Macpherson telescopic damper and coil spring strut, lower wishbone incorporating anti roll bar; rear half elliptic leaf springs with Armstrong lever arm dampers; Girling hydraulic servo disc front 24.8cm (9.75in), drum rear 22.9cm (9in) brakes; Ford-Burman recirculating ball steering; 16.8l (12.5 gal) (15 US gal) fuel tank; 6.40-13 4-ply Nylon Sport tubeless tyres.
DIMENSIONS wheelbase 271.8cm (107in); track 135.25cm (53.25in) front, 135.6cm (53.5in) rear, later 140.3cm (55.25in); length 458.5cm (180.5in); width 175.3cm (69in); height 146cm (57.5in); ground clearance 15.2cm (6in); turning circle 10.7m (35ft).
EQUIPMENT electric windscreen wipers, screen washers, heater opt, radio opt pvc upholstery leather extra, carpet, individual front seats optional, 12 colour options (but see Executive).

PERFORMANCE maximum speed
160.8kph (100.2mph) *The Motor*,
automatic 31.9kph (19.9mph) @
1000rpm; 0-96kph (60mph) 13.4sec;
15.8kg/kW (11.8kg/bhp); fuel
consumption 15.6l/100km (18.1mpg).
PRICE £813 plus PT £169 18 9d,
total £982 18s 9d (£982.94p).
PRODUCTION 77,709, estates 1576.

**True to Dagenham practice
– raw material to finished
product – this Mark III
Zodiac** (right) **was pictured
by the Thames-side foundry.
Zodiac bodywork with extra
rear quarter light gave
an airy feel to the interior.**

1963 Cortina Super and GT 118E

It was not long before Cortina production ramped up, as motor industry jargon had it, to hopeful levels and the 1.5-litre Super arrived with bigger brakes, better trim, and chrome strips down the flanks. Crucially, in view of its impressive performance and influence on the Cortina's public perception, came the Cortina GT with a camshaft designed by Cosworth. Grand Touring was as much part of the motoring lexicon of the 1960s as Chummy and Sedanca de Ville had been in the 1930s. It needed no explanation. It was lower, faster, racier, and lighter. It was also more expensive, and had a silvered facia with lots of round important-looking instruments, and became the basis of Ford's flourishing rally programme with a significant win in the 1964 Safari Rally. This had acquired a reputation as one of the toughest and fastest rallies in the world, Vic Preston won in a Zephyr in 1955 since when it had been dominated by Volkswagen, Mercedes-Benz, and Peugeot all cars renowned for their strength and vigour. Ford had won team prizes in the Safari, but outright victory by Kenyan Ford importer Peter Hughes with the Cortina barely into its stride, gave it a magnificent start. In 1965 notable progress in comfort for production saloon cars was made with the adoption of Aeroflow fresh air ventilation.

INTRODUCTION Super Jan 1963, GT April 1963, production to Oct 1966. BODY saloon 2-door, 4-door; estate 5-door, 5-seats; weight 4-door 850kg (1874b), 2-door 835kg (1841lb), GT 794kg (1750lb).
ENGINE 4-cylinders, in-line; front; 80.96mm x 72.75mm, 1498cc; compr 8.3:1 (GT 9.0:1); 44.7kW (59.9bhp) @ 4600rpm; 29.8kW/l (40bhp/l); 111Nm (81.5 lbft) @ 2300rpm. GT 58.2kW (78bhp) @ 5200rpm; 123Nm (91 lbft) @ 3600rpm.
ENGINE STRUCTURE pushrod ohv, chain-driven camshaft; cast iron cyl head and block; Zenith 33VN2 downdraught carb, GT Weber DCD1 dual barrel; centrifugal and vacuum ign; AC mechanical fuel pump; 5-bearing crank.
TRANSMISSION rwd; Borg & Beck 18.4cm (7.25in) clutch; 4-speed manual gearbox all-synchro; Hardy Spicer open prop shaft; hypoid bevel final drive 3.9:1; Borg Warner Model 35 auto opt.
CHASSIS steel monocoque; ifs by MacPherson struts and anti roll bar (GT 1.9cm (0.75in); live rear axle with half-elliptic springs, telescopic dampers; Girling hydraulic 22.9cm (9in) front

20.3cm (8in) rear drum brakes; GT 24.1cm (9.5in) front discs; Burman recirculating ball steering; 36.4l (8 gal) (9.6 US gal); 5.6 (saloon) 6 (estate) -13, 6-ply tubeless tyres; GT 5.60-13 4-ply.
DIMENSIONS wheelbase 249cm (98in); track 126cm (49.6in), 127cm (50in) estate front ; length 427.5cm (168.3in), estate 428cm (168.5in); width 159cm (62.6in); height 144cm (56.7in), estate 146cm (57.5in), GT 140.3cm (55.25in); ground clearance 16cm (6.3in), estate 17cm (6.7in); 9.6m (31.5ft) turning circle.
EQUIPMENT heater standard, radio, whitewall tyres optional, pvc upholstery, carpets, 11 colours, 5 2-tone optional (not GT).
PERFORMANCE maximum 129.7kph (80.8mph); GT 146.9kph (91.5mph) *The Motor*, 25.8kph (16.1mph) @ 1000rpm; 0-96kph (60mph) 19.0sec, GT 12.1sec; 19kg/kW (14.2kg/bhp), GT 13.6kg/kW (10.2kg/bhp); 10.4l/100km (27.2mpg), GT 10.8l/100km (26.1mpg).
PRICE totals 4-door Super £670, Estate £785, GT £767.
PRODUCTION Super saloon 77,753, GT 76,947, estate 108,219.

Base Cortina had a
slatted painted grille,
Super (right) gained
chrome along the sides
and GT (above) had
a small GT badge
on the rear quarters.

1963 Lotus Cortina

Colin Chapman's designs were long on inspiration but short on quality and reliability. He produced some of the most stimulating cars of the 20th century but they were betrayed by frailty and inconsistency. It was the same for his Lotuses, as well as his consultancy designs, like the A-framed coil-sprung rear suspension and transmission he drew up for the Lotus Cortina. Together with other modifications, such as a partly aluminium-panelled body Chapman designed and Lotus made on the small assembly line in the factory at Cheshunt, they transformed the Cortina into a sporting car with astonishing handling and roadholding. Its merit was demonstrated by Jim Clark when, even with a front wheel about a foot off the ground on corners, the Lotus Cortina was the fastest car on the circuit. It was less satisfactory on real roads, as were later leaf-sprung versions, but on a smooth-surfaced track it was matchless. The twin cam conversion of the strong 5-bearing engine was equally effective and fortunately less frail. Designed by racing engine engineer Harry Mundy, it gave a stirring performance. Achieving reliability was a matter of development, but the axle with its endemic shortcomings, including its effect on the carefully designed production body shell, could not be tolerated. Patience with Chapman ran out and production reverted to Ford.

INTRODUCTION Announced January, delivered summer 1963, produced until November 1966.
BODY saloon, 2-door; 4-seats; weight 775kg (1709lb).
ENGINE 4-cylinders, in-line; front; 82.55mm x 72.75mm, 1558cc; compr 9.5:1; 79kW (106bhp) @ 5500rpm; 50.7kW/l (68bhp/l); 146Nm (108 lbft) @ 4000rpm.
ENGINE STRUCTURE two valves per cylinder, two chain-driven overhead camshafts; cast iron block aluminium cylinder head; two Weber 40DCOE twin choke compound carburettors; centrifugal and vacuum ignition; AC mechanical fuel pump; 5-bearing crankshaft.
TRANSMISSION rear wheel drive; diaphragm spring 20.3cm (8in) sdp clutch; 4-speed manual gearbox all-synchromesh; BRD single piece open prop shaft; hypoid bevel final drive 3.9:1.
CHASSIS steel monocoque structure; ifs by MacPherson struts and anti roll bar; live rear axle with coil springs, A-bracket, radius arms, telescopic dampers; From June 1965 half-elliptic leaf springs, twin radius arms; Girling hydraulic 22.9cm (9in) front, 20.3cm (8in) rear drum brakes; GT 24.1cm (9.5in) front discs; Burman recirculating ball steering; 36.4l (8 gal) (9.6 US gal) fuel tank; 6.00-13 cross-ply tyres, 5.5in rims.
DIMENSIONS wheelbase 249cm (98in); track 130.8cm (51.5in) front, 128.8cm (50.5in) rear; length 427.5cm (168.3in); width 159cm (62.6in); height 136.5cm (53.75in); ground clearance 15.2cm (6in); turning circle 10.4m (34ft).
EQUIPMENT radio optional, safety belts optional, pvc upholstery, moulded rubber floor covering, one only exterior colour white and green, rev limiter at 6500rpm.
PERFORMANCE max speed 173.4kph (108mph) *The Motor*, 25.8kph (17.2mph) @ 1000rpm; 0-96kph (60mph) 10.1sec; 9.8kg/kW (7.3kg/bhp); fuel consumption 13.3l/100km (21.3mpg).
PRICE £910, PT £190 2s 11d, total £1100 2s 11d (£1100.15).
PRODUCTION 3301.

1963 Corsair 120E, GT, 120GT

A cousin for the Cortina, the basis of the Corsair was a Cortina platform with 7.6cm (3in) extra wheelbase, a stylish body and a higher price. Commercially it performed a double function; it made more volume for the Cortina parts it used, and it gave them an upmarket profit. If the Cortina could be said to replace the old Consul, the Corsair was half way towards a Zephyr.

Sir Terence Beckett who, as plain Terry Beckett, was Ford's project engineer in charge of the development of the Cortina, recalled to author Graham Robson: "We needed a replacement for the Classic and we thought of an extension of the Cortina as a way of doing this. It was a useful stopgap and it wasn't expensive. There was a lot of commonality with the Cortina." At 50kg (110.2lb) heavier the Corsair felt more substantial, a perception the self-consciously Thunderbird styling did little to dispel. Commonality with the Cortina extended to scuttle, bulkhead, windscreen, and inner engine bay panels. Ford managed to make a virtue out of the extra floor pan length in the rear, claiming the double skinning of the transmission tunnel was invoked to aid refinement. Corsair suspension was based on GT Cortina components, a steering column gearshift was optional on the 120E, but a floor shift was standard on the GTs.

INTRODUCTION Oct 1963, production until Sept /Oct 1965.
BODY saloon 2-door, 4-door, estate 5-door, 5-seats; 2-door weight 890kg (1962lb), 4-door 896kg (1975lb), GT 4-door 928kg (2046lb).
ENGINE 116E and 116 E/GT 4-cylinders, in-line; front; 80.96mm x 72.75mm, 1498cc; compr 8.3:1, 7.0:1 optional (GT 9.0:1); 44.7kW (59.9bhp) @ 4600rpm; 29.8kW/l (40bhp/l); 110.5Nm (81.5 lbft) @ 2300rpm. GT 58.2kW (78bhp) @ 5200rpm; 38.8kW/l (52.1bhp/l); 123Nm (91 lbft) @ 3600rpm.
ENGINE STRUCTURE pushrod ohv, chain-driven camshaft; cast iron cyl head and block; Zenith 33VN2 downdraught carb, GT Weber 28/36 DCD16/18 dual barrel; centrifugal and vacuum ign; AC mechanical fuel pump; 5-bearing crank.
TRANSMISSION rear wheel drive; Borg & Beck 18.4cm (7.25in) clutch; 4-speed manual gearbox all-synchro; Hardy Spicer open prop shaft; hypoid bevel final drive 3.9:1; Borg Warner Model 35 automatic optional.
CHASSIS steel monocoque structure; ifs by MacPherson struts and anti roll bar, GT 19mm (0.75in); live rear axle with half-elliptic springs, Armstrong telescopic dampers; Girling hydraulic 241mm (9.5in) front discs, 203mm (8in) rear drum brakes; GT vacuum servo; Burman recirculating ball steering; 36.4l (8 gal) (9.6 US gal) fuel tank; 5.60-13, 4-ply tubeless tyres.
DIMENSIONS wheelbase 256.5cm (101in); track 127cm (50in) front, 126cm (49.6in) rear; length 449cm (176.8in); width 161cm (63.4in); height 145cm (57.1in); ground clearance 17cm (6.7in); turning circle 10.2m (33.5ft).
EQUIPMENT heater, radio optional, individual front seats, pvc upholstery, loop pile carpets, 11 colours, 5 2-tone.
PERFORMANCE maximum speed 134.5kph (83.8mph) *The Motor*, GT 147.9kph (92.1mph); 27.9kph (17.4mph) @ 1000rpm; 0-96kph (60mph) 19sec, GT 12.8sec; 20kg/kW (15kg/bhp), GT 16kg/kW (11.9kg/bhp); 26mpg (9.2l/100km).
PRICE de luxe saloon £580, PT £121 7s 11d, £701 7s 11d (£701.40p). GT £847.40p.
PRODUCTION 120E saloons 137,734, GT 21,857.

1964 GT40 Mark I (prototypes, later Mark II, some converted from Mark I)

In 1962 Henry Ford II rescinded American car manufacturers' agreement not to take part in motor racing. It was abrogated at first only in America, but it was not long before Ford, having failed to buy Ferrari for $10million, mounted a challenge in Europe. The Le Mans 24 Hours race was opened to manufacturers' prototypes and Ford created a car to fit the bill. The 1962 Mustang 1 was a 1.7-litre, mid-engined open 2-seater designed by Roy Lunn, while in Britain Eric Broadley had designed the Lola GT, a closed coupe along similar lines. Ford brought them together in Ford Advanced Vehicles, a subsidiary set up in Slough, and by the beginning of 1964 the first cars were finished. Events moved quickly and two crashed the first time out on a track, the Le Mans test weekend, but a GT40 driven by Richie Ginther and Masten Gregory led the race in June before retiring, and another driven by Phil Hill set a new circuit record at 211.4kph (131.7mph). Despite the resources expended on the GT40 design, aided by the latest computer technology, Lunn admitted that: "…some stability phenomenon existed that had not become apparent during the design analytical phase." What this meant was that at speed the car generated some 317.5kg (700lb) of lift, threatening at best instability, at worst flight.

INTRODUCTION April 1964.
BODY coupe; 2-doors, 2-seats; weight 832.4kg (1835lb) dry, 1111.3kg (2450lb) on startline without driver; distribution 43 front 57 rear.
ENGINE 8-cylinders, 90deg V; mid; 95.5mm (later 101.6mm) x 72.9mm, 4195cc (later 4736cc); compr 12.5:1; 261kW (350bhp) @ 7200rpm, later 291kW (390bhp) @ 7000rpm; 62.2kW/l (73.9bhp/l), later 61.4kW/l (82.3bhp/l)); 373Nm (275 lbft) @ 5600rpm, later 441Nm (325 lbft) @ 5000rpm.
ENGINE STRUCTURE pushrod ohv from central camshaft; aluminium cylinder head and block; 4 Weber 48mm dual-choke carburettors; 5-bearing crankshaft, wet-sump. (prototypes of April 1964 had dry-sump 4.2-litre 261kW (350bhp) engine).
TRANSMISSION rwd; 216mm (8.5in) Borg & Beck 3-plate clutch; 4-speed manual Colotti gearbox, no synchro, in unit with transaxle; from 1965 5-speed ZF all-synchromesh.
CHASSIS semi-monocoque hull, 23swg sheet steel (60mm) (.024in) with square tube stiffening, grp body panels from 1968 carbon filament reinforced;

ifs by double wishbones, coil springs, telescopic dampers, anti roll bar; independent rear suspension by double trailing arms, transverse top link and lower wishbone, coil springs, telescopic dampers, anti-roll bar; hydraulic servo disc brakes, from 1968 ventilated discs, 292mm (11.5in); rack and pinion; 139l (30.6 gal) (36.7 US gal) door sill fuel tanks; 6.00-15 front, 9.00-15 rear, later 10.30-15 and 13.50-15 tyres.
DIMENSIONS wheelbase 241.3cm (95in); track front and rear 137.2cm (54in); length 418.1cm (164.6in); width 177.8cm (70in); height 102.9cm (40.5in); ground clearance 12.2cm (4.8in).
EQUIPMENT cockpit and driver's seat ventilation by air-duct front high-pressure point under nose.
PERFORMANCE maximum speed (1966) timed on Mulsanne 301kph (187.5mph), design est 337.1kph (210mph), still
air maximum of early GT40 likely 316.2kph (197mph); 3.2kg/kW (2.4kg/kW), later 2.9kg/kW (2.4kg/bhp).
PRICE n/a.
PRODUCTION 12 prototypes and 87 production GT40s.

Top: near Lochgilphead
on Ecurie Ecosse tour.
Right: Goodwood, December
1965. Graham Hill discusses
Ford's race-spec GT40
with motorsport team
manager Alan Mann.

1965 Corsair V4 and GT

The Corsair's success was based on aspirational owners who valued the practicality of the Cortina, but were looking for something whose doors shut with the solid clunk of a slam-door railway carriage. In its second incarnation the Corsair became the test-bed for a new generation of Ford engines. The V4 was designed to take up less room than a straight four, not that it mattered much in the Corsair, which had an engine bay the same size as before, so it was hard to see the point. Even with a counter-rotating balancer shaft it was no smoother than a straight four; it was heavier, slower, used more fuel, and the GT was little livelier than the ordinary 1700. *The Motor* was exasperated: "the new engine is a little harsh at idling speed … willing … (but) some resonant periods." Fuel consumption deteriorated by 70.6l/100km (4mpg). Aeroflow ventilation and better décor was all very well, but there was little disguising the Transit van refinement, and the extra weight brought woolly lower-geared steering and nose-heavy understeer. Interior improvements included clear round instruments instead of the old model's architectural ovals, and strip-type speedometer. Boot space was generous at 3.3cu m (11.7cu ft). Individual seats and a tall transmission tunnel banished even the option of the bench-style seating treasured by marketing departments since 1946.

INTRODUCTION October 1965; GT 2000 produced to 1969, 1700 de luxe to 1965.
BODY saloon 2-door, 4-door; estate 5-door, 5-seats; weight 2-door 967kg (2131.8lb), 4-door 981kg (2162.7lb), GT 4-door 995kg (2193.6lb).
ENGINE 2720E, GT 2724E; 4-cylinders, 60deg V; front; 93.66mm x 60.35mm, 1663cc; compr 9.1:1, 7.1:1 optional; 57.1kW (76.5bhp) @ 4750rpm; 34.3kW/l (46bhp/l); 127Nm (94 lbft) @ 3000rpm. GT 93.7mm x 72.4mm, 1996cc; 65.6kW (88bhp) @ 4750rpm; 32.9kW/l (44.1bhp/l); 158Nm (116.5 lbft) @ 3600rpm.
ENGINE STRUCTURE pushrod ohv, gear-driven camshaft; cast iron cylinder head and block; Zenith 36 IV downdraught carburettor; centrifugal and vacuum ignition; AC mechanical fuel pump; 3-bearing crankshaft.
TRANSMISSION rear wheel drive; Borg & Beck 8in (203mm) clutch; 4-speed manual all-synchro; Hardy Spicer open prop shaft; hypoid bevel final drive 3.78:1; automatic optional.
CHASSIS steel monocoque structure;

ifs by MacPherson struts and anti roll bar; live rear axle with half-elliptic springs and radius arms on the GT, Armstrong telescopic dampers; Girling hydraulic 24.4cm (9.6in) front discs 22.9cm (9in) rear drum brakes; GT vacuum servo; Burman recirculating ball steering; 45.46l (10 gal) (12 US gal) fuel tank; 5.60-13, 4in rims.
DIMENSIONS wheelbase 256.5cm (101in); track 127cm (50in) front, 126cm (49.6in) rear; length 449cm (176.8in); width 161cm (63.4in); height 145cm (57.1in); ground clearance 17cm (6.7in); turning circle 10.2m (33.5ft).
EQUIPMENT heater, radio optional, individual front seats, pvc upholstery, loop pile carpets, 11 colours, 5 two-tone.
PERFORMANCE maximum speed 141.3kph (88mph) *The Motor*, GT 141.3kph (88mph) *The Autocar*; 28.3kph (17.6mph) @ 1000rpm; 0-96kph (60mph) 15.6sec, GT 14.7sec; 17.2kg/kW (12.8kg/bhp), GT 14.6kg/kW (11.3kg/bhp); fuel consumption 12.6l/100km (22.4mpg).
PRICE £650, PT £135 8s 4d, £785 8s 4d (£785.42); GT total £909.
PRODUCTION 135,000 including GT.

Gearing for Dr Lanchester's counterweighted balancer shafts (below) did not entirely cancel out V4's vibrations.

1965 Transit

Transits were used as fire engines, ambulances, motor caravans, breakdown vehicles, tipper trucks, or dropside lorries. They were made platforms for cherry-pickers, auxiliary power units, generator sets, mobile workshops, security vans, riot police vans, radio and television studios, dustcarts, and milk floats. Their versatile rear-drive structure was integral when they were a van, with the floor welded to inverted full length top-hat section longerons, or when a chassis-cab with closures turning the top-hats into box-section load-bearers. Short wheelbases had plain ladder frames, long wheelbases cruciform bracing. There was a choice of 2 V4 engines or a Perkins diesel, and any number of options on the standard bodywork including sliding doors, side-loading, high roofs, and for buses different trim varying from hard-wearing and practical to luxury. 6 basic models (there were 44 different versions) varied in load capacity from 610kg (12cwt) to 1780kg (35cwt), coaches from 9-seaters to 15-seaters. Short wheelbases came with single rear wheels, long ones with twin. Engineered and built at Langley by a team including Terry (later Sir Terence) Becket and Alex (later Sir Alex) Trotman, production moved to Southampton in 1971. A V6 was added to the engine range, then an automatic, the V4s got more power, and the 2.4-litre Ford diesel replaced the Perkins engine.

INTRODUCTION October 1965. BODY van or chassis-cab; 2-doors, 1 or 2-seats; weight 1837kg (4050lb) to 3266kg (7200lb). ENGINE 4-cylinders, 60deg V; front; 93.6mm x 60.35mm, 1660cc; compr 8.0:1; 48.47kW (65bhp) @ 4750rpm; 29.2kW/l (39.2bhp/l); 117Nm (86.5lbft) @ 3000rpm. 2.0: 93.6 x 72.4mm; 1996cc; compr 8.9:1; 65.62kW (88bhp) @ 4750rpm; 34.4kW/l (44.1bhp/l); 167Nm (123.5lbft) @ 2750rpm. Perkins 4/99 diesel; 1760cc; compr 22:1; 4-cylinders; 30.4kW (40.7bhp) @ 3700rpm; 17.2kW/l (23.1bhp/l); 97Nm (71.5lbft) @ 2250rpm. ENGINE STRUCTURE V4s pushrod ohv; gear-driven side cam, gear-driven balancer shaft; cast iron cyl head, block; single carb, centrifugal and vacuum ign; AC mech fuel pump; 3-bearing crank. TRANSMISSION rwd; Borg & Beck 216mm (8.5in) diaphragm spring clutch; 4-speed manual synchromesh; hypoid bevel final drive 4.111, 4.444, 4.625, 5.143, 5.125:1 according to application; one-piece prop shaft swb, two piece lwb. CHASSIS steel monocoque (but see text); front and rear semi-elliptic springs; differences in dimensions and spring leaves according to application, lwb with slipper-ended rear springs; telesc dampers, heavy-duty option; Lockheed hydraulic brakes, vacuum servo optional, front-rear ratio acc to wheelbase and application; 2-leading shoes at front; 22.9cm (9in) or 25.4cm (10in) dia drums; recirculating ball streering; 42.1l (9.25 gal) 911.1 US gal) fuel tank swb; 68.2l (15 gal) (18 US gal) lwb; 6.50, 7.00, 7.50-14YY tyres depending on application. DIMENSIONS wbase 269.2cm (106in) and 299.7cm (118in); track front 163.8cm (64.5in), rear 153.9cm (60.6in) (twin rear wheels); bodywork length swb to 236.2cm (93in), lwb to 312.4cm (123in); typical van overall length 517.4cm (203.7in); width 205.7cm (81in); height 207.3cm (81.6in); circle 10.4m (34ft) swb, 11.3m (37ft) lwb. PERFORMANCE maximum 125.2kph (78mph) *Commercial Motor* 30cwt van 2.0-litre; 0-50mph (80kph) 26.1sec; 23.9-12.3l/100km (11.8-23mpg) depending on application. PRICE from £545.

Some brand names
became generic; Hoover
and Thermos came to mean
carpet cleaner and vacuum
flask, JCBs were JCBs.
Transit was so universally
understood to mean medium
van or light bus that dealers
could advertise "any
make of Transit supplied."

Right: **boxer Henry Cooper
with his 1965 Transit Custom.**

Essentially a corollary to the introduction of the Transit for capacities of 12cwt to 35cwt, the D-series was to meet the requirements of the heavy end of the commercial market in 3 stages. First came a range covering capacities from 2 to 8 tons, tippers, forward-control tilt-cab inclined engine 6-wheelers, chassis-cab units for special bodywork, together with an articulated tractor unit for gross vehicle weights (gvw) up to 20 tons. There were new engines, a 4161cc 4-cylinder, 5948cc 6-cylinder, and a turbo-diesel 5948cc 6-cylinder. 2 years later the next stage was 4-wheelers with gvws up to 16 tons, and an artic tractor of 28 tons. Cummins and Ford Model 511 V8 diesels were introduced in stage 2 together with, for a time, 6-cylinder 96.2kW (129bhp) and 111kW (149bhp) imported American engines. Heavy-duty vehicles had air-hydraulic brakes as standard and custom cabs were a popular option in the D-series that also extended to PSV chassis. The R192 and R226 (the figures indicating wheelbase in inches), the more powerful available with a 5-speed, could carry up to 53 passengers. Midland Red ordered 100 in 1970 alone and within 2 years 220 were in service with, from 1978 107.38kW (144bhp) turbo-diesels.

The former Thames Trader market (below D-series but heavier than Transit) was filled in 1973 with the A-series, a range of Transit-related light commercials from 30cwt to 5 tons that included tippers, large vans, and small artics. Their engines came from the passenger car range, 2.0-litre V4s, 3.0-litre V6s and 2.4-litre 4-cylinder diesel. There was also the 3.6-litre ohv 4-cylinder 52.2kW (70bhp) diesel dating back to 1954. Standard dual-circuit servo braking systems, optional 4- or 5-speeds for the gearbox, and an unprecedented standard of comfort for the occupants were important novelties.

Beside the D-series came a parallel redesigned normal control chassis with the same range of engines and capacities, known as the K-series, made until 1973. Stage 3 in heavy vehicles was the H-series Transcontinental of 1975, chassis-cabs and trucks between 16-19 tons gvw for 4-wheelers, 24 tons for 6-wheelers, and articulated tractor units of both sorts up to 42 tons. Made in Holland, this was a big range with forward control 3-man tilt cabs, twin-plate clutches, 9-13-speed Fuller constant-mesh gearboxes, single reduction hypoid rear axles, power steering and air brakes. With no suitable engine of its own Ford turned to Cummins for a 264.7kW (355bhp) 14-litre 6-cylinder diesel with turbocharger and aftercooler. In 1977 Ford was making the nation's best-selling car, the Cortina, its best selling tractor, and best-selling commercial vehicle range.

1966 Corsair V4 2000, 2000E saloon, estate car

Second thoughts on the V4 Corsair came not a moment too soon. The estate car introduced at the 1966 Geneva show was not a success; the loading platform was too high. "Not a maid-of-all-work designed to take pigs to market," said *The Autocar*. "The load space is fully carpeted and the sides are trimmed in padded pvc." It was doubtful about the GT badges that still adhered to the Estate Car but much changed in January 1967 when the Corsair's up-market credentials were reinforced by the 2000E. This was essentially a de luxe with the 'E' package for an extra £76. This gained it Executive status, and at only a little over £1,000, it had walnut veneer facia, black leather-looking upholstery, black vinyl roof (with the Aeroflow ventilation extractor vents in the rear quarters tastefully finished black), and fancy wheel trims. The chrome strips were removed from the sides, enhancing dignity, and the individual front seats had reclining backrests. Engine power was raised 5.2kW (7bhp) by means of a progressive double-choke Weber carburettor and new camshaft with 50deg of overlap instead of 34deg. Brake servo, and wide radial-ply Pirelli Cinturato or Goodyear G800 tyres completed a specification that could happily have kept the GT appellation. The back axle radius arms, deleted when the GT was dropped, could be specially requested.

INTRODUCTION 2000 November 1966, production until June 1970; 2000E January 1967, production to June 1970; estate 1966-1968.
BODY saloon 4-door, estate 5-door, 5-seats; weight 4-door 992kg (2187lb), estate 1050kg (2314.8lb).
ENGINE 3006E; 4-cylinders, 60deg V; 93.7mm x 72.4mm, 1996cc; comp 8.9:1; 65.6kW (88bhp) @ 4750rpm; 32.9kW/l (44.1bhp/l); 158Nm (116.5 lbft) @ 3600rpm. After 1967 72.3kW (97bhp) @ 5000rpm; 36.2kW/l (48.6bhp/l); 153Nm (113 lbft) @ 3000rpm.
ENGINE STRUCTURE pushrod overhead valve, gear-driven camshaft; cast iron cylinder head and block; Zenith 36 IV downdraught, 2000E compound Weber 32 DIFA; centrifugal and vacuum ignition; AC mechanical fuel pump; 3-bearing crankshaft.
TRANSMISSION rear wheel drive; Borg & Beck 20.3cm (8in) clutch; 4-speed manual gearbox all-synchro; Hardy Spicer open prop shaft; hypoid bevel final drive 3.78:1; automatic opt.
CHASSIS steel monocoque structure; ifs by MacPherson struts and anti roll bar; live rear axle with half-elliptic springs, (estate stiffer) Armstrong telescopic dampers; Girling hydraulic 24.4cm (9.6in) front discs 22.9cm (9in) rear drum brakes; vacuum servo; Burman recirculating ball steering; 45.5l (10 gal) (12 US gal) fuel tank; 5.60-13, 2000E 165-13, 4.5J rims, estate 6.00-13.
DIMENSIONS wheelbase 256.5cm (101in); track 127cm (50in) front, 126cm (49.6in) rear; length 449cm (176.8in); width 161cm (63.4in); height 145cm (57.1in), estate 146cm (57.5in); ground clearance 17cm (6.7in); turning circle 10.21m (33.5ft).
EQUIPMENT radio standard, cut pile carpets, crushable facia coaming, carpeted boot.
PERFORMANCE maximum speed 146.1kph (91mph) *The Autocar* (estate); 28.3kph (17.6mph) @ 1000rpm; 0-96kph (60mph) 14.0sec; 15.1kg/kW (11.3kg/bhp); fuel consumption 11.4l/100km (24.8mpg).
PRICE £650, PT £135 8s 4d, £785 8s 4d (£785.42); estate total £1112.
PRODUCTION 331,095 all Corsair; 171,144 all V4s; 2000E 31,566; estate car 940.

1966 Zephyr 4 Mark IV 3010E V4 saloon and estate

Bigger than ever, the last Zephyr and Zodiac took bold initiatives. They had independent rear suspension, a long bonnet, short tail, and used compact Vee engines to shift the occupants rearwards instead of giving them more legroom. Shortening the bonnet was bad for a car's proportions, according to the stylists, so the spare wheel was put right at the front, ahead of the radiator, instead of in the boot. The result was radical; distinctive rather than memorable. Disc brakes with a servo optional on 4s, standard on 6s, optional floor shift, overdrive, or automatic transmissions, and the availability of power steering provided a specification that with fuel injection and catalytic converter could have been written in the 1990s. Alas for the shortcomings. Independent rear suspension had been contentious in Europe for years, no car with pretensions could afford to be without it, but Ford adopted a system with less than perfect geometry. Hinged obliquely, it had a short link designed to inhibit rear wheel steer, but not sufficiently so. There was still no consensus on independent rear suspension, beyond suspicion of swing axles like VW or Renault had, and doubt about Mercedes-Benz's low-pivot. Yet even on the press launch of the Mark IV Zephyr in North Africa, it began to look as though the Ford had not got its variant quite right.

INTRODUCTION Dec 1965, production until Dec 1971.
BODY saloon 4-door, estate 5-door, 5-seats; weight 4-door 1250kg (2755.75lb).
ENGINE 3006E; 4-cylinders, 60deg V; 93.7mm x 72.4mm, 1996cc; comp 8.9:1; 61.5kW (82.5bhp) @ 4750rpm; 30.8kW/l (41.3bhp/l); 158Nm (116.5 lbft) @ 3600rpm.
ENGINE STRUCTURE 3010E pushrod overhead valve, gear-driven camshaft; cast iron cylinder head and block; Zenith 36 IVT downdraught; centrifugal and vacuum ignition; AC mechanical fuel pump; automatic choke; 5-bearing crankshaft.
TRANSMISSION rear wheel drive; hydraulic sdp clutch; 4-speed manual gearbox all synchromesh; optional Laycock de Normanville overdrive or 3-speed automatic; final drive 4.4:1.
CHASSIS steel monocoque structure; independent front suspension McPherson struts with co-axial coil springs and dampers and anti roll bar; rear independent semi-trailing arms, coil springs telescopic dampers; hydraulic servo optional,

Girling 244mm (9.6in) disc brakes, vacuum servo; recirculating ball steering; PAS optional; 68.2l (15 gal) (18 US gal) fuel tank; 6.40-13 tyres.
DIMENSIONS wheelbase 292cm (115in); track 145cm (57.1in)front, 147cm (57.9in) rear; length 470cm (185in); width 181cm (71.3in); height 148cm (58.3in); ground clearance 15cm (5.9in); turning circle 11.58m (38ft).
EQUIPMENT safety belts optional; pvc seats, headlining; loop-pile carpet; heater standard.
PERFORMANCE maximum speed 140kph (87.2mph); 31.1kph (19.4mph) @ 1000rpm; 0-96kph (60mph) 17.7sec; 20.3kg/kW (15.1kg/bhp); fuel consumption 12 l/100km (23.5mpg).
PRICE £933 at launch.
PRODUCTION 41,386.

1966 Zephyr 6 Mark IV 3008E V6 saloon and estate

The narrow-angle Vee engines were beginning to settle down and, with the greater smoothness of a 6-cylinder against a 4-cylinder, provided quite refined motoring even if it was never in the same league as a straight 6. The articulated fixed length drive shafts and alloy wishbones were expected to control camber and toe-in both in cornering and with changes in passenger loads. With a heavy weight aboard it was generally successful, the long heavy spare wheel-encumbered front would plough on understeering gently, but unladen the Zephyr oversteered sometimes alarmingly. In 1967 the suspension camber angles were changed to try and reduce the tendency but it was not wholly successful. It also rode bumps badly, transmitting road noise up through the body, and defeating the refinement achieved by the big engine. As tyres became wider power steering became almost essential. Without it, steering at parking speeds was unpleasantly heavy and non power-steered cars were given 6 turns lock to lock to compensate. Following the 1967 facelift that enhanced the front and made Hydrosteer PAS standard, things improved. Most cars' production increased at first, falling away gradually over the years, but the Mark IV Zephyr's decline began almost at once. In its first year 50,593 were made but by 1971 production had shrunk by two-thirds.

PRODUCTION 1966-1971.
BODY saloon; 4-doors, 5-seats; weight 1300kg (2866lb), estate 1385kg (3053.3lb).
ENGINE 6-cylinders, 60deg V; front; 93.66mm x 60.35mm, 2495cc; compr 9.1:1; 83.5kW (112bhp) @ 4750rpm; 33.5kW/l (44.9bhp/l); 186Nm (137.5 lbft) @ 2750rpm.
ENGINE STRUCTURE 3006E pushrod overhead valve, gear-driven camshaft; cast iron cylinder head and block; Zenith 38 IVT downdraught; centrifugal and vacuum ignition; AC mechanical fuel pump; automatic choke; 4-bearing crankshaft.
TRANSMISSION rwd; hydraulic sdp diaphragm spring clutch; 4-speed manual gearbox all synchromesh; optional Laycock de Normanville overdrive or 3-speed automatic Ford C4 or Borg Warner 35; final drive 3.9:1.
CHASSIS steel monocoque structure; ifs by McPherson struts with co-axial coil springs and dampers and anti roll bar; rear independent semi-trailing arms, coil springs telescopic dampers; Girling 244mm (9.6in) disc brakes, vacuum servo; recirculating ball steering;

PAS optional, standard after 1967; 68.2l (15 gal) (18 US gal) fuel tank; 6.70-13 tyres; 14in after 1967.
DIMENSIONS wheelbase 292cm (115in); track 145cm (57.1in) front, 147cm (57.9in) rear; length 470cm (185in); width 181cm (71.3in); height 148cm (58.3in); ground clearance 15cm (5.9in); turning circle 11.9m (39ft).
EQUIPMENT heated rear window optional.
PERFORMANCE maximum speed 154.1kph (96mph) *The Autocar;* 31.1kph (19.4mph) @ 1000rpm; 0-96kph (60mph) 14.6sec; 15.6kg/kW (11.6kg/bhp), estate 16.6kg/kW (12.4kg/bhp); fuel consumption 14.6l/100km (19.4mpg).
PRICE £832, PT £173, total £1005
PRODUCTION 61,031.

The 1967 Zephyr 6 de luxe had a more distinctive front (bottom right) **to distinguish it from the Zephyr 4, p183. An extruded aluminium grille filled the space between the headlights.**

1966 Zodiac Mark IV 3012E

Quad headlights, broad dummy grille bars, turbine-style wheel trims, reclining seats, power steering, and a level of furnishing found only in American cars, kept the Zodiac among the leaders in the luxury car field. Among the standard fittings were a headlamp flasher, reversing lights, cigar lighter, coat hooks, and a vanity mirror behind the passenger side sun visor. There were 3-point safety harnesses with locking inertia reels and the rather large steering wheel was adjustable for height, although not by much more than an inch. The instrument array looked like an aircraft flight deck, the seats were so big there were complaints about sliding about on corners, and the Aeroflow once described as a primitive system of air conditioning was so good that road testers could gleefully report that there should never be any need to open the windows.

Cars were becoming easier to maintain. A Zodiac II of the 1950s demanded application of a grease gun every 1000 miles to 11 places, engine oil changes, and gearbox oil changes. The Mark IV asked for gearbox oil to be changed at 3000 miles then never again, the engine oil at intervals of 6000 miles, and brakes and clutch were expected to adjust themselves for wear with an inspection every year or so. Modern oils and sealed for life bushes had removed nearly all the chores.

PRODUCTION 1966-1971.
BODY saloon; 4-doors, 5-seats; weight 1333kg (2938.7lb), estate 1442kg (3179lb).
ENGINE 6-cylinders, 60deg V; front; 93.66mm x 72.41mm, 2994cc; compr 8.9:1; 95.5kW (128bhp) @ 4600rpm; 31.9kW/l (42.8bhp/l); 239Nm (176 lbft) @ 3000rpm.
ENGINE STRUCTURE 3012E pushrod overhead valve, gear-driven camshaft; cast iron cylinder head and block; Weber 40 DFA twin choke downdraught; centrifugal and vacuum ignition; AC mechanical fuel pump; automatic choke; 4-bearing crankshaft.
TRANSMISSION rear wheel drive; hydraulic sdp diaphragm spring clutch; 4-speed manual gearbox all synchromesh; optional Laycock de Normanville overdrive or 3-speed automatic Ford C4 or Borg Warner 35; final drive 3.7:1.
CHASSIS steel monocoque structure; independent front suspension McPherson struts with co-axial coil springs and dampers and anti roll bar; rear independent semi-trailing arms, coil springs telescopic dampers; Girling disc brakes 244mm (9.6in) front 252mm (9.9in) rear, vacuum servo; recirculating ball steering; PAS standard; 68.2l (15 gal) (18 US gal) fuel tank; 6.70-13 tyres; 14in after 1967.
DIMENSIONS wheelbase 292cm (115in); track 145cm (57.1in) front, 147cm (57.9in) rear; length 472cm (185.8in); width 181cm (71.3in); height 148cm (58.3in); ground clearance 15cm (5.9in); turning circle 11.9m (39ft).
EQUIPMENT heated rear window, cut pile carpet, upholstery cirrus vinyl, leather optional, steering column lock optional, 2 speed wipers.
PERFORMANCE maximum speed 164.5kph (102.5mph) *The Motor;* 19.7mph (31.6kph) @ 1000rpm; 0-60mph (96kph) 11.0sec; 14kg/kW (10.4kg/bhp), estate 15.1kg/kW (11.3kg/bhp); fuel consumption 18.4mpg (15.4l/100km).
PRICE £1010, PT £218 4s 0d, total £1228 4s 0d (£1228.20p).
PRODUCTION 48,846 (including Executive).

1966 GT40 Le Mans winner Mark II works cars

No sooner was 1965 under way than work began on GT40 Mark II. Winning Le Mans 1966 was the aim but by midnight on race day the Ford effort was in ruins; all that was achieved was a lap record and the fastest speed down Mulsanne. Yet development continued with the 7-litre Galaxie V8 used in American saloon car racing. It was not a sophisticated engine, a pushrod, with one 4-choke carburettor, and only gave around 52.2kW (70bhp) per litre against a top flight competitor's 74.6kW (100bhp) per litre. It was heavy, at 272.2kg (600lb) despite aluminium cylinder heads, but reaching peak power at a leisurely 6200rpm, made it extremely reliable, with massive torque that only needed four gears.

Kar Kraft of Detroit developed a strong transaxle from the production Galaxie and the result was race-ready almost at once. A big tough enormously competent car, it competed at the Daytona 24 Hours in February 1966, led almost all the way and took the first three places. It won again at Sebring, came second at Spa, then set new speed records at Le Mans and finished first second and third. Critics complained Ford overwhelmed the opposition, yet Ferrari had around the same number of cars at the start, and all those in with a chance were out by dawn on the second day.

INTRODUCTION February 1966.
BODY coupe; 2-doors, 2-seats; weight 1136.3kg (2505lb), startline 1206.6kg (2660lb).
ENGINE 8-cylinders, 90deg V; mid; 107.5mm x 96.1mm, 6997cc; compr 10.5:1; 361.7kW (485bhp) @ 6200rpm; 69.3bhp/l (51.7kW/L); 475 lbft (644Nm) @ 5000rpm.
ENGINE STRUCTURE pushrod ohv; aluminium cylinder head, cast iron block; Holley 4-choke carburettor; 5-bearing crankshaft, dry-sump.
TRANSMISSION rear wheel drive; Long 2 dry plate clutch; 4-speed manual Ford T-44 synchromesh gearbox in unit with transaxle.
CHASSIS semi-monocoque hull structure, 23swg sheet steel (.024in) with square tube stiffening, grp body panels with carbon filament reinforced; independent front suspension by double wishbones, coil springs, telescopic dampers, anti roll bar; independent rear suspension by double trailing arms, transverse top link and lower wishbone, coil springs, telescopic dampers, anti-roll bar; hydraulic servo disc brakes, ventilated discs, 292mm (11.5in);

rack and pinion steering; 159l (35 gal) (42 US gal) door sill fuel tanks; cast magnesium wheels, 8.00-15 front, 9.50-15 rear.
DIMENSIONS wheelbase 241.3cm (95in); track 144.8cm (57in) front, 142.3cm (56in) rear; length 414cm (163in); width 177.8cm (70in); height 102.8cm (40.5in); ground clearance 10cm (3.94in).
EQUIPMENT cockpit and driver's seat ventilation by air-duct front high-pressure point under nose
PERFORMANCE maximum speed timed on Mulsanne 301kph (187.5mph), design estimated 337kph (210mph), still air maximum of early GT40 likely 316.2kph (197mph); 3.1kg/kW (2.3kg/bhp).
PRODUCTION about 10.

1966 GT 40 Mark III road car

The GT40 could not go on competing as a prototype; it had to graduate to production with 50 cars laid down in order to qualify. However they were by no means all the same, Marks proliferated and many cars that started as Mark Is were converted to Mark IIs, some that began as road cars were converted for racing, many were substantially altered. Only a car-by-car study could provide precise numbers and detailed specifications. A total of 31 Mark I road cars were built but many raced, including the first prototype, chassis GT40/P1013, that competed (and finished) in virtually road-going condition with some 50,000 miles (approx 80,000 kms) on the clock in Portugal's Villa Real 6-hours' race.

The Mark III was the definitive road-going GT40; it was planned to build 20 but in the event only 7 were made, of which 4 were kept by Ford. The engine was detuned, more effective silencers installed, the springing was made more agreeable, the cockpit was properly trimmed and although there was no real luggage space a box in the engine compartment could be pressed into service, although not for anything likely to be affected by heat. The result was surprisingly tractable, Ford ran SNO 250D on the press fleet, and it was possible to use it on the road without causing too much commotion.

INTRODUCTION 1966.
BODY coupe; 2-doors, 2-seats; weight 998kg (2200lb).
ENGINE 8-cylinders, 90deg V; mid; 101.6mm x 72.9mm, 4736cc; compr 10.5:1; 228.2kW (306bhp) @ 6000rpm; 48.2kW/l (64.6bhp/l); 446Nm (329 lbft) @ 4200rpm.
ENGINE STRUCTURE pushrod ohv; aluminium cylinder head, cast iron block; Holley 4-choke carburettor; 5-bearing crankshaft, wet-sump.
TRANSMISSION rear wheel drive; Borg & Beck 2 dry plate clutch; 5-speed manual ZF 5DS-25 all-synchromesh gearbox in unit with transaxle.
CHASSIS semi-monocoque hull structure, 23swg sheet steel (.024in) with square tube stiffening, grp body panels with carbon filament reinforcement; independent front suspension by double wishbones, coil springs, telescopic dampers, anti roll bar; Independent rear suspension by double trailing arms, transverse top link and lower wishbone, coil springs, telescopic dampers, anti-roll bar; hydraulic servo disc brakes, ventilated discs, 292mm (11.5in) front, 285mm (11.2in) rear; rack and pinion steering; 125.5l (27.6 gal) (33.1 US gal) door sill fuel tanks; Borrani wire or cast magnesium wheels, 6.50-15 front, 8.00-15 rear.
DIMENSIONS wheelbase 242.6cm (95.5in); track front and rear 135.3cm (53.25in); length 429.3cm (169in); width 177.8cm (70in); height 104.1cm (41in); ground clearance 10cm (3.94in).
EQUIPMENT cockpit and driver's seat ventilation by air-duct front high-pressure point under nose.
PERFORMANCE maximum speed by design 247kph (154mph), on test approx 257kph (160mph) *The Motor*; 1st 93.1kph (58mph), 2nd 144.5kph (90mph), 3rd 203.9kph (127mph), 4th 228kph (142mph); 0-96kph (60mph) 5.3sec; 0-160.5kph (100mph) 11.8sec *The Motor*; 4.4kg/kW (3.3kg/bhp).
PRODUCTION 7 plus 7 post-production cars, 5 built by Alan Mann Racing.

1966 Cortina Mark II 1300, 1500

Determination to sustain the Cortina's momentum brought a facelift in 1964. The 1966 the launch of the Mark II was within the 4-year model cycle Ford had imposed on itself, and followed by a month, production of the millionth Mark I in September. Mark II was essentially the same platform with a new superstructure, and although the 249cm (98in) wheelbase and 426.7cm (168in) overall length were unchanged, the new body was a useful 61mm (2.4in) wider. The engine bay presswork, the suspension pick-up points, the steelwork round the transmission, and the suspension and steering were much the same as before. Yet what a change the new body made. The flat-sided origami-style sharply-creased Cortina was now quite voluptuous, with a full-width grille incorporating the headlights, and now that the opposition was enthusiastically embracing better heating and fresh-air ventilation systems, Ford enhanced Aeroflow with 25 per cent more through-put. Softer springing and better handling enhanced the car's appeal, while the old 1198cc 3-bearing engine was retained only for some export markets. It was replaced by a 5-bearing 1300, really a short-stroke adaptation of the Mark 1's 1500, with a short block but the same head. Automatic transmission was an option but made the 1300 so feeble it was not popular.

INTRODUCTION October 1966, produced to 1970 (Kent engine from 1967).
BODY saloon; 2-doors, 4-doors 4-seats; estate car 5-door from February 1967; weight from 861kg (1898lb).
ENGINE (1300) 4-cylinders, in-line; front; 80.96mm x 62.99mm, 1298cc; compr 9.0:1; 39.9kW (53.5bhp) @ 5000rpm; 30.7kW/l (41.2bhp/l); 96Nm (71 lbft) @ 2500rpm.
1500: 80.96 x 72.8; 1498cc; 8.3:1; 45.5kW (61bhp) @ 4700rpm; 30.4kW/l (40.7bhp/l); 120Nm (88.5lbft) @ 2500rpm.
ENGINE STRUCTURE pushrod ohv; chain-driven camshaft; cast iron cyl head and block; Ford GPD downdraught carburettor; centrifugal and vacuum ign; mechanical fuel pump; 5-bearing crank.
TRANSMISSION rear wheel drive; diaphragm spring cable operated clutch; 4-speed manual all-synchromesh gearbox; 3-speed automatic optional; hypoid bevel final drive 4.125:1 (1300) 3.89:1 (1500).
CHASSIS steel monocoque; ifs by MacPherson struts and anti roll bar; live rear axle with half-elliptic springs, telescopic dampers, (lever arm on estate cars' rear); Girling hydraulic 229mm (9in) disc brakes at front, 203mm (8in) rear drums; Burman recirculating ball steering; 45.5l (10 gal) (12 US gal) tank; 5.20-13 or 6.00-13 cross-ply, 4in or 4.5in rims.
DIMENSIONS wheelbase 249cm (98in); track front 133cm (52.5in) rear 130cm (51in); length 426.7cm (168in); width 165cm (64.9in); height 144cm (56.5in); ground clearance 13.3cm (5.25in); turning circle 8.53m (28ft).
EQUIPMENT fresh air heater, manual plunger screenwasher, knitweave vinyl upholstery, rubber mat floor covering.
PERFORMANCE maximum speed 129.7kph (80.8mph) (1300) *The Motor*; 25.4kph (15.8mph) @ 1000rpm; 0-96kph (60mph) 20.3sec; 21.6kg/kW (16.1kg/bhp); fuel consumption 27.9mpg (10.1l/100km).
PRICE 1300 4-door £544, £123 13s 4d PT, £668 13s 4d (£668.67p); 1500 Super £755.
PRODUCTION all Mark IIs 1,027,869; standard saloon 14,324 2-door, 4,914 4-door; de luxe 251,537 2-door, 347,462 4-door.

Although still theoretically
optional, the steering column
gearshift and the bench front
seat were consigned to history.

1966 Cortina GT Mark II

The GT was now well established, and was launched with the Mark II Cortina with 4 extra instruments over and above the standard facia layout, a stiffer, lower suspension and, from the beginning of 1967, revised gear ratios. Early cars carried over the old Cortina gear ratios, which even with second held to valve bounce, provided a sluggish response in third. Second was too high or third too low depending how you looked at it, and while it mattered little on other models, it was an irritant on the GT. The ratios had been amended for the 1965 Corsair V4 and the Lotus Cortina within the same gearbox casing, so they were quickly applied to the Mark II GT to go with the revised sporty floor gearshift, soon standard throughout the range. In the autumn of 1967 the entire Mark II range, was re-equipped with the Kent engine, increasing the GT's power by a useful 7.5kW (10bhp) and enhancing performance to close on 160.5kph (100mph) for the saloon, and not much less for the estate car introduced as a somewhat surprising stable-mate. Sporty estate cars like the Lancia High Performance Estate (HPE), Reliant Scimitar GTE, and Volvo 1800ES still lay in the future when Ford applied the GT label to an estate car. "Expensive for a Cortina," said *Autocar*, "but not for what it offers."

INTRODUCTION October 1966, produced until 1970 (Kent engine from 1967).

BODY saloon; 2-doors, 4-doors 4-seats; estate car 5-door from February 1967; weight 2-door 908kg (2002lb).

ENGINE (1300) 4-cylinders, in-line; front; 80.96mm x 72.8mm, 1498cc; compr 9.0:1; 58.2kW (78bhp) @ 5200rpm; 38.8kW/l (52.1bhp/l); 131.5Nm (97 lbft) @ 2500rpm. Kent engine stroke 77.62mm; 1599cc, 65.6kW (88bhp) @ 5200rpm; 41kW/l (55bhp/l); 130Nm (96 lbft) @ 3600rpm.

ENGINE STRUCTURE pushrod ohv; chain-driven camshaft; cast iron cylinder head and block; Weber 28/36. DCD1 (32 DFM Kent) dual choke carburettor; centrifugal and vacuum ignition; mechanical fuel pump; 5-bearing crankshaft.

TRANSMISSION rear wheel drive; diaphragm spring cable-operated clutch; 4-speed manual all-synchromesh gearbox; hypoid bevel final drive 3.89:1.

CHASSIS steel monocoque structure; ifs by MacPherson struts and anti roll bar; live rear axle with half-elliptic springs, radius arms until 1968, telescopic dampers, (lever arm on estate cars' rear); Girling hydraulic 244mm (9.62in) disc brakes at front, 229mm (9in) rear drums; Burman recirculating ball steering; 45.5l (10 gal) (12 US gal) fuel tank; 5.60-13 cross-ply or 165-13 radial-ply, 4in or 4.5in rims.

DIMENSIONS wheelbase 249cm (98in); track front 133cm (52.5in), rear 130cm (51in); length 426.7cm (168in), estate car 431.8cm (170in); width 165cm(64.9in); height 144cm (56.5in); ground clearance 13.3cm (5.25in); turning circle 8.53m (28ft).

EQUIPMENT fresh air heater, manual plunger screenwasher, reclining front seats £25 extra.

PERFORMANCE maximum (estate) 154.1kph (96mph) *Autocar*; 28.1kph (17.5mph) @ 1000rpm; 0-96kph (60mph) 13.0sec; 15.6kg/kW (11.6kg/bhp); 10.9l/100km (26mpg).

PRICE September 1967 GT 2-door £704, PT £161 6s 8d, total £865 6s 8d (£865.33). Estate 1968 total £1084 3s 11d (£1084.20).

PRODUCTION GT 2-door 62,592, 4-door 54,538.

1967 Zodiac Mark IV Executive 3022E

Buyers regarding Zodiacs as aspirational may have been in decline, yet they remained a status symbol despite the lugubrious handling, partly a result of their 57 per cent forward weight bias. Announced at the 1966 Motor Show for the 1967 model year, the Executive was mechanically identical to the Zodiac with the exception of the transmission and steering. The C4 Ford 3-speed automatic provided a certain amount of manual over-ride in L (holding first or second for swift acceleration), D1 (for normal driving), and D2 (smoother running in traffic, and better traction on snow and ice by engaging only 2 and 3 speeds). The Borg Warner fitted later was smoother. Power steering reduced the effort at parking speeds, and the opportunity was taken to raise the ratio to 18.4:1, making for less wheel-twirling. The Executive brought back the sunroof, a popular feature of British cars of the 1930s and 1940s, until discredited by rust and leaks. Ford promised it had been thoroughly tested at MIRA's dust tunnel, in Arctic and tropical weather, and it was wound into position by a foldaway handle. Crushed hide or nylon cloth could be specified for the upholstery, the facia was finished in burr walnut, and the radio had an additional speaker under the rear parcels shelf with a novel control for adjusting the front to rear balance.

INTRODUCTION October 1966, produced until 1971.
BODY saloon; 4-doors, 5-seats; weight 1333kg (2938.7lb).
ENGINE 6-cylinders, 60deg V; front; 93.66mm x 72.41mm, 2994cc; compr 8.9:1; 95.5kW (128bhp) @ 4600rpm; 31.9kW/l (42.8bhp/l); 239Nm (176 lbft) @ 3000rpm.
ENGINE STRUCTURE 3012E pushrod overhead valve, gear-driven camshaft; cast iron cylinder head and block; Weber 40 DFA twin choke downdraught; centrifugal and vacuum ignition; AC mechanical fuel pump; automatic choke; 4-bearing crankshaft.
TRANSMISSION rear wheel drive; 3-speed automatic Ford C4, later Borg Warner 35; 4-speed manual gearbox to special order; overdrive optional; final drive 3.7:1.
CHASSIS steel monocoque structure; independent front suspension McPherson struts with co-axial coil springs and dampers and anti roll bar; rear independent semi-trailing arms, coil springs telescopic dampers; Girling disc brakes 244mm (9.6in) front 256mm (9.9in) rear, vacuum servo; Hydrosteer

PAS; 68.2l (15 gal) (18 US gal) fuel tank; 6.70-14in. radial ply tyres.
DIMENSIONS wheelbase 292cm (115in); track 145cm (57.1in) front, 147cm (57.9in) rear; length 472cm (185.8in); width 181cm (71.3in); height 148cm (58.3in); ground clearance 15cm (5.9in); turning circle 11.9m (39 ft).
EQUIPMENT heated rear window, cut pile carpet, leather optional, steering column lock optional, two speed wipers, sunroof.
PERFORMANCE maximum speed 153.4kph (95.4mph) *The Motor*, 32.1kph (20mph) @ 1000rpm; 0-96kph (60mph) 13.4sec; 14kg/kW (10.4kg/bhp); fuel consumption 15.7l/100km (18mpg).
PRICE 1970 £1414, PT £432 1s 2d, total £1846 1s 2d (£1846.6p).
PRODUCTION 48,846 (all Zodiac).

1967 GT40 Mark IV and J-car

By 1967 developments and redesigns of the GT40 were proliferating along with the outside companies involved making them. The cars were bigger and faster, and while known as J-car and Mark IV in their various guises, the common ingredients were an increase in engine size to 7.0-litre and a hull made of expanded aluminium honeycomb. By 1967 Le Mans there were seven 7.0-litre cars, Carroll Shelby and Holman & Moody with 2 Mark IVs and an improved Mark 2 apiece, with Ford France a Mark 2. There were 2 5.7-litre cars made by John Wyer at Slough, and now called Mirages, and 3 more GT40s running in Group 2 Sports, making 12 cars in all. Dan Gurney and AJ Foyt not only won at record speed, exceeding 5000km (3106.9miles) for the first time, but also won the Index of Thermal Efficiency, a distinction highly regarded in France, and usually won by the French.

The Mirages proved unreliable and raced with 4.7-litre engines, but one of them won outright in the next two years, the first time Le Mans had been won by the same car twice. This sustained the competitive life of the design until the end of the decade in the face of determined opposition by Porsche. Ferrari's domination of Le Mans, which it had won 8 times, including an unbroken run from 1960-1965, was over.

INTRODUCTION 1967.
BODY coupe; 2-doors, 2-seats; 839kg (1850lb) J, 1000kg (2205lb) Mk IV.
ENGINE 8-cylinders, 90deg V; mid; 107.5mm x 96.1mm, 6997cc; compr 10.5:1; 372.9kW (500bhp) @ 5000rpm; 53.3kW/l (71.5bhp/l); 637Nm (470 lbft) @ 5000rpm.
ENGINE STRUCTURE pushrod ohv; aluminium cylinder head, cast iron block; two Holley 4-choke carburettors; 5-bearing crankshaft, dry-sump.
TRANSMISSION rwd; Long 2 dry plate clutch; Ford T-44 4-speed manual all-synchromesh gearbox in unit with transaxle.
CHASSIS semi-monocoque hull structure, with expanded aluminium honeycomb panels 13mm (.5in) and 25mm (1in) thick with square tube stiffening, grp body panels with carbon filament reinforced; ifs by double wishbones, coil springs, telescopic dampers, anti roll bar; irs by double trailing arms, transverse top link and lower wishbone, coil springs, telescopic dampers, anti-roll bar; hydraulic servo disc brakes, ventilated discs, 292mm (11.5in) front and rear; rack and pinion steering; 154.6l (34 gal) (40.8 US gal); door sill fuel tanks; cast magnesium wheels, 8.00-15 front, 12.00-15 rear.
DIMENSIONS wheelbase 241.3cm (95in); track 140cm (55in); length 416.6cm (164in) J, 434.3cm (171cm) Mk IV; width 175.3cm (69in) J, 179cm (70.5in) Mk IV; height 97.8cm (38.5in); ground clearance 10cm (3.94in).
PERFORMANCE maximum 338.7kph (211mph); 2.2kg/kW (2.2kg/bhp) J-car, 2.7kg/kW (2kg/bhp) Mk IV.
PRODUCTION 12 J-cars, 3 Mirages.

Right: **Sebring 12 Hours race. Mario Andretti brings the winning Mark IV Ford that he is sharing with Bruce McLaren into the pits.**

1967 Cortina Mark II 1300 and 1500

The whole rationale of Ford production engineering was to use as many components as many times as possible. Introduced to improve the Mark II Cortina's performance by widening the spread of torque, the Kent engine of 1967 went on to become one of the best-performing Ford engines of modern times. For the next 16 years, besides several marks of Cortina, it saw service in Fiestas, Escorts, and Capris. Its basis was a singularly robust 5-bearing bottom end, and a cylinder block, whose bore centres already matched the Ford production machinery. Its chief novelty lay in a new cylinder head of crossflow pattern that is with the inlet ports on one side, and the exhaust on the other. It was better known as the Crossflow than the Kent. The 1.3 cylinder head was completely flat and the 1.6 had only small recesses. The combustion chambers were entirely contained within the pistons, and the result was a free-revving and almost unburstable engine, which not only became the basis of Ford's mainstream production cars, but was also a resounding success in motor sport. It was used for Formula Ford single seaters and its crankcase and crankshaft were the building blocks for the BDA Ford Cosworths, giving 85.8kW (115bhp) in road tune and anything up to 212.5kW (285bhp) @ 9000rpm for racing.

INTRODUCTION September 1967, produced until 1970.
BODY saloon; 2-doors, 4-doors 4-seats; estate car 5-door; weight 2-door 1600 875kg (1929lb).
ENGINE (1300) 4-cylinders, in-line; front; 80.98mm x 62.99mm, 1298cc; compr 9.0:1; 43.3kw (58bhp) @ 5000rpm; 33.3kW/l (44.7bhp/l); 97Nm (71.5 lbft) @ 2500rpm. 1600 engine stroke 77.62mm; 1599cc; 53kW (71bhp) @ 5200rpm; 33.1kW/l (44.4bhp/l); 124Nm (91.5 lbft) @ 2500rpm.
ENGINE STRUCTURE pushrod ohv; chain-driven camshaft; cast iron cylinder head and block; Ford GPD downdraught carburettor (1600 GT-Weber); centrifugal and vacuum ignition; mechanical fuel pump; 5-bearing crank.
TRANSMISSION rwd; diaphragm spring cable-operated 7.5in (19cm) clutch; 4-speed manual all-synchromesh gearbox; hypoid bevel final drive 4.13:1.
CHASSIS steel monocoque; ifs by MacPherson struts and anti roll bar; live rear axle with half-elliptic springs, radius arms until 1968, telescopic dampers, (lever arm on estate cars' rear); Girling hydraulic 241mm (9.5in)

disc brakes at front, 203mm (8in) rear drums; Burman recirculating ball steering; 45.5l (10 gal) (12 US gal) fuel tank; 5.20-13 radial-ply, 4in rims (1600 5.60-13).
DIMENSIONS wheelbase 249cm (98in); track front 133cm (52.5in), rear 130cm (51in); length 426.7cm (168in), estate car 431.8cm (170in); width 165cm (64.9in); height 144cm 56.5in); ground clearance 16cm (6.3in); turning circle 8.53m (28ft).
EQUIPMENT fresh air heater, manual plunger screenwasher, pvc upholstery, carpet, reclining front seats £25 extra.
PERFORMANCE maximum 140kph (87.2mph) 1600 *The Motor*; 25.4kph (15.8mph) @ 1000rpm, 1600 28kph (17.5mph) @ 1000rpm; 0-96kph (60mph) 15.1sec; 16.5kg/kW (12.3kg/bhp) 1600, 10.6l/100km (26.5mpg).
PRICE September 1967 2-door de luxe £589, plus PT £134 19s 7d, total £723 19s 7d (£723.98p); 4-door Super £659, plus PT £151 0s 5d, total £810 0s 5d (£810.02p).
PRODUCTION Super 2-door saloon 18,950, 4-door 116,143; estate cars 90,290.

Below: **The Kent crossflow engine** with chain-driven camshaft, combustion chambers accurately machined in the piston crowns, and inlet and exhaust on opposite sides.

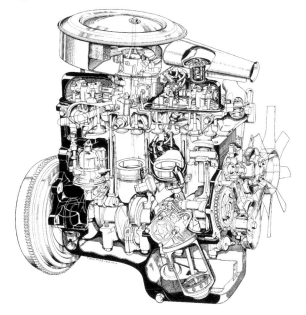

1967 Comuta

The history of electric cars was littered with might-have-beens. The Comuta fulfilled a number of functions. It showed that Ford was aware of electric cars, that it was taking the possibilities seriously and accumulating the necessary engineering expertise. It was good for public relations, the ecology lobby was lending its weight to alternative forms of transport, but just as important it demonstrated what technology was up against in contemplating the abandonment of the internal combustion engine.

The Comuta gave a convincing demonstration of the difficulty of storing sufficient energy in a self-contained small automobile to provide adequate range, adequate performance, in adequate comfort and safety. If Ford Motor Company, with its huge resources in money and manpower, could not solve the electric car's problems, it began to look as though their resolution was a long way off. Driving the Comuta was simple enough, it had an "ignition" switch, a forwards and reverse lever, two pedals, a handbrake, and a steering wheel and whirred quietly into action although not for too long. It broke no new ground in the storage of electrical power and the technology was not much advanced from that of the milk-float. There were plans to make the electric motors bigger to improve the performance but it was not speed that was the problem so much as endurance. Ford's assistant managing director Leonard Crossland dismissed any hopes of putting the Comuta into immediate production, erring on the side of optimism: "We expect electrical cars to be commercially feasible within the next 10 years, although we believe that their uses will be primarily as city centre delivery vans and suburban shopping cars."

INTRODUCTION 1967.
BODY saloon; 2-doors, 2+2-seats; weight 1200lb (544.3kg).
ENGINE 0-cyls, rear; 5bhp (3.7kW) @ 2000rpm; combined 81Nm (60 lbft).
ENGINE STRUCTURE 2 aircraft auxiliary series-wound DC electric motors 147mm (5.5in) dia; transversely mounted; thyristor control.
TRANSMISSION rwd; motors drive inwards through pinion to helical gear driving each rear wheel independently; no differential; final drive 4.05:1.
CHASSIS welded steel backbone chassis forming duct for interior heater; grp bodywork; ifs by forward-facing oblique arms on Neidhart rubber suspension bushes; irs by trailing arms on Neidhart rubber suspension bushes; telescopic dampers; hydraulic drum brakes; 4 mid-mounted 12 volt 85 am hour lead-acid batteries; 4.40 radial ply Goodyear tyres 10in wheels.
DIMENSIONS wheelbase 135.9cm (53.5in); track 111.8cm (44in); length 203.2cm (80in); width 125.7cm (49.5in); height 142.2cm (56in); turning circle 5.49m (18ft).
EQUIPMENT recirculating and fresh air interior heater.
PERFORMANCE max 64.2kph (40mph); 0-48kph (30mph) 12.5-14.0sec; 20.1kph (12.5mph) @ 1000rpm; range 64.4km (40 miles) at 40kph (25mph); restart gradient 1 in 5.
PRODUCTION 2.

Ford's electric vehicle was
demonstrated at Dunton
thirty-five years before Th!nk.

1967 Cortina 1600E

A Cortina aimed at the emerging executive-grade buyer, the 1600E (Ford's third E for Executive model), was introduced at the Paris Motor Show in 1967. It had the GT engine, Lotus suspension, a luxury interior with wood facia, and wide-rimmed Rostyle wheels.

There was a popular fad in the 1960s for one-off versions of production cars trimmed by traditional coachbuilders. It was a sort of social commentary, with pop stars, supermodels and minor royalty feeling obliged to appear democratic, without giving up their well-furnished limousines entirely. Accordingly they had "ordinary" cars like Minis painted, re-equipped, and embellished by their customary coachbuilder. It was not designed to deflect attention, quite the reverse, and the quality was only skin deep, but the idea caught on. Ford had a classless Cortina suitably trimmed by Hooper as a motor show special. Graham Robson described Ford Public Affairs executives Walter Hayes and Harry Calton as the driving forces. The 1600E was the production result with a tasteful coachline, wood-trimmed facia, wood-capped doors, leather-look pvc and central locker armrest. The carpets were thick, the seats reclined, and it did not much matter that the Kent engine's noise problems had not yet been solved and the driveline was harsh.

INTRODUCTION 1967, produced until 1970.
BODY saloon; 4-doors (some 2-doors exported); 4-seats; weight 924kg (2037lb).
ENGINE 4-cylinders, in-line; front; 81.0mm x 77.62mm, 1599cc; compr 9.0:1; 65.6kW (88bhp) @ 5400rpm; 41kW/l (55bhp/l); 130Nm (96lbft) @ 3600rpm.
ENGINE STRUCTURE pushrod ohv; chain-driven camshaft; cast iron cylinder head and block; Weber 32DFM compound carburettor; centrifugal and vacuum ignition; AC mechanical fuel pump; 5-bearing crankshaft.
TRANSMISSION rear wheel drive; diaphragm spring cable-operated Borg & Beck 191mm (7.5in) clutch; 4-speed manual all-synchromesh gearbox; hypoid bevel final drive 3.91:1.
CHASSIS steel monocoque structure; ifs by MacPherson struts and anti roll bar; live rear axle with half-elliptic springs, upper radius arms, telescopic dampers; Girling hydraulic 241mm (9.5in) disc brakes at front, 229mm (9in) rear drums; Burman recirculating ball steering; 45.5l (10 gal) (12 US gal) fuel tank; 165-13 radial-ply tyres, 5.5J rims.
DIMENSIONS wheelbase 249cm (98in); track front 133cm (52.5in); rear 130cm (51in); length 426.7cm (168in), estate car 431.8cm (170in); width 165cm (64.9in); height 144cm (56.5in); ground clearance 14cm (5.5in); turning circle 8.53m (28ft).
EQUIPMENT pvc upholstery, carpet, reclining front seats, radio £27.
PERFORMANCE maximum speed 154.4kph (96.2mph) *The Motor*, 27.6kph (17.2mph) @ 1000rpm; 0-96kph (60mph) 11.8sec; 14.1kg/kW (10.5kg/bhp); fuel consumption 12.2l/100km (23.1mpg).
PRICE February 1968 £799, PT £183 2s 1d, total £982 2s 1d (£982.10).
PRODUCTION 57,524, plus 2563 2-door.

The package was a resounding success, especially since the investment was essentially in the marketing, all the ingredients were already in full production.

1967 Lotus Cortina Mark II, Cortina Twin Cam

Although it lost some of the Mark 1 Lotus-Cortina's glamour, the Mark II's refinement and reliability made it a practical proposition. Production was moved to Dagenham, to the barely concealed relief of Ford executives in charge of warranty claims, and the car was made available in a variety of body colours. Traditionalists could have it in white with a Lotus green stripe but only to special order. There was even some equivocation over the name, Lotus-Cortina gradually giving way to Cortina-Lotus, and finally Cortina Twin Cam to conform with the companion Escort Twin Cam introduced in 1968. The Cortina Lotus's ride height was only about an inch lower than a Cortina GT, there were no aluminium body panels, no lightweight transmission casings (except those homologated for motor sport regulations), no frail A-bracket rear suspension, and it was no longer used as a front-line competition car by the works team. It did not even have a wood rimmed steering wheel. The fat 5.5in wheels and tyres remained, the grille was painted black, the ride was still firm, the gearshift a delight, and the car's new-found reliability found it new customers. Besides the homologated features it was possible to specify a Special Equipment Lotus engine and an ultra-close ratio gearbox for racing.

INTRODUCTION March 1967, production to 1970.
BODY saloon; 2-doors, 4-seats; weight 919kg (2026lb).
ENGINE 4-cylinders, in-line; front; 82.57mm x 72.82mm, 1560cc; compr 9.5:1; 81.7kW (109.5bhp) @ 6000rpm; 52.3kW/l (70.2bhp/l); 144Nm (106.5 lbft) @ 4500rpm.
ENGINE STRUCTURE twin chain-driven overhead camshafts; aluminium cylinder head, cast iron block; Two Weber 40DCOE twin-choke sidedraught carburettors; centrifugal and vacuum ignition; AC mechanical fuel pump; 5-bearing crankshaft.
TRANSMISSION rear wheel drive; Borg & Beck 8in sdp clutch; 4-speed manual all-synchromesh gearbox; semi-floating hypoid bevel final drive 3.77:1.
CHASSIS steel monocoque structure; ifs by MacPherson struts and anti roll bar; live rear axle with half-elliptic springs, radius arms, telescopic dampers; Girling hydraulic 244mm (9.62in) disc brakes at front, 229mm (9in) rear drums; Burman recirculating ball steering; 45.5l (10 gal) (12 US gal) fuel tank; 165 x 13 radial-ply tyres, 5.5J rims.
DIMENSIONS wheelbase 249cm (98in); track front 133cm (52.5in) rear 130cm (51in); length 426.7cm (168in); width 165cm (64.9in); height 141.2cm (55.6in); ground clearance 14cm (5.5in); turning circle 8.53m (28ft).
EQUIPMENT homologated list of 21 high performance racing and rally options, pvc upholstery, carpet.
PERFORMANCE maximum speed 168.7kph (105.1mph) *The Motor*; 28.3kph (17.6mph) @ 1000rpm; 0-96kph (60mph) 9.9sec; 11.2kg/kW (8.4kg/bhp); fuel consumption 12.73l/100km (22.2mpg).
PRICE £869, plus PT £199 2s 11d, total £1068 2s 11d (£1068.15p).
PRODUCTION 4032.

Service intervals were 2,500 miles against 5000 miles for other Cortinas.

Far right: **Gunnar Palm rocks his Lotus Cortina out of mud near Nairobi during a recce for the 1968 Safari Rally.**

1967 Lotus-Ford 49

The inspiration behind Ford in Formula 1 lay with Walter Hayes, a former national newspaper editor who became Director of Public Affairs. Hayes was convinced Colin Chapman had a gift for innovative automotive engineering and was determined Ford should reap the benefit. The catalyst was Keith Duckworth, brilliant racing engine designer, co-founder of Cosworth Engineering, already developing racing engines from Ford components. Hayes commissioned an engine from Cosworth on Ford's behalf, the V8 DFV, and Lotus built a car for it. One of the key features of the engine was that it should form a stressed integral part of the Lotus 49. In a feat unprecedented in modern motor racing the combination won a major world championship race on its first appearance. Two cars were entered for the Dutch Grand Prix at Zandvoort on 4 June 1967, driven by Graham Hill and Jim Clark. A tax exile, Clark had done little testing of it, and Hill led for ten laps before retiring with broken timing gear teeth. Still unfamiliar with the car, Clark came through from 6th place to take the lead, finishing half a minute ahead of Jack Brabham's Repco Brabham, an astonishing achievement. The Lotus-Ford 49 remained a front line racer until 1970. The Cosworth-Ford DFV and its derivatives became the most successful engine in the history of motor racing.

INTRODUCTION April 1967.
BODY open-wheeled racing, 0-doors, 1-seat; weight 500kg (1102lb) dry, 708.5kg (1562lb) on startline.
ENGINE 8-cylinders, 90deg V; mid; 85.74mm x 64.77mm, 2995cc; compr 11.0:1; 305.7kW (410bhp) @ 9000rpm; 102.1kW/l (136.9bhp/l).
ENGINE STRUCTURE 2 gear-driven ohcs per bank, 4 valves per cyl; aluminium cyl head, block, and crankcase; wet cast iron liners; dry sump; Lucas low pressure fuel inj, Lucas transistorised ign, one 10mm Autolite plug per cyl; 5-bg single plane crank, engine wt 167.8kg (370lb).
TRANSMISSION rwd; Borg & Beck 184mm (7.25in) twin plate clutch, Ferodo ceramic lining; ZF 5DS 12 all-synchro manual; spiral bevel final drive, various ratios BRD tubular half shafts.
CHASSIS monocoque in 18swg Alclad, front sub-frame, grp body panelling; cantilevered engine; ifs by unequal length wishbones, inboard coil springs and Armstrong telescopic dampers, anti-roll bar; irs by unequal length wishbones, twin radius arms, outboard coil springs, Armstrong telescopic dampers, anti roll bar; Girling hydraulic disc brakes 305mm (12in) ventilated later solid; Alford & Adler rack and pinion; 68.2l (15 gal) (18 US gal) rubber bag fuel tanks in monocoque side boxes, 45.5l (10 gal) (12 US gal) tank under driver's seat; Firestone tyres, Lotus cast magnesium wheels; 305mm (12in) rims front, 406mm (16in) rear.
DIMENSIONS wheelbase 241.3cm (95in); track 152.4cm (60in) front, 154.9cm (61in) rear; length 401.3cm (158in); height 73.7cm (29in).
PERFORMANCE maximum approx 297kph (185mph); 0-96kph (60mph) approx 4sec; 2.3kg/kW (1.7kg/bhp) on startline.
PRODUCTION 9.

1968 Escort 1100 de luxe, 1300 Super

When planning for the Escort began in 1964, the success likely to attend the Cortina could scarcely have been imagined. There had been a lingering suspicion that Ford was technically in arrears; rivals with front wheel drive and fluid suspension had caught the imagination. Yet Dagenham stuck to its guns, and in 1968 the Anglia replacement was built in new factories on Merseyside in England, and at Saarlouis in Germany. The Escort was conventional front engine rear-drive. Novelty was confined to how it was constructed, with body sides aft of the B-post pressed in one piece, to ensure precise close-fitting door and window apertures. There was a new administration to build it, Ford of Europe, a joined-up reorganisation of dissimilar factories that up till now had been providing different cars for different markets. Soon after the launch, following a press appraisal in Morocco that would become the exemplar for similar events over the next 30 years, it was obvious that not only was the Escort, in the well-worn cliché of *Daily Express* motoring correspondent Basil Cardew "… another winner for Britain." It was a winner for Europe. Production began at Halewood on 17 November 1967, and by its announcement on 17 January 1968 11,300 had been made, 2-door saloons only at first, with 500 being turned out every month.

INTRODUCTION January 1968, produced until to 1974.
BODY saloon; 2-door, 4-door (from 1969);4-seats; weight 745kg (1642lb), 754kg (1662lb) 1300 Super.
ENGINE 4-cylinders, in-line; front; 81mm x 53.3mm, 1098cc; cr 9.0:1; 35.8kW (48bhp) @ 6000rpm; 32.6kW/l (43.7bhp/l); 79Nm (58.5 lbft) @ 3000rpm. 1300 Super: 80.97 x 62.99; 1298cc; 43.25kW (58bhp) @ 5000rpm; 33.3kW/l (44.7bhp/l); 97Nm (71.5 lbft) @ 2500rpm.
ENGINE STRUCTURE pushrod ohv; chain-driven camshaft; cast iron cylinder head and block; Ford GDP downdraught carburettor, mechanical fuel pump; 5-bearing crankshaft.
TRANSMISSION rear wheel drive; Borg & beck diaphragm spring clutch, 165mm (6.5in) 1100, 191mm (7.5in) 1300; 4-speed manual all synchromesh gearbox; hypoid bevel final drive 4.125:1.
CHASSIS steel monocoque; ifs by MacPherson struts; lower links; telescopic dampers; rear live axle with semi-elliptic leaf springs and telescopic dampers; hydraulic 203mm (8in) drum brakes, servo optional £15.37p; rack and pinion steering; 40.9l (9.0 gal) (10.8 US gal) fuel tank 5.50-12 cross ply tubeless tyres, 4.5in rim and 155-12 radial ply tyres £12.29p extra.
DIMENSIONS wheelbase 240cm (94.5in); track front 124.5cm (49in), rear 127cm (50in); length 397.8cm (156.6in); width 157cm (61.8in); height 134.6cm (53in); ground clearance 16cm (6.3in); turning circle 8.84m (29ft).
EQUIPMENT 1100 floor rubber-covered, 1300 carpet; fresh air-blending heater standard; seat belt anchorages built-in; mandatory seat belts £8; inertia reel belts £13; radio £20; metallic paint £6.
PERFORMANCE maximum 127kph (79mph) 1100 *The Autocar*; 24.6kph (15.3mph) @ 1000rpm; 0-96kph (60mph) 22sec; 20.8kg/kW (15.5kg/bhp), 17.4kg/kW (13kg/bhp) 1300; 10.2l/100km (27.6mpg).
PRICE totals with tax; de luxe £635 9s 7d (£635.48p); Super £666 4s 2d (£666.21p) 1300 Super £690 15s 10d (£690.79p)
PRODUCTION 2-door 611,305, 4-door 153,660, estate 130,908.

1968 Escort 1300 GT

After 8 years and 1,300,000 Anglia 105Es, Ford decided that its small car needed more high-performance variants. They had been seen to generate showroom traffic and provided the high-volume versions with a bit of glamour. Accordingly a 1300GT was planned. The Kent engine was provided with a high-lift camshaft, a special inlet manifold, a compound dual-choke Weber carburettor, and the fabricated exhaust manifold already used in the Cortina 1600GT. The GT was the only Escort with two exhaust silencers, one ahead of and one behind the back axle, and disc front brakes with vacuum servo were standard. Its close-ratio gearbox was ingeniously accomplished by altering the constant mesh and third gear train by one tooth in each case. This raised all the gear ratios by around 10%, but changing 3rd from 26/21 to 25/22 almost restored its original value, thus contriving sporting characteristics at the minimum cost. Another novel measure was the deletion, throughout the Escort range, of the customary front anti-roll bar that effectively formed one leg of the lower wishbone in the MacPherson strut. Instead, the Escort had a compression strut angled back to the body shell under the scuttle, and a track control arm pivoting on the main front cross-member. Spring rates for the GT were 135lb/in on the 1100/1300 115lb/in against the old Anglia's 80lb/in.

INTRODUCTION January 1968, produced until 1974.
BODY saloon; 2-door, 4-seats; weight 778kg (1715lb); 4-door from 1969 weight 835kg (1841lb).
ENGINE 4-cylinders, in-line; front; 80.97mm x 62.99mm; 1298cc; compr 9.0:1; 53kW (71bhp) @ 6000rpm; 40.8kW/l (54.7bhp/l); 95Nm (70 lbft) @ 4300rpm.
ENGINE STRUCTURE pushrod ohv; chain-driven camshaft; cast iron cylinder head and block; Weber compound twin choke downdraught carburettor, mechanical fuel pump; 5-bearing crankshaft.
TRANSMISSION rear wheel drive; Borg & Beck diaphragm spring clutch, 190mm (7.5in); 4-speed manual all synchromesh gearbox; hypoid bevel final drive 4.125:1.
CHASSIS steel monocoque structure; independent front suspension by MacPherson struts; lower links; telescopic dampers; rear live axle with semi-elliptic leaf springs and telescopic dampers; Girling hydraulic 218mm (8.6in) front disc brakes, rear 203mm (8in) drum, vacuum servo standard; rack and pinion steering; 40.9l (9.0 gal) (10.8 US gal) fuel tank; 5.5in rim and 155-12 radial ply tyres.
DIMENSIONS wheelbase 240cm (94.5in); track front 124.5cm (49in), rear 127cm (50in); length 397.8cm (156.6in); width 157cm (61.8in); height 134.6cm (53in); ground clearance 15.2cm (6in); turning circle 8.84m (29ft).
EQUIPMENT fresh air-blending heater and heated rear window standard, inertia reel seat belts £15, centre console, £5, radio £35, fabric seat trim £7.
PERFORMANCE maximum speed 154kph (96kph) *The Autocar*; 24.1kph (15mph) @ 1000rpm; 0-96kph (60mph) 12.4sec; 14.7kg/kW (14.2kg/bhp); fuel consumption 10l/100km (28mpg).
PRICE total with tax 1971 £966.11p.
PRODUCTION 1,082,472 Halewood Escorts.

1968 Escort Twin Cam

There was some jostling on the press testing in Morocco for the privilege of driving the Twin Cam, of which there was only one, perhaps two. It was not only the most exciting Escort, it was one of the most exciting small cars of its time and the ancestor of a dynasty of fast Fords. An important asset of a competitions department is its capacity for intrepid experiment. In the case of the Twin Cam Escort, it was the competitions department that spotted a prototype pushrod Escort on test at Boreham, and speculated what it would be like (if it fitted) with a Lotus Cortina engine. It was 136kg (300lb) lighter than a Cortina and yes, it did fit in a strengthened wide wheelarch type 48 bodyshell. Halewood-made production cars were type 49s, homologated for Group 3 competiton, and with their taut handling, stiffened bodyshell, and competition credentials they provided Ford with the ingredients for a remarkable run of sporting successes.

The Twin Cam Escort was faster than an MGB or a Lotus Cortina, a Mini Cooper S or a Sunbeam Rapier. At the new legal British speed limit of 70mph it was tolerably quiet, although above it the resonant noises of a classic competition engine tended to obtrude. It scarcely mattered, the Twin Cam ushered in a new era of small sports saloon.

INTRODUCTION January 1968, produced until 1971.
BODY saloon; 2-door, 4-seats; weight 785kg (1731lb).
ENGINE 4-cylinders, in-line; front; 82.55mm x 72.8mm; 1558cc; compr 9.5:1; 81.7kW (109.5bhp) @ 6000rpm; 52.4kW/l (70.3bhp/l); 144Nm (106.5 lbft) @ 4500rpm.
ENGINE STRUCTURE chain-driven twin overhead camshaft; aluminium cylinder head and cast iron block; two Weber twin choke horizontal 40DCOE carburettors, mechanical fuel pump; 5-bearing crankshaft.
TRANSMISSION rear wheel drive; Borg & Beck diaphragm spring clutch, 203mm (8in); 4-speed manual all synchromesh gearbox; hypoid bevel final drive 3.77:1.
CHASSIS steel monocoque; ifs by MacPherson struts; lower links; telescopic dampers, anti-roll bar; rear live axle and half-elliptic leaf springs with telescopic dampers and radius arms; Girling hydraulic 244mm (9.6in) front disc brakes, rear 229mm (9in) drum, vacuum servo standard; rack and pinion steering; 40.9l (9.0 gal)

(10.8 US gal) fuel tank; 5.5in rim and 165-13 radial ply tyres.
DIMENSIONS wheelbase 240cm (94.5in); track 129.5cm (51in) front, 132.1cm (52in) rear; length 397.8cm (156.6in); width 157.5cm (62in); height 138.4cm (54.5in); ground clearance 15.2cm (6in); turning circle 8.84m (29ft).
EQUIPMENT fresh air-blending heater standard, carpeted floor inertia reel seat belts £15, radio £35, wide range of homologated competition extras, rev limiter at 6500rpm.
PERFORMANCE maximum speed 178.7kph (111.3mph) *Motor*; 28.3kph (17.6mph) @ 1000rpm; 0-96kph (60mph) 8.7sec; 9.6kg/kW (7.2kg/bhp); fuel consumption 12l/100km (23.4mpg).
PRICE total with tax and delivery £1123.17p.
PRODUCTION 1,082,472 Halewood Escorts.

Right: **Morocco, January 1968, the press tests the Ford Escort Twin Cam while Ford minders hover in the background in their still new Zodiac IV.**

1968 3-litre Group 6 F3L Sports Prototype

Short-lived, shapely, but in the end disastrous, designed by Len Bailey and built by Alan Mann at Weybridge, the F3L seemed full of promise. Essentially a two-seater Formula 1 car with a Cosworth DFV engine, the main longitudinal members were side sponsons containing fuel tanks, and a deep central backbone contained the connections to the engine and oil and water radiators. Scuttle and toeboard acted as the main front crossmember that together with the narrow roof formed a rigid roll cage. The BOAC 500 was a 6-hour race for sports cars, and the new Ford prototypes, resplendent in red and gold, competed against Porsches, older GT40s, Lola-Chevrolets and Ferraris, and a gas turbine Howmet. Walter Hayes: "The F3L was to have its debut at Brands, and Jimmy Clark was going to drive it. It was all perfectly clear. Then he rang me up and said 'I can't do it. I know I promised, but Colin (Chapman) says I've got to go to Hockenheim.'"

It did quite well, leading for the first 2 hours, although it gave Bruce McLaren a rough ride on the uneven Brands Hatch surface. When Mike Spence took over it broke a half-shaft. By then news of Clark's death had arrived from Hockenheim. Walter Hayes: "It was one of the very bad moments of my life, standing in the pits at Brands and hearing that Jimmy had died."

He had persuaded Ford Motor Company to create the Ford-Cosworth DFV whose purpose, besides giving Ford a new image, had been to win the world championship again for Jim Clark. The F3L reappeared at the Nürburgring but crashed heavily, badly injuring Chris Irwin. "It was the only car I ever hated in my life," said Hayes. "Alan Mann said he could do it and it would be cheap, and we thought that we needed to replace the GT40 although on reflection we didn't. Sports cars were in decline. I killed that car out of sheer hatred."

INTRODUCTION March 1968.
BODY coupe; 2-doors, 2-seats; weight 671kg (1480lb).
ENGINE 8-cyl, 90deg V; mid; 85.74mm x 64.77mm, 2995cc; compr 11.0:1; 306kW (410bhp) @ 9000rpm; 102kW (137bhp)/l.
ENGINE STRUCTURE two gear-driven ohcs per bank, 4 valves per cylinder; aluminium head, block, and crankcase; wet cast iron liners; dry sump; Lucas low pressure fuel injection, Lucas transistorised ignition, one 10mm Autolite plug per cylinder; 5-bearing single plane crank, engine weight 167.8kg (370lb).
TRANSMISSION rear wheel drive; Borg & Beck 184mm (7.25in) twin plate clutch, Ferodo ceramic lining; 5-speed Hewland manual gearbox; spiral bevel final drive, various ratios BRD tubular half shafts.
CHASSIS monocoque 0.03in (.76mm) malleable aircraft aluminium alloy; double wishbone welded tube ifs with Rose-type inboard joints, co-axial spring and damper units, provision for 4WD; rear suspension Broadley 4-link with trailing radius arms and adjustable transverse links with co-axial spring

Far right: **John Surtees drives the Ford F3L (photo by Classic and Sportscar) and** (below) **unloading from Alan Mann's new 36ft two-deck transporter for a 1968 race at Oulton Park.**

and damper units; hydraulic 292mm (11.5in) disc brakes; body panelled in light alloy with a frontal area 14 sqft (1.3 sqm).
DIMENSIONS wheelbase 221cm (87in); length 421.6cm (166in); height 90.2cm (35.5in).
EQUIPMENT aerodynamic downforce 272kg (600lb); internal ducting behind water radiator; NACA air inlets engine and oil rads.
PERFORMANCE maximum speed 321kph (200mph); 2.2kg/kW (1.6kg/bhp).
PRODUCTION 2.

1969 Capri 1300, 1300GT, 1600, 1600GT

The Car You Always Promised Yourself had a profound effect. In a sense it was like the original Capri of 1961, neither a sports car in the accepted sense, nor an everyday saloon. It created its own niche as a sort of European Mustang and enjoyed astonishing success. The long bonnet, 2+2 seating, and style gave it a cachet hardly any car enjoyed before, and not many would again. The basis was typically Cortina, only the top half was really new, the first engines were wide-ranging, and an important innovation was an array of X, L, XL and R custom pack options, giving customers a wide choice of upholstery and equipment so that they could, in theory at any rate, tailor their Capri to suit themselves. There were dummy air scoops, chrome wheel trims, reclining seats, map-reading light, extra lights and special paint schemes with anti-glare matt black on the bonnet just like real rally cars. Launch prototypes were shown with BDA 16-valve twin cam engines (the Escort was first to get it) but never went into production.

The Capri was destined to be a huge success; it built on Ford's mastery of production engineering through relying on components already in production. It would be made in Britain and Germany, and getting on for 2 million would be sold during the next 17 years.

INTRODUCTION November 1968, produced until December 1973.
BODY coupe; 2-doors, 2+2-seats; weight 1300 880kg (1940lb), 1300 900kg (1984lb), 1600 GT 920kg (2028lb).
ENGINE 1300 4-cylinders, in-line; front; 80.98mm x 62.99mm, 1298cc; compr 9.0:1; 42.5kW (57bhp) @ 5500rpm; 91Nm (70lbft) @ 2500rpm; 32.8kW/l (43.9bhp/l). 1300GT 53.7kW (72bhp) @ 5500rpm. 1600 87.65 x 66mm; 1593cc; 53.7kW (72bhp).
GT 65.6kW (88bhp) @ 5700rpm
ENGINE STRUCTURE pushrod overhead valve, chain-driven camshaft; cast iron cylinder head and block; Ford GPD carburettor; centrifugal and vacuum ignition; mechanical fuel pump; 5-bearing crankshaft. 1300GT and 1600 Weber 320 carburettor; 1600GT Weber compound.
TRANSMISSION rear wheel drive; 19cm (7.5in) diaphragm spring cable-operated clutch; 4-speed manual all-synchromesh gearbox; hypoid bevel final drive 4.125:1 (1300) 3.89:1 (1600). Borg Warner 35 automatic available

1300 GT, 1600, final drive 1600GT 3.777:1.
CHASSIS steel monocoque structure; independent front suspension by MacPherson struts and anti roll bar; live rear axle with half-elliptic springs and radius rods, telescopic dampers; Girling hydraulic 24.1cm (9.5in) disc brakes at front (optional 1300s), 24.4cm (9.6in) GT and 1600; 20.3cm (8in) rear drums; dual circuit; vacuum servo; rack and pinion steering; 48l (10.6 gal) (12.7 US gal) fuel tank; 6.00-13 cross-ply 1300, 165-13 GT and 1600 radial-ply, 4.5rims.
EQUIPMENT SLR pack £79 12s 10d (£79.64p); fixed seat belts £8.49p, inertia reel belts £14.01p.

DIMENSIONS wheelbase 256cm
(100.8in); track front 134.5cm (53in),
rear 132cm (52in); length 426cm
(167.7in); width 164.5cm (64.8in);
height 129cm (50.8in) GT and 1600
128cm (50.4in); ground clearance
11.5cm (4.5in); turning circle 9.75m
(32ft).
PERFORMANCE maximum speed
1300 138kph (86mph), 1300GT
and 1600 150kph (93.4mph),
1600GT 160kph (99.7mph); 1300
26.2kph (16.3mph) @ 1000rpm,
1600GT 28.8kph (17.94mph);
0-100kph (62mph) 19sec; 1600 GT
13sec; 16.8kg/kW (12.5kg/bhp); fuel
consumption 9.1l/100km (31mpg),
9.8l/100km (28.8mpg) 1600GT
PRICE 1300, £682, £890 7s 10d
(£890.39p) including PT; 1300GT £985
70p; 1600 £936.9p; 1600GT £1041.83p.
PRODUCTION 374,700 UK Capris.

1969 Capri 2000 GT, 3000 GT

The one-shape-fits-all recipe of the Capri was well judged. Buyers rang the changes with engines and accessory packs to their hearts' content. Rear axle radius arms had been deleted from Cortina GTs on the grounds of road noise; they were reinstated on the Capri to provide GT handling, and developed with care so that there was negligible sacrifice in noise vibration and harshness, the celebrated NVH that Ford took seriously to compete with classic makes in the sporting or semi-sporting or even quasi-sporting field. By the dawn of the 1970s it did not much matter if a car was sporting or not, but it had to be refined, smooth-running, and if not completely quiet it had to make the right noises. The 2000GT V4 was not quite ready at launch but went into production in March, the V6 3.0-litre following in September. The first addition to the range was the 3000E, technically the same as the 3000GT, but cosmetically upmarket and better equipped. In 1971 the 3.0-litre Essex V6 was revised with better breathing to provide more torque and 138bhp (102.9kW) instead of 128bhp (95.5kW), a change that was never applied to the same engine fitted to soon-to-be-replaced Zodiacs. The German Capri RS2600 was not sold in Britain and only 248 of the dramatic RS3100 with big-bore V6 of 1973 were ever made.

INTRODUCTION November 1968, produced until December 1973.
BODY coupe; 2-doors, 2+2-seats; weight 2000GT 960kg (2116lb), V6 1057kg (2330lb).
ENGINE 2000 4-cylinders, 60deg V; front; 93.66mm x 72.44mm, 1996cc; compr 8.9:1; 68.6kW (92bhp) @ 5250rpm; 34.4kW/l (46.1bhp/l); 141Nm (104lbft) @ 3600rpm. V6 93.66 x 72.4mm; 2994cc, 8.9:1; 95.45 kW (128bhp) @ 4750rpm; 31.9kg/l (42.8bhp/l); 235Nm (173lbft) @ 3000rpm.
ENGINE STRUCTURE pushrod ohv, gear-driven camshaft; cast iron cylinder head and block; Weber 40 compound carburettor; centrifugal and vacuum ignition; mechanical fuel pump; 4-bearing crankshaft. V6 Weber 40DFA carburettor.
TRANSMISSION rear wheel drive; 22.9cm (9.0in) diaphragm spring cable-operated clutch; 4-speed manual all-synchromesh gearbox; hypoid bevel final drive 3.545:1; Borg Warner 35 auto available. V6 3.22:1 final drive.
CHASSIS steel monocoque structure; ifs by MacPherson struts and anti roll bar; live rear axle with half-elliptic springs and radius rods, telescopic dampers; Girling hydraulic disc brakes front, 24.4cm (9.6in); 20.3cm (8in) rear drums; dual circuit; vacuum servo; rack and pinion steering; 48l (10.6 gal) (12.7 US gal) fuel tank; 165-13 radial-ply tyres, 4.5 rims.
DIMENSIONS wheelbase 256cm (100.8in); track 134.5cm (53in) front, 132cm (52in) rear; length 426cm (167.7in); width 164.5cm (64.8in); height 128cm (50.4in); ground clearance 11.5cm (4.5in); turning circle 9.75m (32ft).
EQUIPMENT SLR pack £79 12s 10d (£79.64p); fixed seat belts £8.49p, inertia reel belts £14.01p.
PERFORMANCE maximum speed 171kph (106.5mph), V6 183kph (114mph); 30.6kph (19.1mph) @ 1000rpm, V6 33.4kph (20.8mph); 0-100kph (62mph) 11.3sec, V6 9.2sec; 14kg/kW (10.4kg/bhp); fuel consumption 12.3l/100km (23mpg), V6 12l/100km (23.5mpg).
PRICE £833, £1087 10s 7d (£1087.53p) including PT.
PRODUCTION 374,700 UK Capris.

1970 Escort RS1600

Engine development, inspired by the connections with Cosworth, developer of the brilliantly successful DFV Formula 1 engine, went on apace. 4 valves per cylinder, twin overhead camshaft engines, once the prerogative of the no-expense-spared grand prix car, now became available on a competitively priced popular small saloon. The engine's ancestry was the Cosworth FVA (Four Valve type A) that developed into the Formula 2 unit, which in turn was the prototype of the DFV (Double Four Valve). The new Escort engine was analogous to the Cosworth Formula 2 unit, derated, and with toothed belts instead of gears driving the overhead camshafts. It was thus known as the BDA (Belt Drive type A), the RS from Rallye Sport, evidence of the growing European and in particular German influence on Ford operations. Furthermore while the Twin Cam block was based on the old 1500cc Ford, the BDA was built round the 1600cc Kent block. The small facility at Aveley Essex known as Ford Advanced Vehicles Operation (AVO) could make up to 30 cars a day from body shells and components from Halewood and outside suppliers. The RS1600 was the first AVO car, virtually hand-assembled on the small track. As the Twin Cam was run down, the RS1600 took its place as the front-running Ford sports and competition car.

INTRODUCTION 1970, production until 1974.

BODY saloon; 2-door, 4-seats; weight 785kg (17311lb).

ENGINE 4-cylinders, in-line; front; 80.97mm x 77.6mm; 1601cc; compr 10:1; 89.5kW (120bhp) @ 6500rpm; 55.9kW/l (75bhp/l); 152Nm (112lbft) @ 4000rpm.

ENGINE STRUCTURE belt-driven twin overhead camshaft; 4 valves per cylinder; aluminium cylinder head and cast iron block (aluminium block from 1972); two Weber twin choke horizontal 40DCOE 48 carburettors, mechanical fuel pump; 5-bearing crankshaft.

TRANSMISSION rear wheel drive; Borg & Beck diaphragm spring clutch, 20.3cm (8in); 4-speed manual all synchromesh gearbox; hypoid bevel final drive 3.77:1.

CHASSIS steel monocoque structure; independent front suspension by MacPherson struts; lower links; telescopic dampers, anti-roll bar; rear live axle and half-elliptic leaf springs with telescopic dampers and radius arms; Girling hydraulic 24.4cm (9.6in) front disc brakes, rear 22.9cm (9in) drum, vacuum servo standard; rack and pinion steering; 40.9l (9.0 gal) (10.8 US gal) fuel tank; 5.5in rim and 165-13 radial ply tyres.

DIMENSIONS wheelbase 240cm (94.5in); track front 129.5cm (51in), rear 132.1cm (52in); length 397.8cm (156.6in); width 157.5cm (62in); height 138.4cm (54.5in); ground clearance 15.2cm (6in); turning circle 8.84m (29ft).

EQUIPMENT fresh air-blending heater standard, wide range of homologated competition extras, rev limiter at 6500rpm.

PERFORMANCE maximum speed 182kph (113.4mph) *Motor*; 28.25kph (17.6mph) @ 1000rpm; 0-96kph (0-60mph) 8.3sec; 8.8kg/kW (6.5kg/bhp); fuel consumption 11.2l/100km (25.2mpg).

PRICE total with tax and delivery £1447.

PRODUCTION 947.

Right: Hannu Mikkola and Jim Porter on a special stage during the 1973 Monte Carlo Rally. Escorts driven by Mikkola, Timo Makinen, and Chris Sclater won the team prize and finished 1st and 2nd in the Touring category. RS1600 engine (below) features belt drive for the 2 overhead camshafts and 4 valves per cylinder.

1970 Escort Mexico

The 1968 London-Sydney 10,000mile (approx 16,000km) Marathon had been surprisingly successful. Encouraged, the Daily Mirror sponsored a rally from London, where the 1966 World Cup football series had been staged, to Mexico where the 1970 competition was being held. Timed special stages would be decisive, but with 16,000miles (approx 26,000kms) in prospect, the competitions department needed an Escort to be not only fast but also last the distance. The overhead camshaft engines were now less brittle than their Lotus forbears, but to be on the safe side, a team of cars was built with enlarged 1558cc Kent pushrod engines. 99 competitors started from Wembley Stadium, 71 of whom reached Lisbon a week later. The survivors re-started from Rio de Janeiro and Hannu Mikkola took the lead in his Escort as the field was further depleted. The event was a triumph for Ford, with the manufacturers' team prize and Escorts 1st, 3rd, 5th, and 6th. AVO at once went into production with replicas, the Mexico filling the gap in the sporting range between the GT and the Twin Cam, and with its heavy-duty body becoming a firm favourite with amateur racing and rally drivers. Retailed through a new network of Rallye Sport dealers in 1972, the Mexico's trim was improved to that of the RS1600.

INTRODUCTION 1970, produced until 1974.
BODY saloon; 2-door, 4-seats; weight 891kg (1964lb).
ENGINE 4-cylinders, in-line; front; 80.98mm x 77.62mm; 1599cc ("1601"cc for competition); compr 9.0:1; 64.8kW (86.9bhp) @ 5500rpm; 40.5kW (54.3bhp)/l; 125Nm (92lbft) @ 4000rpm.
ENGINE STRUCTURE pushrod ohv; chain-drive camshaft; 2 valves per cyl; cast iron cyl head and block; Weber 32DFM twin choke compound carb, mechanical fuel pump; 5-bearing crank.
TRANSMISSION rwd; Borg & Beck diaphragm spring clutch, 19cm (7.5in); 4-speed manual all synchro gearbox; hypoid bevel final drive 3.77:1.
CHASSIS steel monocoque; ifs by MacPherson struts; lower links; telescopic dampers, anti-roll bar; rear live axle and half-elliptic leaf springs with telescopic dampers and radius arms; Girling hydraulic 24.4cm (9.6in) front disc brakes, rear 22.7cm (9in) drum, vacuum servo; rack and pinion; 40.9l (9.0 gal) (10.8 US gal) fuel tank; 5.5in rim and 165-13 radial ply tyres.

DIMENSIONS wheelbase 240cm (94.5in); track 129.5cm (51in) front, 132.1cm (52in) rear; length 397.8cm (156.6in); width 157.5cm (62in); height 138.4cm (54.5in); ground clearance 15.2cm (6in); turning circle 8.8m (29ft).
EQUIPMENT heater standard, homologated competition extras, Minilites £109 extra, vinyl seats, pvc headlining; carpets and "Mexico" graphics delete options, Contour driver's seat £18.50, passenger's reclining seat £32.37p, Cibie Oscar lights £7.75p each.
PERFORMANCE maximum 159kph (99mph) Autocar, 28.3kph (17.6mph) @ 1000rpm; 0-96kph (60mph) 10.7sec; 13.8kg/kW (10.3kg/bhp); 10.3l/100km (27.5mpg).
PRICE inc tax and delivery £1150.
PRODUCTION 9382, RS2000 4324.

Top right: **the author was second in a journalists' race at Brands Hatch, overtaken only in the last lap.**

Centre right: **Jimmy Greaves in the 1970 World Cup Rally on Westminster Bridge.**

1970 Cortina Mark III 1297cc, 1599cc

The 4-year model cycle seemed to be working, and Ford confidently moved the 3rd generation Cortina up-market to enhance profitability, but instead of 4 years made it last nearly 6. There were facelifts, the final one in 1975, which was no more than all-black grilles, cloth trim, heated rear windows, and some cosmetic improvements. As a result the Cortina remained best-selling car in Britain 4 years running and the millionth Mark III came that October. The pinched-waist, so called Coke-bottle style, and a wide range of options proved successful, and although the car looked bigger it was the same length as before even though 5cm (2in) wider and 10.2cm (4in) lower. Improved Kent engines with larger inlet valves, new camshaft, changed piston bowl profile and 6 to 10 per cent more power were used for the 1300 and 1600. British and German Escorts were virtually identical but Cologne Cortinas (Fords did not sell as well in Germany) had a distinctly Teutonic style. The German range used its own 1300 and 1600 ohc engines and the Taunus 20M a V6. As part of Ford's multi-national culture the Mark III was dimensioned metrically. The MacPherson strut front suspension that had served well for 20 years was replaced by conventional double wishbone ifs, curiously translated into Fordspeak as SLA (short and long arm).

INTRODUCTION October 1970, produced until 1976.
BODY saloon; 4-doors, 2-doors, 5-seats; estate car 5-doors; weight 2-door 945kg (2083.4lb), 4-door 965kg (2127.4lb), estate 1040kg (2292.8lb).
ENGINE 1300 4-cyls, in-line; front; 80.97mm x 62.99mm, 1298cc; cr 9.0:1; 42.5kW (57bhp) @ 5500rpm; 32.7kW/l (43.9bhp/l); 91Nm (67lbft) @ 3000rpm; 1600 stroke 77.62mm; 1599cc; 50.7kW (68bhp) @ 5200rpm; 115Nm (85lbft) @ 2600rpm.
ENGINE STRUCTURE pushrod ohv; chain-driven camshaft; cast iron cylinder head and block; Ford GPD downdraught carburettor; centrifugal and vacuum ignition; mechanical fuel pump; 5-bearing crankshaft.
TRANSMISSION rwd; diaphragm spring cable operated 7.5in sdp clutch; 4-speed single selector rail all synchromesh gearbox; 3-speed Borg Warner Model 35 automatic optional on 1600; one-piece prop shaft; final drive 1300, 4.11:1; 1600, 3.89:1.
CHASSIS steel monocoque; ifs by coil springs, wishbones, anti-roll bar; rear live axle with coil springs, trailing and semi-trailing radius arms; telescopic dampers; hydraulic servo 24.4cm (9.6in) disc front brakes, 20.3cm (8in) rear drums; rack and pinion steering; 54.6l (12 gal) (14.4 US gal) fuel tank; 5.60-13 4-ply on 4.5J rim, radial-ply, various size options.
DIMENSIONS wheelbase 257.7cm (101.5in); track 142.2cm (56in) front and rear; length 426.7cm (168in); width 170.2cm (67in); height 132.1cm (52in); ground clearance 17.8cm (7in); turning circle 10.36m (34ft).
EQUIPMENT 14 exterior colours, fabric seat trim optional, L Pack, XL Pack options.
PERFORMANCE maximum speed 135.7kph (84.3mph) 1300XL *The Motor*; 24.7kph (15.4mph) @ 1000rpm; 0-96kph (60mph) 18.1sec; 22.2kg/kW (16.6kg/bhp); fuel consumption 12l/100km (23.5mpg).
PRICE at launch: 2-door 1300 £700, total inc PT £913 17s 10d (£913.89p); 1300 XL Estate £1159.33; 1600XL 4-door £1094.6p.
Feb 1972: 1300XL £962.50p, with XL Pack £1080, with styled wheels, radial-ply tyres and cloth trim £1150.73p.
PRODUCTION 1,126,559 all Mark III.

1970 Cortina Mark III 1593cc/1993cc

The 98in (248.92cm) wheelbase platform of the first Cortina lasted through two incarnations, making 8 years, and the 101.5in (257.81cm) wheelbase (within half an inch of Corsair) remained the length of Cortinas to come for the next 12. The Mark III was also intended to replace the Corsair, which accounts for its move up-market, and the stretched platform that was required to provide more room inside. It was also completely new, not only the platform and suspension, but the drivelines too, with the latest thing – overhead cam engines with belt-drive camshafts.

 Even the Kent 1300 and 1600 engines were brought up to date, but since the ohc engines were 1600 and 2000, it meant that the range had two 1600s. The ohc units were accordingly known as 1600GT and 2000GT; they scarcely equated to previous GT Cortinas, but it proved a useful notation to distinguish Cortinas with the US-designed Pinto engine. Planned for an American compact car, the Pinto became part of Ford's new international programme and was used in Taunus, Escort, Capri, Granada, and was even adapted for the Transit van. Tall and 18lb (8.16kg) heavier than the Kent, it required some in-service development before it was as reliable. Unlike the Kent the combustion chambers were in the head, not in the pistons.

INTRODUCTION October 1970, produced until 1976.
BODY saloon; 4-doors, 2-doors, 5-seats; estate car 5-doors; weight 2-door 960kg (2116.4lb), 4-door 980kg (2160.5lb), 1600 estate 1085kg (2392lb).
ENGINE 1600 4-cylinders, in-line; front; 87.75mm x 66mm, 1593cc; compr 9.2:1; 65.6kW (88bhp) @ 5700rpm; 41.2kW/l (55.2bhp/l); 125Nm (92lbft) @ 4000rpm. 2000 90.8mm x 76.95mm; 1993cc; 73.1kW (98bhp) @ 5500rpm; 36.7kW/l (49.2bhp/l); 151Nm (111lbft) @ 4000rpm.
ENGINE STRUCTURE single ohc; toothed belt; opposed ohv; cast iron cyl head and block; Weber 32/36 DGAV (DFAVH 2000) downdraught twin choke carb; centrifugal and vacuum ign; mechanical fuel pump; 5-bearing crank.
TRANSMISSION rwd; diaphragm spring cable operated 8.5in (216mm) sdp clutch; 4-speed single selector rail all synchromesh gearbox; 3-speed Borg Warner Model 35 automatic optional; two-piece prop shaft; hypoid bevel final drive, 3.89 (1600) and 3.444:1 (2000).
CHASSIS steel monocoque; ifs by coil springs, wishbones, anti-roll bar; rear live axle with coil springs, trailing and semi-trailing radius arms; telescopic dampers; hydraulic servo 244mm (9.6in) disc front brakes, 203mm (8in) rear drums; rack and pinion steering; 54.6l (12 gal) (14.4 US gal) fuel tank; 5.60-13 4-ply on 4.5J rim, radial-ply, various size options.
DIMENSIONS wheelbase 257.8cm (101.5in); track 142.2cm (56in) front and rear; length 426.7cm (168in); width 170.2cm (67in); height 132.1cm (52in); ground clearance 17.8cm (7in); turning circle 10.36m (34ft).
EQUIPMENT 14 exterior colours, fabric seat trim optional, L Pack, XL Pack options.
PERFORMANCE maximum 162.5kph (101mph) 2000XL Estate *The Motor*; 26.2kph (16.3mph) @ 1000rpm; 0-96kph (60mph) 14.1sec; 14.6kg/kW (10.9kg/bhp); 7.6l/100km (37.2mpg).
PRICE at launch: 2000 2-door £787, total with PT £1027 9s 5d (£1027.47p); 2000GXL 4-door £133819p; 2000XL Estate £1272.92p. February 1972: £1388.08p with XL Pack, sports wheels, cloth trim.
PRODUCTION 1,126,559 all Mark III.

1970 GT70

Identifying a requirement for a car to enhance Ford's reputation for exciting engineering, the Competitions Department produced a rakish mid-engined coupe. Competitions manager Stuart Turner, together with works driver Roger Clark, decided it was needed after the works Escorts had been badly beaten in the important Monte Carlo Rally. Something more than a motor show concept car was required to take on the Renault Alpine and Porsche 911 in high-speed rallies, or where snow and ice put the Escort at a disadvantage. Placing the engine amidships gave the driver more options in varying conditions, and a prototype was built with a steel platform, glass reinforced plastic body, independent suspension, and a choice of 1.6BDA or V6 RS2600 engines, with a 5-speed ZF transaxle. A potential rally championship car, 6 were planned to study its practicality for production. Regular components were used where possible both for expediency and so that AVO could proceed with production of 500 if it was a success. The design was by Len Bailey, who had been chief designer of the GT40, and World Cup Rally winners Hannu Mikkola and Gunnar Palm were engaged as consultants. Bailey drew up the graceful body, whose efficiency was confirmed by wind-tunnel evaluation, although the cockpit would have been too cramped and hot for a rally car.

INTRODUCTION Brussels Motor Show 1971.
BODY coupe; 2-doors, 2-seats; weight 762kg (1680lb).
ENGINE 6-cylinders, 60deg V; mid; 90mm x 66.8mm, 2520cc; compr 9.0:1; 125bhp (93.2kW) @ 5300rpm; 37kW/l (49.6bhp/l); 201Nm (148lbft) @ 3000rpm (prototype). BDA engine 4-cylinders, in line; 80.98mm x 77.62mm, "1601cc" for competitions; compr 10:1; 89.5kW (120bhp) @ 6,500rpm; 152Nm (112lbft) @ 4000rpm.
ENGINE STRUCTURE pushrod ohv, gear-driven camshaft; cast iron cyl head and block; Solex twin choke 35/35 EEIT carb; mechanical fuel pump; 4-bearing crank. BDA.16 valve, toothed belt dohc; 2 Weber 40DCOE; cast iron block, aluminium head; 5-bearing crank.
TRANSMISSION rear wheel drive; sdp 216mm (8.5in) hydraulic clutch; 5-speed ZF5 DS25 manual all synchro; final drive 4.22:1 (optional Taunus 17M).
CHASSIS perimeter rail 16g steel chassis, floor pan 22g, roll hoop 18g steel tube; (Cortina) ifs by coil springs and double wishbones (with Escort joints); provision for anti roll bar;

telescopic dampers; (Zodiac IV) rear independent by upper link and trailing arm, coil springs and anti-roll bar; brakes, hydraulic no servo (Cortina) disc front 24.4cm (9.6in) rear (Zodiac IV) 25.1cm (9.9in); (Cortina) rack and pinion steering; 54.6l (12 gal) (14.4 US gal) fuel tank; 195/70VR tyres ZZ rims.
DIMENSIONS wheelbase 111.8cm (44in); track 142.2cm (56in) front, 139.7cm (55in) rear; length 388.6cm (153in); width 172.7cm (68in); height 111.8cm (44in); ground clearance 15.2cm (6in); turning circle 9.45m (31ft).
EQUIPMENT laminated windscreen, optional 1600GT engine, optional Essex V6; luggage capacity 283cu m (10cu ft), retractable headlights, contoured ventilated seats, retractable seat belts; (Capri) handbrake switchgear and electricals; (Anglia) heater.
PERFORMANCE maximum speed est for competition version 289kph (180mph); 32.1kph (20mph) @ 1000rpm.
PRICE estimated for a production version, £5000.
PRODUCTION 6 prototypes planned, 5 completed.

The V6 engine proved too heavy for best handling and the final version of the car tuned for French tarmac special stages had the BDA with a Hewland gearbox.

1972 Consul Granada V4 1996cc

It was perhaps only through a certain flamboyance that the Zephyrs and Zodiacs had kept their place in the luxury car world, but by 1971 it was not enough. Pedigree rivals like BMW were becoming more affordable, making executive-class buyers ask why they were paying premium prices for Fords. Premium customers were no longer to be fobbed off with indifferent handling or a quirky appearance. Consequently a new range was introduced, using the old Consul name in conjunction with the new title Granada. Manufactured in West Germany and Britain, with a completely new body shell, the range had a wide choice of engines and a more sophisticated independent rear suspension that did away with the Mark IV Zephyr's rear wheel steer. It also reverted to drum brakes at the back. The first cars were all 4-door saloons, to be followed by estates some 18 months later. More compact than the Mark IV, at 5in (12.7cm) shorter and 4.4in (11.2cm) lower, UK cars had V4 and V6 engines, with German-market cars also having the option of the ohc in-line 4-cylinder. Similar dimensions to the Triumph 2000 and Mercedes-Benz 220 indicated Granada's aspirations; the 58in (147.3cm) shoulder room was generous even though headroom was not, on account of the low build with a low roll-centre only 5.5in (14cm) above the ground.

INTRODUCTION March 1972, production December 1971 to 1974.
BODY saloon; 4-doors, 5-seats; weight 1185kg (2612lb).
ENGINE 4-cylinders, 60deg V; front; 93.7mm x 72.4mm, 1996cc; compr 8.9:1; 60.8kW (81.5bhp) @ 5000rpm; 30.5kW/l (40.8bhp/l); 144Nm (106lbft) @ 3000rpm.
ENGINE STRUCTURE pushrod ohv; gear-driven camshaft; cast iron cylinder heads and block; Ford GPD carburettor, centrifugal and vacuum ignition; mechanical fuel pump; 3-bearing crankshaft
TRANSMISSION rear wheel drive; 21.6cm (8.5in) sdp clutch; 4-speed manual all synchromesh gearbox; optional automatic; hypoid bevel final drive 3.89:1.
CHASSIS steel monocoque structure; independent front suspension, coil springs and double wishbones, anti roll bar; independent rear by semi-trailing arms, coil springs, telescopic dampers; hydraulic vacuum servo dual circuit brakes front disc 26.2cm (10.3in), rear drum 22.9cm (9in); rack and pinion steering; 65l (14.3 gal) (17.2 US gal) fuel tank; 4-ply cross-ply 6.45-14 tyres, 6J wheels optional.
DIMENSIONS wheelbase 277cm (57in); track 151cm (59.5in) front, 154cm (60.6in) rear; length 457cm (179.9in); width 179cm (70.5in); height 137cm (53.9in); ground clearance 13cm (5.1in); turning circle 11m (36ft).
EQUIPMENT cut pile carpet, toughened glass windscreen, safety belts, automatic transmission, sunroof extra, radial ply tyres and 6in rims £57.12, metallic paint £8.84.
PERFORMANCE maximum speed 154kph (95.9mph) *Autocar*; 28.6kph (17.8mph) @ 1000rpm; 0-100kph (62mph) 14.0sec; 19.5kg/kW (14.5kg/bhp); fuel consumption 11.8l/100km (24mpg).
PRICE £1126; £1376.01 incl PT.
PRODUCTION in Britain 58,969, 6002 estates.

233

1972 Consul Granada V6 2495cc, 2995cc

The Granada was not only replacing the Mark IV Zephyr and Zodiac, it was also replacing the Taunus 17M, 20M, and 26M, so it had to cover a wide choice and there was only one bodyshell with which to do it, although Germany had an estate car from the beginning and also the racy 2-door fastback. Comfort was emphasised with long suspension travel, 19.6cm (7.7in) at the front and 22.9cm (9in) at the back, while soft springing and anti-dive geometry gave a supple well controlled smooth ride. Cam Gears made the steering rack with integral power ram, and the rotary valve supplied by Adwest Engineering was similar to the component it supplied to Jaguar. The 2.5-litre car could be a Consul (standard or L trim) or Granada (standard or GXL); the 3.0-litre could be a Consul GT (heavy-duty suspension, 6J wheels, radial-ply tyres, Granada instruments and extra lamps) or Granada with a smarter grille with horizontal chrome bars and smarter side mouldings and GXL spec. Power steering and automatic transmission were standard with GXL together with tinted windows, bumper overriders and a vinyl roof. A heated rear window and radio were standard on the GXL that was welcomed for its real gains in comfort, refinement, and roomy boot within a wheelbase the same as a Jaguar XJ6 and a track slightly wider.

INTRODUCTION March 1972, produced from December 1971-1974. BODY saloon; 4-doors, 5-seats; 2500 1270kg (2800lb), 3000 1300kg (2866lb). ENGINE 2500 6-cyls, 60deg V; front; 93.7mm x 60.3mm, 2495cc; compr 9.0:1; 89.5kW (120bhp) @ 5000rpm; 35.9kW/l (48.1bhp/l); 179Nm (132lbft) @ 3000rpm. 3000: 93.7x72.4mm; 2995cc; 102.9kW (138bhp) @ 5000rpm; 34.4kW/l (46.1bhp/l); 235Nm (173 lbft) @ 3000rpm.
ENGINE STRUCTURE pushrod ohv; gear-driven camshaft; cast iron cyl heads and block; Weber twin choke carb, centrifugal and vacuum ignition; mechanical fuel pump; 4-bearing crank.
TRANSMISSION rwd; 24.1cm (9.5in) sdp clutch; 2-piece propeller shaft; 4-speed manual all synchromesh gearbox; optional automatic; hypoid bevel final drive 3.45:1.
CHASSIS steel monocoque; ifs, coil springs and double wishbones, anti roll bar; independent rear by semi-trailing arms, coil springs, telescopic dampers; hydraulic vacuum servo dual circuit brakes front disc 262mm (10.3in) ventilated on 3000, rear drum 229mm (9in); rack and pinion PAS optional; 65l (14.3 gal) (17.2 US gal); 4-ply cross-ply 6.95S-14 tyres 2500, radial ply 175HR-14 185HR optional 3000; 6J wheels opt.
DIMENSIONS wheelbase 277cm (57in); track 151cm (59.5in) front, 154cm (60.6in) rear; length 457cm (179.9in); width 179cm (70.5in); height 137cm (53.9in); ground clearance 13cm (5.1in); turning circle 11m (36ft).
EQUIPMENT sunroof, cut pile carpet, toughened glass windscreen, safety belts, automatic transmission. optional 6in rims £57.12, metallic paint £8.84.
PERFORMANCE 2500: maximum speed 2500 175kph (109mph) *Autocar*; 31.6kph (19.7mph) @ 1000rpm; 0-100kph (62mph) 10.4sec; 14.2kg/kW (10.6kg/bhp); 13.5l/100km (21mpg). 3000: maximum 182kph (113.4mph) GXL auto *Autocar*, 33.6kph (20.9mph); 0-100kph (62mph) 9.1sec; 12.6kW/l (9.4bhp/l); GXL 14.8l/100km (19.1mpg).
PRICE 2500L £1416 GXL, automatic £1934.
PRODUCTION in Britain 50,747, 7650 estates.
PRODUCTION 374,700 UK Capris.

1973 Escort RS2000

The last Mark I Escort to be built at Aveley, before AVO became a casualty of the continuing oil crisis in 1975, used the American-designed Pinto engine first seen in the Mark III Cortina 2000 of 1970. Ringing the changes with engines was now well-established, and a 2.0-litre Escort was a logical development, aimed at sustaining sales right down to the advent of the Mark II Escort in 1975. The new model's underpinnings were already incorporated in Mark I production during 1973, as part of Ford's Europeanisation programme, and the result was the most refined of all the sporting Mark I Escorts. A small increase in power was achieved over the engine's Cortina installation by introducing an electric fan, and a new aluminium sump and oil pick-up were required to clear the Escort's cross-member. An aluminium bellhousing was provided to raise the engine's resonance threshold to over 6000rpm where in theory it would rarely be heard. Ford works racing driver Gerry Birrell helped in developing the suspension, stiffening the front spring rates by 30 per cent and the rear by 10 per cent. Damper rates were changed to suit, and the ride height lowered, "…working wonders for the comfort and making the RS2000 a much more progressive car when driven to the limits of adhesion," according to *Autocar*.

INTRODUCTION July 1973, production to 1975.
BODY saloon 2-door, 4-seats; weight 915kg (2017.2lb).
ENGINE 4-cylinders, in-line; front; 90.82mm x 76.95mm; 1993cc; compr 9.2:1 74.6kW (100bhp) @ 5750rpm; 37.4kW/l (50.2bhp/l); 1 108lbft (146Nm) @ 3500rpm.
ENGINE STRUCTURE single overhead camshaft, toothed belt drive, opposed ohv; cast iron cylinder head and cast iron block; Weber 32/36 downdraught twin choke carburettor; centrifugal and vacuum ignition; mechanical fuel pump; 5-bearing crankshaft.
TRANSMISSION rear wheel drive; cable operated diaphragm spring clutch, 21.6cm (8.5in); 4-speed manual all synchromesh gearbox; hypoid bevel final drive 3.54:1.
CHASSIS steel monocoque structure; independent front suspension by MacPherson struts; lower links; telescopic dampers, anti-roll bar; rear live axle and half-elliptic leaf springs with telescopic dampers and radius arms; Girling hydraulic 24.4cm (9.62in)

front disc brakes, rear 20.3cm (8in) drum, vacuum servo standard; rack and pinion steering; 40.9l (9 gal) (10.8 US gal) fuel tank; 5.5in rim RS alloy optional wheels; 165-13 radial ply tyres.
DIMENSIONS wheelbase 240cm (94.5in); track front 124.5cm (49in), rear 127cm (50in); length 397.8cm (156.6in); width 157.5cm (62in); height 138.4cm (54.5in); ground clearance 15.2cm (6in); turning circle 8.8m (29ft).
EQUIPMENT fresh air-blending heater, heated rear window, cloth seats pvc headlining; carpeted floor inertia reel seat belts, wide range homologated competition extras, rev limiter at 6500rpm.
PERFORMANCE maximum speed 173.4kph (108mph) *Autocar*; 30kph (18.7mph) @ 1000rpm; 0-96kph (60mph) 9.0sec; 12.3kg/kW (9.2kg/bhp); fuel consumption 10.6l/100km (26.6mpg).
PRICE total with tax and delivery in London £1586.
PRODUCTION 4324 including production at Saarlouis.

1973 Capri RS3100

There were 2 Capri "homologation specials". The rules required 1000 to be built to qualify for motor sporting competition, and Ford Germany produced its RS2600 with the 2637cc V6. This was raced successfully and eventually taken to 2.9 litres, 111.9kW (150bhp) with Kugelfischer fuel injection. The first 50 were light in weight for racing but even fully equipped road versions could reach 120mph (192.6kph). The RS2600 was not sold in Britain but was essentially the prototype of the final Capri, the 3.8i, many years later. Its Halewood equivalent was the RS3100 which in racing form had the Ford-Cosworth 3.4-litre quad-cam V6 conversion. Production never reached 1000, the regulations were loosely applied, and cars passed if it looked as though manufacturers had tried. Sales were overtaken by the Mark II Capri in 1974. Only some 200 road-going cars were ever completed using an overbored gas-flowed 3.0-litre (3091cc) V6 with a Weber carburettor, a rear spoiler soon identified as "ducktail", cast alloy wheels, and racy-looking front quarter bumpers. The basis of the car was largely 3000GT but included ventilated disc brakes as on the RS2600 and incorporated the September 1972 improvements such as a Granada-style facia and matt black panels under the doors. It had firmer, rather than the softer springing used for most of the range.

INTRODUCTION Glasgow Motor Show Nov 1973.
BODY coupe; 2-doors, 2+2-seats; weight 1078kg (2376.6lb).
ENGINE 6-cylinders, 60deg V; front; 95.19mm x 72.4mm, 3091cc; compr 9.0:1; 110.4kW (148bhp) @ 5000rpm; 35.7kW/l (47.9bhp/l); 254Nm (187lbft) @ 3000rpm.
ENGINE STRUCTURE pushrod ohv; gear-drive camshaft; cast iron cylinder head, block; downdraught Weber twin choke carburettor, centrifugal and vacuum ignition; mechanical fuel pump; 4-bearing crankshaft.
TRANSMISSION rear wheel drive; sdp clutch; 4-speed manual synchromesh gearbox; final drive 3.09:1.
CHASSIS steel monocoque structure; ifs by MacPherson struts and anti roll bar; live rear axle with half-elliptic springs anti roll bar, telescopic dampers; Girling hydraulic disc brakes at front, 24.4cm (9.6in); 22.9cm (9in) rear drums; dual circuit; vacuum servo; rack and pinion steering; 48l (10.6 gal) (12.7 US gal) fuel tank; 185-70HR 13 radial-ply tyres, 4.5 rims.
DIMENSIONS wheelbase 256cm (100.8in); track 134.5cm (53in) front, 132cm (52in) rear; length 430.3cm (169.4in); width 164.5cm (64.8in); height 128cm (50.4in); ground clearance 11.5cm (4.5in); turning circle 9.75m (32ft).
PERFORMANCE maximum speed 200kph (125mph) approx; 36.3kph (22.6mph) @ 1000rpm; 0-100kph (62mph) 8.0sec approx; 9.8kg/kW (7.3kg/bhp); fuel consumption approx 10.5l/100km (26.9mpg).
PRICE £2412.64
PRODUCTION 200.

1973 Cortina 2000E

The Cortina's mid-term facelift came as the world oil crisis broke. Inflation, loss of confidence, and international tension hardly made it the best time to move up-market. Yet improvements to the range went ahead and yet another Executive model, the 2000E, was introduced. The two-bay instrument panel was replaced by a comprehensively equipped one extending the width of the car, furnished in the case of the 2000E tastefully in teak. The surviving Kent engine was the 1300, the 1600 Kent replaced by a Pinto, now of 72bhp (53.7kW). Gear ratios, a persistent difficulty with Cortinas, were revised and every model now had anti-roll bars. Spring rates were revised, stiffening the GT and reducing understeer. The 2000E, in addition to deep pile carpets and tree wood (as opposed to lookalike plastic wood) luxury interior was provided with a 1970s fashion statement, a vinyl roof. Shiny wheels, shiny rubbing strips, and door casings to match the Savannah nylon upholstery completed a package instrumental in moving the family car up the aspirational ladder. The 2000E's ride, handling, and performance were well up to the mark. All that lay between it and a real (more expensive) luxury car were refinement and longevity. Ford engineers knew where NVH was coming from, but still often found it impossible to eliminate at the price.

INTRODUCTION 1973, production to 1976.
BODY saloon; 4-doors, 2-doors, 5-seats; estate car 5-doors; weight 4-door 1130kg (2491.2lb).
ENGINE 4-cylinders, in-line; front; 90.8mm x 76.95mm; 1993cc; 73.1kW (98bhp) @ 5500rpm; 36.7kW/l (49.2bhp/l); 150Nm (111lbft) @ 4000rpm.
ENGINE STRUCTURE single overhead camshaft; toothed belt; opposed overhead valve; cast iron cylinder head and block; Weber 32/36 DFAVH downdraught twin choke carburettor; centrifugal and vacuum ignition; mechanical fuel pump; 5-bearing crankshaft.
TRANSMISSION rear wheel drive; diaphragm spring cable operated 216mm (8.5in) sdp clutch; 4-speed single selector rail all synchromesh gearbox; 3-speed Borg Warner Model 35 automatic optional; two-piece prop shaft; hypoid bevel final drive, 3.54:1.
CHASSIS steel monocoque structure; independent front suspension by coil springs, wishbones, anti-roll bar; rear live axle with coil springs, trailing and semi-trailing radius arms, anti-roll bar; telescopic dampers; hydraulic vacuum servo 24.4cm (9.6in) disc front brakes, 20.3cm (8in) rear drums; rack and pinion steering; 54.6l (12 gal) (14.4 US gal) fuel tank; optional 185/70-13, radial-ply 165-13 standard, 5.5in rims.
DIMENSIONS wheelbase 257.8cm (101.5in); track 142.2cm (56in) front and rear; length 426.7cm (168in); width 170.2cm (67in); height 132.1cm (52in); ground clearance 17.8cm (7in); turning circle 10.36m (34ft).
EQUIPMENT rectangular quartz halogen headlamps, centre console, push-button radio standard, seat belts £17.05p, laminated windscreen £28.78p, metallic paint £8.17p. delivery charge included in price.
PERFORMANCE maximum speed 163.7kph (102mph) *Autocar*, 29.3kph (18.2mph) @ 1000rpm; 0-96kph (60mph) 10.3sec; 15.5kg/kW (11.5kg/bhp) 4-door; fuel consumption 10.5l/100km (27mpg).
PRICES 1974 Cortina 1300 £1114; 1300L £1165; 1600XL £1350; 2000E £1637.76p.
PRODUCTION 1,126,559 all Mark III.

Anti-roll bars were incorporated at both ends of the Cortina from 1973, enabling lower rate springs to improve the ride. There had been only one at the front of GTs and GXLs. The 2000E Estate Car was available in 14 colours, six metallic, with the vinyl roof in either black or tobacco. Tinted glass was standard from 1974.

1973 Escort 1300E

Soon after the launch of the Escort, the range was widened with the addition of 1100 and 1300 estates, although a 4-door did not reach production until October 1969. Smooth running of the production lines at Halewood brooked no interruption for special versions, so Ford Advanced Vehicles was set up at Aveley in Essex. Almost a factory within the Ford factory, it was responsible for the racy editions, and also for the first 5000 Executive Escorts.

The 1300E was a costlier 2-door fitted up with pile carpet, wood facia, extra instruments, coachlines, fancy wheel trims, and halogen auxiliary lamps. To emphasise its exclusiveness it was offered with special paintwork that included venetian gold, amber gold metallic, or a fetching metallic purple that set off the chrome flashing round the windows and black vinyl roof. It was based on the Sport, with 13in wheels rather than the full GT, but its "E" for Executive tag (as opposed to "GT") seemed to make insurance companies less suspicious.

Revisions in 1971 brought modest power increases to the range through changes in cam profiles and improvements in combustion chamber design. The de luxe and Super names were abandoned in favour of L and XL, and all were carpeted and better trimmed.

INTRODUCTION 1973 to 1974.
BODY saloon; 2-door, 4-seats; weight 815kg (1796.8lb).
ENGINE 4-cylinders, in-line; front; 80.97mm x 62.99mm; 1298cc; compr 9.2:1; 53.7kW (72bhp) @ 6000rpm; 41.3kW/l (55.5bhp/l); 92Nm (68lbft) @ 4000rpm.
ENGINE STRUCTURE pushrod ohv; chain-driven camshaft; cast iron cylinder head and block; Weber twin choke downdraught carburettor, mechanical fuel pump; 5-bearing crankshaft.
TRANSMISSION rear wheel drive; Borg & beck diaphragm spring clutch, 19.1cm (7.5in); 4-speed manual all synchromesh gearbox; hypoid bevel final drive 4.125:1.
CHASSIS steel monocoque structure; independent front suspension by MacPherson struts; lower links; telescopic dampers; rear live axle with semi-elliptic leaf springs and telescopic dampers; Girling hydraulic 218mm (8.6in) front disc brakes, rear 203mm (8in) drum, vacuum servo standard; rack and pinion steering; 40.9l (9.0 gal) (10.8 US gal) fuel tank; 5.5in rim and 165-13 radial ply tyres.

DIMENSIONS wheelbase 240cm (94.5in); track 124.5cm (49in) front, rear 127cm (50in) rear; length 397.8cm (156.6in); width 156cm (61.8in); height 134.6cm (53in); ground clearance 15.2cm (6in); turning circle 8.84m (29ft).
EQUIPMENT fresh air-blending heater standard, carpeted boot; seat belt anchorages built-in; mandatory seat belts £8; inertia reel belts £13; radio £20; metallic paint £6.
PERFORMANCE maximum speed 149.3kph (93mph) *Motor*; 26.2kph (16.3mph) @ 1000rpm; 0-96kph (60mph) 13.1sec; 15.2kg/kW (11.3kg/bhp); fuel consumption 9.7l/100km (27.3mpg).
PRICE total with tax: £1180.
PRODUCTION 5,000 approx.

Regular Escort prices went up throughout the range, and by 1970 the cheapest was £807 including tax and the XL Estate £1011. Automatic transmission was £120 extra for 1300s including the upper-class 1300E.

1974 Granada Coupe 2994cc, Granada Ghia

Granada up to the waist, the Coupe was a brave entry by Ford Germany to the autobahn-cruiser market. Its racy-looking 2-door body had a long sloping roof and was sold in Britain only in Ghia trim. A 2.0-litre was discontinued in the spring of 1976. Most Coupes were V6s with automatic transmission, and the body style did not survive after 1977. In April 1973 the 2.5-litre saloon was discontinued, and the Ghia appeared both as a saloon and Coupe. The Ghia's distinguishing feature, besides a luxurious interior, was a die-cast grille and headlamp casings that, true to Ford's habit, took the model up the aspirational ladder, encouraging customers to pay a premium in 1974 for a car that cost very little extra to make than it had in 1973. The vinyl roof could be black or a tasteful leather-grained tobacco brown, and upholstery that looked like traditional coachbuilders' west of England broadcloth, was really specially treated brushed nylon Beaumont cloth from which, said Ford, oil, coffee, melted chocolate, and all the usual motoring stains could be easily removed. Footwells were provided with foam underlays to enhance the feeling of cosseted luxury. Granadas' heating and ventilation was revised, and the automatic became the C3 from Ford Bordeaux, similar to the American C4 but more in tune with European driving.

INTRODUCTION January 1974, produced to 1974.
BODY saloon; 2-doors, 5-seats; weight coupe 2.3 1295kg (2855lb), Ghia 3.0 1385kg (3053.4lb).
ENGINE 6-cylinders, 60deg V; front; 93.7mm x 72.4mm, 2995cc; compr 9.0:1; 102.9kW (138bhp) @ 5000rpm; 34.4kW/l (46.1bhp/l); 235Nm (173 lbft) @ 3000rpm.
ENGINE STRUCTURE pushrod ohv; gear-driven camshaft; cast iron cylinder heads and block; Weber twin choke carburettor, centrifugal and vacuum ignition; mechanical fuel pump; 4-bearing crankshaft.
TRANSMISSION rear wheel drive; 24.1cm (9.5in) sdp clutch; 2-piece propeller shaft; 4-speed manual all synchromesh gearbox; optional C3 automatic; hypoid bevel final drive 3.45:1.
CHASSIS steel monocoque structure; independent front suspension, coil springs and double wishbones, anti roll bar; independent rear by semi-trailing arms, coil springs, telescopic dampers; hydraulic vacuum servo dual circuit brakes front disc 26.2cm (10.3in)

ventilated, rear drum 22.9cm (9in); rack and pinion PAS; 65l (14.3 gal) (17.2 US gal) fuel tank; radial ply 175HR-14 185HR optional 185-14 Michelin ZX.
DIMENSIONS wheelbase 277cm (57in); track 151cm (59.5in) front, 154cm (60.6in) rear; length 457cm (179.9in); width 179cm (70.5in); height 137cm (53.9in); ground clearance 13cm (5.1in); turning circle 11m (36ft).
EQUIPMENT sunroof, cut pile carpet, toughened glass windscreen, safety belts, automatic transmission. optional sports wheels £51.54, metallic paint £10.60, laminated windscreen £31.20, manual transmission delete option £114.31.
PERFORMANCE maximum speed Ghia saloon 171kph (106.5mph) *Autocar*, 33.4kph (20.8mph) @ 1000rpm; 0-100kph (62mph) 10.7sec; 13.5kg/kW (10kg/bhp) Ghia 3.0; fuel consumption 13.5l/100km (20.9mpg).
PRICE Ghia saloon £2478.71, £2892 incl car tax and VAT.
PRODUCTION in Britain 50,747 all Granada.

1974 Capri II 1300 and 1600

With the world in the grip of the first oil crisis, manufacturers seized the opportunity to put new model announcements on hold. Not Ford. It took the plunge with the already successful Capri to introduce styling changes, provide more room inside, and while remaining strictly 2+2, introduce the hatchback to make the car far more practical. Folding down the rear seat gave huge luggage capacity. It was surprising really that it had not been done in the first place following the example of the MGB GT. The crease along the body side was discarded, and the dummy air intakes ahead of the rear wheel arch dispensed with, giving a smoother more sophisticated appearance. Slimmer windscreen pillars and bigger windows gave better visibility all round, and although the innovations with their attendant reinforcement round the double-skinned gas-strutted tailgate increased the body weight by 27.2kg (60lb) they were well worthwhile. Using much the same Cortina underpinnings, the 1300 had a pushrod crossflow Kent engine and the 1600 the latest Pinto overhead camshaft engine, giving it a lively turn of speed. The array of trim packs available with the first Capri was reduced; buyers had been confused and in many cases dealers ordering cars for stock failed to identify the most popular options.

INTRODUCTION December 1973, production to October 1976 in Britain and January 1978 in Germany.
BODY coupe; 2-doors, 2+2-seats; weight 1010kg (2226.7lb), 1600 1040kg (2292.8lb).
ENGINE 4-cylinders, in-line; front; 80.98mm x 62.99mm, 1297cc; compr 9.2:1; 42.5kW (57bhp) @ 5500rpm; 32.8kW/l (44bhp/l); 91Nm (67lbft) @ 3000rpm. 1600 87.7 x 66mm; 1593cc; 53.7kW (72bhp) @ 5200rpm; 33.7kW/l (45.2bhp/l); 118Nm (87lbft) @ 3000rpm. 1600GT 65.6kW (88bhp).
ENGINE STRUCTURE 3034E pushrod ohv; chain-driven camshaft; cast iron cyli head, block; Ford GPD carb, centrifugal and vacuum ignition; mechanical fuel pump; 5-bearing crank. 1600 ohc, 1600GT Weber carb.
TRANSMISSION rear wheel drive; 19.1cm (7.5in), 1600 GT 216mm (8.5in) diaphragm spring cable-operated clutch; 4-speed manual all-synchromesh gearbox; hypoid bevel final drive 4.125:1, 1600 3.77:1, 1600GT 3.75:1.
CHASSIS steel monocoque; ifs by MacPherson struts and anti roll bar; live rear axle with half-elliptic springs and anti-roll bar, telescopic dampers; Girling hydraulic disc brakes at front, 24.4cm (9.6in); 20.3cm (8in) rear drums, 1600 22.9cm (9in); dual circuit; opt vacuum servo (1600 std); rack and pinion steering; 57.7l (12.7 gal) (15.2 US gal) fuel tank; 165-13; 185/70-13 optional radial-ply tyres, 5Jrims.
DIMENSIONS wbase 256cm (100.8in); track front 135.4cm (53.3in), rear 138.4cm (54.5in); length 434.1cm (171in); width 169.9cm (66.9in); height 129.8cm (51.1in); ground clearance 10.4cm (4.1in); turning 10.67m (35ft).
EQUIPMENT toughened glass windscreen, laminated extra, brushed nylon seats extra.
PERFORMANCE maximum speed 167kph (104mph) 1600, *Autocar*, 1300 26.2kph (16.3mph), 1600 28.6kph (17.8mph); 1600GT 28.7kph (17.9mph) @ 1000rpm; 0-100kph (62mph) 11.4sec; 1300 23.8kg/kW (17.7kg/bhp), 1600 19.4kg/kW (14.5kg/bhp); 10.2l/100km (27.7mpg).
PRICE 1300L £1336.25, 1600L £1415.83, 1600GT £1632.92.
PRODUCTION 84,400 all Capri II in Britain.

247

1974 Capri II 2000 and 3000

The 2.0-litre overhead camshaft Pinto 4-cylinder engine from the Cortina replaced the V4, and the 3.0-litre V6 Capri was enhanced by an extra 10bhp. Power steering and automatic transmission were popular options, and buyers began taking Capris seriously as competent long distance touring cars, once their racing pedigree and experience improved the performance and handling. The facia and controls had been revised in 1972, and softer spring rates were among radical changes made in the rear suspension to improve the ride. The rear radius arms were replaced by an anti-roll bar, and the rear track was widened by 5.8cm (2.3in). In 1973 the millionth Capri was made, in Cologne as it happened, and the Mark II's revised body shape was made less susceptible to side winds. The 3.0-litre had a new power steering option and bigger brakes. A Ghia Capri went on sale from May 1974 with moulded side rubbing strip, alloy wheels with 5.5J rims, and a vinyl roof, tinted glass, and an extra coat of clear lacquer. The seats were high-backed and the facia panel had a vinyl covering colour-keyed, as they said, to the Rialto material (a velvet-finished brushed nylon) used for the upholstery. Shown at the 1975 Geneva Motor Show as a limited edition, the Capri S had firmer springing, proving so popular it became generally available for 1976.

INTRODUCTION December 1973, production to October 1976 in Britain and January 1978 in Germany.
BODY coupe; 2-doors, 2+2-seats; weight 2.0 1065kg (2348lb), 3.0 1170kg (2579.3lb).
ENGINE 4-cyls, in-line; front; 90.8mm x 76.95mm, 1998cc; compr 9.2:1; 73.1kW (98bhp) @ 5200rpm; 36.6kW/l (49bhp/l); 151Nm (111lbft) @ 3500rpm.
3000: 6-cyls, 60deg V; 93.7 x 72.4mm 9.0:1 compr; 2994cc; 102.9kW (138bhp) @ 5000rpm; 34.4kW/l (46.1bhp/l); 236Nm (174lbft) @ 3000rpm.
ENGINE STRUCTURE chain driven ohc; cast iron cyl head, block; Weber carb, centrifugal and vacuum ignition; mechanical fuel pump; 5-bearing crankshaft. V6 4-bearing; pushrod ohv.
TRANSMISSION rear wheel drive; 21.6cm (8.5in), V6 24.4cm (9.6in) diaphragm spring cable-operated clutch; 4-speed manual all-synchromesh gearbox; hypoid bevel final drive 3.44:1, V6 3.09:1.
CHASSIS steel monocoque; ifs by MacPherson struts and anti roll bar; live rear axle with half-elliptic springs and anti-roll bar, telescopic dampers; Girling hydraulic disc brakes at front, 245mm (9.6in), V6 248mm (9.75in); rear drums 22.9cm (9in); dual circuit; vacuum servo; rack and pinion (PAS optional V6); 57.7l (12.7 gal) (15.24 US gal) fuel tank; 165-13; 185/70-13 optional radial-ply tyres, 5Jrims. V6 185/70-13 standard.
DIMENSIONS wheelbase 256cm (100.8in); track front 135.4cm (53.3in), rear 138.4cm (54.5in); length 434cm (170.9in); width 169.9cm (66.9in); height 129.8cm (51.1in); ground clearance 10.4cm (4.1in); turning circle 10.67m (35ft).
EQUIPMENT toughened glass windscreen, laminated extra, brushed nylon seats extra.
PERFORMANCE maximum speed V6 194.2kph (121mph); 31.3kph (19.5mph) @ 1000rpm, V6 35.2kph (21.9mph) @ 1000rpm; 0-100kph (62mph) V6 8.2sec; fuel consumption Touring DIN V6 10.7l/100km (26.4mpg).
PRICE 2000GT £1687.50, 3000GT £1931.66.
PRODUCTION 84,400 all Capri II in Britain.

1975 Escort Mk II 1098cc

Ford's pan-European policy introduced the underpinnings of the Mark II Escort two years before the demise of the Mark I. Accordingly the new version was essentially a re-skin, providing nearly 25 per cent more window area, and more legroom in the back. Instead of the curvy Mark I it was fashionably upright and square-cut.

The basic layout remained largely Anglia 105E; nothing was changed at Ford unless it was absolutely essential, a principle since Model T days, so handling and general roadworthiness remained good. The platform was adaptable enough to encompass 19 different models at launch. The 1100 was the basic fleet model and soon after it was announced, in July 1975 with the market in deep shock as a result of the unrelenting oil crisis, Ford took the precaution of introducing a cut-price version. This was the Escort Popular 2-door at £1299, with cross-ply tyres and reduced engine power (*Autocar* complained of an engine flat-spot and of having to rev it a lot to make much progress), but it was short-lived. Estate Escorts were Mark II as far as the A pillars; the slightly curved waistline of the Mark I seemed to blend quite well with the front and it was cheaper to keep it. Side mouldings and Sport wheels maintained differentials between L and GL trim options.

INTRODUCTION January 1975, production 1974 to 1980.
BODY saloon, 2-door, 4-door; estate, 4-seats; weight 2-door 875kg (1929lb), estate 1300 920kg (2028.2lb).
ENGINE 4-cylinders, in-line; front; 81mm x 53.3mm, 1098cc; compr 9.0:1; 35.8kW (48bhp) @ 6000rpm; 32.6kW/l (43.7bhp/l); 79Nm (58.5 lbft) @ 3000rpm. Popular 30.6kW (41bhp) @ 5300rpm; 70.5Nm (52lbft) @ 3000rpm.
ENGINE STRUCTURE pushrod ohv; chain-driven camshaft; cast iron cyl head and block; Ford GDP downdraught carburettor 34mm barrel (Popular 30mm barrel), mechanical fuel pump; 5-bearing crankshaft.
TRANSMISSION rwd; diaphragm spring clutch, 191mm (7.5in) 4-speed manual all synchromesh gearbox; hypoid bevel final drive 4.125:1, Popular 3.89:1.
CHASSIS steel monocoque; ifs by MacPherson struts; lower links; telescopic dampers; rear live axle with semi-elliptic leaf springs and telescopic dampers; hydraulic 20.3cm (8in) front drum brakes (discs on L-spec cars), 22.9cm (9in) rear drums; rack and pinion steering; 40.9l (9.0 gal) (10.8 US gal) fuel tank; 155-12 on 4.5rim; or 155-13 steel-braced radial ply tyres, 5in (12.7cm) rim Popular cross-ply 6.00-12.
DIMENSIONS wheelbase 240cm (94.5in); track front 127cm (50in), rear 129.5cm (51in); length 397.8cm (156.6in); width 153.7cm (60.5in); height 141cm (55.5in); ground clearance 14cm (5.5in); turning circle 9.45m (31ft).
EQUIPMENT radio £63.47; remote control door mirror £15.60; rear fog warning lamp £15.80; Popular, rubber floor mats, black-painted trim.
PERFORMANCE maximum speed 1300 149.3kph (93mph) *Autocar*, Popular 123kph (76.6mph) *Motor*; 1300 25.5kph (15.9mph) @ 1000rpm, Popular 26kph (16.2mph); 0-96kph (60mph) 1300 13.5sec, Popular 21.8sec; 25.7kg/kW (19.2kg/bhp) 1300, 28.8kg/kW (21.3kg/bhp) Popular); fuel consumption 1300 9.6l/100km (29.3mpg), Popular 12.2l/100km (34.5mpg).
PRICE totals with tax; 1100 2-door £1440.45; Popular £1299, Popular Plus (radial ply tyres, carpet, etc) £1399.
PRODUCTION Halewood total 960,007, Saarlouis 848,388.

251

1975 Escort Mk II 1297cc, 1599cc

The mainstream replacements for the 7-year-old Mark I Escort were the 1300 and 1600 with the same pushrod Kent engine. The 1600 was an innovation for the Mark II with identical cylinder centres (so the blocks could be bored on the same machines), a longer stroke and a Weber twin choke carburettor. Price inflation was beginning to distort the market, and a mid-range Ford (even a Ghia model) at over £2,000 was surprising. It was the start of a spiral that would make quarterly price increases commonplace. Although the Mark II had only put on around 100lb (45.4kg) over the previous model, a lot of it accounted for by the burden of the bigger windows, the 1100's performance was leisurely for the 1970s. Even fleet buyers tended to go for 1300s. But Ford was now firmly established as meeting the demands of performance-oriented customers, so first and second gearbox ratios were raised and the 1600 and 1600 Sport were welcome. Sport models had reduced ride height and stiffer springs. To keep vibrations from the long-stroke engine in check, a two-piece propeller shaft was introduced for the 1600. Following the introduction of the Mark II Escort, Ford abandoned its policy of including delivery charges in new car prices. Nobody had followed its example, it said, and that made its prices look uncompetitive.

INTRODUCTION January 1975, produced 1974 to 1980.
BODY saloon; 2-door, 4-door, estate, 4-seats; 1300 2-dr 885kg (1951lb), estate 920kg (2028lb), 1600 Ghia 4-dr 955kg (2105.4lb), Sport 930kg (2050.3lb).
ENGINE 4-cyls, in-line; front; 80.98mm x 62.99mm, 1297cc; cr 9.2:1; 42.5kW (57bhp) @ 5500rpm; 32.8kW/l (43.9bhp/l); 91Nm (67lbft) @ 3000rpm. 1300GT: 52.2kW (70bhp) @ 5500rpm; 92Nm (68lbft) @ 4000rpm. 1600: 80.98 x 77.62; 1598cc; 9.0:1; 62.6kW (84bhp) @ 5500rpm; 39.2kW//l (52.6bhp/l); 125Nm (92lbft) @ 3500rpm.
ENGINE STRUCTURE pushrod ohv; chain-driven camshaft; cast iron cyl head and block; Ford GDP downdraught carb 1300GT & 1600 Weber twin-choke; mechanical fuel pump; 5-bearing crankshaft.
TRANSMISSION rwd; diaphragm spring clutch, 191mm (7.5in) 4-speed manual all synchromesh; hypoid bevel final drive 3.89:1; GT, 1600 Sport 4.125:1; 1600 GT 3.54:1.
CHASSIS steel monocoque; ifs by MacPherson struts; lower links; telesc

dampers; rear live axle with semi-elliptic leaf springs and telescopic dampers; hydraulic 244mm (9.6in) front disc brakes, 203mm (8in) or 229mm (9in) rear drums, vacuum servo, divided hydraulic circuits; rack and pinion; 40.9l (9.0 gal) (10.8 US gal); 155SR-13in tyres, 5in rims. Sport 175/70SR-13in.
DIMENSIONS wbase 240cm (94.5in); track front 127cm (50in), rear 129.5cm (51in); l 397.8am (156.6in); w 153.7cm (60.5in); ht 141cm (55.5in); clearance 14cm (5.5in); turning circle 9.45m (31ft).
EQUIPMENT Ford Bordeaux automatic £145.67; radio £63.47; remote control door mirror £15.60; rear fog warning lamp £15.80.
PERFORMANCE maximum 149.3kph (93mph) 1300 *Autocar*; 27.5kph (17.1mph) 1300, 26.2kph (16.3mph) @ 1000rpm GT; 30.5kph (19mph) 1600; 0-96kph (60mph) 13.5 sec; 20.8kg/kW (15.5kg/bhp) 1300; 9.6l/100km (29.3mpg).
PRICE totals with tax; 1300 4-door £1558.62; 1300 Ghia 4-door £2067.57; 1600 Sport 2-door £1860.48.
PRODUCTION Halewood total 960,007, Saarlouis 848,388.

Right: 250 Boreham record car. Skinny high-pressure tyres and freak driving produced 2.38l/ 100km (118.7mpg) from an Escort 1300.

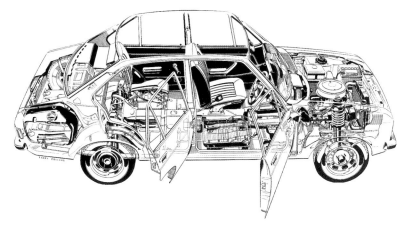

253

1975 Escort RS1800; 1976 RS 2000

All sporting Escorts had lapsed, so when the Mark II appeared there were no Mexicos or RS models. In March 1975 the Pinto-engined RS2000 due for production by the end of the year was shown, together with the prototype BDA-engined RS1800, due on sale in June in small numbers befitting a hand-built competition car. With AVO closed down, high-performance Escorts with all 3 engine options (the RS Mexico would follow in 1976), were built at Saarlouis. The successful RS2000, which had a restyled sloping polyurethane front unlike the RS1800, was shown at the 1975 Geneva Motor Show. Both had 2-door reinforced body shells with stronger suspension pick-ups, and a heavy-duty front cross-member. The new front claimed to improve aerodynamics, reducing front-end lift by 25 per cent, (also declared to be more pedestrian-friendly) while the small back spoiler was said to diminish it at the rear by 60 per cent. Overall aerodynamic drag was down 16 per cent. The gearbox was the standard close-ratio GT and two radius arms replaced the front anti-roll bar, so Ford said, to improve the ride of the firmly sprung car. The interior continued the competition theme with black headlining, black cloth trim and carpet, and lightweight seats. In September 1978 an enhanced RS 2000 Custom was brought out with Recaro seats and alloy wheels.

INTRODUCTION March 1975 and 1976. Production to 1978.
BODY saloon; 2-door; RS1800 900kg (1984.1lb), RS2000 925kg (2039.3lb).
ENGINE 4-cylinders, in-line; front; 86.75mm x 77.62mm, 1837cc; compr 10.0:1; 85.8kW (115bhp) @ 6000rpm; 46.7kW/l (62.6bhp/l); 163Nm (120 lbft) @ 4000rpm. RS2000: 90.8 x 76.95; 1993cc; 9.2:1; 82kW (110bhp) @ 5500rpm; 41.2kW/l (55.2bhp/l); 161Nm (119lbft) @ 3500rpm.
ENGINE STRUCTURE RS1800 BDA twin belt-driven ohc; 16-valve; 2000 single belt driven ohc 8-valve; 1800 aluminium block and head, 2000 cast iron block, aluminium head; downdraught Weber twin-choke carb; mechanical fuel pump; 5-bearing crank.
TRANSMISSION rwd; diaphragm spring clutch, 191mm (7.5in) 4-speed manual all synchromesh gearbox (RS2000 Type E) (RS1800 close-ratio); hypoid bevel final drive 3.54:1.
CHASSIS steel monocoque; ifs by MacPherson struts; lower links, anti-roll bar; telescopic dampers; rear live axle with semi-elliptic leaf springs, radius arms, and telescopic dampers; hydraulic

244mm (9.6in) front disc brakes, 203mm (8in) or 229mm (9in) rear drums, vacuum servo, divided hydraulic circuits; rack and pinion steering; 40.9l (9.0 gal) (10.8 US gal) fuel tank; cast aluminium alloy wheels 155SR-13in tyres 5.5in (1800) and 6in (2000) rims. Sport 175/70HR-13in.
DIMENSIONS wheelbase 240cm (94.5in); track front 127cm (50in), rear 129.5cm (51in); length 397.8cm (156.6in); width 157cm (61.8in); height 141cm (55.5in); ground clearance 14cm (5.5in); turning circle 9.45m (31ft).
EQUIPMENT Ford Bordeaux automatic £145.67; radio £63.47; remote control door mirror £15.60; rear fog warning lamp £15.80.
PERFORMANCE maximum speed RS2000 173.7kph (108.2mph) *Motor*; 29.7kph (18.5mph) @ 1000rpm; 0-96kph (60mph) 8.5sec; 10.5kg/kW (7.8kg/bhp) 1800, 11.3kg/kW (8.4kg/bhp) RS2000; 37.7kph (23.5mph).
PRICE totals with tax; 1975 RS2000 £2857, 1977 £3519. 1977 RS1800 £3786.
PRODUCTION RS1800 109 sold UK; RS2000 10,039 sold UK.

Far right: **Roger Clark and Jim Porter raise the dust on the way to scoring their sixth victory in the Scottish Rally. In 1975 their Cossack RS1800 was producing 179kW (240bhp) and reached 60mph in less than 6 sec.**

1976 Escort RS Mexico

The Mark II Escort Mexico, with a 1.6-litre Pinto engine and looking much like any other Escort, never quite caught on. The RS 2000 was almost as fast as the small-scale production RS 1800, but the Mexico never seemed to find its niche, was discontinued in 1978, and a hybrid RS2000 produced instead with Mexico interior and steel wheels.

The rationale behind the original Mexico had been a competition car with stamina, so the engine was a regular cast-iron Kent crossflow. For the Mark II it inherited a Pinto ohc engine with 2 valves per cylinder, much like the RS2000's but smaller and with its own cylinder block casting. The gearbox in the first series of Mark II Mexicos was the Ford Type 3 three-rail shift; later cars had the German Type E single-rail shift as used for the RS2000. Some Mexicos were badged 1600GT and some were redesignated RS Mexico. The interior had the facia layout of the Sport pack on 1300 and 1600, against the RS models' centre consoles and clocks. Towards the end of the Mark II's production span special editions came thick and fast such as the Escort Harrier, which was a series of 1500 cars based on the 1600 Sport with Recaro seats, rear spoiler, and alloy RS wheels to commemorate the eighth successive win in the RAC Rally.

INTRODUCTION 1976, production to 1978.
BODY saloon; 2-door; weight 920kg (2028.2lb).
ENGINE 4-cylinders, in-line; front; 87.65mm x 66mm, 1593cc; compr 9.2:1; 70.8kW (95bhp) @ 5750rpm; 44.5kW/l (59.6bhp/l); 125Nm (92 lbft) @ 4000rpm.
ENGINE STRUCTURE single belt driven ohc 8-valve; cast iron block aluminium head; downdraught Weber twin-choke carburettor; mechanical fuel pump; 5-bearing crankshaft.
TRANSMISSION rear wheel drive; diaphragm spring clutch, 191mm (7.5in) 4-speed manual all synchromesh gearbox; hypoid bevel final drive 3.54:1.
CHASSIS steel monocoque structure; independent front suspension by MacPherson struts; lower links, anti-roll bar; telescopic dampers; rear live axle with semi-elliptic leaf springs, radius arms, and telescopic dampers; hydraulic 244mm (9.6in) front disc brakes, 229mm (9in) rear drums, vacuum servo, divided hydraulic circuits; rack and pinion steering; 40.9l (9.0 gal) (10.8 US gal) fuel tank; cast aluminium alloy wheels 175/70HR-13in tyres, 6in rims (steel wheels optional).
DIMENSIONS wheelbase 240cm (94.5in); track front 127cm (50in), rear 129.5cm (51in); length 397.8cm (156.6in); width 157cm (61.8in); height 141cm (55.5in); ground clearance 14cm (5.5in); turning circle 9.45m (31ft).
EQUIPMENT radio £63.47; remote control door mirror £15.60; rear fog warning lamp £15.80.
PERFORMANCE maximum speed 172kph (107.1mph) *Ford*; 29.7kph (18.5mph) @ 1000rpm; 13kg/kW (9.7kg/bhp); 0-96kph (60mph) 10.5sec; fuel consumption 9.2l/100km (30.71mpg).
PRICE totals with tax; 1977 Mexico £2978.
PRODUCTION approx 2290 UK registered.

1976 Cortina Mark IV 1297cc, 1593cc, 1993cc

By the middle of the 1970s the Coke-bottle fashion was passing. Ford's new designer Uwe Bahnsen was given the job of co-ordinating Cortina design for Ford Europe using the existing platform. The German and British editions were now almost fully integrated, sporty versions were dropped in favour of business and executive versions, and as before, a wide range of options meant Cortina customers could, in theory at any rate, tailor their cars to their precise specifications. As ever theory and practice did not always coincide, and choosy customers often found that ringing too many changes on what was on offer at a dealer delayed delivery. The Mark IV had a more European stance than the Detroit-inspired Mark III, it was crisper and more upright, with 15 per cent more glass. And because Cologne and Dagenham were not yet completely in step the German Taunus range appeared 6 months ahead of Britain's. Also the bigger German versions still used the 1999cc and 2293cc Cologne V6, and no Taunus employed the UK-only Kent 4-cylinder.

In the aftermath of the oil crisis some economy models were introduced. There was an entry-level 36.9kW (49.5bhp) 1300 Kent engine and a 44kW (59bhp) 1600 Pinto but they sold slowly.

INTRODUCTION October 1976, produced to 1979.
BODY 1300 saloon, 2-dr, 4-dr; 1600 and 2000 4-door, estate; 5-seats; 1300 1000kg (2205lb), 1600 1035kg (2282lb).
ENGINE 1300 4-cyls, in-line; front; 81mm x 63mm, 1297cc; compr 9.2:1; 36.9kW (49.5bhp) @ 5000rpm; 28.5kW/1 (38.2bhp/l); 87Nm (64 lbft) @ 3000rpm. 1600 87.7m x 66mm; 1593cc; 44kW (59bhp) @ 4500rpm or 53.7kW (72bhp) @ 5000rpm; 111 or 118Nm (82 or 87 lbft) torque.
ENGINE STRUCTURE Kent pushrod ohv; Pinto single ohc; toothed belt; opposed ohv; cast iron cyl head, block; Ford GPD carb (2000 Weber 32/36 DGAV downdraught twin choke); mechanical fuel pump; 5-bearing crank.
TRANSMISSION rwd; diaphragm spring cable-operated 216mm (8.5in) sdp clutch; 4-spd single selector rail all synchro; 3-speed Borg Warner Model 35 auto opt (not 1300 or economy 1600); 2-piece prop shaft (not 1300, 1600); hypoid bevel final drive, 4.11 (1300); 3.78 and 3.89 (1600s); 3.75:1 (2000).
CHASSIS steel monocoque; ifs by coil springs, wishbones, anti-roll bar; rear live axle with coil springs, trailing and semi-trailing radius arms; telescopic dampers; hydraulic vacuum servo 248mm (9.75in) disc front brakes, 203mm (8in) rear drums, 227mm (9in on 2000); rack & pinion, PAS opt 2000; 54.6l (12 gal) (14.4 US gal); opt 185/70-13, radial-ply 165-13 standard, 4.5 or 5.5in rims.
DIMENSIONS wb 257.8cm (101.5in); track front 144.5cm (56.9in), rear 142.2cm (56in); l 432.6cm (170.3in); w 170.2cm (67in); h 132cm (52in); clear 17.8cm (7in); turning 10.4m (34ft).
EQUIPMENT heated rear window, radial-ply tyres, brake servo, front discs, 2-speed wipers, electric screenwash, reversing lights, cigar lighter, dipping mirror, carpets standard through range.
PERFORMANCE maximum 160.5kph (100mph) 2000 Ghia *Autocar*; 28.7kph (17.9mph) @ 1000rpm; 0-96kph (60mph) 11sec; 1600 23.5kW/kg (17.5kg/bhp); 11.7l/10km (24.1mpg).
PRICE at launch 1300 2-door £1950.39, 4-door £2029.95; 1600GL 4-door £2548.26, estate £2822.04; 2000 Ghia 4-door £3120.97.
PRODUCTION 1,131,850 all Mark IV.

The Cortina's move
up-market continued with
four sorts of trim, Standard,
L, GL, and Ghia, reflecting
equipment and luxury.

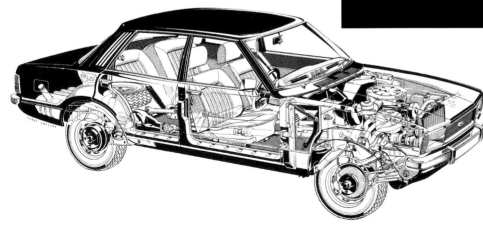

1976 Fiesta 957cc/1117cc

Ford's return to the small-car market was previewed as the Bobcat supermini prototype shown in 1976. The first front wheel drive Ford, first transverse-engined Ford, and the smallest capacity Ford since the 1950s, it was notable for the diversity of the plants that produced it. Bodies and engines were made in two new plants at Valencia Spain, transmissions at Bordeaux France, and cylinder blocks, radiators at Dagenham, and carburettors in Belfast. Assembly was at Valencia, Cologne, Saarlouis Belgium and later Dagenham, and it quickly became Europe's fastest-selling car, with 0.5 million made in the first year and 3 million by the time of its first face-lift in 1984. Technically not very daring, it remained a 3-door hatchback until 1989 and there was no automatic option until Continuously Variable Transmission (CVT) became available. The design brief specified a 90 inch (228.6cm) wheelbase, which was 7.6cm (3in) longer than a Fiat 127 (to which the Fiesta bore a resemblance), and 11.4cm (4.5in) shorter than an Escort. To achieve the necessary economy and performance the weight target was 700kg (1543.2lb). Fiestas went on sale in most of Europe during 1976, right hand drive models reaching Britain in February 1977 in base, S, and Ghia configurations. A 1978 special edition coincided with the 75th anniversary of Ford Motor Company.

INTRODUCTION 1976, produced until 1983.
BODY saloon; 2-doors, 4-seats; weight 730kg (1609.4lb).
ENGINE 4-cylinders, transverse; front; 74mm x 55.7mm, 957cc; compr 9.0:1; (lc 8.3:1 29.8kW (40bhp) @ 6000rpm); 33.6kW (45bhp) @ 6000rpm; 35kW/l (47bhp/l); 65Nm (47.7lbft) @ 3000rpm.
1.1: 74 x 65mm; 1117cc; 39.52kW (53bhp) @ 6000rpm; 35.4kW/l (47.4bhp/l); 80Nm (59lbft).
ENGINE STRUCTURE pushrod ohv; chain-driven camshaft; cast iron cylinder head, block; Ford sonic idle carburettor, mechanical fuel pump; 3-bearing crankshaft.
TRANSMISSION front wheel drive; 16.5cm (6.5in) sdp clutch; 4-spd manual synchromesh gearbox; final drive helical spur, 957cc 4.29:1; 1117cc 4.056:1.
CHASSIS steel monocoque structure; independent front suspension by MacPherson struts, coil springs; rear suspension dead axle, trailing links, Panhard rod; telescopic dampers; hydraulic, vacuum servo 221mm (8.7in) front disc brakes; rear drums 178mm

(7.0in); rack and pinion steering; 34l (7.5 gal) (9 US gal) fuel tank; Michelin ZX radial-ply 135-12 or 145-12 tyres.
DIMENSIONS wheelbase 228.6cm (90in); track 133.5cm (52.6in) front, 132cm (52in) rear; length 356.5cm (140.4in); width 156.5cm (61.6in); height 136cm (53.5in); ground clearance 14cm (5.5in); turning circle 9.45m (31ft).
EQUIPMENT pvc upholstery, cloth on Ghia, carpets, laminated windscreen.
PERFORMANCE maximum speed 957cc 126.8kph (79mph), 1117cc 138kph (86mph) *Autocar*; 24kph (15mph) or 24.9kph (15.5mph) @ 1000rpm; 0-100kph (62mph) 19.6sec or 15.7sec; 21.7kg/kW (16.2kg/bhp);fuel consumption 8l/100km (35.3mpg) or 8.4l/100km (33.6mpg).
PRICE basic Fiesta £1856, L £2079, Ghia £2657; 1.1L £2179, 1.1 Ghia £2757.
PRODUCTION Fiesta in Britain 307,600.

Right: **Fiesta Sandpiper, a special edition.**

1977 Fiesta 1297cc

The engine for the first Fiesta was essentially a crossflow Kent, dating back to the 105E Anglia, and turned sideways. Kents however invariably had a bore of 81mm whatever their capacity, and the same cylinder spacing, a legacy of the machinery on which they were produced. The Fiesta had a shrunken Kent with 74mm bores and a shorter block, hence it had a shorter crankshaft, which Ford decided could manage perfectly well on 3 main bearings instead of the usual 5. The strokes chosen were 55.7mm giving a capacity of 957cc, and 65mm giving 1117cc. By 1977 the engineering work necessary to get a 5 main bearing, markedly over-square, 81mm bore power unit to fit into the Fiesta's engine space had been carried out, notwithstanding the difficulty of changing the clutch without first removing the engine. This had been thought essential for the fleet buyer market in the small capacity classes. Among the modifications necessary were new engine and gearbox mountings, a bigger radiator, and a higher final drive ratio. The 1300 was available as an S with thicker anti-roll bar, stiffer springs, adjustable dampers, and fashionable (for a time) striped upholstery rather like a deckchair. The alternative was a Ghia with all-round comfort and luxury trim. Both models had 155SR-12 tyres and the same rather wide-ratio gearbox.

INTRODUCTION 1976, produced until 1983.
BODY saloon; 2-doors, 4-seats; weight 885kg (1951lb).
ENGINE 4-cylinders, transverse; front; 81mm x 63mm, 1298cc; compr 9.2:1; 49.2kW (66bhp) @ 5600rpm; 37.9kW/l (50.8bhp/l); 92Nm (68lbft) @ 3250rpm.
ENGINE STRUCTURE pushrod ohv; chain-driven camshaft; cast iron cylinder head, block; Weber dual choke carburettor, mechanical fuel pump; 5-bearing crankshaft.
TRANSMISSION front wheel drive; sdp clutch; 4-speed manual synchro gearbox; final drive helical spur, 3.842:1.
CHASSIS steel monocoque structure; ifs by MacPherson struts, coil springs; rear suspension dead axle, trailing links, Panhard rod; telescopic dampers; hydraulic, vacuum servo 22.1cm (8.7in) front disc drum brakes; rear drums 178mm (7.0in); rack and pinion steering; 34l (7.5 gal) (9 US gal) fuel tank; Michelin ZX radial-ply 155SR-12 tyres; aluminium alloy wheels.
DIMENSIONS wheelbase 228.6cm (90in); track 133.5cm (52.6in) front, 132cm (52in) rear; length 356.5cm (140.4in); width 156.5cm (61.6in); height 136cm (53.5in); ground clearance 14cm (5.5in); turning circle 9.45m (31ft).
EQUIPMENT pvc upholstery, cloth on Ghia, carpets, laminated windscreen.
PERFORMANCE maximum speed 151kph (94.1mph) *Autocar*; 26.97kph (16.8mph) @ 1000rpm; 0-100kph (62mph) 13.7sec; 18kg/kW (13.4kg/bhp); fuel consumption 8.9l/100km (31.7mpg).
PRICE 1300S £2844.
PRODUCTION Fiesta in Britain 307,600.

263

1977 Cortina Mark IV V6 2293cc

In pre-rationalisation days Ford Cologne and Ford Dagenham had both developed 60-degree V6 engines. A common policy seemed unnecessary in the 1960s. The markets were different, the cars were different; it was blandly assumed they would remain different. The Cologne engine was compact and light, and in the tradition of the Ford V8 since the 1930s the drive to the central camshaft was by gears. The Essex engine was strong, but it was heavy, and in view of the Cologne engine's scope for development (it had already been used successfully in racing) it was chosen for the most up-market Cortina yet, which under inflationary pressure was the first Cortina to break the £4000 barrier.

As a measure of how money had been devalued, when the first Cortina came out in 1962, £4,000 would have bought an Aston Martin DB4 or gone two-thirds of the way towards a Rolls-Royce Silver Cloud. Changed days. Yet the Cortina IV 2300 was more than 15 years ahead of Cortina I in terms of equipment, furnishings, technical sophistication, and performance. S for Sport was largely a trim and suspension term, not a measure of speed, and the extra weight of the V6 meant uprated front springs anyway. Gas-filled dampers came in and the S had seats striped in the style of seaside deck chairs.

INTRODUCTION September 1977, production to 1979.
BODY saloon, 4-door; 5-seats; estate, 5-door; weight saloon 1090kg (2403lb).
ENGINE 6-cylinders, 60deg V; front; 90mm x 60.14mm, 2294cc; compr 8.75:1; 80.5kW (108bhp) @ 5000rpm; 35.1kW/l (47.1bhp/l); 176Nm (130lbft) @ 3000rpm.
ENGINE STRUCTURE pushrod ohv, gear-driven camshaft; cast iron cylinder head and block; Solex twin choke 35/35 EEIT carburettor; mechanical fuel pump; 4-bearing crankshaft.
TRANSMISSION rear wheel drive; diaphragm spring cable operated 216mm (8.5in) sdp clutch; 4-speed single selector rail all synchromesh gearbox; 3-speed Borg Warner Model 35 automatic optional; 2-piece prop shaft; hypoid bevel final drive, 3.44:1.
CHASSIS steel monocoque structure; ifs by coil springs, wishbones, anti-roll bar; rear live axle with coil springs, trailing and semi-trailing radius arms; telescopic dampers; hydraulic vacuum servo 248mm (9.75in) disc front brakes, 229mm (9in) rear drums; rack and pinion steering; (PAS standard);

54.6l (12 gal (14.4 US gal) fuel tank; 185/70-13, radial-ply tyres; 5.5in rims.
DIMENSIONS wheelbase 257.8cm (101.5in); track front 144.5cm (56.9in), rear 142.2cm (56in); length 432.6cm (170.3in); width 170.2cm (67in); height 132.1cm (52in); ground clearance 17.8cm (7in); turning circle 10.36m (34ft).
EQUIPMENT heated rear window, radial-ply tyres, brake servo, front discs, 2-speed wipers, electric screenwash, reversing lights, cigar lighter, dipping mirror, carpets standard alloy wheels optional.
PERFORMANCE maximum speed 158.9kph (99mph) 2.3 Ghia auto *Autocar*; 31.6kph (19.7mph) @ 1000rpm; 0-96kph (60mph) 12.2sec; 13.5kg/kW (10.1kg/bhp); fuel consumption 12.4l/100km (22.8mpg).
PRICE £4126 S, £4445 Ghia.
PRODUCTION 1,131,850 all Mark IV.

1977 Granada Mark II 1993cc/2293

Retaining much of the original platform and suspension, the Mark II Granada took on a crisper appearance. Assembled in Germany, the UK V6 engines were discarded in favour of smaller and lighter German ones, and fuel injection was introduced to cope with increasingly demanding American emission legislation. In anticipation of its adoption in Europe, fuel injection and electronic ignition enabled the necessary control of the combustion process. Ford was among the the advocates of lean-burn, wanting to reduce noxious emissions by more complete combustion but over-ruled by those who bargained for catalytic converters at the expense of heavy fuel consumption. The 2.0-litre in-line four was no longer offered in its 55.9kW (75bhp) economy form, and it was joined by a 2.3-litre V6 with only 6.7kW (9bhp) extra but a good deal more torque. The German V6 was nearly 22kg (48.5lb) lighter than the older Essex, and although incapable of stretching beyond 2.8 litres it was much smoother and free-revving. Practical benefits of the new big Fords included Ghias with electric windows and central locking, and an extension of the intervals between major services to 12,000 miles. The new 2.0-litre weighed a useful 50kg (110lb) less than its predecessor through increasing enlightenment provided by computer aided design.

INTRODUCTION production December 1976 - 1978 in Cologne. BODY saloon; 4-doors, 5-seats; weight 2.0 1300kg (2866lb), 2.3 1310kg (2888lb), 5-door estate 1395kg (3075.4lb). ENGINE 2.0: 4-cylinders, in-line; front; 90.8mm x 76.95mm, 1998cc; compr 9.2: 73.8kW (99bhp) @ 5200rpm; 37kW/l (49.5bhp/l); 151Nm (111 lbft) @ 4000rpm. 2.3: 60deg V6; 90 x 60.14mm; 2294cc; compr 8.75; 80.5kW (108bhp) @ 5000rpm; 35.1kW/l (47.1bhp/l); 176Nm (130lbft) @ 3000rpm. ENGINE STRUCTURE belt-driven overhead camshaft; cast iron cylinder head, block; Weber twin choke variable carburettor, mechanical fuel pump; 5-bearing crankshaft. V6 chain-driven camshaft, pushrod ohv; Solex twin choke; 4-bearing crank. TRANSMISSION rear wheel drive; diaphragm spring sdp clutch; 4-speed manual synchromesh gearbox; C3 automatic optional £320.70; final drive hypoid bevel 3.89:1. V6 3.64:1. CHASSIS steel monocoque structure; ifs by coil springs and double wishbones; irs by coil springs and semi-trailing arms; front anti roll bar; telescopic dampers; hydraulic vacuum servo brakes, front 262mm (10.3in) discs rear 229mm (9in) drums; dual circuit; rack and pinion steering PAS optional (£210.50); 65l (14.3gal) (17.2 US gal) fuel tank; radial-ply 175SR-14 tyres 5.5in rims. V6 185-14. DIMENSIONS wheelbase 277cm (109in); track 151.5cm (59.7in) front, 153cm (60.2in) rear; length 463.3cm (182.4in); width 179cm (70.5in); height 142cm (55.9in); ground clearance 15cm (5.9in); turning circle 11.2m (36.75ft). EQUIPMENT seat belts standard, optional central locking (£111.57), remote control mirror (£93.59), electric aerial (£39.88), sun roof (£174.26), front electric windows £141.02). PERFORMANCE maximum 164kph (102.2mph), V6 automatic 158kph (98.4mph) *Autocar*; 29.7kph (18.5mph) @ 1000rpm, V6 31.5kph (19.6mph) @ 1000rpm; 0-100kph (62mph) 11.9sec, V6 auto 14.5sec;17.6kg/kW (13.1kg/bhp); fuel consumption 13.4l/100km (21.1mpg), V6 13.7l/100km (20.6mpg). PRICE £4516.54, 2.3V6 £5260.94. PRODUCTION total Granada 639,440.

1977 Granada Mk II 2.8, 2.8Fi

Bosch K-Jetronic fuel injection was already available in Germany when it was included in the specification of the new Granada. The additional 18.6kW (25bhp) made a marked difference in speed and acceleration with scarcely any penalty in fuel consumption, such was the efficiency that attended it with the same overall gearing. One of the new body's novelties, consequence of an era in which drag coefficients were being freely bandied about, was its Cd. Ford claimed the new car had 3.2 per cent less drag than its predecessor, which may not have been saying much, but a good deal of the improvement was said to come from the rearwards slant of the radiator grille. Its slats were cunningly arranged to admit cooling air at slow speeds when it was needed most, but built up a boundary-layer that rendered the grille aerodynamically solid at high speeds, diverting air over the nose of the car. The grille was supplemented by a small beard-type spoiler that swept the slipstream aside reducing rear-end lift by a remarkable 38 per cent. In August 1979 the 2.3-litre came in for a number of modifications, the engine power was increased to 114bhp (85kW) and there were improvements to trim and equipment. In 1981 the entire range was revised with major alterations to the suspension settings and cosmetic details inside.

INTRODUCTION production Dec 1976 -1978 in Cologne.
BODY saloon; 4-doors, 5-seats; 1360kg (2998.3lb), estate 1455kg (3207.7lb).
ENGINE 6-cylinders, 60deg V; front; 93.0mm x 68.5mm, 2792cc; compr 9.2:1; 100.7kW (135bhp) @ 5200rpm; 36.1kW/l (48.4bhp/l); 216Nm (159lbft) @ 3000rpm. 2.8i: 119.3kW (160bhp) @ 5700rpm; 221Nm (163lbft) @ 4300rpm.
ENGINE STRUCTURE pushrod ohv, chain-driven camshaft; Solex twin choke carb; cast iron cyl head, block; mechanical fuel pump; 4-bearing crank, 2.8i Bosch K-Jetronic mechnical fuel inj.
TRANSMISSION rwd; diaphragm spring sdp clutch; 4-speed manual synchromesh gearbox; automatic option; final drive hypoid bevel 3.45:1.
CHASSIS steel monocoque; ifs by coil springs and double wishbones; irs by coil springs and semi-trailing arms; front anti roll bar; telescopic dampers; hydraulic vacuum servo brakes, front 262mm (10.3in) ventilated discs rear 229mm (9in) drums; dual circuit; rack and pinion PAS; 65l (14.3 gal) (17.2 US gal) fuel tank; radial-ply 175SR-14 tyres 5.5in rims. V6 185-14.
DIMENSIONS wheelbase 277cm (109.1in); track 151.5cm (59.7in) front, 153cm (60.2in) rear; length 463.3cm (182.4in); width 179cm (70.5in); height 142cm (55.9in); ground clearance 15cm (5.9in); turning circle 11.2m (36.75ft).
EQUIPMENT seat belts standard, optional central locking (£107.38), remote control mirror (£22.50), sun roof (£167.80), tinted glass £52.33.
PERFORMANCE max speed 2.8i 187.8kph (117mph) *Autocar*, 33.2kph (20.7mph) @ 1000rpm; 0-100kph (62mph) 8.9sec; 13.5kg/kW (10.1kg/bhp); 13.6l/100km (20.8mpg).
PRICE 2800GL automatic std £5913; 2800i GL£61502800i Ghia £7315; 2800iGL Estate £6849 .
PRODUCTION total Granada 639,440.

Granada service intervals were extended to 12,000 miles for everything except a change of engine oil and filter. Greasing was eliminated and with breakerless ignition routine tasks were all but banished.

1977 Granada Mk II 2.1D 2112cc diesel

Ford's plans to make its own diesel developed in arrears of the market demand, especially in Continental Europe, and it had to turn to Peugeot for a suitable engine for the Granada. Its own light commercial diesels could not be made sufficiently refined for use in a car so the 4.90 used in the Peugeot 504 was adapted instead. It was used both as a 1.9-litre and 2.1-litre, only the larger sold in Britain, after some detail work to make it fit the Granada. The sump was redesigned, engine accessories repositioned, and the power of the glow-plugs was increased to speed cold starts. Ford also installed bigger air, oil, and fuel filters with the objective of extending the interval between oil changes to match that of petrol-engined cars. It was not quite achieved. Oil changes were still required every 3000miles (4828km) filters at 6000miles (9656km) and fuel filters frequently.

Peugeot's altruism in the sale of an important engine to a rival did not extend to offering Ford a new 2.3-litre diesel it had developed. *Autocar* reported that its existence was revealed only after Ford had signed up to the existing engines, leaving it a generation behind in a growing European market, even though diesel cars were still regarded with some reserve in Britain, suitable at best as taxis.

INTRODUCTION production December 1976-1978 in Cologne.
BODY saloon; 4-doors, 5-seats; weight 1310kg (2888lb).
ENGINE 4-cylinders, in-line; front; 88mm x 80mm, 1948cc; compr 21.8:1; 47kW (63bhp) @ 5200rpm; 24.1kW/l (32.3bhp/l); 122Nm (90lbft) @ 2000rpm.
ENGINE STRUCTURE pushrod ohv, chain-driven camshaft; Bosch fuel injection; cast iron cylinder head, block; mechanical fuel pump; 5-bearing crankshaft.
TRANSMISSION rear wheel drive; diaphragm spring sdp clutch; 4-speed manual synchromesh gearbox; final drive hypoid bevel 3.89:1.
CHASSIS steel monocoque structure; ifs by coil springs and double wishbones; independent rear suspension by coil springs and semi-trailing arms; front anti roll bar; telescopic dampers; hydraulic vacuum servo brakes, front 262mm (10.3in) discs rear 229mm (9in) drums; dual circuit; rack and pinion steering, PAS optional £219.50; 65l (14.3gal) (17.2 US gal) fuel tank; radial-ply 175SR-14 tyres 5.5in rims.

DIMENSIONS wheelbase 277cm (109.1in); track front 151.5cm (59.7in), rear 153cm (60.2in); length 463.3cm (182.4in); width 179cm (70.5in); height 142cm (55.9in); ground clearance 15cm (5.9in); turning circle 11.2m (36.75ft).
EQUIPMENT seat belts standard, optional central locking (£111.57).
PERFORMANCE maximum speed 2.8i 187.8kph (117mph) *Autocar*; 29.7kph (18.5mph) @ 1000rpm; 0-100kph (62mph) 27.2sec; 27.9kg/kW (20.8kg/bhp); fuel consumption 9.4l/100km (30.1mpg).
PRICE £5087 .
PRODUCTION total Granada 639,440.

An engine oil change and fuel filter replacement was required every 3,000 miles on Granada diesels. Ford warranty terms remained at 12 months but there was no upper limit on mileage covered in the first year. The Peugeot 504 L cost £4517.

1978 Capri III 1600/2000

Not much sheet metal changed for the 1978 Capri facelift. The front was tidied up with four round headlamps instead of two rectangular ones, and a spoiler and a slatted grille were added. Aerodynamics improved the drag factor by 6 per cent (12.6 per cent with the rear spoiler) from Cd 0.4 to 0.374 and, together with recalibration of the carburettor, gave a small saving in fuel but little in the way of increased speed. Although Ford's official figures (given here) made the car's weight much the same as the Mark II, road test weighbridge figures showed the increase that invariably followed the introduction of the new model. The 1600GT 65.6kW (88bhp) was dropped in 1980, and the 1300, restored to normal Kent specifications giving 42.5kW (57bhp) @ 5500rpm and 91Nm (67lbft) of torque, was discontinued in 1982. All models except the 1300 gained Bilstein gas-filled dampers, and the 1600 and 2000 were available in GL or S trim. S-specification cars had a bootlid spoiler, a shaded "sidewinder" stripe and Recaro competition style seats with head restraints incorporating a mesh-filled ring to help rearwards visibility. Its wider tyres made the steering heavier but the firmer suspension proved popular with keen drivers. The Capri generated a lot of special editions, among them the 1600cc Capri GT4 of which 1500 were made in February 1980.

INTRODUCTION 1978, production to 1986.
BODY coupe; 2-doors, 4-seats; weight 1600 1050kg (2314.8lb), 2000 1060kg (2336.9lb).
ENGINE 4-cylinders, in-line; front; 87.6mm x 66mm, 1593cc; compr 9.2:1; 53.7kW (72bhp) @ 5200rpm; 33.7kW/l (45.2bhp/l); 118Nm (87 lbft) @ 2700rpm. 1600GT/S: 65.62kW (88bhp) @ 5700rpm. 2000: 90.82 x 76.95; 1993cc; 68.6kW (92bhp) @ 5200rpm; 34.4kW/l (46bhp/l).
ENGINE STRUCTURE ohc, toothed belt; cast iron cylinder head, block; Ford single venturi carburettor, GT/S 2000 Weber twin-choke; 5-bearing crankshaft.
TRANSMISSION rear wheel drive; sdp clutch; 4-speed manual synchro gearbox; optional C3 automatic; final drive 3.77, GT/S 3.75, 2000 3.44:1, auto 3.75, 3.44, 3.09.
CHASSIS steel monocoque structure; independent front suspension by MacPherson struts; rear suspension semi-elliptic springs; anti roll bars; gas-filled telescopic dampers; hydraulic vacuum servo brakes, front disc 244mm (9.6in) dia, rear 229mm (9in) drums,

dual circuit; rack and pinion steering; 57.7l (12.7 gal) (15.2 US gal) fuel tank; 165SR-13 radial-ply tyres, 5Jrims.
DIMENSIONS wheelbase 256cm (100.8in); track front 135.5cm (53.4in), rear 138.5cm (54.5in); length 437.5cm (172.2in); width 170cm (66.9in); height 136cm (53.5in); ground clearance 11.5cm (4.5in); turning circle 10.8m (35.43ft).
EQUIPMENT 2-speed wipers; hazard warning lights; electric screenwash; cloth upholstery; laminated windscreen.
PERFORMANCE maximum speed 1600S 159kph (99mph), 2000 167kph (104mph) *Autocar*; 1600 28.6kph (17.8mph) @ 1000rpm, 1600S 28.9kph (18mph) @ 1000rpm, 2000 31.3kph (19.5mph) @ 1000rpm; 0-100kph (62mph) 1600 12.7sec, 2000 11.2sec; 1600 19.6kg/kW (14.6kg/bhp), 2000 15.5kg/kW (11.5kg/bhp); fuel consumption 10.2-9.8l/100km (27.7-28.8mpg).
PRICE Sept 1978 1300£2959, 1600S £3069, 2000S £4192.
PRODUCTION Cologne (all Capris 1,886,647).

Above: **Anxious as ever
to emphasise the Capri's
accommodation,** Ford issued
this picture showing how
deceptive it was. True.
It would carry four people and
their luggage even if the "Plus
Twos" were not quite full size.

1978 Capri III 3000; 1981 2.8i

The 3.0-litre Capri did not continue entirely unchanged until the model ceased production in 1986. The more efficient and clean-burning fuel injected 2.8i was announced in March 1981, first fruit of the newly established Special Vehicle Engineering department at Dunton, although it was another 3 months before it went on sale. The 2.8i was much the same as the 3.0 but the engine was a high-revving 160bhp (119.3kW) Cologne V6, the suspension was stiffened, and the ventilated alloy wheels had wider tyres. Handling was much improved, fresh paintwork and graphics made the car look better, and while it ultimately failed to sustain Capri sales, it improved the model's image throughout its run-out phase. In January 1983 the 2.8i was given a 5-speed gearbox and later the same year the entire range was trimmed, L, GL, and Ghia were discontinued leaving only 1.6LS, 2.0S, and 2.8i. For the 1985 model year the 2.8i Injection Special was provided with a limited slip differential. The Capri lasted far longer than anyone would have predicted in 1969, production continuing until just before Christmas 1986 after nearly 1.9 million had been made. It was not only a marketing success, it was a production triumph, shadowing other models in the Ford range, mainly Cortinas, and provided substantial economies of scale in the production of all the common components.

INTRODUCTION 1978, production to 1986.
BODY coupe; 2-doors, 4-seats; weight 1170kg (2579.4lb).
ENGINE Essex 6-cylinders, 60deg V; front; 93.7mm x 72.4mm, 2994cc; compr 9.0:1; 102.9kW (138bhp) @ 5000rpm; 34.4kW/l (46.1bhp/l); 236Nm (174lbft) @ 3000rpm.
 ENGINE STRUCTURE pushrod ohv, gear-drive camshaft; cast iron cylinder head and block; Weber twin-choke downdraught carburettor; 4-bearing crankshaft.
TRANSMISSION rear wheel drive; sdp clutch; 4-speed manual synchro gearbox; optional C3 automatic; final drive 3.09:1.
CHASSIS steel monocoque structure; independent front suspension by MacPherson struts; rear suspension semi-elliptic springs; anti roll bars; gas-filled telescopic dampers; hydraulic vacuum servo brakes, front disc 248mm (9.75in) dia, rear 229mm (9in) drums, dual circuit; rack and pinion PAS; 57.7l (12.7 gal) (15.2 US gal) fuel tank; 185/70 HR-13 radial-ply tyres, 5.5Jrims.
DIMENSIONS wheelbase 256cm (100.8in); track front 135.5cm (53.4in), rear 138.5cm (54.5in); length 437.5cm (172.2in); width 170cm (66.9in); height 136cm (53.5in); grd clearance 11.5cm (4.5in); turning circle 10.8m (35.4ft).
EQUIPMENT 2-speed and intermittent wipers; hazard warning lights; electric screenwash; cloth upholstery; laminated windscreen.
PERFORMANCE maximum speed 188kph (117mph) *Autocar*; 35kph (21.8mph) @ 1000rpm; 0-100kph (62mph) 8.6sec; 11.4kg/kW (8.5kg/bhp); fuel consumption 14.5l/100km (19.5mpg).
PRICE Mar 1978 £4422.
2.8i June 1981 £7993.
PRODUCTION Cologne (all Capris 1,886,647) (Capri III 324,045).

1981 2.8i:
WEIGHT 1230kg (2711.6lb)
ENGINE Cologne V6; 93.0 x 68.5mm; 2792cc; compr 9.2; breakerless ignition; Bosch K-Jetronic fuel injection; 119.3kW (160bhp) @ 5700rpm; 42.7kW/l (57.3bhp/l); 220Nm (162lbft) @ 4200rpm.
TRANSMISSION diaphragm spring

clutch.
CHASSIS 24mm (0.9in) front,
14mm (0.55in) rear anti-roll bars;
10.3in (26.2cm) ventilated front discs;
59.1l (13 gal) (15.6 US gal) fuel tank;
205/60VR-13 tyres 7in rims, alloy
wheels.
PERFORMANCE max speed
203.9kph (127mph); 0-62 7.9sec;
34kph (21.2mph) @ 1000rpm;
10.3kg/kW (7.7kg/bhp);
13.3l/100km (21.3mpg).
PRODUCTION 1987 Capri 280,500.

Britain was always
the strongest market
for the Capri, so much
so that the final 12 months'
production from Cologne
was exclusively right hand
drive. The last 280 made
were known as Capri 280
Brooklands with metallic
green paint and leather
interior.

1979 Cortina Mark V 1297cc

Cortinas were built in 4 European factories, Dagenham (from 1962), Genk in Belgium (from 1977), Amsterdam (1967-1975) and Cork (from 1978). Dagenham also sent CKD kits to Australia and South Africa, but the sales peak of 290,972 in 1967 was not repeated, and 1975 in the wake of the oil crisis represented a low point of 141,060, even though one new car in three sold in Britain was a Ford. Nevertheless with the announcement in August of the Mark V, it looked as though its best days were behind it, and a shot in the arm was required to see it through to the 1980s. Known as the Cortina 80, its platform remained that of the Mark III, detail changes freshened up the appearance, and following yet another world oil crisis, fuel economy was pursued by reducing weight. Appearance grew closer to the Granada (and Taunus), and Ford cheerfully admitted copying details, such as tail light clusters, from Mercedes-Benz as signals of quality. There was indeed a big effort to improve quality. Customers were disillusioned over European cars' readiness to rust, and many Japanese imports were more reliable for longer than their UK counterparts. Ford was by no means the worst culprit for body decay but it was time to improve matters, and Cortinas were now wax-injected and had chip-resistant pvc applied underneath.

INTRODUCTION September 1979, produced until 1982.
BODY saloon, 2-door, 4-door; 5-seats; weight 965kg (2127.4lb).
ENGINE 4-cylinders, in-line; front; 81mm x 63mm, 1297cc; compr 9.2:1; 45.6kW (61.2bhp) @ 6000rpm; 35.2kW/l (47.2bhp/l); 92Nm (68lbft) @ 3000rpm.
ENGINE STRUCTURE pushrod ohv; chain-driven camshaft; cast iron cylinder head and block; Ford Motorcraft constant vacuum VV carburettor; mechanical fuel pump; 5-bearing crankshaft.
TRANSMISSION rear wheel drive; diaphragm spring cable operated 216mm (8.5in) sdp clutch; 4-speed single selector rail all synchromesh gearbox; one-piece prop shaft; hypoid bevel final drive, 4.44:1.
CHASSIS steel monocoque structure; independent front suspension by coil springs, wishbones, anti-roll bar; rear live axle with coil springs, trailing and semi-trailing radius arms; gas-filled telescopic dampers; hydraulic vacuum servo 248mm (9.75in) disc front brakes, 203mm (8in) rear drums; rack and pinion steering; 54.6l (12 gal) (14.4 US gal) fuel tank; optional 165-13, radial-ply, 4.5 or 5.5in rims.
DIMENSIONS wheelbase 257.8cm (101.5in); track front 144.5cm (56.9in), rear 142.2cm (56in); length 432.6cm (170.3in); width 170.2cm (67in); height 132.1cm (52in); ground clearance 17.8cm (7in); turning circle 10.36m (34ft).
EQUIPMENT heated rear window, radial-ply tyres, brake servo, front discs, 2-speed wipers, electric screenwash, reversing lights, cigar lighter, dipping mirror, carpets standard throughout range, viscous fan drive, laminated windscreen.
PERFORMANCE maximum speed 139.7kph (87mph) *Ford*; 24.2kph (15.1mph) @ 1000rpm; 0-96kph (60mph) 16.1sec; 21.2kg/kW (15.8kg/bhp); fuel consumption approx 11.3l/100km (25mpg).
PRICE at launch 4-door £3475; L £3677; L 4-door £3806.
PRODUCTION 1,131,850 all Mark IV and V.

KEY

1. Viscous-coupled thermostatic fan on all engines for improved economy and reduced noise

2. New variable-venturi carburettor on 1300 and 1600cc (except 91 PS)

3. Improved heating and ventilation with centre fresh-air vents and side-window demisting

4. New open-framed head restraints

5. Increased glass area allowing better vision all round

6. New wrap-round tail lamp clusters with integral fog lamps for saloons

7. Tough plastic bumper end-caps front and rear

8. New corrosion protection system integrated with multi-stage paint process

9. New more comfortable seats with sprung platform construction, infinitely-variable backrest adjustment and seat-mounted belt stalks

10. Revised spring and damper settings all-round and 'S' pack option in lieu of 'S' derivative

11. New wrap-round front indicators for improved safety

12. Deeper front spoiler for increased stability

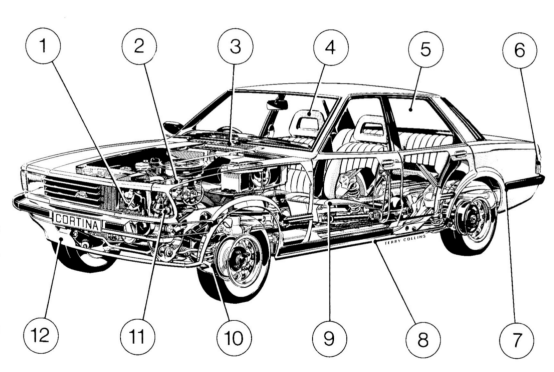

1979 Cortina Mark V 1593cc/1993cc

The Kent engine fitted to the 1300 Mark V Cortina was something of an aberration. An essential element of the change from Mark IV to V was the harmony achieved with Cologne, whose 1300 had a small Pinto engine. Throughout the rest of the range however engines proliferated, the 1600 available in two states of tune, and the 2000 increased in power through reduced valve spring loading and running the fan through a viscous coupling. When the engine was cold the fan ran slowly, using scarcely any engine power, when hot it was speeded up but never to more than 3000rpm, saving more than 2bhp (1.5kW) and quite a lot of fuel. The economy 1600 used the ingenious new downdraught Ford/Motorcraft VV constant vacuum carburettor, a complex instrument designed on similar principles to the well-established sidedraught SU, or Zenith-Stromberg. In the 1970s it still looked as though emission control regulations might be met without resorting to fuel injection by means of this variable venturi (hence VV). Ford claimed it reduced carbon monoxide emissions by 30 per cent. The 1600 for Ghia saloons and estate cars had a different cam profile and a Weber compound dual-choke carburettor, giving it more power than the former Cortina GT. The usual equipment packs of L, GL, and Ghia remained on offer.

INTRODUCTION September 1979, production to 1982.
BODY saloon, 2-door, 4-door; 5-seats estate car 5-door; weight saloon 1060kg (2336.9lb) or 1085kg (2392lb).
ENGINE 1600 4-cylinders, in-line; front; 87.7mm x 66mm; 1593cc; 9.2:1; 56.3kW (75.5bhp) @ 5500rpm or 92.5bhp (69kW) @ 5900rpm; 35.3kg/l (58.1bhp/l) or 43.3kW/l (58.1bhp/l); 119Nm (87.5 lbft) @ 2800rpm or 126Nm (93 lbft) @ 4000rpm. 2000 90.8 x 76.95; 1993cc; 76.1kW (102bhp) @ 5400rpm; 38.2kW/l (51.2bhp/l); 155Nm (114lbft) @ 4000rpm.
ENGINE STRUCTURE Pinto single ohc; toothed belt; opposed ohv; cast iron cylinder head and block; Ford/Motorcraft VV carburettor (or Weber 32/36 downdraught twin choke); mechanical fuel pump; 5-bearing crankshaft.
TRANSMISSION rear wheel drive; diaphragm spring cable operated 216mm (8.5in) sdp clutch; 4-speed single selector rail all synchromesh gearbox; 3-speed Borg Warner Model 35 automatic optional; 2-piece prop shaft; hypoid bevel final drive, 3.78, 3.89, and 3.45:1, automatic 3.89, and 3.75.
CHASSIS steel monocoque structure; ifs by coil springs, wishbones, anti-roll bar; rear live axle with coil springs, trailing and semi-trailing radius arms; telescopic dampers; hydraulic vacuum servo 24.8cm (9.75in) disc front brakes, 20.3cm (8in) rear drums, 22.9cm (9in) on 2000; rack and pinion steering; (PAS optional); 54.6l (12 gal) (14.4 US gal) fuel tank; optional 185/70-13, radial-ply 165-13 standard, 4.5 or 5.5in rims.
DIMENSIONS wheelbase 257.8cm (101.5in); track front 144.5cm (56.9in), rear 142.2cm (56in); length 432.6cm (170.3in); width 170.2cm (67in); height 132.1cm (52in); ground clearance 17.8cm (7in); turning circle 10.36m (34ft).
EQUIPMENT heated rear window, radial-ply tyres, brake servo, front discs, 2-speed wipers, electric screenwash, reversing lights, cigar lighter, dipping mirror, carpets standard throughout range.
PRODUCTION 1,131,850 all Mark IV and V.

PERFORMANCE 1600L
maximum speed 146.1kph
(91mph) *Autocar*; 28.4kph
(17.7mph) @ 1000rpm
0-96kph (60mph) 13.6sec;
18.8kg/kW (14kg/bhp); fuel
consumption 9.6l/100km
(29.3mpg).
PRICE 1600 4-door £3675;
1600L 4-door £4006; 1600GL
£4394; 2000GL £4634; 2000
Ghia £5380; 1600 Estate £4083;
2000GL Estate £5080.

1979 Cortina Mark V V6 2293cc

One of the marketing ploys for the Cortina's final fling was the distribution of specification packs. There was no base-level or L-spec 2300, no 2-door version, and only GLs or Ghias. There was a profound rationale for this; flagship cars had to keep their dignity, and once the customer went for an expensive model it helped profitability to load it up with options.

More options made it more expensive, but since it was possible to price many of the items at a premium, it was good business. L-spec replaced the base model's rubber floor mats with carpet and brightwork was added. GL brought seat head restraints, map pockets in the door casings, clock, central console, wooden instrument panel, and a proper side moulding on the body, not just a painted line. A Ghia had cut-pile carpet, cloth-faced door casings, wooden door cappings, a light in the boot, a light in the glovebox, alloy wheels, fatter tyres, and the extra *cachet* of Ghia heraldry and script that let everybody see it was the most expensive Cortina you could get. The run-out phase produced some special editions of the 1300, 1600 and 2000.

Chairman Sam Toy drove the final Cortina off the line at Dagenham on Thursday 22 July 1982, 20 years after the first one, and after 4,279,079 of all 5 Marks had been built.

INTRODUCTION September 1979, production to 1982.
BODY saloon, 4-door; 5-seats; estate car 5-door; weight saloon 1080kg (2381lb).
ENGINE 6-cylinders, 60deg V; front; 90mm x 60.14mm, 2294cc; compr 9.2:1; 86.5kW (116bhp) @ 5500rpm; 37.7kW/l (50.6bhp/l); 178Nm (131.5 lbft) @ 3000rpm.
ENGINE STRUCTURE pushrod ohv, gear-driven camshaft; cast iron cylinder head and block; Solex twin choke 35/35 EEIT carburettor; mechanical fuel pump; 4-bearing crankshaft.
TRANSMISSION rear wheel drive; diaphragm spring cable operated 216mm (8.5in) sdp clutch; 4-speed single selector rail all synchromesh gearbox; 3-speed Borg Warner Model 35 automatic optional; 2-piece prop shaft; hypoid bevel final drive, 3.44:1.
CHASSIS steel monocoque structure; ifs by coil springs, wishbones, anti-roll bar; rear live axle with coil springs, trailing and semi-trailing radius arms; telescopic dampers; hydraulic vacuum servo 248mm (9.75in) disc front brakes, 229mm (9in) rear drums; rack and pinion steering; (PAS standard); 54.6l (12 gal (14.4 US gal) fuel tank; 185/70-13, radial-ply tyres; 5.5in rims.
DIMENSIONS wheelbase 257.8cm (101.5in); track front 144.5cm (56.9in), rear 142.2cm (56in); length 432.6cm (170.3in); width 170.2cm (67in); height 132.1cm (52in); ground clearance 17.8cm (7in); turning circle 10.36m (34ft).
EQUIPMENT heated rear window, radial-ply tyres, brake servo, front discs, 2-speed wipers, electric screenwash, reversing lights, cigar lighter, dipping mirror, carpets standard alloy wheels optional.
PERFORMANCE maximum speed 176kph (109.6mph), automatic 168kph (104.7mph) *Ford;* 31.4kph (19.6mph) @ 1000rpm; 0-96kph (60mph) 10.3sec, automatic 12.2sec; 12.5kg/kW (9.3kg/bhp); fuel consumption 10.9km/l (30.7mpg).
PRICE at launch 2300 Ghia 4-door £5989 GL Estate £5,689.
PRODUCTION 1,131,850 all Mark IV and V.

1980 Escort III 1117cc/1296cc ohc

The third Escort was launched just as Britain was poised for the Metro. Press and government created a lot of interest in a car expected to make or break BL. A fortnight before it was to be launched, Ford replaced its best-selling Escort with another best-selling Escort. The Metro was not eclipsed, but technically the Escort was more than a match for it, having at last gone over to front wheel drive and appearing with a new range of Compound Valve angle Hemispherical chamber (CVH) overhead camshaft engines. Only the 1100 Escort came with a Valencia Fiesta pushrod engine, 3-door, 5-door, and 3-door estate versions were available from the start, and a van followed closely. New from end to end the well-rounded model programme was a triumph of production engineering, but no sooner had the car appeared than the press raised heavy criticism of its ride quality. Developed at Dunton and tested exhaustively on Ford's extensive proving ground at Lommel in Belgium, it was too firmly sprung, so spring rates and damper settings had to be modified to take account of the complaints. Promoted not very effectively as a "world car" the Escort bore little resemblance to its North American counterpart of the same name but did use the same gearbox as the (25 per cent Ford-owned) Mazda 323.

IINTRODUCTION September 1980, production to 1986.
BODY saloon; 3 or 5-doors, 5-seats; weight 3-door 765kg (1686.5lb); 5-door 835kg (1840.8lb); estate 820kg (1807.8lb).
ENGINE 4-cylinders, in-line; front; transverse; 73.96mm x 64.98mm, 1117cc; compr 9.0:1; 40.6kW (54.4bhp) @ 5700rpm; 36.3kW/l (48.7bhp/l); 80Nm (59lbft) @ 4000rpm.
1300 CVH 79.96 x 64.62mm; 1295cc; 9.5:1; 43.5kW (58.3bhp) @ 6000rpm; 33.6kW (45bhp)/l; 84Nm (62lbft) @ 4000rpm.
ENGINE STRUCTURE 1100 Valencia pushrod, chain-drive camshaft; iron head and block. 1300 CVH, belt-driven overhead camshaft; hydraulic tappets; aluminium cylinder head; Motorcraft VV carburettor; 1100 3-bearing 1300 5-bearing crankshaft.
TRANSMISSION front wheel drive; sdp diaphragm spring clutch; gearbox 4-speed synchromesh; final drive 4.06:1, 1300 3.84:1.
CHASSIS steel monocoque; MacPherson strut independent front suspension; independent rear by coil springs, pressed lateral arms and trailing tie-bars; 1300 front anti-roll bar; telescopic dampers; hydraulic (1300 servo) brakes, front 24cm (9.45in) dia discs, rear 18cm (7.09in) drums, dual circuit, rack and pinion steering; 40l (8.8 gal) (10.6 US gal) fuel tank; 145SR13, 155SR13, or 175/70 SR/HR13 tyres 4.5 or 5J rims.
DIMENSIONS wheelbase 239.5cm (94.3in); track 138.5cm (54.5in) front, 143cm (56.3in) rear; length 397cm (156.3in), estate 411.5cm (162in); width 164cm (64.6in); height 140cm (55.12n), estate 137.5cm (54.1in); ground clearance 14cm (5.5in); turning circle 10.5m (34.45ft).
PERFORMANCE maximum speed 146kph (90.9mph), 1300 160kph (99.7mph); 26.8kph (16.69mph), 1300 29kph (18.1mph) @ 1000rpm; 0-100kph (62mph) 13.6sec, 1300 11.3sec; 18.8kg/kW (14.1kg/bhp); fuel consumption 8l/100km (35.3mpg), 1300 7.7l/100km (36.7mpg).
PRICE 1.1 3-door £3374; 1.3 3-door £3543; 1.3 Ghia 5-door £4876.
PRODUCTION 1,857,000 all Mk III.

1980 Escort III 1596cc/1608cc diesel

The notchback was either an inspired innovation or else designers were unable to make up their minds about 2-box or 3-box cars. Ford preferred to call Escort's 2 and a half box rear a "bustle". The term did not catch on. It was much the same size as its rear-drive predecessor although the roof was 5.08cm (2in) lower and track 10.16cm (4in) wider. By the 1980s mathematical analysis of design by computers was commonplace and, with the demand for fuel economy, saving weight was a priority. The Mark III Escort with no long propeller shaft or rear axle casing achieved a useful reduction of around 15 per cent, 108.9kg (240lb), getting down to a competitive weight for its class. Code-named Erika, it required an investment of £500 million, and occupied 500 engineers for 5 years. The work was facilitated by the 1978 establishment of a data link between Merkenich in Germany, Dunton in Essex, and Dearborn. The body stress model was calculated so carefully that, as famously described by Egon Gögel, chief of vehicle programmes engineering, "The roof is an inactive area – it only serves to keep the rain out." Stout roof edge framing carried the body stresses and the roof itself had no cross-bracing. The same went for the boot floor. "If we didn't need it to keep the luggage in, we'd take it out."

INTRODUCTION September 1980, production to 1986; diesel introduced 1983.
BODY saloon; 3 or 5-doors, 5-seats; weight 3-door 795kg (1752.7lb); 5-door diesel 915kg (2017.2lb).
ENGINE 4-cylinders, in-line; front; transverse; 79.96mm x 79.52mm, 1597cc; compr 9.5:1; 70.5kW (94.5bhp) @ 5700rpm; 44.1kW /l (59.2bhp)/l; 132Nm (97 lbft) @ 4000rpm (opt 58kW (77.8bhp) @ 5800rpm). Diesel 80 x 80mm; 1608cc; 21.5:1; 39.5kW (53bhp) @ 4800rpm; 24.6kW (32.9bhp)/l; 95Nm (70 lbft) @ 3000rpm.
ENGINE STRUCTURE 1600 CVH, belt-driven ohc; hydraulic tappets; aluminium cyl head; Weber twin choke DFT or Motorcraft VV carburettor; electronic ignition; 5-bearing crankshaft. Diesel Ford KHD ohc.
TRANSMISSION front wheel drive; sdp diaphragm spring clutch; gearbox 4-speed synchromesh; final drive Weber CVH 3.84:1, VV 3.58:1. diesel 3.58:1.
CHASSIS steel monocoque; ifs by MacPherson strut; irs by coil springs, pressed lateral arms and trailing tie-bars; front anti-roll bar; telescopic dampers,

Weber car Bilstein gas-filled; hydraulic servo brakes, front 24cm (9.5in) dia ventilated (not diesel) discs, rear 18cm (7.1in) drums, dual circuit, rack and pinion steering; 40l (8.8 gal) (10.6 US gal) fuel tank; tyres 185/60HR14 5.5J rims or 175/70HR13 5J rims; diesel 155SR13, or 175/70 SR/HR13 tyres.
DIMENSIONS wheelbase 239.5cm (94.3in); track 138.5cm (54.5in) front, 143cm (56.3in) rear; length 397cm (156.3in), estate 411.5cm (162in); width 164cm (64.6in); height 140cm (55.1in), estate 137.5cm (54.1in); ground clearance 14cm (5.5in); turning circle 10.5m (34.5ft).
EQUIPMENT Weber car alloy wheels.
PERFORMANCE maximum 182kph (113.4mph), diesel 146kph (90.9mph); 29kph (18.1mph) diesel 39kph (24.3mph) @ 1000rpm; 0-100kph (62mph) 9.7sec, diesel 18.1sec; 11.3kg/kW (8.4kg/bhp), diesel 23.2kg/kW (17.3kg/bhp); 8.9l/100km (31.7mpg) diesel 5.8l/100km (48.7mpg).
PRICE 1.6GL 3-door £4021, Ghia 5-door £5033; 1985 1.6 GL diesel 5-door £7075.
PRODUCTION 1,857,000 all Mk III.

1981 Fiesta XR2

The first 100mph Fiesta, second product of Dunton's Special Vehicle Engineering, was based on the 1300S, with a 1.6-litre Kent engine and stiffened suspension. It was introduced in September, following a series of Fiesta challenge races, and cars built with competitions department at Boreham-designed X-pack parts. The engine already had considerable success in North America, and was a combination of the Federal US specification bottom end, and a 1600GT cylinder head and camshaft as used on Mark II Cortinas and some Escorts. The 32/34 DFTA Weber carburettor was mounted on a 1300-pattern (but bigger bore) manifold, and the exhaust was a unique 4-into-2 cast iron arrangement. Novel breakerless ignition was introduced. The gearbox was an Escort pattern, and the perforated aluminium alloy wheels were Wolfrace Sonics like those of the 2.8i Capri, but an inch narrower. The 1300S spring rates were retained, with the same anti-roll bar at the back, and the ride height was lowered by an inch at the front by altering the spring pan on the MacPherson strut. The tie bar to the front frame was also lowered to reduce rearwards pitch on acceleration, not so much for occupant comfort as to lessen changes in driveshaft angles that created torque steer, often a nuisance with lightly laden powerful front wheel drive cars.

INTRODUCTION 1981, production to 1983.
BODY saloon; 3-doors, 5-seats; weight 800kg (1763.7lb).
ENGINE 4-cylinders, in-line; front; transverse; 80.98mm x 77.62mm, 1599cc; compr 9.0:1; 62kW (83.1bhp) @ 5500rpm; 38.8kW/l (52bhp/l); 125Nm (92lbft) @ 5500rpm.
ENGINE STRUCTURE Kent; pushrod, chain-driven camshaft; 2 valves; cast iron cylinder head and block; Weber 34DFTA carburettor, transistorised ignition; 5-bearing crankshaft.
TRANSMISSION front wheel drive; sdp clutch; gearbox 4-speed synchromesh; final drive 3.58:1.
CHASSIS steel monocoque structure; ifs by MacPherson struts, coil springs; anti-roll bar; rear suspension dead axle, trailing links, Panhard rod; telescopic dampers; hydraulic, vacuum servo 247mm (9.7in) front disc brakes; rear drums 178mm (7in); rack and pinion steering; 34l (7.5 gal) (9 US gal) fuel tank; 185/60HR 13 tyres; aluminium alloy wheels, 6J rims.
DIMENSIONS wheelbase 228.6cm (90in); track 133.5cm (52.6in) front, 132cm (52in) rear; length 356.5cm (140.4in); width 156.5cm (61.6in); height 136cm (53.5in); ground clearance 14cm (5.5in); turning circle 9.45m (31ft).
PERFORMANCE maximum speed 170kph (105.9mph); 29.7kph (18.5mph) @ 1000rpm; 0-100kph (62mph) 10.1sec; 12.8kg/kW (9.6kg/bhp); fuel consumption 8.6l/100km (32.9mpg).
PRICE 1982 £5150.
PRODUCTION April 1981 Fiesta production passes 2m.

Four gears and only 84bhp (62.6kW) were not the ingredients of a sporty car despite appearances. The first XR2 lasted barely two years.

1981 Probe III

As a result of 2 world oil crises, the spiralling cost of fuel, and apprehension over the future of oil supplies, car buyers sought economy. They did not want to give up the customary comfort, convenience, and speed of their cars, so designers had to explore new ways of meeting their requirements. One way lay through good aerodynamics. A slippery shape not only improved fuel consumption, it could also be turned to advantage by providing cars with a fresh new look. Until now a car's coefficient of wind resistance (Cd) was largely academic; it scarcely mattered that a Cortina was something like 0.44. When Probe III was shown as a concept car, there was little attempt to disguise its relationship with the approaching Cortina replacement. A good deal of education was required to prepare public taste. Executives in charge of the new car realised it was fairly radical and remained unsure if the customers were ready for it.

Probe III's body was a complex of features, few of which would have made much difference aerodynamically on their own. Flush windows, the shape of the corner pillars, elimination of roof gutters and drip channels, flush wheel discs, rear spats, and plastic skirts, wings, and spoilers combined to give a drag coefficient of 0.22. The curved side windows only wound down after the glass had first been moved inwards rather like an aircraft door. Underneath, the airflow was managed just as carefully as it was on top. The exhaust was entirely enclosed within the under-tray, and elaborate arrangements were made for insulating its heat and noise. The under-car air management system involved a scoop that would require to be retracted on rough roads, or to clear town-road obstructions such as manhole covers, as it would only work if it were close to road level.

That was not all. Probe III was equipped with car-of-the-future features including digital instruments and the Auto Leading and Information (ALI) system built into the facia, giving the driver route instructions to a programmed destination by means of arrows on an animated diagram. It was said that the aerodynamics were so good that a 1600cc engine, suitably geared, would drive it at 120mph (192.6kph) and provide spectacular economy at lower speeds.

Probe III was not a runner. It only had one opening door. Probes IV and V were even more radical, built in America in 1983 and 1985 with more extreme aerodynamics, such as enclosure of the front wheels by plastic membranes and Cd figures of 0.15 and 0.137. Pure research vehicles, they explored design initiatives but were well removed from any production capability.

1981 Escort III XR3, XR3i

Ahead of the launch of the Mark III Escort, all the old RS models were discarded. They were to be replaced by only one, the XR3, which appeared first using the 1600 with the CVH hydraulic tappet engine. In October 1982 the XR3 became the XR3i with fuel injection, having already gained the 5-speed gearbox now available throughout the range either as standard or as an option. The XR3 accounted for one Escort in 10 and was entirely separate from the RS1600i, a notable competition-tuned specialist road car sold in small numbers in 1982-1983.

Besides fuel injection the XR3i gained a new high-efficiency exhaust system and an oil-water intercooler to help it withstand prolonged operation at high speeds. The electronic ignition was provided with an over-run cutoff to avoid fuel wasteage, and reprogrammed with a revised advance curve. Girth of the front anti-roll bar was increased from 22mm (.87in) to 24mm (.94in) and at the back linear rate springs replaced dual rate. Ride heights were reduced by 30mm (1.2in) in front and 20mm (.8in) at the rear and the struts were now Girling Monotubes. Environmental concerns about asbestos were extending throughout the industry, and the XR3i was one of the first Fords to use brake linings free of the material.

INTRODUCTION 1981, production to 1986.
BODY saloon; 3-doors, 5-seats; weight 895kg (1973lb), cabriolet 970kg (2138.5lb).
ENGINE 4-cylinders, in-line; front; transverse; 80mm x 79.5mm, 1598cc; compr 9.5:1; 70.5kW (94.5bhp) @ 6000rpm; 44.1kW/l (59.1bhp/l); 132Nm (97 lbft) @ 4000rpm. XR3i 77kW (103.3bhp) @ 6000rpm; 48.1kW/l (64.6bhp/l); 138Nm (102 lbft) @ 4800rpm.
ENGINE STRUCTURE CVH; belt-driven ohc; 2 valves, hydraulic tappets; aluminium cyl head, iron block; twin choke Weber DFT carburettor, transistorised ignition; 5-bearing crank. XR3i Bosch K-Jetronic fuel injection.
TRANSMISSION front wheel drive; sdp clutch; gearbox 5-speed synchro; final drive 3.84:1. XR3i 4.29:1.
CHASSIS steel monocoque; MacPherson strut independent front suspension; independent rear by coil springs, pressed lateral arms and trailing tie-bars; front anti-roll bar; telescopic dampers, Bilstein gas-filled; hydraulic servo brakes, front 24cm (9.5in) dia

ventilated discs, rear 18cm (7.1in) drums, dual circuit, rack and pinion steering; 40l (8.8 gal) (10.6 US gal) fuel tank; tyres 185/60HR14 5.5J rims or 175/70HR13 5J rims.
DIMENSIONS wheelbase 239.5cm (94.3in); track front 138.5cm (54.5in), rear 143cm (56.3in); length 397cm (156.3in), estate 411.5cm (162in); width 164cm (64.6in; height 140cm (55.1in), XRi 137cm (53.9in); ground clearance 14cm (5.5in); turning circle 10.5m (34.45ft).
EQUIPMENT cloth seats, carpet standard. rear seats belts, central locking, electric windows, manual sunroof £247, radio cassette player £136, optional extras.
PERFORMANCE maximum speed 182kph (113.4mph), XR3i 186kph (115.9mph); 29kph (18.1mph), XR3i 32.5kph (20.2mph) @ 1000rpm; 0-100kph (62mph) 9.7sec, XR3i 9.6sec; 12.7kg/kW (9.5kg/bhp); fuel consumption 7.7l/100km (36.7mpg), XR3i 8.1l/100km (34.9mpg).
PRICE 1981 XR3 £5750; 1983 XR3i £6278.
PRODUCTION 1,857,000 all Mk III.

Far right: **XR3**, with cutaway
Collins of its fuel injected
successor **XR3i** (below).
Among the safety items were
removal of the fuel tank away
from its vulnerable site beside
the rear-end accident, and
the telescopic cranked
steering column.

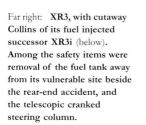

1982 Sierra 1294cc/1593cc

The Sierra was in many respects an unwelcome contrast to the dapper Cortina that embodied fashion. It had been crisp, dignified, and a byword for the stylish family car. Sierra's principal demerit lay in not being front wheel drive. Ford still had a disparate family of engines, not many could be satisfactorily turned sideways and mounted on suitable transmissions so claimed rear wheel drive was a matter of preference. It did not ring true. The market wanted front wheel drive, Vauxhall had brought in a front drive Cavalier, and Ford looked behindhand technically. Probe III's flush-fitting windows were abandoned. The radical styling had gone badly wrong due, it was said, to managerial faint-heartedness just as the design was frozen for production, yet it was not very long before rivals were following Ford's aerodynamic example. An economy version of the 1.6 offered at launch had identical power and torque, but employed a sophisticated ignition system similar in principle to that used with the Bosch Motronic fuel injection. A 1984 version known as E-Max was a development of this with an 81.3 x 77mm, 1599cc engine. Once again power remained at 55.9kW (75bhp) but developed at 5300rpm instead of 4300rpm. Torque increased from 88 to 91lbft and fuel savings were between 7 and 13 per cent.

INTRODUCTION September 1982, production to 1987.
BODY saloon; 5-doors, 5-seats; weight 990kg (2182.6lb), estate 1040kg (2292.8lb).
ENGINE 4-cylinders, in-line; front; 79mm x 66mm, 1294cc; compr 9.1:1; 44kW (59bhp) @ 5700rpm; 34kW/l (45.6bhp/l); 98Nm (72lbft) @ 3100rpm.
1.6: 87.65 x 66mm; 1593cc; 9.2:1; 55kW (73.8bhp) @ 5300rpm; 34.5kW/l (46.3bhp/l); 120 Nm (88.5lbft) @ 2900rpm.
ENGINE STRUCTURE belt driven overhead camshaft; 2 valves; iron cylinder head, block; Ford variable venturi carburettor, breakerless electronic ignition; 5-bearing crankshaft.
TRANSMISSION rear wheel drive; sdp diaphragm spring clutch; gearbox 4-speed synchromesh, 5-speed optional; final drive 3.77:1.
1.6: C3 3-speed automatic optional, 3.61:1 or 3.92:1, estate 1.6 4-speed manual, 3.62:1; economy model 3.14:1, estate 3.92. 5-speed 3.62, 3.38, 3.92.
CHASSIS steel monocoque; independent front suspension by MacPherson struts; independent rear suspension by semi-trailing arms and coil springs; front anti roll bar; telescopic dampers; hydraulic servo brakes, front 24cm (9.5in) dia disc, rear 20.3cm (8in) dia drums, dual circuit; rack and pinion steering; 60l (13.2 gal) (15.8 US gal) fuel tank; 165SR13 or 185/70SR13 tyres 4.5 or 5.5J rims. 1.6: 195/70HR13.
DIMENSIONS wheelbase 261cm (102.8in); track 145cm (57.1in) front, 147cm (57.9in) rear; length 439.5cm (173in), estate 449cm (176.8in); width 170cm (66.9in); height 136cm (53.5in), estate 139cm (54.7in); ground clearance 12cm (4.7in); turning circle 10.6m (34.78ft).
EQUIPMENT cloth trim, laminated windscreen standard. 5-speed gearbox £150.
PERFORMANCE maximum speed 152kph (94.7mph), 1.6: 165kph (102.8mph); 29kph (18mph) @ 1000rpm, 1.6 various; 0-100kph (62mph) 18.1sec,. 1.6 14sec, automatic 17.2sec; 22.5kg/kW (16.8kg/bhp); fuel consumption 7.9l/100km (35.8mpg).
PRICE 1.3 £4783; 1.6 £5071; estate £5548; 1.6 Ghia £7365.

1982 Sierra 1993/1998cc

Better-class Sierras got 5-speed gearboxes, all 4 of the straight-4s were Pinto-engined and all were hatchbacks, unlike the Vauxhall Cavalier, which gave customers the choice of a 4-door. The Sierra's behaviour in cross winds brought an early modification with small "ears" in the rear quarters, aerodynamic spoilers said to keep the car straight and stable. Cost-effective independent rear suspensions had proved elusive on mid-size and large Fords, so the Sierra had an ingenious 7cm (2.75in) dia bent tube sub-frame combined with modestly angled semi trailing arms. Compromise had to be reached on the angle, as 26deg for the Granada had brought too much camber change so the Sierra was pitched at 18deg. The aluminium final drive casing was bolted to the frame front and rear, the rear dampers were repositioned within the springs on estate cars, which also had the option of Nivomat ride height levelling. At the front, crash test requirements brought the 24mm (0.94in) anti-roll bar behind the wheel line, instead of ahead as was customary with MacPherson struts The Sierra lost Ford primacy in a market it had dominated for 20 years. It would be a decade before it found its feet again with the Mondeo and, in mounting a defence of the styling, had to issue a denial it was planning an emergency re-skin to prop up sales.

INTRODUCTION September 1982, production to 1987.
BODY saloon; 5-doors, 5-seats; weight 1025kg (2260lb), estate 1065kg (2348lb), V6 saloon 1070kg (2359lb).
ENGINE 4-cylinders, in-line; front; 90.82mm x 76.95mm, 1993cc; compr 9.2:1; 77kW (103.3bhp) @ 5200rpm; 38.6kW/l (51.8bhp/l); 157Nm (116lbft) @ 4000rpm.
V6: 84 x 60.1mm; 1998cc; 9.1:1; 66kW (88.5bhp) @ 5000rpm; 33kW (44.25bhp)/l; 150 Nm (111lbft) @ 3000rpm.
ENGINE STRUCTURE belt driven overhead camshaft; 2 valves; iron cyl head, block; Weber 32/36DGAV carburettor, breakerless electronic ignition; 5-bearing crank. V6 gear-driven central camshaft, 4-bearing crank, twin-choke Solex EEIT carburettor.
TRANSMISSION rwd; sdp diaphragm spring clutch; gearbox 4-speed synchro, 5-speed optional; final drive 3.38:1. C3 3-speed auto optional, 3.38:1. V6 manual 3.38:1, estate 3.62:1, also auto.
CHASSIS steel monocoque; ifs by MacPherson struts; irs by semi-trailing arms and coil springs; front anti roll bar; telescopic dampers; Nivomat ride height levelling option on estate cars; hydraulic servo brakes, front 24cm (9.45in) dia ventilated disc, rear 22.9cm (9in) dia drums, dual circuit; rack and pinion steering, PAS optional; 60l (13.2 gal) (15.8 US gal) fuel tank; 165HR13 or 175/70HR13 tyres 4.5 or 5.5J rims. Estate 175 or 195/70HR13.
DIMENSIONS wheelbase 261cm (102.8in); track 145cm (57.1in) front, 147cm (57.9in) rear; length 439.5cm (173in), estate 449cm (176.8in); width 170cm (66.9in); height 136cm (53.5in), estate 139cm (54.7in); ground clearance 12cm (4.7in); turning circle 10.6m (34.8ft).
EQUIPMENT cloth trim, laminated windscreen standard. 5-speed gearbox £150.
PERFORMANCE maximum speed 185kph (115.2mph), V6 176kph (109.6mph); 32.3kph (20.1mph), V6 32.3kph (20.1mph) @ 1000rpm; 0-100kph (62mph) 10.4sec, auto 12.8sec; fuel consumption 7.9l/100km (35.8mpg), V6 9.7l/100km (29.1mpg).
PRICE 2.0GL £6524.

1982 Sierra diesel 2304cc

Sierra engines were something of a muddle due to the transition to Ford of Europe and a legacy of too many power units. The petrol range comprised 3 4-cylinder in-line Pintos, 4 including the economy model, and 2.3 and 2.8 Cologne V6s. One of the Pintos was 1993cc and one V6 1998cc, an anomaly explained by a German market preference for the V6 even though it gave less power, and was heavier at 167.8kg (370lb) against 137kg (302lb). In the absence of its own diesel, not due until 1984, Ford turned to Peugeot, one of Europe's main producers of car-sized diesel engines, for a suitable unit. Peugeot's 2.1-litre was already installed in the Granada and, since it had just moved on to a 2.5-litre engine for its own cars, it was able to offer Ford the 2.3-litre. Diesels were still relatively unsophisticated, so hydraulically damped mountings that extended throughout the petrol range as well, were welcome. All models had underbonnet sound-damping material, the thickness of which was increased to 30mm (1.18in) on the diesel. With little more power than a 1.3-litre, a heavy flywheel, and ponderous handling due to the heavy weight over the front wheels, the diesel was so sluggish that press road tests were not encouraged. 3-door Sierras, available with every engine except the V6, were discontinued after 3 years.

INTRODUCTION Sept 1982, production to 1987.
BODY saloon; 5-doors, 5-seats; weight 1156kg (2548.5lb), estate 1195kg (2634.5lb).
ENGINE 4-cylinders, in-line; front; 94mm x 83mm, 2304cc; compr 22.2:1; 49kW (65.7bhp) @ 4200rpm; 21.3kW/l (28.5bhp/l); 139Nm (102.5lbft) @ 2000rpm.
ENGINE STRUCTURE LXD2; pushrod ohv, chain-driven camshaft; 2 valves; aluminium cylinder head, iron block inclined 20deg right; Bosch EP/VAC injection; 5-bearing crankshaft.
TRANSMISSION rear wheel drive; sdp diaphragm spring clutch; gearbox 5-speed synchromesh; final drive 3.14:1.
CHASSIS steel monocoque; independent front suspension by MacPherson struts; independent rear suspension by semi-trailing arms and coil springs; front anti roll bar; telescopic dampers; estate, self-levelling rear; hydraulic servo brakes, front 240mm (9.5in) dia ventilated disc, rear 229mm (9in) dia drums, dual circuit; rack and pinion steering, PAS optional; 60l (13.2gal) (15.8 US gal) fuel tank;

165SR13 or 175/70SR13 tyres 4.5 or 5.5J rims, estate 175 or 195/70HR13.
DIMENSIONS wheelbase 261cm (102.8in); track 145cm (57.1in) front, 147cm (57.9in) rear; length 439.5cm (173in), estate 449cm (176.8in); width 170cm (66.9in); height 136cm (53.5in), estate 139cm (54.7in); ground clearance 12cm (4.7in); turning circle 10.6m (34.8ft).
EQUIPMENT cloth trim, laminated windscreen standard. 5-speed gearbox £150.
PERFORMANCE maximum speed 155kph (96.6mph); 42.2kph (26.3mph) @ 1000rpm; 0-100kph (62mph) 19.1sec; 23.6kg/kW (17.6kg/bhp), estate 24.4kg/kW (18.2kg/bhp); fuel consumption 6.7mpg (42.2l/100km).
PRICE 3-door £5749, 5-door L £6421, GL Estate £7711.

1982 Sierra 2.3 V6

Unlike the V6 Cortina which had sold well, the Sierra V6 survived only 2 years. The Ghia V6 was given the further refinement of self-levelling suspension, but it was not enough, and by 1984 it was discontinued. A 1979 novelty on the Taunus/ Cortina V6 engine was breakerless transistorised ignition using a magnetic reluctance triggering system. Extended now to the entire range except the 1.6 economy version, the ignition was set on the production line using microwaves directed through a spark plug to detect TDC with the engine running on the test bed. A crank angle probe over the flywheel ring gear then set the ignition timing within half a degree's tolerance. Automatic transmission did not do a lot for a vigorous performance, and economy was not a strong point either, with one road test recording a worst of 15.4l/100km (18.3mpg), so with a meagre 59.1l (13 gal) fuel tank the useful range was less than 400km (about 250mls). The best of the Ghia Sierra lay in the 1980s advances in refinement and comfort that included details which would in due course be taken for granted, but which were only now appearing on popular cars. Delayed action interior lights, illuminated vanity mirrors, footwell-mounted lights, lockable compartments, carpeted boot, and cassette holders for the built-in radio/cassette player were still by no means commonplace.

INTRODUCTION September 1982, production to 1987.
BODY saloon; 5-doors, 5-seats; weight 1115kg (2458lb), estate 1155kg (2546.3lb).
ENGINE 6-cylinders, 60deg V; front; 90mm x 60.1mm, 2294cc; compr 9:1; 84kW (112.6bhp) @ 5300rpm; 36.6kW (49.1bhp)/l; 176Nm (130lbft) @ 3000rpm.
ENGINE STRUCTURE gear-driven central camshaft; pushrod ohv; 2 valves; iron cylinder head, block; Solex 35/35 EEIT carburettor; breakerless ignition; 4-bearing crankshaft.
TRANSMISSION rear wheel drive; sdp diaphragm spring clutch; gearbox 4-speed synchromesh; final drive 3.14:1; estate 3.38:1; optional 5-speed, optional C3 automatic.
CHASSIS steel monocoque structure; independent front suspension by MacPherson struts; independent rear suspension by semi-trailing arms and coil springs; front anti roll bar; telescopic dampers; estate, self-levelling rear; hydraulic servo brakes, front 24cm (9.5in) dia ventilated disc, rear 22.9cm (9in) dia drums, dual circuit; rack and pinion steering, PAS optional; 60l (13.2gal) (15.8 US gal) fuel tank; 165HR13 or 175/70HR13 tyres 4.5 or 5.5J rims, estate 175 or 195/70HR13.
DIMENSIONS wheelbase 261cm (102.8in); track 145cm (57.1in) front, 147cm (57.9in) rear; length 439.5cm (173.1in), estate 449cm (176.8in); width 170cm (66.9in); height 136cm (53.5in), estate 139cm (54.7in); ground clearance 12cm (4.7in); turning circle 10.6m (34.78ft).
EQUIPMENT PAS £355.66, rear seat belts £93.87, heated driver's seat £71.59, electric rear windows £126.13, trip computer £195.25.
PERFORMANCE maximum speed 190kph (118.4mph), automatic 182kph (113.4mph); 34.8kph (21.7mph) @ 1000rpm; 0-100kph (62mph) 10.5sec; 13.3kg/kW (9.9kg/bhp), estate 13.8kg/kW (10.3kg/bhp); fuel consumption 9.2l/100km (30.7mpg), auto 10l/100km (28.25mpg).
PRICE GL £8061, Ghia £9355, GL Estate £8597.

1983 Fiesta II 957cc/1117cc

Second thoughts on the Fiesta produced detail changes. Ford would have been forgiven for pressing on with none at all, since the car had sold well ever since 1977, late special editions such as the Fiesta Finesse ran to 12,000 and over 300,000 were built in Britain alone. The facelift gave it a less erect front in the interests of slipperier aerodynamics despite adding to overall length, and provided extra crushable material to meet the ever more demanding impact test criteria. The two Valencia engines gained little in power, made a small improvement in torque, and new 5-speed gearboxes permitted higher gearing. The suspension was revised to accommodate high-pressure 13in instead of 12in tyres, and comfort and equipment improved. Useful gains in economy were previewed in 1981 with the Fuel Economy Research Vehicle (FERV), which among other things was the result of much laboratory work evaluating 11 different inlet port types and 3 sorts of combustion chamber, resulting in a new cylinder head with smaller-section inlet ports and smaller valves. The objective was improved swirl for better combustion and increased compression. New cam profiles and an exhaust system that kept the flow from adjoining cylinders apart to reduce back pressure improved consumption by 18-22 per cent at 75mph and 11-34 per cent on the urban cycle.

INTRODUCTION August 1983, production to 1989.
BODY saloon; 3-doors, 5-seats; weight 750kg (1653.5lb), 1.1 755kg (1664.5lb).
ENGINE 4-cylinders, in-line; front; transverse; 73.96mm x 55.7mm, 957cc; compr 8.5:1; 33kW (44.25bhp) @ 5750rpm; 34.5kW/l (46.2bhp/l); 68Nm (50 lbft) @ 3700rpm.
1.1: 73.96 x 64.98mm; 1117cc; 9.5:1; 37kW (49.6bhp) @ 5000rpm; 33.1kW (44.4bhp)/l; 83Nm (61lbft) @ 2700rpm.
ENGINE STRUCTURE pushrod ohv; chain-driven camshaft; 2-valves; iron cylinder head, block; inverse Ford-Motorcraft carburettor; 3-bearing crankshaft.
1.1: carburettor VV.
TRANSMISSION front wheel drive; sdp clutch; gearbox 4-speed synchro; final drive 4.06:1, or 4.29 or 3.84.
1.1: 3.583:1 or 3.842:1 with optional 5-speed gearbox.
CHASSIS steel monocoque structure; ifs by MacPherson struts, coil springs; rear suspension dead axle, trailing links, Panhard rod; telescopic dampers; hydraulic, vacuum servo 22.1cm (8.7in)
front disc brakes; rear drums 17.8cm (7in); rack and pinion steering; 34l (7.5gal) (9 US gal) fuel tank; radial-ply 135SR-13 tyres or 155/70SR13, 4.5 or 5J rims.
DIMENSIONS wheelbase 228.6cm (90in); track 136.5cm (53.7in) front, 132cm (52in) rear; length 365cm (143.7in); width 158.5cm (62.4in); height 136cm (53.5in); ground clearance 14cm (5.5in); turning circle 10.3m (33.8ft).
PERFORMANCE maximum speed 137kph (85.4mph); 25.9kph (16.1mph) @ 1000rpm (4.06:1); 0-100kph (62mph) 19.8sec; 22.7kg/kW (16.9kg/bhp), 1.1 20.4kg/kW (17kg/bhp); fuel consumption 6.43l/100km (43.9mpg).
PRICE L £4320, 1.1 Ghia £5100.
PRODUCTION 1,980,100 all Fiesta II.

1983 Fiesta II 1298cc/ (from 1986)1392cc

The 1.3 added to the range, and the 1.4 Compound Valve Hemispherical (CVH) ohc hydraulic tappet engines represented a move to regain Ford's reputation for technical innovation, somewhat lost when the Sierra remained in the shrinking world of rear wheel drive mass-market cars. Alterations to the front presswork were not merely cosmetic, but necessary to provide space for the extra length of the transverse CVH engine and five-speed transaxle. Aft of the A-pillars Fiesta was largely unaltered, but the new front gave a marginal improvement to Cd through smoother lines at the critical front corners. Fuel economy was of growing importance in Britain where the price of petrol was about the break the £1 a gallon barrier and looked like doubling. It did so within the year, so the Fiesta's overdrive 5th gear, standard on the CVH and diesel and an optional extra on the 1100, was timely. The 13in tyres were run at 2.67kg-cm (38psi) front and 2.88kg-cm (41psi) rear to lower rolling resistance, the resulting harsher ride being countered by a more compliant bush for the front suspension tie rod. The tyre treatment was claimed to give a 2.5 per cent improvement in economy, and among the suspension and steering changes were non-stiction top mounts for the front struts, a 3.3cm (1.3in) wider track, and revised rack and pinion.

INTRODUCTION August 1983, production to 1989.
BODY saloon; 3-doors, 5-seats; weight 775kg (1708.5lb).
ENGINE 4-cylinders, in-line; front; transverse; 79.96mm x 64.5mm, 1297cc; compr 9.5:1; 50.5kW (67.7bhp) @ 6000rpm; 39.2kW/l (52.2bhp/l); 100Nm (78 lbft) @ 4000rpm. Replaced 1986 by "lean-burn" 77.24 x 74.3mm; 1392cc; 9.5:1; 55kW (73.76bhp) @ 5600rpm; 39.5kW/l (53bhp/l); 109Nm (80 lbft) @ 4000rpm. With catalytic converter compr 8.5:1; 51.5kW (69.1bhp); 37kW/l (49.6bhp/l); 103Nm (76 lbft).
ENGINE STRUCTURE CVH belt-driven overhead camshaft, hydraulic tappets; 2-valves; aluminium cylinder head, iron block; inverse Ford-Motorcraft VV carburettor; 5-bearing crankshaft. Lean-burn, Weber DFM. Catalytic converter, fuel injection.
TRANSMISSION front wheel drive; sdp clutch; gearbox 5-speed synchromesh; final drive 3.842:1.
CHASSIS steel monocoque structure; ifs by MacPherson struts, coil springs; lean-burn car anti-roll bar; rear suspension dead axle, trailing links, Panhard rod; telescopic dampers; hydraulic, vacuum servo 22.1cm (8.7in) front disc brakes; rear drums 17.8cm (7in); rack and pinion steering; 34l (7.5 gal) (8.9 US gal) fuel tank; radial-ply 155/70SR-13 tyres, 4.5 or 5J rims.
DIMENSIONS wheelbase 228.6cm (90in); track 136.5cm (53.7in) front, 132cm (52in) rear; length 365cm (143.7in); width 158.5cm (62.4in); height 136cm (53.5in); ground clearance 14cm (5.5in); turning circle 10.3m (33.8ft).
PERFORMANCE maximum speed 163kph (101.5mph), lean-burn 165kph (102.8mph), catalyser 161kph (100.3mph); 34.7kph (21.6mph) @ 1000rpm; 0-100kph (62mph) 12.2sec. (12.1sec) (13sec);15.3kg/kW (11.4kg/bhp); fuel consumption 7.5l/100km (37.9mpg), cat 7.6l/100km (37.2mpg).
PRICE L £5336, Ghia £5657. 1986 1.4 Ghia £6507.
PRODUCTION 1,980,100 all Fiesta II.

1983 Fiesta II diesel 1608cc

Ford took time over introducing its own diesel. It waited until it was quite certain that demand was going to be sustained, and governments were not going to go back on their taxation policy that generally (except in Britain) encouraged diesel as a key ingredient of good national housekeeping. It embarked in 1981 on a joint research programme with Klockner-Humboldt-Deutz AG, German van and lorry manufacturers, waiting for diesel cars to pass 5 per cent as a trigger for production for the European market. It also waited until it had available production plant made redundant by the conclusion of the Kent engine programme. Its new 1.6-litre diesel was first employed on the Escort and Orion, and would remain a Ford mainstay until the turn of the century. Previewed in May 1983, the new engine had an overhead camshaft, was cast iron throughout, and was on hydraulic mounts to reduce body resonances. Apart from the cylinder spacing there were no hand-me-downs on the new engine. It had conventional indirect injection, a combination gear and toothed belt drive to the overhead camshaft, and slightly offset in-line vertical valves. "Square" bore and stroke dimensions of 80mm would give a capacity of 1608.5cc, yet according to German type-approval papers it could be between 1606.5 and 1611.7 depending on the 1mm machining tolerances.

INTRODUCTION August 1983, production to 1989.
BODY saloon; 3-doors, 5-seats; weight 835kg (1840.8lb).
ENGINE 4-cylinders, in-line; front; transverse; 80mm x 80mm, 1608cc; compr 21.5:1; 39.5kW (53bhp) @ 4800rpm; 24.6kW/l (32.9bhp/l); 95Nm (70 lbft) @ 3000rpm.
ENGINE STRUCTURE Ford/KHD; 2 in-line valves, belt-driven overhead camshaft; iron cylinder head and block; mechanical fuel injection; 5-bearing crankshaft.
TRANSMISSION front wheel drive; sdp clutch; gearbox 5-speed synchromesh; final drive 3.333:1.
CHASSIS steel monocoque structure; ifs by MacPherson struts, coil springs; rear suspension dead axle, trailing links, Panhard rod; telescopic dampers; hydraulic, vacuum servo 22.1cm (8.7in) front disc brakes; rear drums 17.8cm (7in); rack and pinion steering; 34l (7.5 gal) (8.98 US gal) fuel tank; radial-ply 155/70SR-13 tyres.
DIMENSIONS wheelbase 228.6cm (90in), track 136.5cm (53.7in) front, 132cm (52in) rear; length 365cm (143.7in), width 158.5cm (62.4in); height 136cm (53.5in); ground clearance 14cm (5.5in); turning circle 10.3m (33.8ft).
PERFORMANCE maximum speed 148kph (92.2ph); 39.8kph (24.8mph) @ 1000rpm; 0-100kph (62mph) 17.3sec; 21.1kg/kW (15.8kg/bhp); fuel consumption 5.1l/100km (55.1mpg).
PRICE L 1986, 1.6L £6002.
PRODUCTION 1,980,100 all Fiesta II.

When Escort and Orion diesels were increased from 1608cc to 1753cc in the autumn of 1988, the Fiesta, due to be phased out soon afterwards, remained as it was.

1983 Orion 1296cc/1597cc/1608cc diesel

The Orion was in almost every respect a booted Escort, despite Ford's advocacy of it as a separate model line. It was 10 years before the fiction was ended and the non-hatchback Escort became known simply as an Escort saloon.

The Orion's family role was emphasised by the absence of anything racy from its range. It was to be a conventional 3-box car throughout its life, staid, routine, catering for a substantial number of buyers to whom ostentation was anathema. It also had the virtue, through its stiffer bodyshell and enclosed boot instead of a hatchback, of being a good deal quieter and more refined than the Escort. Although quite a lot of the body panels were common to both cars, the roof-line was notably different as well as the back, so it was able to accommodate a roomier rear seat. True to its market aims, the Orion's rear backrest sloped at 27 degrees instead of 24 degrees, and legroom was increased to 101.6cm (40in) against the Escort's 96.5cm (38in). This was a class-leading dimension, and together with a generous 15.7 cu ft lockable secure boot sustained its market appeal. There were three trim levels, GL, Ghia, and Injection, and four engine options, 1300, 1600, 1600 injection, and 1600 diesel, the first Ford to get its own Dagenham-made compression ignition engine.

INTRODUCTION July 1983, production to 1986.
BODY saloon; 4-doors, 5-seats; 875kg (1929lb), 1.6 890kg (1962lb), auto 925kg (2039.3lb), diesel 935kg (2061.3lb).
ENGINE 4-cylinders, in-line; front; transverse; 79.96mm x 64.5mm, 1297cc; compr 9.5:1; 50.5kW (67.7bhp) @ 6000rpm; 39.2kW/l (52.2bhp/l); 100Nm (74lbft) @ 3500rpm. 1.6:76.96 x 79.5mm; 1597cc; 58kW (77.8bhp) @ 5800rpm; 36.3kW/l (48.7bhp/l); 125Nm (92 lbft) @ 3000rpm. Injection model 77kW (103.3bhp), 48.2kW/l (64.7bhp/l; 138Nm (102 lbft) @ 4800rpm. diesel 1608cc; 39.5kW (53bhp); 24.6kW/l (32.9bhp/l).
ENGINE STRUCTURE CVH belt-driven ohc; 2-valves; aluminium cylinder head, iron block; Ford VV carburettor; 5-bearing crankshaft. Injection Bosch K-Jetronic. Diesel Ford KHD; ohc; parallel valves.
TRANSMISSION front wheel drive; sdp clutch; 4-speed synchromesh; 5-speed optional; final drive 3.84:1. 1.6 3.58:1, automatic optional 3.31:1. Injection 3.84:1, diesel 3.58.

CHASSIS steel monocoque; ifs by MacPherson strut; irs by coil springs, pressed lateral arms and trailing tie-bars; front anti-roll bar; telesc dampers (1.6 front and rear); hydraulic servo brakes, front 240mm (9.4in) dia (1.6 ventilated) discs, rear 180mm (7.1in) drums, dual circuit, rack and pinion; 40l (8.8 gal) (10.6 US gal); 155SR13, or 175/70 HR13 tyres, 5J rims.
DIMENSIONS wheelbase 240cm (94.5in); track 140cm (55.1in) front, 142.4cm (56.1in) rear; length 419.5cm (165.2in); width 164cm (64.6in); height 139.5cm (54.9in); grd clearance 14cm (5.5in); turning circle 10.6m (34.8ft).
EQUIPMENT GL, Ghia and Injection trim levels, all with electric boot release.
PERFORMANCE maximum 157kph (97.8mph), inj 186kph (116mph), diesel 150kph (93.4mph); 29kph (18mph) @ 1000rpm, inj 36.4kph (22.67mph), diesel 38.9kph (24.23mph); 0-100kph (62mph) 13.6sec, inj 9.6sec, diesel 18.8sec; 17.3kg/kW (12.9kg/bhp), 1.6 15.3kg/kW (11.4kg/bhp), diesel 23.7kg/kW (17.7kg/bhp); 7.4l/100km (38.4mpg), inj 8l/100km (35.5mpg), diesel 4.9l/100km (57.3mpg).

PRICE 1.3GL £5905, 1.6 Ghia
7235, 1.6i Ghia £7435, 1.6 GL
diesel 1985 £7075.
PRODUCTION 1,857,000
all Escort III models.

Below: **controversial rear
suspension developed for
the Escort and Orion. Spring
rates, pivot points, and rear
wheel location were all in
dispute until Ford solved
the problem and produced
one of the best handling and
riding cars of its generation.**

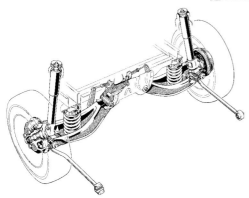

1983 Escort RS1600i

Shown as a prototype in the autumn of 1981, RS1600i was an XR3 with an 85.8kW (115bhp) fuel injection engine, lowered suspension, and elaborate aerodynamics, intended as a Group A motor sport homologation special. Subject to delays, it tentatively went on sale in the spring of 1982, but deliveries of right hand drive cars did not begin until the end of the year. Since the Advanced Vehicles Operation (AVO) had closed in 1974, responsibility for fast Fords had been taken by the Motorsport and Rallye Sport (hence RS) divisions in Germany under Mike Kranefuss. Suspension changes included different struts, anti-dive geometry, Koni dampers, thick anti-roll bars, and an aluminium front cross-member. Overall gearing was raised from 4.29:1 on the XR3i to 3.84:1, and in compensation 5th gear was lower, 0.83:1 against the standard car's 0.75. The result was not entirely satisfactory, with top speed in 5th scarcely faster than 4th. External differences were a striped bonnet, a deep front spoiler and a biplane rear wing. The CVH engine was provided with a special cam, solid valve lifters and a high-compression head, the road-going car providing a racy feel but some coughing and spluttering on start-up. The performance was lively, but the RS1600i was only really quick in race tune with the engine producing half as much power again.

INTRODUCTION 1982, production to 1983.
BODY saloon; 2-doors, 5-seats; weight 920kg (2028.2lb).
ENGINE 4-cylinders, in-line; front; transverse; 79.96mm x 79.52mm, 1596cc; compr 9.9:1; 85.8kW (115bhp) @ 6000rpm; 53.7kW/l (72.1bhp/l); 148 (109lbft) @ 5250rpm.
ENGINE STRUCTURE belt-driven overhead camshaft; 2-valves; aluminium cylinder head, finned aluminium rocker cover, iron block; Bosch K-Jetronic fuel injection, breakerless ignition; 5-bearing crankshaft.
TRANSMISSION front wheel drive; 20.3cm (8in) diaphragm spring clutch; gearbox 5-speed synchromesh; helical spur final drive 3.84:1.
CHASSIS steel monocoque; ifs by MacPherson struts, coil springs and anti-roll bar; independent variable rate rear suspension by coil springs telescopic dampers and anti roll bar; hydraulic vacuum servo brakes, front 23.9cm (9.4in) dia disc, rear 17.78cm (7in) dia drums, dual circuit; rack and pinion stering; 48l (10.6 gal) (12.7 US gal) fuel tank; SP Sport Super D4 195/50VR15 tyres 6in rims, alloy wheels.
DIMENSIONS wheelbase 240cm (94.5in); track 140cm (55.1in) front, 142.5cm (56.1in) rear; length 397cm (156.3in); width 164cm (64.6in); height 137cm (53.9in); ground clearance 14cm (5.5in); turning circle 10.6m (34.8ft).
EQUIPMENT central locking £136.36, front electric windows £161.41, manual sunroof £258.98, tinted windows £43.08, black paint £80.68, radio cassette £143.25.
PERFORMANCE maximum speed 187kph (116.5mph) *Autocar*; 33.1kph (20.6mph) @ 1000rpm; 0-100kph (62mph) 8.7sec; 10.7kg/kW (8kg/bhp); fuel consumption 10l/100km (28.25mpg).
PRICE £6834.
PRODUCTION 8659.

Group A/N regulations demanded the production of 5000 RS1600i Escorts, but demand was so strong getting on for 9,000 were made. Distinctive appearance with strobe bonnet stripes, alloy wheels, and Recaro seats.

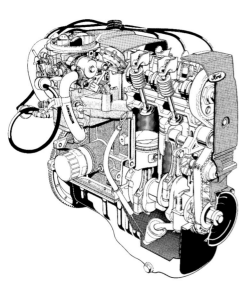

Above: **Ford 1.6 Compound Valve angle Hemispherical chamber (CVH) overhead camshaft engine.**

1983 Sierra XR4i

The most radically-styled Sierra, indeed the most radical-looking Ford since the original Probe III concept car, the XR4i featured not only a dramatic biplane rear spoiler but also a unique 3-window side. On sale from June, it had the Cologne V6 engine of the Capri 2.8i and the same 5-speed transmission with close-ratio gears. It faced competition from the Audi Coupe and BMW 320i, the stylish 3-door body and aerodynamic aids distancing it from the run-of-the-mill Sierra even though a major part of its rationale was to provide the range with some much needed glamour. The lower bodywork was wrapped in polycarbonate cladding, faired round the wheelarches to promote good airflow past the wheels, always a difficult area for aerodynamicists. The wheels stuck further out into the airstream owing to their wide low-profile tyres, and as an additional cosmetic feature the cladding had a contrasting inlaid coloured strip. Suspension modifications included a thicker front anti-roll bar and the addition of a 10mm (.39in) one at the back. Gas filled dampers and bigger brakes completed the performance package. Nothing was skimped on comfort and trim; the interior was equipped with Ghia-style upholstery and accessories, which added to the speed but did not save weight. Despite 3-door bodywork this was the heaviest Sierra yet, heavier than a 2.8i Capri.

INTRODUCTION April 1983, production to 1985.
BODY saloon; 3-doors, 5-seats; weight 1175kg (2590.4lb).
ENGINE 6-cylinders, 60deg V; front; 93mm x 68.5mm, 2792cc; compr 9.2:1; 110.5kW (148.2bhp) @ 5700rpm; 39.5kW/l (53.1bhp/l); 216Nm (159 lbft) @ 3800rpm.
ENGINE STRUCTURE gear-driven central camshaft; pushrod ohv; 2-valves; iron cylinder head, block; Bosch K-Jetronic mechanical fuel injection; breakerless ignition; 4-bearing crankshaft.
TRANSMISSION rear wheel drive; diaphragm spring sdp clutch; gearbox 5-speed synchromesh; final drive 3.62:1.
CHASSIS steel monocoque; independent front suspension by MacPherson struts; independent rear suspension by semi-trailing arms and coil springs; front and rear anti roll bars; telescopic dampers; hydraulic servo brakes, front 26cm (10.2in) dia ventilated disc, rear 26cm (10in) dia drums, dual circuit; rack and pinion steering, PAS optional; 60l (13.2gal) (15.9 US gal) fuel tank; 195/60VR14 tyres 5.5J rims.
DIMENSIONS wheelbase 261cm (102.8in); track 145cm (57.1in) front, 147cm (57.9in) rear; length 446cm (175.6in); width 173cm (68.1in); height 139cm (54.7in); ground clearance 12cm (4.7in); turning circle 10.6m (34.8ft).
EQUIPMENT Ford active warning system for fluid levels, brake pad wear; Ford FM/MW/LW radio cassette player.
PERFORMANCE maximum speed 210kph (130.81mph) *Autocar*, 36.2kph (22.6mph) @ 1000rpm; 0-100kph (62mph) 7.7sec;10.6kg/kW (7.9kg/bhp); fuel consumption 13.3l/100km (21.2mpg).
PRICE 1984 £9946.
PRODUCTION 27,400.

1984 Fiesta II XR2 1597cc

Expanding the Fiesta range, the XR2 had 5 gears and a 71.6kW (96bhp) version of the CVH engine as used in the original Escort XR3. Low-profile tyres, bigger brakes, up-rated springs and gas-filled dampers, a rear anti-roll bar, wheelarch extensions in smart black plastic and quasi-aerodynamic trappings round the rear window provided the sporting ingredients. Yet it was still a mildly tuned engine; the Escort had already gone on to fuel injection, but the Fiesta stuck with a Weber twin-choke downdraught carburettor, with a special inlet manifold to ensure everything fitted within the smaller space. The principal feature was an aluminium cylinder head with valves inclined at 45deg and skewed in relation to one another in plan view by 7deg. This gave the compound valve angle of the title and, by its nature, a near-hemispherical combustion chamber. The design represented yet another triumph of Ford minimalism, by working the valves through a single overhead cam spun by a toothed belt. Inclined valves customarily had to be operated by two cams, or a complicated system of rockers, but the 7deg inclination allowed them to be operated by only one through American-style hydraulic tappets, unusual in a small European engine. XR2 was energetic rather than truly swift and suffered through its thick anti roll bar from a somewhat choppy ride.

INTRODUCTION June 1984, production to 1989.
BODY saloon; 3-doors, 5-seats; weight 840kg (1852lb).
ENGINE 4-cylinders, in-line; front; transverse; 79.96mm x 79.5mm, 1597cc; compr 9.5:1; 70kW (93.9bhp) @ 5750rpm; 43.8kW/l (58.8bhp/l); 132Nm (97 lbft) @ 4000rpm.
ENGINE STRUCTURE CVH belt-driven overhead camshaft, hydraulic tappets; 2-valves; aluminium cylinder head, iron block; Weber twin-variable-choke downdraught carburettor; breakerless ignition; 5-bearing crankshaft.
TRANSMISSION front wheel drive; sdp 20.3cm (8in) clutch; gearbox 5-speed synchromesh; final drive 3.58:1.
CHASSIS steel monocoque structure; ifs by MacPherson struts, coil springs; rear suspension dead axle, trailing links, Panhard rod, anti-roll bar; telescopic dampers; hydraulic, vacuum servo 23.9cm (9.4in) front disc drum brakes; rear drums 17.8cm (7in); rack and pinion steering; 34l (7.5 gal) (8.9 US gal) fuel tank; radial-ply 185/60HR-13 tyres 6J rims.

DIMENSIONS wheelbase 228.6cm (90in); track 138.5cm (54.5in) front, 134cm (52.8in) rear; length 371cm (146.1in); width 162cm (63.8in); height 136cm (53.5in); ground clearance 14cm (5.5in); turning circle 10.3m (33.79ft).
EQUIPMENT 2-speed intermittent wipers, cloth upholstery, foam headlining, laminated windscreen.
PERFORMANCE maximum speed 165kph (102.8mph) *Autocar*; 27.8kph (17.3mph) @ 1000rpm; 0-100kph (62mph) 10.2sec; 12kg/kW (8.9kg/bhp); fuel consumption 9.4l/100km (30.1mpg).
PRICE £5713.
PRODUCTION 1,980,100 all Fiesta II.

1984 Tickford Capri

The Capri may have lacked sophistication but it had a certain appeal in its simplicity, compact dimensions, versatility and good value. Its charm was not unlike that of the pre-war V8, and enjoyed by a wide clientele for much the same reasons. Encouraging sales of the 2.8i perhaps gave it delusions of grandeur, and under the same prompting that created the successful E for Executive versions of the Zephyr, Cortina, Corsair, and Escort, Ford and Tickford (then a division of Aston Martin) decided to develop a special premium-priced Capri. Connolly leather was used for the upholstery, later with velour inserts, and Wilton carpet for the floor. The walnut veneer facia was later changed to black ash. The engine was turbocharged, intercooled, oil-radiatored, and provided with a bigger water radiator. A Getrag gearbox was tried, limited slip differential installed, and overall gearing raised. Air dams, bibs, spoilers, ducts, and wheel discs improved the Capri's aerodynamics a little. Biggest change was to the suspension, in which former grand prix driver John Miles, by then a road tester with *Autocar*, played a pivotal role. He found that better rear axle location was vital because in hard cornering the single-leaf sprung standard axle moved as much as 3.8cm (1.5in) sideways, partly due to deflection in the rubber bushes in the spring eyes.

INTRODUCTION September 1983, production to 1986.
BODY coupe; 2-doors, 4-seats; weight 1230kg (2712lb).
ENGINE Cologne 60deg V6; front; 93.0mm x 68.5mm; 2792cc; compr 9.2:1; 152.9kW (205bhp) @ 5000rpm; 54.8kW/l (73.4bhp/l); 192Nm (260lbft) @ 3500rpm.
ENGINE STRUCTURE gear-driven camshaft, pushrod ohv; cast iron cyl head, block; breakerless ign; Bosch K-Jetronic mechanical fuel inj; IHI RHB6 turbocharger with 0.6kg-cm (8.5psi) boost and integral wastegate, equal-length stainless steel manifolds; 4-bearing crankshaft.
TRANSMISSION rwd; diaphragm spring sdp clutch; 4-speed manual synchromesh gearbox; final drive 3.09:1.
CHASSIS steel monocoque; ifs by MacPherson struts; rear susp semi-elliptic springs; 24mm (0.9in) front, 14mm (0.6in) rear anti-roll bars; gas-filled telesc dampers; hydraulic vacuum servo brakes, 26.2cm (10.3in) ventil front discs (9.75in) dia, rear 22.9cm (9in) drums, dual circuit; rack and pinion PAS; 59.1l (13gal) (15.6 US gal); 205/ 60VR13 radial-ply, 7J rims; alloy wheels.
DIMENSIONS wbase 256cm (100.8in); track 140cm (55.1in) front, 143cm (56.3in) rear; length 437.5cm (172.2in); width 170cm (66.9in); height 136cm (53.5in); ground clearance 11.5cm (4.5in); turning circle 10.8m (35.43ft).
EQUIPMENT leather and velour upholstery, black ash facia, two pearlescent colours, white and flaxen mist.
PERFORMANCE maximum over 225kph (140.2mph); 41.4kph (25.8mph) @ 1000rpm; 0-100kph (62mph) 6.2sec; 8kg/kW (6kg/bhp); standard non-turbo 2.8i 14.5l/100km (19.5mpg).
PRICE PRICE £18,581.

The Tickford Capri was shown at Birmingham in 1982 and went into production in 1983 priced around £15,000. It was still being made in 1986 but at £18,581 the Capri's essential ingredient of good value had disappeared, and it was no match for even a bottom of the range Porsche.

1984 Escort RS Turbo, Escort Cabriolet

The RS Turbo and the Escort Cabriolet were important developments. The RS was a limited production homologation special, designed under the talented Rod Mansfield at Special Vehicle Engineering (SVE) at Dunton, and could be configured to almost any specification. It aimed to meet the regulations for international rallies yet remain flexible enough to suit each event. Replacing the discontinued RS1600i, it used the XR3i as a basis, with a turbocharged version of the 1.6-litre CVH. It also had a viscous coupling limited slip differential, the first application for this ingenious component which helped banish front wheel drive torque steer. There were the customary extended wheel arches for large fat wheels, Recaro seats, and measures to minimise turbo lag. In 1986 the RS Turbo graduated from pure homologation special to proper road car with softer springing, higher gearing, and glass reinforced plastic bodywork panelling. The Cabriolet cost £2000 more than an ordinary Escort and there was a choice of Ghia or XR3i with either 58.9kW (79bhp) or 78.3kW (105bhp) CVH engines. A practical conversion, it was made by the specialists in open-topped bodies, Karmann in Germany, with little loss of interior accommodation except for a smaller boot to give space for the top to fold down.

Specification for RS
INTRODUCTION 1984, production to 1990.
BODY saloon; 2-doors, 5-seats; weight 940kg (2072lb), Cabriolet 970kg (2138.5lb).
ENGINE 4-cylinders, in-line; front; transverse; 79.96mm x 79.52mm, 1597cc; compr 8.3:1; 97kW (130.1bhp) @ 6000rpm; 60.7kW/l (81.5bhp/l); 180Nm (133lbft) @ 5250rpm. Cabriolet: 77kW (103.3bhp) @ 6000rpm; 48.3kW/l (64.7bhp/l); 138Nm (102lbft) @ 4800rpm.
ENGINE STRUCTURE CVH belt-driven overhead camshaft; 2-valves; hydraulic tappets aluminium cylinder head and block; KE-Jetronic fuel injection; Garrett TO3 turbocharger; intercooler; breakerless ignition; 5-bearing crankshaft. Cabriolet Bosch K-Jetronic, non-turbo.
TRANSMISSION front wheel drive; 20.3cm (8in) diaphragm spring clutch; gearbox 5-speed synchromesh; helical spur final drive 4.27:1; Ferguson limited slip differential. Cabriolet 4.29:1.
CHASSIS steel monocoque; ifs by MacPherson struts, coil springs; irs variable rate by coil springs; telescopic dampers, front and rear anti roll bars; hydraulic vacuum servo brakes, front 23.9cm (9.4in) dia ventilated discs, rear 20.1cm (7.9in) drums; dual circuit; rack and pinion steering; 48l (10.6 gal) (12.7 US gal) fuel tank; SP Sport Super D4 195/50VR15 tyres 6in rims, alloy wheels. Cabriolet 185/60HR14.
DIMENSIONS wheelbase 240cm (94.5in); track 140cm (55.1in) front, 142.5cm (56.1in) rear; length 397cm (156.3in); width 164cm (64.6in); height 137cm (53.9in); ground clearance 14cm (5.5in); turning circle 10.6m (34.78ft).
EQUIPMENT halogen headlights, reversing light, 2-speed and intermittent wipers, laminated windscreen.
PERFORMANCE maximum speed 200kph (124.6mph), Cabriolet 186kph (115.9mph); 32.7kph (20.4mph) @ 1000rpm; 0-100kph (62mph) 8.2sec, Cabriolet 9.7sec; 9.7kg/kW (7.2kg/bhp), Cabriolet 12.6kg/kW (9.4kg/bhp); 10l/100km (28.3mpg), Cabriolet 8.4l/100km (33.8mpg).
PRICE RS £9951, 1.6i Cabriolet £9253.
PRODUCTION RS Turbo 8604, Cabriolet 27,900.

1985 Sierra XR4x4

A rearrangement of the Sierra range took place in 1984 with the E-Max 1.6-litre economy model, using a revised Pinto engine of 81.3mm x 77mm instead of 87.67mm x 61mm. Power and torque were about the same as before and there was a useful gain in fuel consumption. The newly introduced 3-door body shell was abandoned together with the 2.3-litre V6, while a CVH taxation special was introduced for the business market, on which a 1.8-litre limit had been imposed by income tax "benefit in kind" legislation. An alternative over the 1.8 limit was a new 2.0-litre 85.8kW (115bhp) Sierra with L-Jetronic fuel injection. The major development of 1985 was Ford employing 4-wheel drive for rallying, in common with the XR4x4 using two viscous coupling limited-slip differentials in its determination to match the opposing works teams from Peugeot and Audi. Drawing on Ferguson FF Developments' experience (going back to 4x4 Capris in 1970) 4-wheel drive was used on sporting Sierras and Escort RS Cosworths on and off for the next decade. In 1986 Ford confirmed its commitment to the wide non-competition 4-wheel drive market with a 4x4 Ghia Estate with similar running gear to the XR. The XR4x4 was announced with the 2.0, but by the time it went on sale in May 1985 it was a V6 with K-Jetronic.

INTRODUCTION February 1985, on sale May, production to 1990. Specification for V6 2792cc.
BODY saloon; 5-doors, 5-seats; weight 1175kg (2590lb).
ENGINE 6-cylinders, in 60deg V; front; 93mm x 68.5mm, 2792cc; compr 9.2:1; 110.5kW (148.2bhp) @ 5700rpm; 39.5kW /l (53.1bhp/l); 216Nm (159 lbft) @ 3800rpm. 2.0: 4-cylinders; 90.82 x 76.95mm; 1993cc; 9.2:1; 84.5kW (113.3bhp) @ 5200rpm; 42.4kW (56.9bhp/l); 157Nm (116 lbft) @ 4000rpm.
ENGINE STRUCTURE central gear-driven camshaft; pushrods; 2-valves; iron cyl head, block; Bosch K-Jetronic mechanical fuel inj; 4-bearing crank. 2.0 belt-driven ohc; Bosch electronic L-Jetronic and Ford EEC-IV engine management; 5-bearing crankshaft.
TRANSMISSION four wheel drive by Borg Warner Morse Hi-Vo chain and viscous coupling; front drive shaft through engine sump; sdp clutch; gearbox 5-speed synchromesh; 37 per cent drive to front, 63 per cent to rear; final drive 3.36:1.
CHASSIS steel monocoque; ifs by MacPherson struts; independent rear suspension by semi-trailing arms and coil springs; front and rear anti roll bars; telescopic dampers; hydraulic servo brakes, front 26cm (10.2in) dia ventilated disc, rear 25.2cm (9.9in) dia drums, dual circuit; rack and pinion PAS; 60l (13.2gal) (15.8 US gal) fuel tank; 195/60VR14 tyres 5.5J rims.
DIMENSIONS track 145cm (57.1in) front, 147cm (57.9in) rear; length 446cm (175.6in); width 173cm (68.1in); height 139cm (54.7in); ground clearance 12cm (4.7in); turning circle 10.6m (34.78ft).
EQUIPMENT split rear seats, door mirror remote control, front electric windows, heated rear window, tinted glass, tailgate wash-wipe, alloy wheels, central locking, radio cassette all standard.
PERFORMANCE maximum speed 201kph (125.2mph) *Autocar*. 2.0 190kph (118.35mph) estimate; 36.2kph (22.6mph) @ 1000rpm; 0-100kph (62mph) 8.4sec *Autocar*. 2.0 0-100kph 9.4sec estimate; 10.5kg/kW (7.9kg/bhp); 13.8l/100km (20.5mpg).
PRICE £11,500.
PRODUCTION 23,540.

1985 Sierra RS Cosworth

Launched in March for the Geneva Motor Show, a whole year would elapse before deliveries began of the road car with probably the biggest rear wing ever. Its purpose was Group A Touring Car Racing, for which 5,000 had to be produced, and although it had the structure of an ordinary Sierra 3-door (stiffer and lighter than the 5-door) and made a splendid road-burner, its speed and performance were aimed at motor sport. A newly developed Cosworth-designed engine round the Pinto cylinder block had a turbocharger and a 16-valve twin-cam head, and following its homologation in 1987, race-prepared engines were giving 223.7kW (300bhp). It even had its cam covers painted vivid red in the best Testarossa tradition, sharing with Ferrari Weber fuel injection and a Marelli electronic ignition system similar to that used in Formula 1. Drive was through a Borg Warner close-ratio gearbox supplied ready-built from the US, and the final drive had a viscous coupled limited slip differential. Ford fitted its own electronic anti-lock braking. Two journalists on the press launch vividly recalled sweeping down a motorway, easily keeping station with a Boeing jetliner on its final approach to the runway of the nearby airport, at around 240kph (150mph). The Boeing's wings were keeping it flying, the Cozzie's were keeping it on the ground, and steady as a rock.

INTRODUCTION March 1985, production to 1986.
BODY saloon; 3-doors, 5-seats; weight 1240kg (2734lb).
ENGINE 4-cylinders, in-line; front; 90.82mm x 76.95mm, 1994cc; compr 8.0:1; 150kW (201.2bhp) @ 6000rpm; 75.2kW/l (101bhp/l); 276Nm (204 lbft) @ 4500rpm.
ENGINE STRUCTURE 2 belt driven overhead camshafts; 4-valves; aluminium cylinder head, iron block; Weber electronic fuel injection, Marelli electronic breakerless ignition; 5-bearing crankshaft; Garrett T3 turbocharger, boost 0.65bar (9psi); intercooler; two electric cooling fans.
TRANSMISSION rear wheel drive; sdp diaphragm spring self-adjusting clutch; Borg Warner manual gearbox 5-speed synchromesh; final drive 3.64:1; limited slip differential.
CHASSIS steel monocoque; ifs by MacPherson struts; anti-roll bars front and back; irs by semi-trailing arms, coil springs, telescopic dampers; hydraulic servo brakes, front 28.3cm (11.1in) dia ventilated disc, rear 27.3cm (10.75in) dia disc, dual circuit, ABS; variable ratio rack and pinion PAS; 65l (14.3 gal) (17.1 US gal) fuel tank; 205/50VR15 tyres, 7Jrims.
DIMENSIONS wheelbase 261cm (102.8in); track 144cm (56.7in) front, 144.5cm (56.9in) rear; length 446cm (175.6in); width 173cm (68.1in); height 137.5cm (54.1in); ground clearance 12cm (4.7in); turning circle 10.6m (34.8ft).
EQUIPMENT electric windows, Recaro seats with height and rake adjustment in Roma cashmere fabric, leather-bound steering wheel all standard.
PERFORMANCE maximum speed 240kph (149.5mph); 36.7kph (22.9mph) @ 1000rpm. 0-100kph (62mph) 6.8sec; 8.3kg/kW (6.2kg/bhp); 14.3l/100km (19.8mpg) *Autocar*.
PRICE £15,950 (1986).
PRODUCTION 6021.

Not many years after 75kW (100bhp) per litre was regarded as appropriate for a fragile racing unit, the RS Cosworth was tractable and untemperamental on the road.

1985 Granada/Scorpio 1796cc/1993cc

Demand for big Fords was at best inconsistent when decisions about a new Granada were being taken. Developing as many variants as possible was a pressing need, so a common platform for both cars was tempting. "Platform" roughly corresponded to the old chassis, a framework comprising engine and transmission, suspension and running gear, on which a variety of bodies could be mounted. It was not possible to separate them. In a monocoque hull, body and platform were wholly integrated, but it was feasible within one design to make different wheelbases, different tracks, and different bodywork styles. It was a subtler conception than the old Consul and Zephyr of the 1950s, where one was merely a stretched version of the other, with the addition or subtraction of a couple of cylinders and almost everything else identical. The large Granada bore no more than a family resemblance to the mid-size Sierra, and although both were hatchbacks, following the example of Rover and Renault in the luxury market, many customers would scarcely make the connection. In the UK top of the range models were known as Granada Scorpios, lesser variants were Granadas. It was the first volume production car with electronic ABS as standard from launch, and following the Sierra's near-miss in 1983, it was voted Car of the Year for 1986.

INTRODUCTION 1985, produced until 1998.
BODY saloon; 5-doors, 5-seats; weight 1180kg (2601.4lb), 2.0 1185kg (2612.5lb).
ENGINE 4-cylinders, in-line; front; 86.2mm x 76.95mm, 1796cc; compr 9.5:1; 66kW (88.5bhp) @ 5400rpm; 36.7kW (49.3bhp/l); 140Nm (103lbft) @ 3500rpm.
2.0: 90.82 x 76.95mm; 1993cc; 9.2:1; 77kW (103.3bhp) @ 5200rpm; 38.6kW/l (51.8bhp/l); 157Nm (116lbft) @ 4000rpm.
ENGINE STRUCTURE belt-driven overhead camshaft; 2-valves; iron cylinder head, block; twin venturi Pierburg downdraught carburettor; Ford ESC II electronic ignition; 5-bearing crankshaft. 2.0 twin venturi Weber.
TRANSMISSION rwd; cable-operated 21.6cm (8.5in) sdp clutch; gearbox 5-speed synchromesh; final drive 3.92:1. 2.0: 3.62:1, A4LD automatic option.
CHASSIS steel monocoque; ifs by offset coil sprung MacPherson struts, telescopic twin-tube dampers, anti-roll bar; rear suspension independent with progressive rate coil springs, 18deg

semi-trailing arms, telescopic dampers; anti roll bar; automatic self-levelling electric-pumped pneumatic optional; hydraulic servo brakes, front 26cm (10.2in) dia ventilated discs, rear 25.3cm (10in) dia discs, dual circuit, ATE electronic ABS; rack and pinion, hydraulic variable ratio PAS optional; 70l (15.4gal) (18.5 US gal) fuel tank; 175TR14 or 185/70HR14 tyres, 5.5 or 6J rims.
DIMENSIONS wheelbase 276cm (108.7in); track front and rear 147.5cm (58.1in); length 467cm (183.9in); width 176cm (69.3in); height 144cm (56.7in); ground clearance 12cm (4.7in); turning circle 11m (36.1ft).
EQUIPMENT steering wheel adjustable for rake and reach, asymmetrically split rear seat backrests, warning module for fluids and brake pads.
PERFORMANCE maximum 179kph (111.5mph), 2.0 188kph (117.1mph); 36.1kph (22.5mph) @ 1000rpm, 2.0 39.1kph (24.4mph); 0-100kph (62mph) 13.1sec, 2.0 11.5sec; 17.9kg/kW (13.3kg/bhp), 2.0 15.4kg/kW (11.5kg/bhp); 7.9l/100km (35.8mpg). PRICE 1.8GL £9974, 2.0L £9663.

1985 Granada/Scorpio 2.0 EFI, V6EFI

Despite looking fashionably slippery the Granada was not especially aerodynamic. Like the Chrysler Airflow of the 1930s it appeared more efficient than it really was, with a Cd of 0.34 instead of the current best practice of under 0.30. With a smaller frontal area than its Cd 0.44 predecessor however, the real drag figure was much the same as the benchmark Audi 100. Detailing was better than the Sierra with flush bonded windows, small air intakes, recessed drip rails, and wiper blades that parked out of the draught. Yet by the 1980s luxury-car buyers were tending towards established prestige makes, mostly German, and while Granada sales in Britain were satisfactory they did not make headway in the rest of Europe. Its 4-cylinder petrol engines were Pinto-based, with the same 76.95mm bore and 86.2 (1.8-litre) or 90.82mm (2.0-litre) stroke. Among the changes that came with the 2.0-litre's Bosch L-Jetronic fuel injection was an intricate cast aluminium inlet manifold with tuned length tracts, of a sort that would gain increasing favour with many designers in years to come. New V6 engines were expected in 1987, so the 1985 one was essentially a stop-gap. It was the end of 1986 before the new engines were announced and the winter of 1986-1987 before the much-altered 60deg V6s of 2.4-litres and 2.9-litres were put into production.

Specification for 2.0 EFI.
INTRODUCTION 1985, production to 1998.
BODY saloon; 5-doors, 5-seats; weight 1185kg (2612.5lb), V6 1310kg (2888lb).
ENGINE 4-cylinders, in-line; front; 90.82mm x 76.95mm, 1993cc; compr 9.2:1; 84.5kW (113.3bhp) @ 5200rpm; 42.4kW (56.9bhp/l); 157Nm (116 lbft) @ 4000rpm. V6: 93 x 68.5mm; 2792cc; 110.5kW (148.2bhp) @ 5800rpm; 39.6kW (53.1bhp/l); 219Nm (161lbft) @ 3000rpm.
ENGINE STRUCTURE belt-driven overhead camshaft; 2-valves; iron cylinder head, block; Bosch L-Jetronic fuel injection; Ford EEC IV engine management; 5-bearing crank.
V6 gear-driven central camshaft; 4-bearing crankshaft; Bosch LE-Jetronic.
TRANSMISSION rwd; cable-operated 21.59cm (8.5in) sdp clutch; gearbox 5-speed synchromesh; final drive 3.92:1. limited slip 3.64; A4LD automatic option. V6: 3.36 or 3.64:1.
CHASSIS steel monocoque; ifs by offset coil sprung MacPherson struts, telescopic twin-tube dampers, anti-roll bar; irs with progressive rate coil springs, 18deg semi-trailing arms, telescopic dampers; anti roll bar; automatic self-levelling electric-pumped pneumatic optional; hydraulic servo brakes, front 26cm (10.2in) dia ventilated discs, rear 25.3cm (9.96in) dia discs, dual circuit, ATE electronic ABS; rack and pinion, hydraulic variable ratio PAS optional, standard on V6; 70l (15.4 gal) (18.5 US gal) tank; 185/70HR14 tyres; 6J rims.
DIMENSIONS wheelbase 276cm (108.7in); track 147.5cm (58.1in); length 467cm (183.9in); width 176cm (69.3in); height 144cm (56.7in); ground clearance 12cm (4.7in); turning circle 11m (36.1ft).
EQUIPMENT steering wheel adjustable for rake and reach, asymmetrically split rear seat backrests, warning module for fluids and brake pads.
PERFORMANCE maximum 193kph (120.2mph), V6 208kph (129.6mph); 35.6kph (22.2mph) @ 1000rpm, V6 41.2kph (25.7mph); 0-100kph (62mph) 10.6sec, V6 9.6sec, auto 11.7sec; 14kg/kW (10.5kg/bhp), V6 11.9kg/kW (8.8kg/bhp); 8.6l/100km (32.9mpg), V6 9.3l/100km (30.4mpg).
PRICE 2.0iGL £10,831, 2.0i Ghia £12,056, 2.8i Ghia £14,306.

1985 Granada/Scorpio diesel

It was small wonder that diesel-engined large Fords did not make big inroads into the market. Peugeot supplied the 2.1D 2112cc diesel of 1977 that gave 47kW (63bhp), before being replaced by the 2498cc of 51.5kW (69bhp) at 4200rpm. By 1983 the Granada was mature enough to be described by *Autocar* as "much improved," although still not giving much in the way of speed with a maximum of 139.7kph (87mph), or accleration at nearly 28sec to reach 62mph. An estate car weighed in at 1425kg (3141.6lb) and compared poorly against Rover, Citroen, Vauxhall, Mercedes-Benz, and Peugeot rivals. *Autocar* described the performance as "acceptable" and the car as a "good all-rounder" as well as a cheaper alternative to the others. In 1985 the Scorpio was introduced at the Geneva Motor Show in the spring, the 4x4 in the autumn at Frankfurt, and the diesel in January 1986, still with the 51.5kW (69bhp) Peugeot engine. It was 1988 before a newer one, as used in the Peugeot Express van and turbocharged to 68.6kW (92bhp), was fitted giving a top speed around 173kph (108mph) and cutting the 0-62mph to 13.1sec. The opportunity was taken to fit an M75 gearbox at the same time. The turbo-diesel produced 203Nm (150lbft) of torque at 2250rpm against the non-turbo's 148Nm 109lbft and most buyers found extra layers of sound-deadening welcome.

INTRODUCTION 1985, production to 1998.
BODY saloon; 5-doors, 5-seats; weight 1350kg (2976lb).
ENGINE 4-cylinders, in-line; front; 94mm x 90mm, 2498cc; compr 23:1; 51kW (68.4bhp) @ 4500rpm; 20.4kW/l (27.4bhp/l); 148Nm (109 lbft) @ 2000rpm.
ENGINE STRUCTURE Peugeot XD3 chain-driven camshaft, pushrod ohv; 2-valves; iron cylinder head, block; Bosch EP/VAC fuel injection; 5-bearing crankshaft; block inclined right.
TRANSMISSION rear wheel drive; cable-operated 21.6cm (8.5in) sdp clutch; gearbox 5-speed synchromesh; final drive 3.89:1.
CHASSIS steel monocoque; ifs by offset coil sprung MacPherson struts, telescopic twin-tube dampers, anti-roll bar; rear suspension independent with progressive rate coil springs, 18deg semi-trailing arms, telescopic dampers; anti roll bar; automatic self-levelling electric-pumped pneumatic optional; hydraulic servo brakes, front 26cm (10.2in) dia ventilated discs, rear 25.3cm (10in) dia discs, dual circuit, ATE

electronic ABS; rack and pinion, hydraulic variable ratio PAS; 70l (15.4 gal) (18.5 US gal) fuel tank; 175TR14 or 185/70HR14tyres, 5.5 or 6J rims.
DIMENSIONS wheelbase 276cm (108.7in); track front and rear 147.5cm (58.1in); length 467cm (183.9in); width 176cm (69.3in); height 144cm (56.7in); ground clearance 12cm (4.7in); turning circle 11m (36.1ft).
EQUIPMENT steering wheel adjustable for rake and reach, asymmetrically split rear seat backrests, warning module for fluids and brake pads.
PERFORMANCE maximum speed 158kph (98.4mph); 39.1kph (24.4mph) @ 1000rpm; 0-100kph (62mph) 19.4sec; 26.5kg/kW (19.7kg/bhp); fuel consumption 7.3l/100km (38.7mpg).
PRICE 2.5LD £10,682.

1985 Granada/Scorpio 4x4

It was debatable how much of the 4x4's crisp handling and responsiveness was to the credit of its 4-wheel drive, and how much to firmer springing and low profile tyres. Either way it was probably the best Scorpio of all. Jensens of 1966, the VW Iltis of 1977, and Audi's pioneering work with the quattro of 1980 had made 4-wheel drive not only respectable, but almost commonplace by the time Ford got round to it. And while some manufacturers with front-drive transverse-engined cars went to tortuous lengths to transmit drive round corners, Ford had only to adapt the rear-drive Scorpio/Sierra driveline to achieve its object. The epicyclic centre differential sent only 34 per cent of the traction to the front wheels, so the Scorpio's tendency to understeer towards the outside of corners was all but eliminated; it ran true on the motorway and kept an astonishingly firm grip in all weathers. Together with the anti-lock brakes since launch standard on all Granadas, the 4x4 Scorpio was exemplary for all year round mobility. A special feature of the Ford 4x4 was a viscous coupling between central and rear differentials to subdue wheelspin. In December 1986 the Scorpio gained the 2.9-litre V6 with similar power but more mid-range pull, making the performance livelier at some expense in fuel consumption.

INTRODUCTION 1985, production to 1998.
BODY saloon; 5-doors, 5-seats; weight 1385kg (3053.4lb).
ENGINE 6-cylinders, 60deg V; front; 93mm x 68.5mm, 2792cc; compr 9.2:1; 110.5kW (148.2bhp) @ 5800rpm; 39.6kW/l (53.1bhp/l); 219Nm (161 lbft) @ 3000rpm.
ENGINE STRUCTURE gear-driven central camshaft; 2-valves; iron cylinder head, block; Bosch LE-Jetronic fuel injection; Ford EEC IV engine management; 4-bearing crankshaft.
TRANSMISSION four wheel drive by Borg Warner Morse Hi-Vo chain and viscous coupling; front drive shaft through engine sump; sdp clutch; gearbox 5-speed synchromesh; 37 per cent drive to front, 63 per cent to rear; final drive 3.36:1.
CHASSIS steel monocoque; ifs by offset coil sprung MacPherson struts, telescopic twin-tube dampers, anti-roll bar; irs with progressive rate coil springs, 18deg semi-trailing arms, telescopic dampers; anti roll bar; automatic self-levelling electric-pumped pneumatic optional; hydraulic servo brakes, front 26cm (10.2in) dia ventilated discs, rear 25.3cm (9.96in) dia discs, dual circuit, ATE electronic ABS; rack and pinion, hydraulic variable ratio PAS; 70l (15.4gal) (18.5 US gal) fuel tank; 205/60 VR15tyres; 6J rims.
DIMENSIONS wheelbase 276.5cm (108.9in); track front 147.5cm (58.1in), rear 148cm (58.3in); length 467cm (183.9in); width 176cm (69.3in); height 143.5cm (56.5in); ground clearance 12cm (4.7in); turning circle 11m (36.1ft).
EQUIPMENT steering wheel adjustable for rake and reach, asymmetrically split rear seat backrests, warning module for fluids and brake pads.
PERFORMANCE maximum speed 203kph (126.5mph); 41.2kph (25.7mph) @ 1000rpm; 0-100kph (62mph) 9.9sec;12.5kg/kW (9.3kg/bhp); fuel consumption 12.8l/100km (22.1mpg) *The Sunday Times.*
PRICE £19,680.

The author's Scorpio (bottom left) photographed at the site of the 1906 French Grand Prix. The tunnels below the road ran to the pits.

"Two winters and 25,000 miles ... have revealed no shortcomings and many advantages... makes the standard two wheel drive car feel soggy and unresponsive. Air conditioning and leather upholstery lift the price of the Scorpio well beyond £20,000 ... dynamically it bears comparison with BMW, Mercedes-Benz, and Audi. Qualitatively it has come through with credit." The Sunday Times

1985 RS200

Designed as a Group B rally car, the RS200 was turbocharged, mid-engined, light, 4-wheel driven, fast on any surface, getting its substantial power down through fat tyres, and was the most expensive Ford to date. Group B regulations demanded a production run of 200 cars, so Reliant of Tamworth was commissioned to build them. The prototype was announced in 1984, it did not reach production until 1986, and although it held great promise, its rallying career was cut dramatically short. In the Rally of Portugal, notorious for spectators flooding the special stages, an RS200 went off, killing 3. Then in the Tour de Corse Henri Toivonen and Sergio Cresto died when their Lancia Delta S4 crashed and caught fire. The Federation Internationale du Sport Automobile (FISA) immediately banned aerodynamic devices on Group B cars and called a halt to the entire class from 1987. Ford was one of the manufacturers that had invested large sums in the category and, faced with the prospect of scrapping the entire production run, converted them from stark rally cars to Ghia luxury specification trimmed by Tickford, and put them on sale. Costly, noisy, high-revving, and physically demanding to drive, with a GRP body, cramped interior and lacking an effective heater, the RS200 was spectacularly fast with astonishing roadholding and a surprisingly supple ride.

INTRODUCTION Turin Show 1984, production to 1986.
BODY coupe; 2-doors, 2-seats; weight 1180kg (2601.4lb), rally spec 1050kg (2315lb).
ENGINE 4-cyls, in-line; mid; 86mm x 77.62mm, 1803cc; cr 8.2:1; 184kW (246.7bhp) @ 6500rpm; 102.1kW/l (136.8bhp/l); 292Nm (215 lbft) @ 4500rpm. Rally versions 283kW (380bhp), track 485kW (650bhp).
ENGINE STRUCTURE BDT (Belt Drive camshafts Turbocharged) inclined 23deg right; 2 belt-driven overhead cams; 4-valves; aluminium cylinder head, block; Bosch fuel inj, EEC-IV engine management; 5-bearing crankshaft; Garrett T03/04 turbocharger .8bar (11.6psi), rally version 1.2bar (17.4psi).
TRANSMISSION 4wd with optional rear-drive only; torque split 37% front 63% rear; lockable centre differential splits 50/50; 5-spd all-indirect gearbox at front separate from engine; diaphragm spring twin plate AP 18.4cm (7.25in) clutch; helical spur primary drive; final drive epicyclic Ferguson with viscous coupling limited slip 4.375:1.

CHASSIS stressed platform; floor and bulkheads Ciba-Geigy honeycomb sandwich; steel front and rear extensions; bolt-on tubular stiffening subframes link suspension towers to central structure; ifs and irs by double wishbones with twin coil spring damper units and anti-roll bars, adjustable at front; adjustable toe-in control link at rear, alternative ride heights, adjustable spring platform positions; hydraulic servo brakes, 28.5cm (11in) dia ventilated discs, dual circuit; rack and pinion; 2 fuel tanks 73.6l (16.2 gal) (19.4 US gal) & 41.8l (9.2 gal) (11 US gal) total 115.4l (25.4 gal) (30.4 US gal); Pirelli P700 225/50VR16 tyres, 8in rims, Speedline 3-piece composite alloys.
DIMENSIONS wheelbase 253cm (99.6in); track 150cm (59.1in) front, 149.7cm (58.9in) rear; length 400cm (157.5in); width 176.5cm (69.5in); height varies about 132cm (52in); ground clearance varies about 18cm (7.1in); turning circle 9.6m (31.5ft).
EQUIPMENT road car had insulated cover to sound-damp engine, grey carpet, cloth seats, leather-rimmed steering wheel, no radio.

PERFORMANCE maximum speed 225kph (140.2mph); 32.4kph (20.2mph) @ 1000rpm; 0-100kph (62mph) 6.1sec *Autocar*; 6.4kg/kW (4.8kg/bhp); fuel consumption 17l/100km (16.6mpg). PRICE £45,000. PRODUCTION 200.

Pure-bred rally car with **GRP** 2-seat body on a steel monocoque, the RS200 went to 7400rpm before rev limiter came in. Gear speeds were 59.4kph (37mph), 102.7kph (64mph), 142.9kph (89mph), and 179.8kph (112mph). Stig Blomqvist gave buyers demo drives at Boreham.

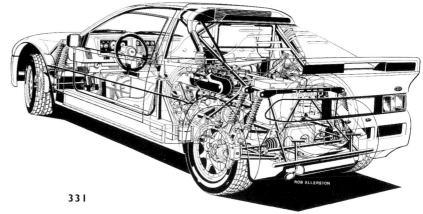

ROB ALLERSTON

1986 Fiesta II 1.4 CVH

The most contentious aspect of proliferating emission laws was how to achieve the necessary reduction in poisonous carbon monoxide (CO) and oxides of nitrogen (Nox). The choice lay between cleaning up the exhaust after it had left the engine, by means of catalytic converters, or trying to make the combustion process more complete beforehand. Ford advocated the latter course and developed its Compound Valve angle Hemispherical chamber (CVH) technology in its pursuit. Cars with catalytic converters needed to run on an air/fuel mixture of 14.7:1 otherwise the cleansing process would not work. This stoichimetric ratio, as it was known, was critical, but unfortunately was responsible for catalytic converter cars using more fuel. In 1986 Ford redesigned the CVH's combustion chambers and piston crowns to promote complete combustion, allowing stoichimetric ratios of 17 or 18:1 so less fuel was used. The 1986 Fiesta did 5.4l/100km (52.3mpg) at 90kph (56mph), and 6.8l/100km (41.5mpg) at 120kph (75mph). Power went up roughly 9 per cent, using low-friction piston rings and a sequential carburettor with a manual choke. It was to no avail. Legislators went for catalytic converters, carburettors were abandoned and electronic engine management developed. Fiestas were later provided with a bigger 40l (8.8 gal) fuel tank.

INTRODUCTION February 1986, production to 1989.
BODY saloon; 3-doors, 5-seats; weight 780kg (1719.5lb).
ENGINE 4-cylinders, in-line; front; transverse; 77.24mm x 74.3mm, 1392cc; compr 9.5:1; 55kW (73.8bhp) @ 5600rpm; 39.5kW/l (53bhp/l); 109Nm (80 lbft) @ 4000rpm. With catalyser 44kW (59bhp).
ENGINE STRUCTURE CVH single belt-driven overhead camshaft; 2-valves; hydraulic tappets; aluminium cylinder head, iron block; twin choke Weber DFM carburettor; 5-bearing crankshaft.
TRANSMISSION front rear wheel drive; sdp clutch; gearbox 5-speed synchromesh; automatic; final drive 3.842:1.
CHASSIS steel monocoque structure; ifs by MacPherson struts, coil springs; anti-roll bar; rear suspension dead axle, trailing links, Panhard rod; telescopic dampers; hydraulic, vacuum servo 22.1cm (8.7in) front disc brakes; rear drums 17.78cm (7.0in); rack and pinion steering; 34l (7.5 gal) (8.9 US gal) fuel tank; radial-ply 155/70SR-13 tyres, 4.5 or 5J rims.

DIMENSIONS wheelbase 228.6cm (90in); track 136.5cm (53.7in) front, 132cm (52in) rear; length 365cm (143.7in); width 158.5cm (62.4in); height 136cm (53.5in); ground clearance 14cm (5.5in); turning circle 10.3m (33.79ft).
EQUIPMENT flush wheel covers, cloth seats, body graphics.
PERFORMANCE maximum speed 165kph (102.8mph); 34.7kph (21.6mph) @ 1000rpm; 0-100kph (62mph) 12.1sec; 14.2kg/kW (10.6kg/bhp), with catalyser 17.7kg/kW (13.2kg/bhp); fuel consumption 6.9l/100km (40.9mpg).
PRICE 1.4L £6140, 1.4 Ghia £7554.

CVH engine: 1.4 (right) exhaust side showing the toothed belt drive to the overhead camshaft and hydraulic tappets with the pressed steel rockers. **1.8 Escort CVH induction side** (far right) shows small depressions in the piston crown with cutaways for the valve heads.

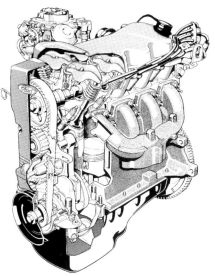

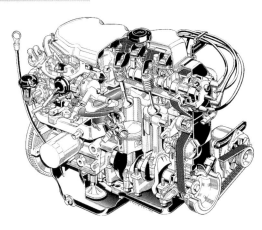

1986 Escort 1117cc/1297cc

The mid-term facelift for Escort and Orion included a new facia and a reallocation of engines that would see them through until the end of the decade. As a sort of Mark IV Escort, there was not much new about it, beyond the new Lucas Stop Control System (SCS), a starter-system anti-lock braking that was optional throughout the range and standard on the RS Turbo. Visual changes were limited to a soft-look front, and a modest lip on the tailgate. There were 5 engine capacities including the unaltered 1.6 diesel. The petrol engines were 1.1-litre, 1.3-litre, 1.4CVH, and 1.6CVH, with carburettor, fuel injection, or turbocharger. The 1.3 with 5-speed overdrive gearbox was the most economical, with new European Legislative Average (ELA) consumption (urban cycle x2 plus steady speed figures divided by 4 in an effort to de-mysticise the official EEC figures) of 6.4l/100km (44.4mpg) which was better than the 1.1-litre by some 3.2per cent even though it was quite a lot faster. Much of the credit for the superior economy was down to the high 5th gear. It was now acknowledged that the early Escort's indifferent ride was due to dampers that had been set to give more resilience on bump than rebound. The rear suspension gave more track-change than it should have; geometry changes were brought in to put things right.

INTRODUCTION Jan 1986, production to 1990.
BODY saloon; 3-doors, 5-seats; weight 825kg (1819lb), 5-door 845kg (1863lb), cabriolet 925kg (2039lb), 3-door estate 850kg (1874lb), 1.3 add 15kg (33.1lb).
ENGINE 4-cylinders, in-line; front; transverse; 73.96mm x 64.98mm, 1117cc; compr 9.5:1; 37kW (49.6bhp) @ 5000rpm; 33.1kW/l (44.4bhp)/l; 83Nm (61 lbft) @ 2700rpm. 1.3: 73.96 x 75.48mm; 1297cc; 9.3:1; 44kW (59bhp) @ 5000rpm; 33kW/l (44.25bhp/l); 100Nm (73 lbft) @ 3000rpm.
ENGINE STRUCTURE pushrod ohv, chain-driven camshaft; 2-valves; iron cylinder head, block; Motorcraft VV carburettor; 3-bearing crankshaft. 1.3, 5-bearing.
TRANSMISSION front wheel drive; sdp diaphragm spring clutch; gearbox 4-speed synchromesh, 5-speed optional; final drive 3.84 or 4.06:1.
CHASSIS steel monocoque; independent front suspension by MacPherson struts, lower track control arms, anti-roll bar; independent rear suspension by transverse arms and longitudinal tie-bars, coil springs; telescopic dampers; hydraulic vacuum servo brakes, front 23.9cm (9.4in) dia discs, rear 18cm (7.1in) dia drums, dual circuit; rack and pinion steering; 48l (10.6 gal) (12.7 US gal) fuel tank; 145SR13 tyres, 4.5 rims.
DIMENSIONS wheelbase 240cm (94.5in); track front 140.5cm (55.31in), rear 142.5cm (56.1in); length 405cm (159.5in), estate 408cm (160.6in); width 164cm (64.6in); height 137cm (53.9in); ground clearance 14cm (5.5in); turning circle 10.6m (34.8ft).
EQUIPMENT Lucas Girling Stop Control System (SCS) £330.
PERFORMANCE maximum speed 145kph (90.3mph), 1.3 157kph (97.8mph); 28.4kph (17.7mph) @ 1000rpm; 0-100kph (62mph) 18.2sec, 1.3 15.4sec; 22.3kg/kW (16.6kg/bhp), 1.3 19.1kg/kW (14.2kg/bhp); fuel consumption 6.4l/100km (44.4mpg) 1.3.
PRICE 1.1 Popular 3-door £4921; 1.3L 3-door £5930; 1.3L Estate 3-door £6382.
PRODUCTION 1,885,000 all models.

Mid-term changes included
a more pedestrian-friendly
front. Different levels of trim
and equipment distinguished
the **Escort Popular** (above)
from the **Escort L** (right) .

1986 Escort 1392cc/1597cc

The Escort's surviving CVH engines, of which Bridgend had already made 2.5m, had high compression ratios making the combustion chambers not so much hemispherical, like half an orange, as the peel squeezed between the humped pistons and valves in the aluminium heads. Only the fuel injection versions had combustion chambers true to the old description. Now they became more heart-shaped rather than half-round recesses in the cast aluminium cylinder head. To try and make it easier to burn weaker mixtures, the swirl effect was developed, increasing the turbulence of the incoming charge and making it burn faster. Lean mixtures ignited too slowly. Other improvements to the CVH included a revised water pump, with a cast rotor and a straight inlet pipe. Keen attention was paid to engine breathing in an effort to meet emission requirements, and the new pump met the demands of the RS Turbo, now in main line production. It was no longer a small-numbers specialist build job, each of which could be modified in any number of ways. Standard on the RS also was SCS anti-lock brakes, available as an option (£330 against the Granada's £800 ABS) throughout the range. The Escort now had Granada-style instrumentation and switchgear, and there was the option of the Granada's electrically heated windscreen to ward off misting and icing.

Specification for 1.4, 1.6, 1.6i, XR3i.
INTRODUCTION Jan 1986, production to 1990.
BODY saloon; 3-doors, 5-seats; weight 850kg (1874lb), 5-door 870kg (1918lb), cabriolet 950kg (2094.4lb); 5-door estate 895kg (1973lb). 1.6 add 10kg (22lb). XR3i 945kg (2083.4lb); cabriolet 995kg (2193.6lb)
ENGINE 4-cylinders, in-line; front; transverse; 77.24mm x 74.3mm, 1392cc; compr 9.5:1; 55kW (73.8bhp) @ 5600rpm; 39.5kW/l (53bhp/l); 109Nm (80 lbft) @ 4000rpm. With catalytic converter: compr 8.5:1; 54.5kW (73.08bhp) @ 5600rpm; 39.1kW/l (52.5bhp/l); 103Nm (76 lbft) @ 4000rpm. 1.6: 79.96 x 79.52mm; 1598cc; 9.5:1; 66kW (88.5bhp) @ 5800rpm; 41.3kW /l (55.4bhp/l); 133Nm (98 lbft) @ 4000rpm. 1.6i: 77kW (103.3bhp) @ 6000rpm; 48.3kW /l (64.5bhp/l); 138Nm (102 lbft) @ 4800rpm. 1.6i with catalytic converter: compr 8.5:1; 66kW (88.51bhp) @5800rpm, 41.3kW/l (55.4bhp/l; 123Nm (91 lbft) @ 4600rpm.
ENGINE STRUCTURE CVH belt-driven ohc; 2-valves; hydraulic tappets; aluminium cyl head, iron block; Weber 2V carburettor; electronic ignition; 5-bearing crankshaft. 1.6i mechanical Bosch KE-Jetronic fuel injection.
TRANSMISSION front wheel drive; sdp 19cm (7.5in) diaphragm spring clutch; 4-speed synchromesh, 5-speed optional; final drive 3.84 or 4.06:1. 1.6: 21.8cm (8.6in) clutch; opt ATX automatic, 3.58:1 final drive 3.31 automatic. 1.6i: 4.27:1.
CHASSIS steel monocoque; ifs by MacPherson struts, lower track control arms, anti-roll bar; irs by transverse arms and longitudinal tie-bars, coil springs; telescopic dampers; hydraulic vacuum servo brakes, front 23.9cm (9.4in) dia ventilated discs, rear 18cm (7.1in) dia drums, dual circuit; rack and pinion steering; 48l (10.6 gal) (12.7 US gal) fuel tank; 155SR13 or 175/70SR13 tyres, 4.5 rims.
DIMENSIONS wheelbase 240cm (94.5in); track front 140.5cm (55.3in), rear 142.5cm (56.1in); length 405cm (159.5in), estate 408cm (160.6in); width 164cm (64.6in); height 137cm (53.9in); ground clearance 14cm (5.5in); turning circle 10.6m (34.78ft).

EQUIPMENT Lucas Girling Stop
Control System (SCS) £330, automatic
£467.
PERFORMANCE maximum speed
167kph (104mph), 165kph (102.8mph)
with cat. 1.6i 185kph (115.2mph),
178kph (110.9mph) with cat. 28.8kph
(17.9mph)
@ 1000rpm, 1.6i 32.6kph (20.3mph);
0-100kph (62mph) 12.7sec, 13.3sec
with cat. 1.6i 10.5sec, 11.5 with cat.
15.5kg/kW (11.5kg/bhp), 1.6 13kg/kW
(9.7kg/bhp); fuel consumption 6.8l/
100km (41.5mpg), 1.6i with cat 7.9l/
100km (35.9mpg).
PRICE 1.4GL 5-door £6919; 1.6L
£6712; 1.6 Ghia 5-door £7746.
PRODUCTION 1,885,000 all models.

1986 Escort diesel 1608cc/1753cc

From its launch in April 1984, the small Ford diesel faced an uphill task in competition with the 1.9-litre Peugeot 309 and Citroen BX, later 205 and Visa. The BX was Britain's best-selling diesel in 1987. One small diesel in 3 came from PSA against Ford's one in 5. Fiat went for bigger capacity diesels to address the power deficit between them and petrol engines, encouraging Ford to follow suit with the first production engine to use a thermoset plastic manifold, the result of a £50million research programme at the Dunton R&D centre. Plastics under the bonnet faced a hostile environment, but they led to lighter engines and could be made with such accuracy that machining was eliminated, so they were cheap. The new-found power improved the 0-62mph time by 2sec and the engine was also quieter than its predecessor. At the same time as the new diesel, the 1.3 petrol was provided with electronic ignition giving an extra 2.2kW (3bhp); road speeds were not much altered but there was a claimed 18 per cent improvement in economy. Escort and Orion also gained variable ratio steering, lighter at slow speeds.

Introduced as a 1608cc, the Escort and Orion diesels were enlarged in 1988 to 1753cc, raising power to 44.7 kW (60bhp) and torque from 95Nm (70 lbft) to 110Nm (81 lbft).

INTRODUCTION January 1986, modified MY 1989, production to 1990.
BODY saloon; 3-doors, 5-seats; weight 910kg (2006lb), 5-door 930kg (2050.3lb), 3-door estate 935kg (2061.3lb).
ENGINE 4-cylinders, in-line; front; transverse; 80mm x 80mm, 1608cc; compr 21.5:1; 39.5kW (52.97bhp) @ 4800rpm; 24.6kW/l (32.9bhp/l); 95Nm (70 lbft) @ 3000rpm.
ENGINE STRUCTURE Ford KHD, belt-driven overhead camshaft; 2-valves; iron cylinder head, block; mechanical fuel injection; 5-bearing crankshaft.
TRANSMISSION front wheel drive; sdp diaphragm spring 19.1cm (7.5in) clutch; gearbox 5-speed synchromesh; final drive 3.84.
CHASSIS steel monocoque; independent front suspension by MacPherson struts, lower track control arms, anti-roll bar; independent rear suspension by transverse arms and longitudinal tie-bars, coil springs; telescopic dampers; hydraulic vacuum servo brakes, front 23.9cm (9.4in) dia discs, rear 18cm (7.1in) dia drums, dual circuit; rack and pinion steering;

48l (10.6gal) (12.7 US gal) fuel tank; 155SR13 tyres, 5in rims.
DIMENSIONS wheelbase 240cm (94.5in); track front 140.5cm (55.3in), rear 142.5cm (56.1in); length 405cm (159.5in), estate 408cm (160.6in); width 164cm (64.6in); height 137cm (53.9in); ground clearance 14cm (5.5in); turning circle 10.6m (34.78ft).
EQUIPMENT Lucas Girling Stop Control System (SCS) £330.
PERFORMANCE maximum speed 146kph (90.9mph); 36.2kph (22.65mph) @ 1000rpm; 0-100kph (62mph) 18.9sec; 23kg/kW (17.2kg/bhp); fuel consumption 5.2l/100km (54.3mpg).
PRICE 3-door £6079; L 5-door £7091; GL estate 5-door £7943.
PRODUCTION 1,885,000 all models.

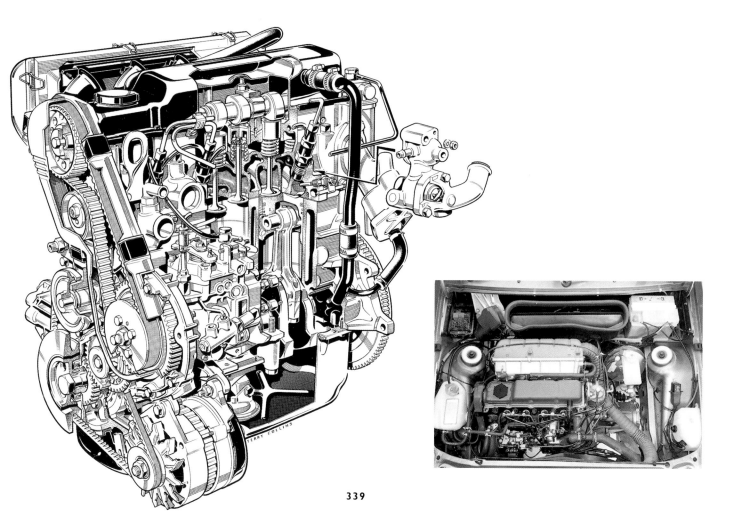

TERRY COLLINS

339

1986 Orion

The 3-box design of the Orion appealed to a clientele that would never buy a hatchback Escort, and preferred to distance itself from the hurly-burly high-speed world of rallying where the Escort had been a consistent front-runner. Orion customers were far more interested in safety features such as anti-lock brakes; skidding for them remained an unrelenting nightmare, and if safer brakes could be managed within a smaller budget than the £800 or so asked for it in the Granada, so much the better. The German Anti Block Systeme (ABS), at its sophisticated electronic best, was still a premium-priced option when Lucas-Girling came along with its Stop Control System (SCS). Offered as standard on 1.6 Turbo and XR3i Escorts, or for £330 on 1.4 and 1.6CVH Orions and Escorts, SCS worked well with one wheel on the snowy verge and the other on (relatively) grippy wet tarmac. Its hydro-mechanical system provided commendable security against wheel-locking in emergencies. It was a modest success but never quite as effective as an electronic one, and once real ABS became cheaper it was discarded. In 1989 there was an attempt to revive the E for Executive suffix that had been applied so successfully to Escorts, Cortinas, and Corsairs, but the 1600E Orion was little more than a reissue of the 1.6 Ghia and was short-lived.

Specification 1.4, 1.6, 1.6i
INTRODUCTION January 1986, produced until 1990.
BODY saloon; 4-doors, 5-seats; weight 875kg (1929lb).
ENGINE 4-cylinders, in-line; front; transverse; 77.24mm x 74.3mm, 1392cc; compr 9.5:1; 55kW (73.8bhp) @ 5600rpm; 39.5kW/l (53bhp/l); 109Nm (80 lbft) @ 4000rpm. With catalytic converter compr 8.5:1; 54.5kW (73bhp) @ 5600rpm; 39.1kW /l (52.5bhp/l); 103Nm (76 lbft) @ 4000rpm. 1.6, 79.96 x 79.52mm; 1598cc; 9.5:1; 66kW (88.5bhp) @ 5800rpm; 41.3kW/l (55.4bhp/l); 133Nm (98 lbft) @ 4000rpm. 1.6i 77kW (103.3bhp) @ 6000rpm; 48.3kW/l (64.6bhp)/l; 138Nm (102 lbft) @ 4800rpm. 1.6i with catalytic converter compr 8.5:1; 66kW (88.5bhp) @ 5800rpm; 41.3kW/l (55.4bhp/l); 123Nm (91 lb ft) @ 4600rpm.
ENGINE STRUCTURE CVH belt-driven overhead camshaft; 2-valves; hydraulic tappets; aluminium cylinder head, iron block; Weber DFM carburettor; electronic ignition; 5-bearing crankshaft. 1.6i mechanical

Bosch KE-Jetronic fuel injection.
TRANSMISSION front wheel drive; sdp 19cm (7.5in) diaphragm spring clutch; gearbox 4-speed synchromesh, 5-speed optional; final drive 3.84 or 4.06:1. 1.6, 21.84cm (8.6in) clutch; optional ATX automatic, 3.58:1 final drive 3.31 automatic. 1.6i 4.27:1.
CHASSIS steel monocoque; ifs by MacPherson struts, lower track control arms, anti-roll bar; irs by transverse arms and longitudinal tie-bars, coil springs; telescopic dampers; hydraulic vacuum servo brakes, front 23.9cm (9.4in) dia ventilated discs, rear 18cm (7.1in) dia drums, dual circuit; rack and pinion; 48l (10.6gal) (12.7 US gal) tank; 155SR13 or 175/70SR13 tyres, 4.5 rims. 1.6i 185/60HR14, 5.5 or 6J rims.
DIMENSIONS wheelbase 240cm (94.5in); track front 140.5cm (55.3in), rear 142.5cm (56.1in); length 421.5cm (165.9in); width 164cm (64.6in); height 139.5cm (54.9in); ground clearance 14cm (5.5in); turning circle 10.6m (34.78ft).
EQUIPMENT Lucas Girling Stop Control System (SCS) £330, automatic £467.

PERFORMANCE maximum speed
167kph (104mph), 165kph (102.8mph)
with cat, 1.6i 185kph (115.2mph),
178kph (110.9mph) with cat; 32.6kph
(20.3mph)@ 1000rpm; 0-100kph
(62mph) 12.9sec, 13.3sec with cat,
1.6i 10.5sec, 11.5 with cat; 15.9kg/kW
(11.9kg/bhp); fuel consumption 6.8l/
100km (41.5mpg), 1.6i with cat 7.9l/
100km (35.9mpg).
PRICE 1.4L £6455; 1.6 Ghia £8159;
1.6i Ghia £7586.
PRODUCTION 1,885,000 all models.

341

1987 Sierra

Alterations ensured Sierra's survival, and although it never found a place in the nation's heart like the Cortina did, it sold steadily to the end. By the spring of 1987 there were 18 Sierras and Sapphires with petrol engines from 1.6 to 2.0-litre, and a 2.3-litre diesel. Trim options ranged from basic to Ghia, although this had more to do with marketing demarcations than the value of extras. A curiosity of the UK fleet market was that cars, like office carpets or the key to the executive toilet, carried distinctions of status as surely as the pips and crowns on officers' uniforms. Two-tone paint, plush upholstery, central locking, a box to store cassettes in, tinted windows, a sunroof, and a rev counter hardly amounted to £1000 extra, although crucial in the commercial pecking order. Biggest change to the appearance was more glass area. Among revisions in May 1988 was the replacement of the British-built 1.8-litre Pinto engine by a one built in America, with different cylinder dimensions but the same power output. Also in 1988 the MT75 5-speed gearbox, bigger and with a synchromesh reverse, was introduced for the more powerful ends of Sierra and Scorpio ranges. In 1989 a new 8-valve 2.0-litre twin cam engine replaced older 2.0-litre Pintos, giving 81.3kW (109bhp) on a carburettor or 93.2kW (125bhp) with fuel injection.

INTRODUCTION February 1987, production to 1992. Specification 2.0EFI and 2.3diesel. BODY saloon; 5-doors, 5-seats; weight 1060kg (2337lb), estate 1090kg (2403lb), 2.3D 1165kg (2568.4lb). ENGINE 4-cylinders, in-line; front; 90.82mm x 76.95mm, 1993cc; compr 9.2:1; 85kW (114bhp) @ 5500rpm; 42.6kW/l (57.2bhp/l); 160Nm (118 lbft) @ 4000rpm. With catalyser compr 8.5:1; 74kW (99.2bhp) @ 5100rpm; 37.2kW/l (49.8bhp/l); 148Nm (109 lbft) @ 4000rpm; (lead-free fuel specific). 2.3 94 x 83mm; 2304cc; cr 22.2:1; 49kW (65.7bhp) @ 4200rpm; 21.3kW/l (28.5bhp/l); 139Nm (103 lbft) @ 2000rpm. ENGINE STRUCTURE 1 belt-driven overhead camshaft; 2-valves; iron cylinder head, block; Bosch L-Jetronic electronic fuel injection, electronic ignition; 5-bearing crankshaft. 2.3 LXD2 block inclined 20deg to right; chain-driven lateral camshaft; aluminium cylinder head; Bosch EP/VAC injection. TRANSMISSION rear wheel drive; sdp diaphragm spring clutch; gearbox 5-speed synchromesh; A4LD (automatic

4-speed Lock-up Overdrive) optional; final drive 3.92 or 3.62:1 with catalyser-equipped cars. 2.3, 3.14 or 3.38:1. CHASSIS steel monocoque structure; MacPherson strut independent front suspension; anti roll bar; independent rear suspension by semi-trailing arms, coil springs; telescopic dampers (GLS and Ghia gas-filled); estate self-levelling; hydraulic servo brakes, front 23.9cm (9.4in) dia ventilated disc, rear 20.3cm (8in) dia drums, 24.2cm (9.5in) discs with optional ABS, dual circuit, rack and pinion PAS; 60l (13.2 gal) (15.8 US gal) fuel tank; 195/60HR14 tyres, 5.5in rims, Ghia alloy wheels. 2.3tyres 165SR/TR 13/14. Estate 175SR/TR 13/14. DIMENSIONS wheelbase 261cm (102.8in); track front 145cm (57.1in), rear 147cm (57.9in); length 442.5cm (174.2in); width 169.5cm (66.7in); height 136cm (53.5in); ground clearance 12cm (4.7in); turning circle 10.6m (34.78ft). EQUIPMENT electrically heated windscreen, 60/40 split rear seat back, high-security locking system, integral radio aerials. Automatic £554.

PERFORMANCE maximum speed 190kph (118.4mph), automatic 184kph (114.6mph), with catalyser 181kph (112.7mph) or 178kph (110.9mph) auto, 2.3 154kph (95.93mph); 33.7kph (21mph) @ 1000rpm, 2.3 42.2kph (26.3mph); 0-100kph (62mph) 11.2sec, 2.3 19.1sec; 12.5kg/kW (9.3kg/bhp), 2.3 23.8kg/kW (17.7kg/bhp); fuel consumption 8.5l/100km (33.2mpg), 2.3 6.6l/100km (42.8mpg).

PRICE 1.6 £7347, 2.0LX £8569, 2.0i Ghia £10,995, 2.3GLD Estate £9889.

PRODUCTION 974,00 all Sierras.

343

1987 Sapphire

It took 4 years to get round to making a Sierra with a boot instead of a hatchback. When the Sierra was facelifted, the Sapphire was enlisted in the battle with the Vauxhall Cavalier, and in defence of Ford's 27% share of the UK market. In one typical January-May the Cavalier was ahead of Sierra with 54,087 sales against 48,290, but in May the Ford edged ahead with 10,028 against 8,984. The traditional fleet market was still strong; company representatives and their contents' insurers often preferring the security of a lockable boot rather than a hatchback with breakable windows, despite its large capacity. One survey showed 4 buyers out of 5 demanding more security, so Ford spent £228million on adding a boot and making other changes. The resulting stiffer shell with its bonded-in big back window was quieter, and although quite shallow with the spare wheel underneath, had useful carrying capacity. Volkswagen had its Jetta, Austin Rover its Montego, Vauxhall had had a 4-door Cavalier from the beginning, and Ford itself had the Orion, all essentially notchback versions of an existing model. There were minor engineering changes including stiffer suspension, but little to the bodywork beyond detail revisions to the front. These were extended throughout the Sierra/Sapphire range, making it a touch less radical but more generally popular.

INTRODUCTION February 1987, production to 1992.
Specification 2.0EFI and 1.6 carburettor.
BODY saloon; 4-doors, 5-seats; weight 1095kg (2414lb), 1.6 1025kg (2259.7lb).
ENGINE 4-cylinders, in-line; front; 90.82mm x 76.95mm, 1993cc; cr 9.2:1; 85kW (114bhp) @ 5500rpm; 42.6kW/l (57.2bhp/l); 160Nm (118 lbft) @ 4000rpm. With catalyser cr 8.5:1; 74kW (99.2bhp) @ 5100rpm; 37.2kW/l (49.8bhp/l); 148Nm (109 lbft) @ 4000rpm; (lead-free fuel specific). 1.6 81.3 x 76.95mm; 1598cc; compr 9.5:1; 55kW (73.8bhp) @ 4900rpm; 34.5kW/l (46.2bhp/l); 123Nm (91 lbft) @ 2900rpm.
ENGINE STRUCTURE 1 belt-driven overhead camshaft; 2-valves; iron cylinder head, block; Bosch L-Jetronic electronic fuel injection, electronic ignition; 5-bearing crankshaft. 1.6 Weber 2V carburettor.
TRANSMISSION rear wheel drive; sdp diaphragm spring clutch; gearbox 5-speed synchromesh; A4LD (automatic 4-speed Lock-up Overdrive) optional; final drive 3.92 or 3.62:1 with catalyser-equipped cars. 1.6 4-speed, final drive

3.62:1; 5-speed optional.
CHASSIS steel monocoque structure; MacPherson strut independent front suspension; anti roll bar; independent rear suspension by semi-trailing arms, coil springs; telescopic dampers (GLS and Ghia gas-filled); hydraulic servo brakes, front 23.9cm (9.4in) dia ventilated disc, rear 20.3cm (8in) dia drums, 24.2cm (9.5in) discs with optional ABS, dual circuit, rack and pinion PAS optional; 60l (13.2 gal) (15.8 US gal) fuel tank; 195/60HR14 tyres, 5.5in rims, Ghia alloy wheels.
DIMENSIONS wheelbase 261cm (102.8in); track front 145cm (57.1in) rear 147cm (57.9in); length 446.5cm (175.8in); width 170cm (66.9in); height 136cm (53.5in); ground clearance 12cm (4.7in); turning circle 10.6m (34.8ft).
EQUIPMENT electrically heated windscreen £104, trip computer £121, automatic £554, PAS £505, air conditioning £718, Teves ABS £934, headlamp washers £145, trailer coupling £295, high-security locking system, integral radio aerials, electric fan.
PERFORMANCE maximum speed 190kph (118.4mph), automatic 184kph

(114.6mph), with catalyser 181kph
(112.7mph) or 178kph (110.9mph)
auto, 1.6 165kph (102.8mph); 33.7kph
(21mph) @ 1000rpm, 1.6 29.9kph
(18.6mph); 0-100kph (62mph) 11.2sec,
1.6 14.2sec; 12.9kg/kW (9.6kg/bhp),
1.6 18.6kg/kW (13.9kg/bhp); fuel
consumption 8.5l/100km (33.2mpg),
1.6 7.56l/100km (37.4mpg).
PRICE 1.6 £7272, 2.3D £7741,
2.0iGLS £9680, 2.0i Ghia £10,845.
PRODUCTION 974,00 all Sierras.

345

1987 Sierra Cosworth RS500

Following on the success of the 1985-1986 Sierra RS Cosworth, the RS500 evolved as an even more potent Group A racer. Only 500 (thus RS for RennSport 500) had to be manufactured to qualify as "production" according to Touring Car regulations and although it was nominally no more powerful and not much faster than the road-going car, the RS500's engine could be made to produce more than 500bhp (372.9kW) reliably and consistently. It became almost unbeatable in Group A until the rules were changed to its disadvantage. Sold through specially designated Ford RS dealers this "Evolution" (in touring car race jargon) had a 167kW (224bhp) version of the Cosworth engine, the additional 14.9kW (20bhp) gained by a Garrett T31/T04 turbocharger and enlarged air-to-air intercooler and induction system, twin fuel injectors to each cylinder, pressurised oil cooling to each piston, and larger capacity oil and water pumps. Cooling ducts behind apertures in the front bumper directed air to the intercooler and brakes. Aerodynamic devices included a splitter to enhance downforce, a small lip on the trailing edge of the rear wing, and an extra spoiler on the tailgate. Aston Martin Tickford gained the half million pound contract to build 15 cars a day; most of them were painted black, with white or blue metallic available to special order only.

INTRODUCTION 1987 production. BODY saloon; 3-doors, 5-seats; weight 1240kg (2733.7lb). ENGINE 4-cylinders, in-line; front; 90.8mm x 77.0mm, 1994cc; compr 8.0:1; 167kW (224bhp) @ 6000rpm; 83.8kW/l (112.4bhp/l); 280Nm (207 lbft) @ 4500rpm. ENGINE STRUCTURE two belt-driven ohcs; 4-valves inclined at 45deg; hydraulic tappets; aluminium cyl head, iron block; Weber-Marelli electronic twin-nozzle fuel injection and engine management; 5-bearing crankshaft; Garrett T31/T04 .55bar (7.98psi) turbocharger with air to air intercooler. TRANSMISSION rwd; sdp diaphragm spring clutch; gearbox 5-speed synchromesh; final drive 3.64:1 with viscous-coupling limited slip differential. CHASSIS steel monocoque; MacPherson strut ifs; irs by semi-trailing arms, coil springs; telescopic dampers anti roll bars front and rear; hydraulic servo brakes, front 28.3cm (11.1in) dia ventilated disc, rear 27.2cm (10.7in) dia discs with Teves ABS, dual circuit, rack and pinion PAS; 65l (14.3 gal) (17.1 US gal) fuel tank; 205/50VR15 tyres, 7J rims, alloy wheels. DIMENSIONS wheelbase 261cm (102.8in); track front 144cm (56.7in), rear 144.5cm (56.9in); length 446cm (175.6in); width 173cm (68.1in); height 137.5cm (54.1in); ground clearance 12cm (4.7in); turning circle 10.3m (33.79ft). EQUIPMENT front aerodynamic splitter, rear wing. PERFORMANCE maximum speed 246kph (153.2mph); 36.7kph (22.9mph) @ 1000rpm; 0-100kph (62mph) 6.2sec; 7.4kg/kW (5.5kg/bhp); fuel consumption 11.2l/100km (25.2mpg). PRICE £19,950. PRODUCTION 500.

Right: Dr Jonathan Palmer flew his helicopter to Boreham to put his new turbocharged Sierra RS Cosworth through its paces during his first season driving with the Formula 1 Tyrrell team. Ironically it was a season when he was the consistent winner among the non-turbo cars.

347

1987 Fiesta II CVT

Continuously Variable Transmission or Constant Velocity Transmission (CVT) or CTX as Ford preferred to call it, was introduced on the engaging but ultimately unsuccessful Daf air-cooled flat-twin of 1959. It was fully automatic, with a centrifugal clutch, limited-slip differential, and V-belts running in moveable pulleys. It was simple and efficient, the only point of debate was whether it was worthy because it was cheap, or because it banished gearchanging from small cars. It was only practical because its power losses were negligible, unlike those of conventional automatics with oil-churning torque converters. The solitary control for the driver was a forward and reverse lever, although it took 20 years' development with V-belts manufactured in steel segments instead of rubber and textiles, and redesigned to push and not pull, before the CVT was fit for anything as powerful as a Fiesta. The engine still whirred a great deal as it got up to speed ahead, it seemed, of the gearbox. But it was economical, and with electronic controls the constant buzziness of the engine was curbed although not cured. CVT was optional on the Fiesta and, since it was a joint development between Ford and Fiat, also on the Fiat Uno. Most customers did not seem ready for CVT and continued to elect for the clutch and manual gearbox to which they were long accustomed.

INTRODUCTION 1987, produced until 1989.
BODY saloon; 3-doors, 5-seats; weight 785kg (1730.6lb).
ENGINE 4-cylinders, in-line; front; transverse; 73.96 x 64.98mm; 1117cc; 9.5:1; 37kW (49.6bhp) @ 5000rpm; 33.1kW/l (44.4bhp/l); 83Nm (61 lbft) @ 2700rpm.
ENGINE STRUCTURE pushrod ohv; chain-driven camshaft; 2-valves; iron cylinder head, block; inverse Ford-Motorcraft VV carburettor; contact-breaker ignition; 3-bearing crankshaft.
TRANSMISSION front wheel drive; automatic continuously variable from 3.67 and 0.63, final drive 3.84:1; single epicyclic gearset for forward and reverse; hydro-mechanical valve block controls ratio selection and wet multi-plate startup clutches.
CHASSIS steel monocoque structure; ifs by MacPherson struts, coil springs; rear suspension dead axle, trailing links, Panhard rod; telescopic dampers; hydraulic, vacuum servo 22.1cm (8.7in) front disc brakes; rear drums 17.8cm (7in); rack and pinion steering; 34l (7.5 gal) (9 US gal) fuel tank; radial-ply 135SR-13 tyres or 155/70SR13, 4.5 or 5J rims.
DIMENSIONS wheelbase 228.6cm (90in); track front 136.5cm (53.7in), rear 132cm (52in); length 365cm (143.7in); width 158.5cm (62.4in); height 136cm (53.5in); ground clearance 14cm (5.5in); turning circle 10.3m (33.79ft).
EQUIPMENT Ghia trim options.
PERFORMANCE maximum speed 140kph (87.2mph); high ratio 41.3kph (25.7mph) @ 1000rpm; 0-100kph (62mph) 18sec; 21.2kg/kW (15.8kg/bhp); fuel consumption 6.3l/100km (44.8mpg).
PRICE L £4320, 1.1 Ghia £5100.
PRODUCTION 1,980,100 all Fiesta II.

In 1987 the Constant Velocity Transmission (CVT) developed jointly with Fiat from Daf patents went on sale but probably owing to its curious driving character never really took on despite its technical merit. Segmented steel belt is at top left of Terry Collins's cutaway.

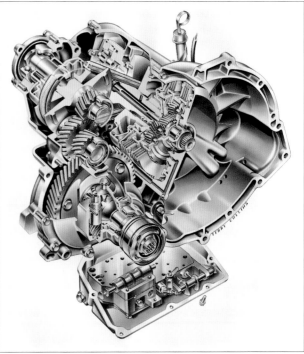

349

1988 Sierra Cosworth and Sierra Sapphire RS Cosworth

Production of the 3-door Sierra launched at Frankfurt in 1985 stopped as planned after 5000 had been made for homologation in Group A. Five hundred of the powerful RS500 version were made in 1987, then in 1988 came the less assertive road-going 4-door Sapphire edition with similar engine and transmission, but although still often called RS it was more of a road car than a detuned racer. With its stiffer bodyshell it reached out to the autobahn-cruising high-speed business market dominated by the classic German makes. Ford's aspirations towards BMW and Mercedes-Benz had been confined to reproducing features, tail-lights, or trim, but now it had a refined road car that reached 60mph almost as quickly as a Porsche 944 Turbo and faster than a 928. It outran an Aston Martin V8, a Ferrari Testarossa would be hard-pressed to keep up until 160kph (about 100mph), and soaked up bumps serenely. Earlier versions had the stiff twitchy feel of a car designed for grip at the expense of comfort. The Design Council praised its value for money. Against a BMW 535iSE at £23,575, an M5 at £34,850, or a Mercedes-Benz 300SE at £27.250 it looked a bargain, even if the pile of the carpets was not so deep, nor the castings finished quite as smoothly as cars from the very top drawer. Genk production began in November 1987.

INTRODUCTION Nov 1987, production to 1990.
BODY saloon; 3-doors, 5-seats; weight 1250kg (2755.8lb).
ENGINE 4-cylinders, in-line; front; 90.82mm x 76.95mm, 1994cc; compr 8.0:1; 150kW (201.2bhp) @ 6000rpm; 75.2kW/l (100.9bhp/l); 276Nm (204 lbft) @ 4500rpm.
ENGINE STRUCTURE 2 belt driven overhead camshafts; 4-valves; aluminium cylinder head, iron block; Weber electronic fuel injection, Marelli electronic breakerless ignition; 5-bearing crankshaft; Garrett T03 B turbocharger, boost 0.65bar (9psi); intercooler; two electric cooling fans.
TRANSMISSION rear wheel drive; sdp diaphragm spring self-adjusting clutch; Borg Warner manual gearbox 5-speed synchromesh; final drive 3.64:1; limited slip differential.
CHASSIS steel monocoque; ifs by MacPherson struts; anti-roll bars front and back; irs semi-trailing arms, coil springs, telescopic dampers; hydraulic servo disc brakes, front 283mm (11.1in) dia ventilated disc, rear 273m (10.8in) dia disc, dual circuit, Teves ABS;

variable ratio rack and pinion PAS; 65l (14.3 gal) (17.1 US gal) fuel tank; 205/50VR15 tyres, 7J rims.
DIMENSIONS wheelbase 261cm (102.8in); track 145cm (57.1in) front, 146cm (57.5in) rear; length 449.5cm (177in); width 170cm (66.9in); height 137cm (53.9in); ground clearance 12cm (4.7in); turning circle 10.6m (34.8ft).
EQUIPMENT electric windows, Recaro seats with height and rake adjustment in Roma cashmere fabric, leather-bound steering wheel all standard.
PERFORMANCE maximum speed 242kph (150.7mph); 36.7kph (22.9mph) @ 1000rpm; 0-100kph (62mph) 6.5sec; 8.3kg/kW (62.kg/bhp); fuel consumption 10.3l/100km (27.4mpg).
PRICE £19,500.
PRODUCTION 11,000.

351

1989 Fiesta III 1001cc/1119cc Popular and Popular Plus

The general arrangement of the third generation Fiesta was much as before on a new platform, the suspension was the same, but the bodyshell was 10.2cm (4in) longer and 5.1cm (2in) wider. The wheelbase was increased 15.2cm (6in), and for the first time came with the option of 3 or 5 doors. Torsion beam rear suspension replaced the old dead rear axle, and the MacPherson struts at the front were modified, with the lower arms relocated on double bonded vertical bushes. Engine changes were introduced to meet European emission control regulations that would eventually demand catalytic converters. High Compression Swirl (HCS) combustion chambers with new combustion chamber shapes, port profiles, and manifolds contributed to the debate on the merits of lean-burn against exhaust scrubbing, as the better means of reducing noxious fumes. The increase in space inside was welcome, as was the 45% bigger boot and the 10% more glass, but the low-geared steering and unresponsive handling made the Fiesta rather a dull car. Still a best seller for 10 of the previous 12 years, Fiesta production had reached 5m, 1.2m of which were sold in Britain, and it was soon to edge Sierra off the production line at Dagenham. Overall cost of ownership was taken seriously, with claims that average service costs were 27% lower.

INTRODUCTION January 1989.
BODY saloon; 3/5-doors, 5-seats; 779kg (1717.4lb), 1.1 785kg (1730.6lb).
ENGINE 4-cylinders, in-line; front; transverse; 68.7mm x 67.5mm, 1001cc; compr 9.5:1; 33kW (44.3bhp) @ 5000rpm; 33kW (44.2bhp)/l; 74Nm (55 lbft) @ 3000rpm. 1.1: 68.7 x 75.5mm; 1119cc; 40kW (53.6bhp) @ 5200rpm; 35.7kW (47.9bhp)/l; 86Nm (63 lbft) @ 2700rpm. 1.1 with catalytic converter: compr 8.8:1; 37kW (49.6bhp) @ 5200rpm; 33.2kW (44.3bhp)/l; 83Nm (61 lbft) @ 3000rpm.
ENGINE STRUCTURE HCS pushrod ohv, chain-drive camshaft; 2-valves; iron cylinder head, block; twin choke downdraught Weber carburettor, breakerless electronic ignition; 3-bearing crankshaft.
TRANSMISSION front wheel drive; sdp diaphragm spring clutch; gearbox 4-speed synchromesh; final drive 4.06:1. 1.1 5-speed optional; CTX automatic optional with 3.84:1 final drive.
CHASSIS steel monocoque; ifs by MacPherson struts; irs by trailing arms, torsion beams, coil springs; telescopic dampers; hydraulic brakes, front 24cm (9.5in) dia discs, rear 180mm (7.5in) dia drums, dual circuit, SCS optional; rack and pinion steering; 42l (9.2gal) (11.1 US gal) fuel tank; 135SR13 tyres 4.5 or 5J rims. 1.1 145SR13, 155/70SR13, 165/65SR13.
DIMENSIONS wheelbase 244.5cm (96.3in); track 139cm (54.7in) front, 138.5cm (54.5in) rear; length 374cm (147.2in); width 161cm (63.4in); height 132.5cm (52.2in); ground clearance 14cm (5.5in); turning circle 9.8m (32.2ft).
EQUIPMENT radio/cassette, four speakers, tinted glass, sunroof, metallic paint all standard.
PERFORMANCE maximum 139kph (86.6mph), 1.1 145kph (90.3mph), *Autocar*; 24.7kph (15.4mph) @ 1000rpm, 1.1 33.5kph (20.9mph) 5-speed; 0-100kph (62mph) 20.2sec, 1.1 15.3sec *Autocar*, 23.6kg/kW (17.6kg/bhp), 19.6kg/kW (14.6kg/bhp) 1.1; 8.5l/100km (33.2mpg) 1.1.
PRICE Popular 1.0 3-door £5199, 5-door £5476; Popular Plus 3-door £5877; Pop Plus 1.1 3-door £6183, 5-door £6460; 1.1L 3-door £6645, 5-door £6922, LX £7570.

1989 Fiesta III 1392cc/1596cc

All the engines were modified for Fiesta III. Iron "Valencia" pushrod engines had new cranks and pistons, producing different bore/stroke ratios. The former 957cc engine was over-square at 74x55.7mm, and became 68.7x67.5mm, giving a capacity of 1001cc. Power was unchanged but it was produced at 700rpm less. The High Compression Swirl (HCS) pushrod engines were equipped with fully transistorised ignition using a single flywheel sensor and a pair of dual output coils instead of the old coil and distributor. The 1.1-litre was given a longer-stroke crank to increase the swept volume; it now had a 75.5mm throw making it 1119cc, improving economy, raising an extra few bhp and more torque. Of the Compound Valve Hemispherical (CVH) overhead cam engines the 1.4-litre gained in power and was the first Ford engine to meet the impending European Emission Standards for 1996. The 1.6-litre was a detuned version of the former carburettor XR2 with 67.1kW (90bhp) instead of 70.8kW (95bhp). An additional 1.6-litre was a 16-valve Zetec twin cam as used in the Escort and Mondeo giving 0-60mph acceleration in a fraction over 10sec. Fiestas' variable ratio rack and pinion steering was not unduly heavy but the optional power assistance reduced the turns lock to lock from the manual's 4.6 to 2.8, enhancing feel and control.

INTRODUCTION January 1989. BODY saloon; 3/5-doors, 5-seats; weight 815kg (1796.8lb); 1.6 835kg (1840.8lb).
ENGINE 4-cylinders, in-line; front; transverse; 77.2mm x 74.3mm, 1391cc; compr 9.5:1; 55kW (73.8bhp) @ 5600rpm; 39.5kW (53bhp)/l; 109Nm (80 lbft) @ 4000rpm. 1.6, 80 x 79.5mm; 1598cc; 66kW (88.5bhp) @ 5800rpm; 41.3kW (55.4bhp)/l; 133Nm (98 lbft) @ 4000rpm.
ENGINE STRUCTURE CVH belt-driven overhead camshaft; 2-valves; hydraulic tappets; aluminium cylinder head, iron block; twin choke downdraught Weber DFM carburettor, breakerless electronic ignition; 5-bearing crankshaft. 1.6 Weber 2V.
TRANSMISSION front wheel drive; sdp diaphragm spring clutch; gearbox 5-speed synchromesh; final drive 4.06:1, cat 3.84:1; CTX automatic optional with 3.84:1 final drive 1.6.
CHASSIS steel monocoque; ifs by MacPherson struts; irs by trailing arms, torsion beams, coil springs; telescopic dampers; 1.6 front anti-roll bar; hydraulic vacuum servo brakes, front

240mm (9.5in) dia discs, ventilated on 1.6; rear 180mm (7.5in) dia drums, dual circuit, SCS optional; rack and pinion steering; 42l (9.2 gal) (11.1 US gal) fuel tank; 145SR13, 155/70SR13, 165/65SR13 tyres, 5J rims.
DIMENSIONS wheelbase 244.5cm (96.3in); track 139cm (54.7in) front, 138.5cm (54.5in) rear; length 374cm (147.2in); width 161cm (63.4in); height 132.5cm (52.2in); ground clearance 14cm (5.5in); turning circle 9.8m (32.2ft).
EQUIPMENT radio/cassette, four speakers, tinted glass, sunroof, metallic paint all standard.
PERFORMANCE maximum speed 165kph (102.8mph), 1.6 174kph (108.4mph); 33.5kph (20.9mph) @ 1000rpm; 0-100kph (62mph) 12sec, 1.6 10.3sec; 14.8kg/kW (11kg/bhp), 12.7kg/kW (9.4kg/bhp) 1.6; fuel consumption 7.2l/100km (39.2mpg).
PRICE 1.4LX 3-door £7992, 1.6S £7865.

A new trim level LX was introduced between the L and Ghia.

1989 Fiesta III Diesel. Experimental 2-stroke

Even with a larger, more powerful version of Ford's diesel the Fiesta was never going to be lively. Its official fuel consumption figures were not as good as before on the urban cycle or at a constant 90kph (56mph), but at 120kph (75mph) it still managed 5.6l/100km (50.4mpg) and its acceleration was slightly faster than a 1.1-litre petrol car with the optional 5-speed gearbox. In 1992 Ford revealed an experiment to equip the Fiesta with an engine that looked as though it had been consigned, through its inability to meet increasingly demanding emission regulations, to the dustbin of technology in the 1960s. A 2-stroke was equipped with a compressed air fuel metering system so precise that its emissions were relatively clean. Unburnt hydrocarbons no longer escaped in such profusion and the virtues of fewer moving parts, no valves, springs, camshaft, or pushrods, 30 per cent less weight, 12 per cent better economy, and 10 per cent more power, persuaded Ford to set up a programme running 3-cylinder 1200cc 2-strokes in 50 Fiestas for field trials. They were astonishingly smooth-running with none of the popping and banging associated with old-style 2-strokes. A tank under the bonnet supplied oil to the engine for 12,500 miles without refilling, but it turned out to be problematical in service and the experiment was concluded.

INTRODUCTION January 1989.
BODY saloon; 3/5-doors, 5-seats; weight 870kg (1918lb).
ENGINE 4-cylinders, in-line; front; transverse; 82.5mm x 82mm, 1753cc; compr 21.5:1; 44kW (59bhp) @ 4800rpm; 25.1kW (33.7bhp)/l; 110Nm (81 lbft) @ 2500rpm. 2 stroke, 1.2-litre; 3-cylinders; 59.7kW (80bhp) @ 5500rpm; 122Nm (90 lbft) @ 4000rpm.
ENGINE STRUCTURE Ford/KHD belt-driven ohc; 2-valves; iron cylinder head, block; mechanical fuel injection; 5-bearing crankshaft. 2str, reed valve intakes; Sarich forced-air 6bar (87.02psi) fuel injection system by reciprocating pump driven off the crankshaft; sealed crankcase; engine 100mm (3.9in) lower, 70mm (2.8in) narrower than 4-cylinder; roller-bearing forged one-piece crankshaft; catalytic converter.
TRANSMISSION front wheel drive; sdp diaphragm spring 191mm (7.5in) clutch; gearbox 5-speed synchromesh; final drive 3.59.
CHASSIS steel monocoque; ifs by MacPherson struts; irs by trailing arms, torsion beams, coil springs; telescopic dampers; hydraulic brakes, front 240mm (9.5in) dia discs, rear 180mm (7.5in) dia drums, dual circuit, SCS optional; rack and pinion steering; 42l (9.2 gal) (11.1 US gal) fuel tank; 145SR13 tyres.
DIMENSIONS wheelbase 244.5cm (96.3in); track 139cm (54.7in) front, 138.5cm (54.5in) rear; length 374cm (147.2in); width 161cm (63.4in); height 132.5cm (52.2in); ground clearance 14cm (5.5in); turning circle 9.8m (32.2ft).
EQUIPMENT radio/cassette, four speakers, tinted glass, sunroof, metallic paint all standard.
PERFORMANCE maximum 152kph (94.7mph), 2stroke 168kph (104.7mph); 29.7kph (18.5mph) @ 1000rpm; 0-100kph (62mph) 16sec, 2stroke 10.7sec;19.8kg/kW (14.7kg/bhp); fuel consumption 5.1l/100km (55.4mpg), 2stroke 5.7l/100km (49.6mpg).
PRICE L 1.8D 3-door £7467, LX 1.8D 5-door £8392.

Right: police surveillance. Experiments with orbital engines were carried out over big mileages as patrol cars.

1989 Fiesta XR2i

Fast Fiestas began with the XR2 from 1981-1983, continuing in 1984-1989 with the restyled body. It gained the 1.6 CVH engine and 5-speed gearbox, handled well and safely, and with a top speed comfortably over 168kph (105mph) was a firm favourite with keen young drivers. The 1989-1992 XR2i had the Mark III body, was still a 2-door, and with fuel injection (necessary for catalytic converter cars) had a real turn of speed. The suspension was tightened down making it a more sporting car than its predecessors and although it never gained the reputation of a VW Golf GTi, was nevertheless a worthy contender in the hot hatch market. Alloy wheels became standard in the summer of 1990. Fastest Fiesta was the RS Turbo of 1990, based on the XR2i, with a 99.2kW (133bhp) CVH engine similar to the Escort RS Turbo and although not notably economical at 12.3-11.3l/100km (23-25mpg) it reached 60mph in under 8 seconds and had a top speed of 207kph (130mph). Wide wheels and fat fashionable low profile tyres made the steering heavy at parking speed, PAS was not considered necessary and kept the price under £12,000 It had only a brief production run, being overtaken by the 16 valve RS1800 in 1992. "More fun than a Ferrari at 10 per cent of the price," according to *The Sunday Times*.

INTRODUCTION January 1989.
BODY saloon; 3/5-doors, 5-seats; weight 890kg (19623lb).
ENGINE 4-cylinders, in-line; front; transverse; 80mm x 79.5mm, 1598cc; compr 9.75:1; 81kW (108.6bhp) @ 6000rpm; 50.7kW (68bhp)/l; 138Nm (102 lbft) @ 2800rpm. With catalytic converter 76kW (101.9bhp) @ 6000rpm; 47.6kW (63.8bhp)/l; 135Nm (100 lbft) @ 2800rpm.
ENGINE STRUCTURE CVH belt-driven ohc; hydraulic tappets; 2-valves; aluminium cylinder head, iron block; mechanical fuel injection, breakerless electronic ignition; 5-bearing crankshaft.
TRANSMISSION front wheel drive; sdp diaphragm spring clutch; gearbox 5-speed synchromesh; final drive 4.06:1.
CHASSIS steel monocoque; ifs by MacPherson struts; irs by trailing arms, torsion beams, coil springs; telescopic dampers; hydraulic brakes, front 24cm (9.5in) dia discs, rear 18cm (7.5in) dia drums, dual circuit, SCS optional; rack and pinion steering; 42l (9.24gal) fuel tank; 185/60HR13 tyres 5.5J rims.
DIMENSIONS wheelbase 244.5cm (96.3in); track 141cm (55.5in) front,

138cm (54.3in) rear; length 380cm (149.6in); width 163cm (64.2in); height 132.5cm (52.2in); ground clearance 14cm (5.5in); turning circle 9.8m (32.2ft).
EQUIPMENT radio/cassette, four speakers, tinted glass, sunroof, metallic paint all standard.
PERFORMANCE maximum 192kph (119.6mph), 187kph (116.5mph) with cat; 32.9kph (20.5mph) @ 1000rpm; 0-100kph (62mph) 9.8sec, 10.1sec with cat; 11kg/kW (8.2kg/bhp); fuel consumption 8.2l/100km (34.3mpg) *Autocar*.
PRICE £9995.

Omitted from the model lineup when the new Fiesta was launched at the beginning of 1989 owing to the priority given to the mainstream Popular and LX, the XR2 brought the total of Fiesta models to 18 and was distinguished by body coloured bumpers and flared wheel arches to accommodate the wide wheels and fat tyres.

1990 Escort revision

The Escort and Orion had a lot of life in them yet, but only 2 years elapsed before their next makeover. A world wide best seller for 8 years out of 9, despite differences in the Transatlantic "Escort", Ford was unnerved by criticism of the Sierra but determined to do something about the Escort's less than rapturous reception. It spent £1billion redeveloping it for the 1991 model year. Based on a number of customer surveys it was provided with more elbow-room; the body engineers found 7.6cm (3in) extra inside between the B-pillars, while making the outside only 4.6cm (1.8in) wider. The wheelbase was stretched by 12.7cm (5in) and the torsion beam rear suspension was new. Equipment levels were enhanced with power steering, air-conditioning, electronic anti-lock brakes, height and tilt seat adjustments, and an adjustable steering column available either as standard or an option. Even the basic Escort Popular gained height-adjustable front seat belts. Orions, representing 26% of Escort sales, gained 6% more boot space, and among the 6 engine options were fuel injection and electronic ignition. The RS2000 was available with the 3-door body and prices were only increased by 3%. The Cabriolet lent the range some sparkle with RS2000 firm suspension, and a stiffened body made, as before, by Wilhelm Karmann GmbH of Osnabruck.

Spec 1.4LX non-catalytic converter as sold in Britain.
INTRODUCTION August 1990.
BODY saloon; 3-doors, 5-seats; weight 930kg (2050lb), 5-door 950kg (2094.4lb), Orion 985kg (2171.5lb), estate 1005kg (2215.6lb).
ENGINE 4-cylinders, in-line; front; transverse; 77.24mm x 74.3mm, 1392cc; compr 8.5:1; 52kW (69.7bhp) @ 5600rpm; 37.4kW (50.1bhp)/l; 103Nm (76 lbft) @ 4000rpm. Without catalytic converter 54kW (72.4bhp) @ 5500rpm, 108Nm (80 lbft) @ 4000rpm.
ENGINE STRUCTURE CVH belt-driven overhead camshaft; hydraulic tappets; 2-valves; aluminium cylinder head, iron block; electronic fuel injection (non-cat twin choke carburettor); electronic ignition; 5-bearing crankshaft.
TRANSMISSION front wheel drive; sdp clutch; gearbox 5-speed synchromesh; CTX automatic opt; limited slip differential; final drive 4.059:1, 3.824:1 non-cat, 3.84:1 with CTX.
CHASSIS steel monocoque structure; independent front suspension by MacPherson struts, anti-roll bar; semi independent rear suspension by trailing arms, torsion beam axle, telescopic dampers; hydraulic servo brakes, front dia 23.9cm (9.4in) ventilated discs, rear 18cm (7.1in) dia drums, dual circuit, Teves ABS optional; variable rate rack and pinion steering; 55l (12.1 gal) (14.5 US gal) fuel tank; 175/70R13tyres, 5J rims.
DIMENSIONS wheelbase 252.5cm (99.4in); track 144cm (56.7in) front, 146cm (57.5in) rear; length 403.5cm (158.9in). Orion 423cm (166.5in), estate 427cm (168.1in); width 169cm (66.5in); height 139.5cm (54.9in); estate 141.5cm (55.7in); turning circle 10m (32.8ft).
EQUIPMENT ABS £435; automatic £760; metallic paint £175. 4-speaker radio cassette, tinted windows, sunroof standard.
PERFORMANCE maximum speed 164kph (102.2mph). *Autocar*; 34.4kph (21.4mph) @ 1000rpm.; 0-100kph (62mph) 12.8sec.; 17.9kg/kW (13.3kg/bhp); fuel consumption 9.7l/100km (29.1mpg).
PRICE £9470.

1990 Granada Scorpio saloon

Selling enlarged Sierras to discriminating executives was not getting any easier, and ever since their introduction in 1985 the Granada and Scorpio had been available only as hatchbacks. Notchbacks met the demand for a lockable boot, and sheltered rear-seat occupants from draughts when the hatch opened. 3-box saloons were quieter and more refined and, with new twin-cam engines, the Granada was growing sophisticated. The gearbox was improved; just as well in view of growing opposition from Rover, working to overcome its quality problems, and improved Vauxhall Carltons and Senators. The Vauxhall Cavalier was once again the best-selling car in Britain, dislodging Ford from market leadership. Scorpio saloon's announcement at the Brussels Motor Show in January focussed Ford's attantion on Continental European that bought Fiestas, Escorts, and Sierras, but not many Granadas. Ford was fourth in Europe behind Volkswagen-Audi, Fiat-Lancia-Alfa, and Peugeot-Citroen. The Scorpio was its response to Europeans who regarded large Fords with disdain. The British had bought big Fords since the Zephyr and Zodiac of the 1950s. In the UK one large car in 4 was a Ford. Things were about to change, even though each clientele may have regarded Ford's takeover of Jaguar as buying its way into the aristocracy.

Spec 2.0i and 2.9V6.
INTRODUCTION January 1990, production to 1992.
BODY saloon; 4/5-doors, 5-seats; weight 1245kg (2744.7lb), 2.9V6 1315kg (2900lb).
ENGINE 4-cylinders, in-line; front; 86mm x 86mm, 1998cc; compr 10.3:1; 88kW (118bhp) @ 5500rpm; 44.5kW (59.1bhp)/l; 171Nm (126 lbft) @ 2500rpm.
Without catalytic converter 92kW (123.4bhp) @ 5500rpm; 46kW (61.8bhp)/l; 174Nm (87 lbft) @ 2500rpm.
V6 6-cylinders 60 deg V; 93 x 72mm; 2935cc; compr 9.5:1; 107kW (143.5bhp) @ 5500rpm; 36.3kW (48.9bhp)/l; 228Nm (168 lbft) @ 3000rpm. Non-cat 110kW (147.5bhp) @ 5700rpm; 37.8kW (50.3bhp)/l; 233Nm (172 lbft) @ 3000rpm.
ENGINE STRUCTURE 2 chain driven ohcs; 2-valves; aluminium cyl head, iron block; electronic fuel inj, breakerless ignition; 5-bearing crank. V6 hydraulic tappets; chain-driven central camshaft; iron heads and block; 4-bearing crank; Bosch LE/L Jetronic fuel injection.

TRANSMISSION rwd; sdp clutch; gearbox 5-speed synchromesh; 4-speed automatic opt; final drive 3.92:1, 3.62:1, 3.64:1 with limited slip differential. V6 final drive 3.64 or 3.36; opt 4x4 34/66 torque split front/rear; 3.62:1 final drive.
CHASSIS steel monocoque; ifs by MacPherson struts; anti roll bar; irs by semi-trailing arms, coil springs; telescopic dampers; hydraulic servo disc brakes, front 26cm (10.24in) dia ventilated, rear 25.3cm (9.96in) dia, Teves ABS; rack and pinion variable ratio PAS; 70l (15.4 gal) (18.5 US gal) tyres, 6Jrims. 4x4 205/60VR15.
DIMENSIONS wbase 276cm (108.7in); track 147.5cm (58.1in) front, 150cm (59.1in) rear, 4x4 148cm (58.3in) front; length 467cm (183.9in), saloon 474.5cm (186.8in); width 176cm (69.3in), 4x4 176.5cm (69.5in); height 144cm (56.7in), 4x4 143.5cm (56.5in); ground clearance 12cm (4.7in); turning circle 11m (36.1ft).
EQUIPMENT CD player £215, traction pack £650. Alloy wheels, ABS, automatic, PAS, electric seats, leather trim, 6-speaker radio cassette all included in price.

PERFORMANCE maximum speed
180kph (112.1mph) 2.0i automatic
Autocar; 35.5kph (22.1mph) @
1000rpm; 0-100kph (62mph) 11.6sec;
14.1kg/kW (10.6kg/bhp), V6 12.3kg/
kW (9.2kg/bhp); fuel consumption
11.2l/100km (25.2mpg).
PRICE 2.0i automatic £19,245, 2.9EFi
Ghia X £20,895, Scorpio 4x4 £25,350.
PRODUCTION.

1990 Sapphire RS Cosworth 4x4

Cosworth's evolution from racing and high performance engines to production engines was profound. Mercedes-Benz employed it to engineer the 190 2.5-1619, its castings techniques were world-class, and Ford used it to stiffen V6 engine blocks to reduce resonant noise, making them paragons of smoothness and power. Cosworth reduced turbo lag to an absolute minimum. 4-wheel drive was more or less obligatory for rallying as well as being important for high-speed driving in all weathers. The 4-door Sierra Sapphire body was the stiffest and lightest in the range, so all the elements were brought together with the MT75 gearbox, in probably the most accomplished Sierra model yet. The Sierra may not have been as universally loved as many Fords, but the Sapphire Cozzie 4x4 was such a tempting target for car thieves that it had to be equipped with a special alarm system, and sales were very nearly killed off by the steep rise in its insurance premiums. It was well equipped, with leather upholstery optional, which went some way towards justifying its premium price. This was really Ford's third try at the performance market and its best and most civilised by far, with neither freakish tyres nor uncomfortably hard springing. The technical difficulties of equipping 4x4s with ABS brakes were overcome and all Ford 4x4s now had them.

INTRODUCTION Feb 1990, production to 1992.

BODY saloon; 4-doors, 5-seats; weight 1290kg (2844lb).

ENGINE 4-cylinders, in-line; front; 90.8mm x 77mm, 1994cc; compr 8:1; 162kW (217.2bhp) @ 6000rpm; 81.2kW (108.9bhp)/l; 290Nm (214 lbft) @ 3500rpm.

ENGINE STRUCTURE 2 belt-drive overhead camshafts; 4-valves; aluminium cylinder head, iron block; Weber-Marelli electronic fuel injection and engine management; 5-bearing crankshaft; Garrett T.03B turbocharger .7bar (10.15psi); air/air intercooler.

TRANSMISSION four wheel drive; sdp clutch; MT75 gearbox 5-speed synchromesh; torque split 34/66 front/rear; limited slip differentials; final drive 3.62:1.

CHASSIS steel monocoque structure; independent front suspension by MacPherson struts; anti-roll bar; independent rear suspension by semi-trailing arms, coil springs; anti roll bar; telescopic dampers; hydraulic servo disc brakes, front 28.3cm (11.14in) dia ventilated, rear 27.2cm (10.71in)

dia, Teves ABS; rack and pinion PAS; 60l (13.2 gal) (15.8 US gal) fuel tank; 205/50VR15 tyres 7Jrims.

DIMENSIONS wheelbase 261cm (102.8in); track front 145cm (57.1in) rear 147cm (57.9in); length 449.5cm (177in); width 170cm (66.9in); height 135cm (53.2in); turning circle 11m (36.1ft).

EQUIPMENT leather upholstery £500, metallic paint £175. ABS, alloy wheels, PAS, electric windows all standard.

PERFORMANCE maximum speed 232kph (144.5mph) *Autocar*, 35.8kph (22.3mph) @ 1000rpm; 0-100kph (62mph) 6.6sec; 8kg/kW (5.9kg/bhp); fuel consumption 13.1l/100km (21.6mpg).

PRICE £24,995.

PRODUCTION 9250.

1991 Escort XR3i, RS2000

Ford celebrated a year's production of the Mark IV Escort by putting the high-performance versions, previewed the year before, on sale. "The Champ is Back" Ford advertising cheerfully asserted at the Earls Court Motorfair, the former London Motor Show in October, at which the RS2000 appeared with a 111.9kW (150bhp) 2.0-litre 16 valve twin cam engine, disc brakes on all four wheels, and profoundly improved handling. 3 Escorts were shown with the new engine, built in a new plant at Bridgend in South Wales, and called the Zeta. Lancia soon complained about the name; too close to Beta they said, so it was changed to Zetec.

The new factory cost £500million, and could make 500,000 engines a year, more than enough for the entire Escort range. The Zetec, engineered for transverse mounting and front wheel drive, was also to be a key ingredient in the Sierra's successor, the Mondeo, 2 years hence. Yet even Ford admitted the engine had had a protracted birth. As late as October 1991 no promises were being made about which Escorts and Orions it would be fitted in, beyond top of the range models already committed to. Consequently most 1.6-litre Escorts were still sold with the 10 year old CVH. Disc brakes were standardised on fast Fords, so was ABS, PAS, and MTX75 close-ratio gears.

INTRODUCTION October 1991.
BODY saloon; 3-doors, 5-seats; weight 1090kg (2403lb), RS 1110kg (2447lb).
ENGINE 4-cylinders, in-line; front; transverse; 80.6mm x 88mm, 1796cc; compr 10:1; 96kW (128.7bhp) @ 6250rpm; 53.5kW (71.7bhp)/l; 162Nm (119 lbft) @ 4500rpm. RS 86 x 86mm; 1998cc; compr 10.3:1; 110kW (147.5bhp) @ 6000rpm; 55.1kW (73.8bhp)/l; 190Nm (140 lbft) @ 4500rpm
ENGINE STRUCTURE Zetec 2 belt-driven overhead camshafts; 4-valves; hydraulic tappets; aluminium cylinder head, iron block; electronic multi-point injection, mapped ignition; 5-bearing crankshaft. RS chain-driven camshafts
TRANSMISSION front wheel drive; sdp clutch; gearbox 5-speed synchromesh; final drive 3.82:1.
CHASSIS steel monocoque; independent front suspension by MacPherson struts, anti-roll bar; rear suspension, torsion beam, trailing arms, coil springs, anti roll bar, telescopic dampers; hydraulic servo disc brakes, 26cm (10.24in) dia front (ventilated) and rear, ABS optional; rack and pinion

PAS; 55l (12 gal) (14.5 US gal) fuel tank; 185/60VR14tyres 6Jrims. RS 195/50VR15 tyres.
DIMENSIONS wheelbase 252.5cm (99.4in); track front 144cm (56.7in), rear 146cm (57.5in); length 403.5cm (158.9in); width 169cm (66.5in); height 139.5cm (54.9in); turning circle 10m (32.8ft).
EQUIPMENT ABS £505. central locking, electric front windows, electric mirrors, alloy wheels, sunroof, radio cassette, PAS all standard.
PERFORMANCE maximum speed 200.7kph (125mph) *Autocar*; 33kph (20.6mph) @ 1000rpm; 0-100kph (62mph) 8.6sec, RS 8.4sec; 11.4kg/kW (8.5kg/bhp), RS 10.1kg/kW) (7.5kg/bhp); fuel consumption 9.9l/100km (28.6mpg).
PRICE £13,990.
PRODUCTION.

XR3i (right) **and RS200** (far right) **with Zeta, soon to be renamed Zetec engines.**

367

1991 Scorpio V6 24v

"The new Scorpio is either a Jaguar in a plain wrapper or far too good a car to be a Ford. At £27,383 it rubs shoulders with BMWs and Mercedes-Benzes, yet in anything less than a perfect light it could be mistaken for a commonplace Granada at half the price. It is fast enough and very nearly refined enough to be handed to Ford's Coventry subsidiary to be restyled as the medium-sized Jaguar needed for the 1990s. Taking an engine designed by Cosworth Engineering would not cause Jaguar to lose face. It might hurt to inherit a chassis derived from the humble Sierra but even this has been purified to near-Jaguar standards, though it needs improvements to make the ride smoother. Ford is not planning to use the Scorpio as a basis for a Jaguar but it must be tempting to apply the up-market label and design a body more sophisticated than the rather stodgy six year old Granada... Unfortunately the engine is paired with Ford's A4LD automatic, which changes grear with an audible thump, a matter of calibration to put right says Ford." How prescient of *The Sunday Times* in April 1991, to outline Ford's policy for the Coventry subsidiary acquired in 1989. Ford was careful not to associate the 24-valve Scorpio too closely to Cosworth, it was not a Cosworth Scorpio like a Cosworth Sierra, but it was a sure sign of things to come.

INTRODUCTION January 1991.
BODY saloon; 4-doors, 5-seats; weight 1385kg (3053.4lb).
ENGINE 6-cylinders, 60deg V; front; 93mm x 72mm, 2935cc; compr 9.7:1; 143kW (191.8bhp) @ 5750rpm; 48.7kW (65.3bhp)/l; 275Nm (203 lbft) @ 4500rpm.
ENGINE STRUCTURE 2 chain-driven overhead camshafts per bank; 4-valves; hydraulic tappets; aluminium cylinder heads, iron block; multi-point Bosch LH-Jetronic fuel injection Ford EEC IV engine management; 4-bearing crankshaft, two 3-way catalytic converters.
TRANSMISSION rear wheel drive; A4LDE Automatic 4-speed Lock-up overDrive; final drive 3.64:1, limited slip differential.
CHASSIS steel monocoque; independent front suspension by struts, coil springs, telescopic dampers, anti-roll bar; independent rear suspension by semi-trailing arms, coil springs, anti roll bar, telescopic dampers; hydraulic servo ventilated disc brakes, front 27.8cm (10.9in) dia, rear 27.3cm (10.75in) dia, ABS; rack and pinion PAS; 70l (15.4gal)

(18.4 US gal) fuel tank; 205/50ZR16 tyres, 6.5Jrims.
DIMENSIONS wheelbase 276cm (108.7in); track 149cm (58.7in) front, 151cm (59.5in) rear; length 474.5cm (186.8in), 5-door 467cm (183.9in); width 176.5cm (69.5in); height 141cm (55.5in); ground clearance 12cm (4.7in); turning circle 11m (36.1ft).
EQUIPMENT alloy wheels, ABS, PAS, air conditioning, electric seats and windows, mirrors and sunroof, cruise control, trip computer, CD player, choice of leather or cloth all standard.
PERFORMANCE maximum speed 225kph (140.2mph); 41kph (25.5mph) @ 1000rpm; 0-100kph (62mph) 8.8sec; 9.7kg/kW (7.2kg/bhp); fuel consumption 12.8l/100km (22mpg)
Autocar.
PRICE £26,800.

1992 Escort RS Cosworth

Having taken part in rallies since 1990, the RS Cosworth Escort finally went on sale in the spring of 1992. Essentially a cut-down Sierra Cosworth 4x4 platform with an Escort top half, it had a high-mounted rear aerofoil to provide essential downforce at speed and was only ever available with 3 doors. The full-sized Sierra Cosworth 4x4 continued in production until the end of 1992, but the smaller car's light weight and responsive handling gave it the edge in competition. In standard road trim the Cosworth YB 16 valve 2.0-litre turbocharged engine gave 169.3kW (227bhp) but works rally cars were developed with anything up to 298kW (400bhp). The handling was astonishingly well controlled and precise, with little of the nervousness associated with quasi-competition cars. Indeed, with performance in the order of a 1960s Ford V8-engined Cobra, the RS in prudent hands had an almost unprecedented margin of safety. A 7-speed gearbox was listed among the homologated optional extras for competition. In due course the authorities deemed such power outputs hazardous and put a limit on turbocharger pressures. The car's preoccupation lay with rallying. Unaffordable insurance premiums restricted its sales, leading to the abandonment of XR titles in 1994, and the confinement of RS to small runs of specialist rally cars.

INTRODUCTION May 1992.
BODY saloon; 3-doors, 5-seats; weight 1275kg (2811lb).
ENGINE 4-cylinders, in-line; front; longitudinal; 90.82mm x 76.95mm, 1994cc; compr 8:1; 162kW (217.2bhp) @ 6250rpm; 81.2kW (108.9bhp)/l; 294Nm (217 lbft) @ 3500rpm.
ENGINE STRUCTURE Zetec 2 belt-driven overhead camshafts; 4-valves; hydraulic tappets; aluminium cylinder head, iron block; Weber-Marelli electronic multi-point injection, mapped ignition; 5-bearing crankshaft, Garrett T3/T04B turbocharger .8bar (11.6psi), with air/air intercooler.
TRANSMISSION four wheel drive; sdp clutch; gearbox 5-speed synchromesh; central planetary differential, torque split 34/66 or 40/60 with viscous coupling; final drive 3.62:1.
CHASSIS steel monocoque structure; independent front suspension by MacPherson struts, anti-roll bar; rear suspension, torsion beam, trailing arms, coil springs, anti roll bar, telescopic dampers; hydraulic servo ventilated disc brakes, 27.8cm (10.9in) dia front and rear, Teves ABS; rack and pinion PAS;

65l (14.3gal) (17.1 US gal) fuel tank; 225/45ZR16 tyres 8Jrims.
DIMENSIONS wheelbase 255cm (100.4in); track 146.5cm (57.7in) front, 148cm (58.3in) rear; length 414cm (163in); width 174cm (68.5in); height 142.5cm (56.1in); turning circle 10.5m (34.5ft).
EQUIPMENT central locking, electric front windows, electric mirrors, alloy wheels, sunroof, radio cassette, PAS all standard.
PERFORMANCE maximum speed 225kph (140.2mph); 38.1kph (23.7mph) @ 1000rpm; 0-100kph (62mph) 6.1sec; 7.9kg/kW (5.9kg/bhp); fuel consumption 11l/100km (25.7mpg).
PRICE £22,050, Lux £25,590.

Far right: **François Delacour and Daniel Grataloup (RS Cosworth) celebrate Ford's first victory in the Monte Carlo rally for 41 years.**

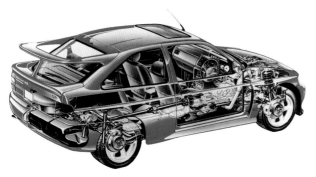

1992 Fiesta RS 1800, RS Turbo

The Peugeot 205 GTi was dominating speedy small cars, and the Fiesta XR2 was not the answer even after becoming XR2i in 1989. At around 190kph (118mph) it was fast, but lacked the Peugeot's precision, quick steering, and exquisite balance. The RS Turbo at the Turin Motor Show in April 1990 still fell short. It was coarse and ill-mannered, and although 1.6sec faster than the XR2i to 100kph (62mph), it was slower than the lighter Renault 5GT Turbo. The Fiesta's CVH engine was based on the Escort's with a Garrett T02 turbocharger and air-to-air intercooler. The steering was higher-geared at 3.75 turns from lock to lock instead of 4.2, yet still felt unworthy. The Turbo did not last and in 1992 the RS1800 resurrected the name of an Escort rather than a Fiesta. It was slower than the Turbo, with a 16-valve version of an engine still called Zeta rather than Zetec, but overall a substantial improvement despite its choppy ride, a result of the addition of a rear anti-roll bar. The smooth-running engine was a revelation after the uncouth turbo, it had ample torque, and was agreeably economical.

The RS Fiesta had Recaro seats, 5-spoke alloy wheels, and the obligatory cosmetic bounce provided by a colour-keyed spoiler, even though the steering had reverted to over 4 turns lock to lock.

Spec RS, 1800 RS Turbo items labelled RST.
BODY saloon; 3/5-doors, 5-seats; weight 995kg (2193.6lb), RST 920kg (2028lb).
ENGINE 4-cylinders, in-line; front; transverse; 80.6mm x 88mm, 1796cc; compr 10:1; 96kW (128.7bhp) @ 6250rpm; 54.6kW (71.7bhp)/l; 162Nm (120 lbft) @ 4500rpm. RST 80 x 79.5mm; 1598cc; compr 8.2:1; 98kW (131.4bhp) @ 5500rpm; 61.3kW (82.2bhp)/l; 184Nm (136 lbft) @ 2400rpm.
ENGINE STRUCTURE Zeta, 2 belt-driven overhead camshafts; hydraulic tappets; 4-valves; aluminium cylinder head, iron block; electronic fuel injection, breakerless electronic ignition; 5-bearing crankshaft. RST CVH 1 ohc; 2-valves; Bosch K-Jetronic injection; GarrettT02 turbocharger, intercooler.
TRANSMISSION front wheel drive; sdp diaphragm spring clutch; gearbox 5-speed synchromesh; final drive 3.82:1.
CHASSIS steel monocoque; independent front suspension by MacPherson struts; independent rear suspension by trailing arms, torsion beams, coil springs; telescopic dampers; anti-roll bars front and back; hydraulic brakes, front 24cm (9.5in) dia ventilated discs, rear 18cm (7.5in) dia drums; rack and pinion steering; 42l (9.2gal) (11.1 US gal) fuel tank; 185/55VR14 tyres 5.5J rims.
DIMENSIONS wheelbase 244.5cm (96.3in); track front 140.5cm (55.3in), rear 137.5cm (54.1in); length 380cm (149.6in); width 163cm (64.2in); height 132.5cm (52.2in); ground clearance 14cm (5.5in); turning circle 9.8m (32.2ft).
EQUIPMENT radio/cassette, 4-speakers, tinted glass, sunroof, metallic paint all standard.
PERFORMANCE maximum speed 200kph (124.6mph), RST 205kph (127.7mph); 30kph (18.7mph) @ 1000rpm, RST 33.8kph (21.1mph) @ 1000rpm; 0-100kph (62mph) 8.5sec, RST 8.2sec; 10.4kg/kW (7.7kg/bhp), RST 9.4kg/kW (7kg/bhp); fuel consumption 8l/100km (35.3mpg).
PRICE RS Turbo 1991 £11,731, RS1800 1992 £11,615.

1992 16v Zetec Fiesta, Escort, Orion

If the new Zetec engine was a long time coming, it was worth the wait. Ford's first mass-market 16-valve 1.8-litre was planned for February 1992, beginning with a 1.6-litre for all three small and medium-sized Fords, Fiesta, Escort, and Orion as well as van derivatives. A more powerful 1.8 was phased in over several months later and a 2.0-litre Zetec was planned for the Mondeo still fully a year away. The dohc RS2000 Escort remained and the existing CVH 1.1-litre and 1.4-litre engines were planned to go on for a further 3 years. The Zetec, as it would be known after Lancia complained about calling it Zeta, was to be produced in Cologne and Mexico as well as Bridgend, which together had a production capacity of a million a year. Developed by Dunton and Cologne, the design was thoroughly up to date without being radical. There was no variable valve timing such as Honda had introduced, or far-reaching structural innovations like Rover's bolted-sandwich K-series. Zetec's lightweight valve gear with low-mass anti-syphon hydraulic tappets revved smoothly up to 7000rpm before hitting the rev limiter, its cylinder dimensions were "under-square" and although its block was cast iron in the interests of noise absorption the 1.8 was still a lightweight. Cam belt replacement was specified at 90,000km (56,000miles), much the same as most

of the opposition, after 150,000 hours of dynamometer testing, and a total of 1260 prototype engines had been made, 320 of which were installed in vehicles that covered more than 10m kilometres (6m miles). In its first form the Zeta was available in two power variants, and it subsequently became available in a variety of sizes. The Zeta was made from high quality materials together with Ford's well-established manufacturing economies. Following a tradition going back to the 1930s the bores could be machined on the same machinery as its predecessor. The cylinder centres were exactly the same as those of the CVH it replaced.

INTRODUCTION as Zeta 1798cc, October 1991.
ENGINE weight 122kg (269lb) with oil and principal fixtures; 4-cyls, in-line; front; transverse; 80.6mm x 88mm, 1798cc; compr 10:1; 77kW (103.3bhp) @ 5500rpm, 42.8kW (57.4bhp)/l; or 96kW (128.7bhp) @ 6250rpm, 53kW (71.6bhp)/l; 153Nm (113 lbft) @ 4000rpm or 162Nm (120 lbft) @ 4500rpm.
ENGINE STRUCTURE 2 HSN (highly saturated nitrile) toothed belt-driven ohcs; 4-valves, inlet 32mm (1.26in), exhaust 28mm (1.1in); low-mass anti-syphon hydraulic tappets; cyl head die-cast aluminium, sand-cast grey iron block; chilled cast iron camshafts; high-silicon al pistons; forged steel connecting rods; shell-moulded cast-iron crank with 5 main bearings and 8 counterweights; structural al oil pan; sequential multi-point fuel inj; 16-bit EEC IV engine management computer with 56kB memory; 3-way cat; fuel requirement 95RON unleaded.

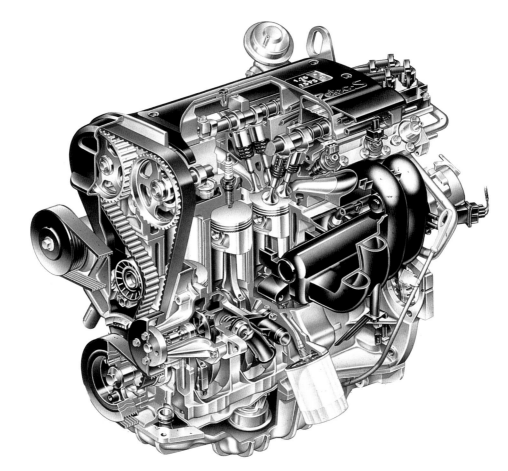

Expert in small high-revving
multi-cylinder lightweight
aluminium engines, Japanese
motorcycle manufacturer
Yamaha was involved in
designing and building
1991 prototype Zetec-SEs.

1992 Escort/Orion revisions

A good record in the market disguised misgivings about the Escort and Orion that surfaced soon after their announcement. Ford reacted with astonishing speed and had a facelift under development within months. Renovations surfaced after only 2 years, not only improving the ride and handling, but also the appearance. Styling leadership, from which Ford had gained much advantage since the Zephyr and Zodiac of the 1950s, had seemed to slip from its grasp. There had been eccentricities, like the Mark IV Zephyr, but by and large Fords had been fashionable, well proportioned, and appealing. The Sierra had shaken confidence, so during the second half of 1992 Escorts and Orions were given a new nose cone and separate air intake grille, a new rear with bigger tail lights and back window. Road behaviour benefited from extra internal stiffening including thicker-gauge steel in the forward bulkhead, and a facia cross member that braced the steering column to absorb side impacts better. Absorption of frontal crash loads was enhanced with beams extending forward of the suspension turrets and the middle of the car now became an effective safety cage. Power steering became standard throughout the Zetec-engined range, CTX automatic was made available, and substantial price cuts to the outgoing models were passed on to the new ones.

Spec 1.6i 16v.
INTRODUCTION September 1992.
BODY saloon; 3-doors, 5-seats; weight 1085kg (2392lb), 5-doors 1105kg (2436lb), Orion 4-doors 1110kg (2447lb), cabriolet 2-door 1110kg (2447lb), estate car 5-doors 1135kg (2502lb).
ENGINE 4-cylinders, in-line; front; transverse; 76mm x 88mm, 1597cc; compr 10.3:1; 66kW (88.5bhp) @ 5500rpm; 41.3kW (55.4bhp)/l; 134Nm (99 lbft) @ 4000rpm.
ENGINE STRUCTURE 2 belt-driven overhead camshafts; 4-valves; hydraulic tappets; cylinder head aluminium, iron block; 5-bearing crankshaft; sequential multi-point fuel injection; EEC IV engine management; 3-way catalytic converter.
TRANSMISSION front wheel drive; sdp clutch; MTX75 gearbox 5-spd synchromesh; final drive 3.82:1.
CHASSIS steel monocoque; independent front suspension by MacPherson struts, anti-roll bar; rear suspension, torsion beam, trailing arms, coil springs, anti roll bar, telescopic dampers; hydraulic servo brakes,

260mm (10.2in) dia front ventilated discs, rear 203mm (8in) drums, Teves ABS optional; rack and pinion PAS; 55l (12.1gal) (14.5 US gal) fuel tank; 175/70TR13tyres 5Jrims, 155TR13 or 185/60HR14 6Jrims.
DIMENSIONS wheelbase 252.5cm (99.4in) track 144cm (56.7in) front, 146cm (57.5in) rear; length 403.5cm (158.9in), Cabrio 410.5cm (161.6in), Orion 423cm (166.5in), estate 427cm (168.1in); width 169cm (66.5in); height 139.5cm (54.9in), estate 141cm (55.5in); turning circle 10m (32.8ft).
EQUIPMENT CD player £367, ABS £504, manual sunroof, ally wheels, PAS, standard.
PERFORMANCE maximum speed 178.2kph (111mph) *Autocar*, 36.5kph (22.7mph) @ 1000rpm; 0-100kph (62mph) 11.9sec; 16.4kg/kW (12.2kg/bhp); fuel consumption 9.2l/100km (30.7mpg).
PRICE 1.6i LX £11885, 1.6i Ghia 5-door £12,440, Orion 1.8 16v Ghia £12,590, 1.6i LX Estate £12,325.

1993 Maverick 2.4 and 2.7 diesel

Ford was never entirely happy with joint ventures, except those in which it had the upper hand as with its takeover of Jaguar. The co-operative arrangement with Nissan, under which a new factory was established in Spain to make a strong 4x4, proved short-lived. The Ford Maverick and Nissan Terrano II produced in the former Spanish Motor Iberica SA factory at Barcelona were identical except in badging and cosmetics. The vehicles were designed by Nissan in 2 wheelbases with 3-doors or 5-doors, had a stout separate chassis with the body mounted at 10 points, and a choice of petrol or diesel engines. They were sold through separate dealer organisations, they gave a good account of themselves off-road, and although not as refined on-road as rivals such as Land Rover Discovery or Vauxhall Frontera, their build quality was superior to both. In the interests of economy Maverick ran for the most part in rear wheel drive The 4x4 market showed strong growth, it was a new product line for Ford, the diesel had a welcome power increase to 92kW (123.4bhp) in 1996 with the addition of an intercooler, but the arrangement with Nissan lasted only 5 years. Double-headed marketing proved fractious, dealers disliked being second-guessed on trade-in prices for a virtually identical model, and in the end Ford decided to make its own 4x4.

INTRODUCTION June 1993.
BODY saloon; 3-doors, 5-seats; weight 1620kg (3571.5lb), 5-door 5-7 seats 1750kg (3858lb), diesels 1730kg (3814lb) and 1850kg (4078.5lb).
ENGINE 4-cylinders, in-line; front; 89mm x 96mm, 2389cc; compr 8.6:1; 91kW (122bhp) @ 5200rpm; 38.1kW (51.1bhp)/l; 197Nm (145 lbft) @ 4000rpm. Diesel 96 x 92mm; 2663cc; compr 21.9:1; 73kW (97.9bhp) @ 4000rpm; 27.4kW (36.7bhp)/l; 221Nm (163 lbft) @ 2200rpm.
ENGINE STRUCTURE Z24 chain driven ohc; 3-valves (2 inlet); aluminium cyl head, iron block; electronic fuel inj; breakerless ignition; 5-bearing crank. Diesel TD27T 2-valves; pushrod; gear driven side camshaft; turbocharger.
TRANSMISSION rwd, selectable 4wd; transfer box for high (1.0) or low (2.02) ratio; 244mm (9.61in) hydraulic sdp clutch; gearbox 5-speed synchromesh; final drive 4.63:1, auto-locking front hubs, limited slip rear axle diff lock.
CHASSIS box-section ladder frame; ifs by double wishbones and torsion bars, anti-roll bar; rear suspension live axle, five-bar multi-link, coil springs, anti-roll bar; telescopic dampers; hydraulic servo brakes, front ventilated discs, rear drums; recirculating ball PAS; 72l (15.8 gal) (7 US gal) fuel tank, 80l (17.6 gal) (21.1 US gal) on lwb; 215SR15tyres, 6Jrims.
DIMENSIONS wheelbase 245cm (96.5in), lwb 265cm (104.3in); track front 145.5cm (57.3in), rear 143cm (56.3in); length 410.5cm (161.6in), lwb 458.5cm (180.5in); width 173.5cm (68.3in); height 180.5cm (71.1in), lwb 181cm (71.3in); ground clearance 21cm (8.3in); turning circle 10.8m (35.4ft), lwb 11.4m (37.4ft); approach angle 35deg, departure angle 36.5deg (lwb 26.5deg) wading depth 45cm (17.7in).
EQUIPMENT alloy wheels on GLX, air conditioning, leather optional. Rear screen wash-wipe, cloth upholstery, RDS radio cassette standard. Accessories included roof rails, nudge bars, running boards, tow bar, lamp guards. 14 equipment packs. 2 solid colours, 8 metallic no extra cost.
PERFORMANCE maximum 159kph (99mph), diesel 147kph (91.6mph); 34.9kph (21.7mph) @ 1000rpm; 0-100kph (62mph) 12.3sec, diesel 19sec;

17.8kg/kW (13.3kg/bhp, diesel 23.7kg/kW (17.7kg/bhp); 14.9l/100km (19mpg), diesel 10.2l/100km (27.6mph). PRICE swb petrol £15,000; swb diesel £15,500; lwb petrol £17,700, diesel £18,200; lwb GLX petrol £19,200, diesel £19,700.

The author's Maverick and accessories. (Above) the pull-out tray that transformed dog-carrying and (right) with Thule luggage carrier increasing the holiday loads carried with all three rows of seats occupied.

1993 Mondeo 1.6/1.8/2.0

The Mondeo was acclaimed critically and commercially from the beginning. Its election as Car of the Year, when opposition from the Citroen Xantia and Mercedes-Benz C-class was keen, was testament to qualities worthy of the Cortina in its heyday.

When the Mondeo was announced it was said to be a car for the world, an ambition that had been on Ford's wish-list since the Model T, and no more realistic in the 1990s than it had been in the 1920s. Buyers in different countries had wanted different Escorts, so European and American models had gone their separate ways before production even started. It was much the same with Mondeo although it took a little longer, and some innovations such as driver airbags, obligatory in America were incorporated on UK cars too although half the size. Mondeo was launched as a 4-door saloon, a 5-door hatchback that looked like a saloon, and an estate car. A 4x4 was listed. Five years and £3billion were spent on 5 levels of trim and a new range of engines to provide front wheel drive in the mainstream market. No Sierra engine survived, the Mondeo's was mounted transversely, and the only similarity was size (The Mondeo was 5cm (1.97in) shorter), and it turned out to be a perfect fit for British garages.

Spec for 1.8i and 2.0; for 1.6 engine spec see 1992 16v Zetec.
INTRODUCTION January 1993.
BODY saloon; 4-doors, 5-seats; 1225kg (2700.6lb), 5-door 1245kg (2745lb), estate 1270kg (2800lb); 2.0i plus approx 10kg (22lb).
ENGINE 4-cylinders, in-line; front; transverse; 80.6mm x 88mm, 1796cc; compr 10:1; 85kW (114bhp) @ 5750rpm; 47.3kW (63.5bhp)/l; 158Nm (117 lbft) @ 3750rpm. 2.0 84.8 x 88mm; 1988cc; 100kW (134.1bhp) @ 6000rpm; 50.3kW (67.5bhp)/l; 180Nm (133 lbft) @ 4000rpm.
ENGINE STRUCTURE 2 belt-driven ohcs; 4-valves; hydraulic tappets; cylinder head aluminium, iron block; 5-bearing crankshaft; sequential multi-point fuel injection; EEC IV engine management; 3-way catalytic converter.
TRANSMISSION front wheel drive; sdp clutch; MTX75 gearbox 5-spd synchromesh; CD4E automatic option; final drive 4.06:1, automatic 3.92:1.
CHASSIS steel monocoque; ifs by MacPherson struts, coil; springs offset, lower A-arms, anti-roll bar; Quadralink strut-type irs with coil springs; anti roll bar; telescopic dampers, transverse and trailing arms; hydraulic servo brakes, front 260mm (10.2in) dia ventil discs, rear 228mm (9in) dia drums, ABS opt; r&p PAS; 61.5l (13.5 gal) (16.2 US gal); 185/65HR14, 195/60HR15tyres, 5.5J rims, Si 205/55VR15 6J rims.
DIMENSIONS wheelbase 270.5cm (106.5in); track front 150.5cm (59.25in), rear 148.5cm (58.5in), estate 150.5cm (59.25in) rear; length 448cm (176.4in), estate 463cm (182.3in); width 175cm (68.9in); height 143cm (56.3in), 5-door 142.5cm (56.1in), estate 144cm (56.7in); ground clearance 12cm (4.7in); turning circle 10.9m (35.8ft).
EQUIPMENT Base, LX, GLX, Ghia, and Si, central locking, driver's airbag, alarm, seatbelt pre-tensioners, and cupholders standard. Traction control, adaptive damping, and cruise control optional on up-market models.
PERFORMANCE maximum 196kph (122mph) *Autocar*; 35kph (21.8mph) @ 1000rpm; 0-100kph (62mph) 9.6sec; 14.4kg/kW (10.7kg/bhp); fuel consumption 10.1l/100km (28mpg).
PRICE 1.6i 4 door £11,200; 2.0iGhia £17,450; 1.8iGLX Estate £14,155.

1993 Mondeo 1.8 turbodiesel

The Mondeo was made with exterior body panels and almost half the monocoque in galvanised steel. It was heavier than the Sierra not because the body was over-engineered, computer design analyses saw to that, but because of the mechanical sophistication the customers were now demanding. The 5-link rear suspension was every bit as heavy as the old Sierra's live rear axle and long transmission shaft. The chassis tuning to meet the new standards had been carried out by development and testing chief Richard Parry-Jones, and technical counsellor Jackie Stewart. Together they spent 2 years evaluating and fine-tuning prototypes. The challenge was balance. "You can cut down on the compliant bushes that make the car supple and quiet, and make the Mondeo handle like a racing car. Or you can beef them up and make it seem like a limousine, but also make it feel unresponsive." Stewart gave an assurance that Ford's fabled bean-counters had never stood in their way. "Throughout the programme we were never refused any change we wanted to make on the grounds of cost." The diesel was no longer a poor relation in the engine range, was taken seriously with a turbocharger and intercooler as the market grew more encouraging, yet like the 1.6 and 1.8 petrol, it was not initially available in Ghia trim.

INTRODUCTION January 1993.
BODY Saloon; 4-doors, 5-seats; weight 1285kg (2833lb), 5-door 1305kg (2877lb), estate 1330kg (2932lb).
ENGINE 4-cylinders, in-line; front; transverse; 82.5mm x 82mm, 1753cc; compr 21.5:1; 65kW (87.2bhp) @ 4500rpm; 37.1kW (49.7bhp)/l; 178Nm (131 lbft) @ 2200rpm.
ENGINE STRUCTURE Ford/KHD; gear and belt-driven overhead camshaft; 2-valves; iron cylinder head and block; 5-bearing crankshaft; indirect mechanical fuel injection, Garrett AiResearch T3 turbocharger with intercooler.
TRANSMISSION front wheel drive; sdp clutch; MTX75 gearbox 5-spd synchromesh; final drive 4.06:1.
CHASSIS steel monocoque; independent front suspension by MacPherson struts, coil springs offset, lower A-arms, anti-roll bar; Quadralink strut-type independent rear suspension with coil springs; anti roll bar; telescopic dampers, transverse and trailing arms; hydraulic servo brakes, front 260mm (10.2in) dia ventilated discs, rear 228mm (9in) dia drums, ABS optional; rack and pinion PAS; 61.5l (13.5 gal) (16.2 US gal) fuel tank; 185/65HR14, 195/60HR15 tyres, 5.5J rims.
DIMENSIONS wheelbase 270.5cm (106.5in); track front 150.5cm (59.25in), rear 148.5cm (58.5in), estate rear 150.5cm (59.25in); length 448cm (176.4in), estate 463cm (182.3in); width 175cm (68.9in); height 143cm (56.3in), 5-door 142.5cm (56.1in), estate 144cm (56.7in); ground clearance 12cm (4.7in); turning circle 10.9m (35.8ft).
EQUIPMENT Base, LX, GLX, central locking, driver's airbag, alarm, seatbelt pre-tensioners, and cupholders standard.
PERFORMANCE maximum speed 175kph (109mph) *Autocar*; 39.8kph (24.8mph) @ 1000rpm; 0-100kph (62mph) 14.7sec; 19.8kg/kW (14.7kg/bhp); fuel consumption 7.9l/100km (36mpg).
PRICE 1.8TD LX £13,470; estate £14,575.

1993 Escort RS2000 4x4

Announced at the Geneva Motor Show in March, and expected to be in production by year's end, it was summer 1994 before Escort RS2000 4x4s went on sale. Difficulties at Saarlouis were blamed but in reality engineers were so busy on mainstream cars that none could be spared to develop small-production speciality vehicles. Transverse-engined, unlike the Sierra 4x4, it had the same twin-cam engine as the standard RS2000 with 3 differentials. In the middle, as it were, was a planetary drive differential, splitting the power and torque 40 per cent to the front, 60 per cent to the rear for sportier handing than the regular front drive car. Escort floorpans were designed with 4x4 in mind and the rear diff was accommodated without intruding on boot space. Instead of the standard car's semi-independent trailing arm and torsion beam axle, the rear final drive was bolted into its own sub-frame, and the back wheels hung on independent semi-trailing arms. The result was astonishing grip and handling in the wet, or on rally special stages, but the additional weight of, and power losses in the complicated drivelines, shaved half a second off the 0-100kph (62mph) time and around 3kph (2mph) off the top speed. It was not much, but together with the higher price buyers seemed to be put off, and not many were sold.

INTRODUCTION August 1993.
BODY saloon; 3-doors, 5-seats; weight 1240kg (2733.7lb).
ENGINE 4-cylinders, in-line; front; transverse; 86mm x 86mm; 1998cc; compr 10.3:1; 110kW (147.5bhp) @ 6000rpm; 55.1kW (73.8bhp)/l; 190Nm (140 lbft) @ 4500rpm.
ENGINE STRUCTURE 2 chain-driven overhead camshafts; 4-valves; hydraulic tappets; aluminium cylinder head, iron block; electronic multi-point injection, mapped ignition; 5-bearing crankshaft.
TRANSMISSION 4 wheel drive; sdp clutch; gearbox 5-speed synchromesh; central planetary differential, torque split 34/66 or 40/60 with viscous coupling; final drive 3.56:1.
CHASSIS steel monocoque; independent front suspension by MacPherson struts, anti-roll bar; rear suspension, torsion beam, trailing arms, coil springs, anti roll bar, telescopic dampers; hydraulic servo disc brakes, 26cm (10.2in) dia front (ventilated) and 27cm (10.6in) rear, ABS; rack and pinion PAS; 55l (12.1gal) (14.5 US gal) fuel tank; 195/50VR15tyres, 6J rims.

DIMENSIONS wheelbase 252.5cm (99.4in); track 144cm (56.7in) front, 146cm (57.5in) rear; length 403.5cm (158.9in); width 169cm (66.5in); height 139.5cm (54.9in); turning circle 10m (32.8ft).
EQUIPMENT central locking, electric front windows, electric mirrors, alloy wheels, sunroof, radio cassette, PAS all standard.
PERFORMANCE maximum speed 208kph (129.6mph); 32.5kph (20.2mph) @ 1000rpm; 0-100kph (62mph) 8.7sec; 11.3kg/kW (8.4kg/bhp); fuel consumption 9.9l/100km (28.6mpg).
PRICE £16,310

1994 Mondeo V6

As a world car the Mondeo was launched in the United States as the Ford Contour and Mercury Mystique, the smaller with a 2.0-litre 4-cylinder made in Chihuahua Mexico, and the larger 2.5-litre 24-valve quad-cam 60deg V6 that would become famous as Duratec. With Ford engineering at full stretch, Porsche Engineering at Weissach was recruited as a consultant in the design of the Duratec, an all-aluminium modular V6, usually joined to CD4E, Ford's first automatic transaxle designed for full electronic control. Duratec formed the basis of a family of engines between 2.0 and 3.0 litres. It was light, only some 18kg (40lb) heavier than a Zetec 4-cylinder, and it not only had to fit inside the small space available but was also required to deliver good low-speed pulling power. It had to be versatile enough for regular slow-speed passenger cars as well as high-performance sports saloons, and in its leisurely applications it was important not to feel like a quad-cam multi-valve unit needing high revs to get the best out of it. Bruce Coventry, head of V6 development said: "Low-end torque establishes the character of a vehicle and there won't be a 4-valve V6 that can match our torque curve. From 1500rpm to almost 5200rpm the torque doesn't vary by more than 5 per cent, so the usable power is good throughout the mid range."

INTRODUCTION January 1994.
BODY saloon; 4-doors, 5-seats; weight 1320kg (2910lb), 5-door 1330kg (2932lb), estate 1380kg (3042.4lb).
ENGINE 6-cylinders, 60deg V; front; transverse; 82.4mm x 79.5mm, 2544cc; compr 9.7:1; 125kW (167.6bhp) @ 6250rpm; 49.1kW (65.9bhp)/l; 220Nm (162 lbft) @ 4250rpm.
ENGINE STRUCTURE 2 chain-driven ohcs per bank; 4-valves; aluminium cylinder heads and block; 4-bearing crankshaft; sequential multi-point fuel injection; electronic engine management.
TRANSMISSION front wheel drive; sdp clutch; 5-speed synchromesh; CD4E automatic option; final drive 4.06:1, automatic 3.77:1.
CHASSIS steel monocoque; ifs by MacPherson struts, coil; springs offset, lower A-arms, anti-roll bar; Quadralink strut-type irs with coil springs; anti roll bar; telescopic dampers, transverse and trailing arms; hydraulic servo ventilated disc brakes, front 27.8cm (10.9in) dia, rear 25.2cm (9.9in) dia, ABS; rack and pinion PAS; 61.5l (13.5gal) (16.2 US gal)fuel tank; 195/60VR15tyres, 5.5J rims. 205/55ZR15, 205/50ZR16 6/6,

5.7J rims.
DIMENSIONS wheelbase 270.5cm (106.5in); track front 150.5cm (59.25in), rear 148.5cm (58.5in), estate 150.5cm (59.25in) rear; length 448cm (176.4in), estate 463cm (182.3in); width 175cm (68.9in); height 143cm (56.3in), 5-door 142.5cm (56.1in), estate 144cm (56.7in); ground clearance 12cm (4.7in); turning circle 10.9m (35.8ft).
EQUIPMENT traction control, air conditioning, ABS, central locking, driver's airbag, alarm, seatbelt pre-tensioners, and cupholders standard, cruise control, leather trim optional.
PERFORMANCE maximum 225kph (140.2mph); 35.5kph@ 1000rpm; 0-100kph (62mph) 8.6sec, auto 10.4sec; 10.6kg/kW (7.9kg/bhp), estate 11kg/kW (8.2kg/bhp); 9.1l/100km (31mpg). PRICE £15,970, Ghia £19,950, estate £20,995.

Design brief for the Mondeo V6 aimed at longer service intervals. The all aluminium engine needed only fluid and filter changes for its first 160,000km (100,000miles).

1994 Probe 2.0, 2.5 V6

In a bold initiative to re-enter a market that it had dominated with the Capri, Ford brought in the Probe sports coupe early in 1994. It had an intricate pedigree. It was engineered by Mazda in which Ford had a quarter share, based on the Mazda 626 and MX-6 platform, and was assembled using engines and transmissions from Japan in a jointly owned factory at Flat Rock in the United States. It had already been on sale for two years and one version of its V6 engine was successful in the British Touring Car Championship (BTCC) works Mondeo.

There was more than nostalgia for the Capri behind the Probe; there was competition from the Vauxhall Calibra, and in a sense it represented a return to Ford roots, as the first whole-car import from the United States since Trafford Park days.

The suspension was retuned for Europe, stiffening the front struts and Mondeo-like Quadralink rear suspension, to provide a firmer ride than its US counterparts, and *Motor Trend* voted it Car of the Year. It cost $13,685 and $16,015 in the US or about £9,120 and £10,700 at the current exchange rate, yet even with the addition of VAT it sold in Britain close to Calibra prices. It did not reach British buyers with the three-year warranty it enjoyed in America.

INTRODUCTION 1994.
BODY coupe; 2-doors, 4-seats; weight 1220kg (2689.6lb), automatic 1250kg (2755.8lb), V6 1325kg (2921.1lb).
ENGINE 4-cylinders, in-line; front; transverse; 83mm x 92mm, 1991cc; compr 9:1; 88kW (118bhp) @ 5500rpm; 44.2kW (59.3bhp)/l; 173Nm (128 lbft) @ 4500rpm. V6 6-cylinders in 60deg V; 84.5 x 74.2mm; 2497cc; compr 9.2:1; 122kW (163.6bhp) @ 5600rpm; 48.9kW (65.6bhp)/l; 217Nm (161 lbft) @ 4000rpm.
ENGINE STRUCTURE 99A 2 belt-driven ohcs; 4-valves; aluminium cyl head, iron block; Mitsubishi electronic fuel injection, electronic engine management; 5-bearing crankshaft. V6 99B 2 gear and belt-driven ohcs, al heads and block; 4-bearing crank; Nippon Denso fuel injection.
TRANSMISSION front wheel drive; sdp clutch; gearbox 5-speed synchromesh; automatic optional; final drive 4:1, 3.77:1 automatic.
CHASSIS steel monocoque; ifs by struts, coil springs, anti-roll bar; irs by multi-link, coil springs, anti roll bar; telescopic dampers; hydraulic servo brakes, front 25.8cm (10.16in) dia ventilated discs, rear drums, or 25.8cm (10.16in) discs when fitted with Sumitomo anti-lock braking; rack and pinion PAS; 59l (12.97gal) fuel tank; 195/65SR14, 205/55SR/HR15 or 225/50VR16 tyres, 5.5,6 or 7J rims.
DIMENSIONS wheelbase 261cm (102.8in); track front 152cm (59.8in); length 454cm (178.8in); width 177.5cm (69.9in); height 131cm (51.57in); ground clearance 16cm (6.3in); turning circle 11.2m (36.8ft).
EQUIPMENT alloy wheels, 2 airbags, electric windows and mirrors standard, leather trim sunroof in Plus Pack.
PERFORMANCE maximum speed 190kph (118.35mph), V6 215kph (133.92mph); 37.7kph (23.48mph) @ 1000rpm, V6 31.7kph (19.75mph); 0-100kph (62mph) 10.4sec, V6 7.9sec; 13.9kg/kW (10.3kg/bhp), V6 10.9kg/kW (8.1kg/bhp); fuel consumption 9.42l/100km (30mpg), V6 11.8l/100km (24mpg).
PRICE 2.0 16v £16,230, 2.5 24v £19,735.

1994 Scorpio revision

Scorpio received mixed reviews after the Paris Motor Show. The oval grille and ellipsoidal headlights, intended to add distinction, were met with something approaching disbelief. The centre section, the most expensive bit of a car to change, was the same as before, the hatchback abandoned, and even though up-market versions were redesigned with wood and leather inside, and prices followed those of Vauxhall and Rover it was the big Ford's last hoorah. The 4-cylinder 16-valve 2.0-litre and Cologne 12-valve 2.9-litre V-6 engines were carried over, and there was a top version with the Cosworth 24-valve. The slow 12-valve V-6 was due to be dropped, but the 2.5-litre turbo-diesel survived.

Large Fords never sold in big numbers, Britain was usually their best market; on the Continent they tended to be outshone by big Opels. The abandonment of the Granada name was imminent, and this Scorpio became the last of a line that went back 45 years to the Zephyr and Zodiac of the 1950s. "Ford is unlikely to stretch a front wheel drive Mondeo the way it did a rear-drive Sierra when the Scorpio's replacement is due towards the end of the decade. The next big Ford could be called a Jaguar as a means of beating at last Vauxhall, Rover, and Opel." *The Sunday Times,* 31 July 1994.

INTRODUCTION January 1991.
BODY saloon; 4-doors, 5-seats; weight 1545kg (3406lb).
ENGINE 6-cylinders, 60deg V; front; 93mm x 72mm, 2935cc; compr 9.7:1; 152kW (203.8bhp) @ 6000rpm; 51.8kW (69.4bhp)/l; 282Nm (208 lbft) @ 4200rpm.
ENGINE STRUCTURE 2 chain-driven overhead camshafts per bank; 4-valves; aluminium cylinder heads, iron block; multi-point Bosch LH-Jetronic fuel injection Ford EEC IV engine management; 4-bearing crankshaft, two 3-way catalytic converters.
TRANSMISSION rear wheel drive; A4LDE Automatic 4-speed Lock-up overDrive; final drive 3.64:1, limited slip differential.
CHASSIS steel monocoque structure; independent front suspension by struts, coil springs, telescopic dampers, anti-roll bar; independent rear suspension by semi-trailing arms, coil springs, anti roll bar, telescopic dampers; hydraulic servo ventilated disc brakes, front 27.8cm (10.9in) dia, rear 27.3cm (10.75in) dia, ABS; rack and pinion PAS; 70l (15.4gal) (18.5 US gal) fuel tank;

205/50ZR16 tyres, 6.5Jrims.
DIMENSIONS wheelbase 276cm (108.7in); track 149cm (58.7in) front, 151cm (59.5in) rear; length 474.5cm (186.8in), 5-door 467cm (183.9in); width 176.5cm (69.5in); height 141cm (55.5in); ground clearance 12cm (4.7in); turning circle 11m (36.1ft).
EQUIPMENT alloy wheels, ABS, PAS, air conditioning, electric seats and windows, mirrors and sunroof, cruise control, trip computer, CD player, choice of leather or cloth all standard.
PERFORMANCE maximum speed 225kph (140.2mph); 41kph (25.5mph) @ 1000rpm; 0-100kph (62mph) 8.8sec; 10.2kg/kW (7.6kg/bhp); fuel con 12.8l/100km (22mpg) *Autocar.*
PRICE £26,800.

In 1993 the 2.5-litre diesel supplied by Peugeot was replaced by a turbocharged unit made by the Italian VM company, raising power output from 68.6kW (92bhp) to 85.8kW (115bhp) and improving performance.

1995 Galaxy 2.0 and V6

Multi purpose vehicles (MPVs), also known quaintly as "people-movers", became one of the fastest-growing automotive sectors with sales doubling since 1990 and forecasts of attaining one new car in 25 within 5 years. Their essential features were 3 rows of flexible seating, a one-box body with steeply sloping windscreen, and the category was dominated by the Renault Espace. Opportunists came in with converted forward-control vans, their engines concealed in unlikely places and suffering a turbulent ride. They were short-lived. Ford and Volkswagen established a joint £1.6billion factory AutoEuropa in Portugal (Setubal according to Ford, Palmela if you believed VW) to produce one with a flat floor, hinged and not sliding doors, seats for 6 that could swivel or be taken out altogether, all within the road space of a Mondeo Estate. Responsibility for the design and engineering lay with VW, production with Ford, so in theory both companies did what they were best at, and unlike Ford's joint venture with Nissan, the Galaxy and VW Sharan (and for a time the Seat Alhambra) coexisted successfully well into the 21st century. Under the codename VX62 the Galaxy used the old 16v 2.0 Scorpio engine and Volkswagen's V6 codenamed VR6. Front suspension was modelled on the Passat, with Ford-inspired MacPherson struts.

INTRODUCTION February 1995.
BODY minivan; 5-doors, 6-seats; weight 1560kg (3439.2lb), V6 1670kg (3681.7lb).
ENGINE 4-cylinders, in-line; front, transverse; 86mm x 86mm, 1998cc; compr 9.8:1; 85kW (114bhp) @ 5500rpm; 42.5kW/l (57.1bhp/l); 167 Nm (123 lbft) @ 2300rpm. V6: 15deg 81 x 90.3mm; 2792cc; compr 10:1; 128kW (171.7bhp) @ 5800rpm; 45.8kg (61.5bhp)/l; 235Nm (173 lbft) @ 4200rpm.
ENGINE STRUCTURE Zetec 2 belt-driven ohc; 4 valve; aluminium cyl head and block; fuel injection, electronic ignition; 5-bearing crank. V6: 2 valves per cyl; sohc per block; aluminium heads, iron block.
TRANSMISSION front wheel drive; 5-speed manual synchromesh gearbox; 4-speed automatic option; final drive 4.53:1, automatic 4.24; V6 4.06:1 automatic 3.94.
CHASSIS steel monocoque; ifs by MacPherson struts, lower wishbones, anti-roll bar; irs, semi-trailing arms on sub-frames, coil springs, anti roll bar; telescopic dampers; hydraulic servo disc brakes, front 28.8cm (11.3in) dia ventilated, rear 28cm (11in) dia solid, ABS; rack and pinion PAS; 75 (16.5gal) (19.74 US gal) fuel tank; 195/65 TR14 tyres, 6J rims, V6 205/60 HR15.
DIMENSIONS wheelbase 283.5cm (111.6in); track 154cm (60.6in) front, 151cm (59.5in) rear; length 461.5cm (181.7in); width 180cm (70.9in); height 172.5cm (67.9in); ground clearance 15cm (5.9in); turning circle 11.7m (38.4ft).
EQUIPMENT V6 electronic traction control standard.
PERFORMANCE maximum speed 176.6kph(110mph), V6 204kph (127.1mph); 31.9kph (19.9mph) @ 1000rpm; 0-100kph (62mph) 12.0sec, V6 10.6sec; 18.4kg/kW (13.7kg/bhp), V6 13kg/kW (9.7kg/bhp); fuel consumption approx 8.8l/100km (32mpg), V6 9.9l/100km (28.6mpg).
PRICE 2.0 Aspen £15,995; GLX V6 £20,550, Ghia V6 £23,300.

Three levels of trim were offered; Aspen, GLX, and Ghia.

1995 Galaxy turbodiesel, 2.3, and 4x4

Galaxy's Volkswagen turbocharged diesel engine provided good economy and a moderate turn of speed. By the time the Ford 2.3 petrol engine was introduced in March 1997 the model was already taking 30 per cent of the MPV market, its total of 15,000 outselling the VW Sharan in Britain by 8000 in 1996. The new engine, developed by Cosworth, also found a home in the Scorpio and, coming between the 2.0 and V6, soon accounted for up to half of the Galaxys sold. It almost matched the V6's performance while offering something close to the 2.0-litre's economy. The GLX 2.3 had anti-lock brakes, driver's airbag, and electric windows, and the Ghia added alloy wheels, roof rails, and a heated windscreen. There was also a Ghia X with a CD player, fog lights, cruise control, fuel computer, and air conditioning. The VW Sharan did not get the 2.3 engine but it did have an exclusive 82kW (110bhp) Audi/VW turbodiesel. The 4-wheel drive Galaxy introduced in January 1997 competed with sports utilities and came only with the 2.8-litre V6 engine and automatic transmission. The VW Synchro system sent nearly 100 per cent of torque to the front wheels until slippery conditions were encountered. A viscous coupling then diverted up to 75 per cent to whichever wheels could make best use of it.

INTRODUCTIONS February 1995. BODY minivan; 5-doors, 6-seats; weight 1670kg (3681.7lb), 2.3 1565kg (3450.2lb), 4x4 1840kg (4056.5lb). ENGINE 4-cylinders, in-line; front, transverse; 79.5mm x 95.5mm, 1896cc; compr 19.5:1; 66kW (88.5bhp) @ 4000rpm; 34.8kW (46.7bhp)/l; 197Nm (145 lbft) @ 1940rpm. 2.3: 108.1kW (145bhp); 203 Nm (150 lbft). ENGINE STRUCTURE Single ohc, cast iron cylinder head and block; Bosch VE fuel injection with electronic engine management; turbocharger, air/air intercooler; 5-bearing crankshaft. TRANSMISSION front wheel drive; 5-speed manual synchromesh gearbox; final drive 4.24:1. 2.3 4.53:1, automatic 4.24. 4x4 3.94:1. CHASSIS steel monocoque structure; independent front suspension by MacPherson struts, lower wishbones, anti-roll bar; independent rear suspension, semi-trailing arms on sub-frames, coil springs, anti roll bar; telescopic dampers; hydraulic servo disc brakes, front 28.8cm (11.3in) dia ventilated, rear 28cm (11in) dia solid, ABS; rack and pinion PAS; 75 (16.5 gal)

(19.7 US gal) fuel tank; 195/65 TR14 tyres, 6J rims, V6 205/60 HR15. DIMENSIONS wheelbase 283.5cm (111.6in); track front 154cm (60.6in), rear 151cm (59.5in); length 461.5cm (181.7in); width 180cm (70.9in); height 172.5cm (67.9in); ground clearance 15cm (5.9in); turning circle 11.7m (38.4ft). PERFORMANCE maximum speed 257kph (160mph) *Ford*, 2.3 194.2kph (121mph); 40.7kph (25.4mph) @ 1000rpm TD; 0-100kph (62mph) 18sec, 2.3 10.1sec, 4x4 11.6sec; 25.3kg/kW (18.9lg/bhp) TD; fuel consumption approx 6.7l/100km (42.4mpg), 2.3 10l/100km (28mpg). PRICE Aspen TD £16,995, Ghia TD £20,450. 2.3 GLX £20,205; Ghia £21,585, Ghia X £22,635. 4x4 Ghia £25,750, Ghia X 4x4 £26,810.

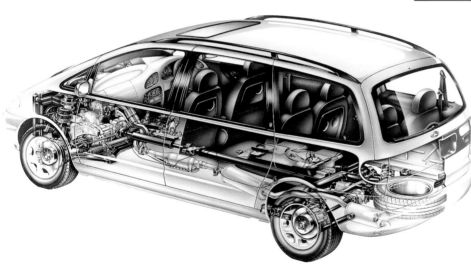

1995 Explorer

A huge success in America, where it outsold all its rivals until suffering in the Firestone tyre debacle, the Explorer was previewed with its native V8 engine in 1995. By the time it appeared at the Birmingham Motor Show in October 1996 it was re-equipped with a new sohc V6 and engineered for right hand drive. Ford was keen to remain in the market for Sports Utility Vehicles (SUVs) following the demise of the Maverick. British drivers generally liked their tough nature and the Explorer exemplified the rugged, businesslike qualities from the spiritual home of the SUV even though it would not be available with its 156.6kW (210bhp) V8 or as the up-market Mercury Mountaineer. Still the new engine that replaced an older 119.3kW (160bhp) V6 gave a good account of itself and was only 3.7kW (5bhp) short. Its automatic was a smooth-shifting 5-speeder, and the UK market did not import the short wheelbase 2-door version, which had a reputation for over-sensitive handling unsuitable for Europe. Unusually for an American SUV the Explorer was not of unitary construction. It was based on the ladder frame chassis originally designed for the Ranger pick-up. Bulky and not as refined as its European rivals, but enormously roomy and well equipped, the Explorer remained the world's most successful SUV with over 2m sold.

INTRODUCTION December 1996. BODY saloon; 5-doors, 5-seats. ENGINE 6-cylinders, 60deg V; front; 100.3mm x 84.3mm, 4014cc; compr 9.7:1; 153kW (205.2bhp) @ 5250rpm; 38.1kW (51.1bhp)/l; 353Nm (260 lbft) @ 3000rpm.
ENGINE STRUCTURE chain-driven single ohc per bank; aluminium cylinder heads, cast iron block; Ford EEC-V electronic fuel injection; 4-bearing crankshaft.
TRANSMISSION rear wheel drive; electrically engaged 4 wheel drive; 5-speed automatic; final drive 3.73:1; limited slip differential.
CHASSIS ladder frame chassis; ifs by short and long arm links, torsion bars, anti-roll bar; rear suspension live axle, leaf springs, anti roll bar; telescopic dampers; hydraulic servo brakes, front 28.6cm (11.3in) dia ventilated, rear 28.5cm (11.2in) dia discs, ABS; rack and pinion PAS; 72l (15.8gal) (19 US gal) fuel tank; 225/705 R16 tyres, 7J rims.
DIMENSIONS wheelbase 283cm (111.4in); track 149cm (58.7in); length 453cm (178.4in); width 188cm (74in); height 180cm (70.9in); ground clearance 20cm (7.9in); turning circle 12.5m (41ft).
EQUIPMENT central locking, electric mirrors, seat adjusters, sunroof, and windows, stereo, air conditioning, leather upholstery £1000. 3-year warranty.
PERFORMANCE maximum speed 171kph (106.5mph) *Ford*; 49.1kph (30.6mph) @ 1000rpm; 0-100kph (62mph) 10.9sec; fuel consumption 15.1l/100km (18.7mpg) *Autocar*.
PRICE 2000 4.0 XLT £26,400, 4.0 North Face £27,900.

1995 Escort 1.8i 16v

In a bold return to a 4-year model cycle the Escort was once again rejuvenated with a revised front, a small oval grille, a completely redesigned facia, and a great deal of effort was expended on build quality and the elimination of noise vibration and harshness (NVH). The CE99 programme (subsequently CW170) was co-ordinated with an American initiative codenamed Helios that began as a response to the approaching Chrysler Neon of which much was expected. With the mid-1990s emphasis on the globalisation of Ford there was talk of the Escort being a world car on the lines of the Toyota Corolla, but not for the first time this proved illusory.

Mechanically much the same as before, the new Escort was a quieter, more refined car that slightly cast aside the model's traditional emphasis on speed and power. Its launch followed the withdrawal in 1994 of the XR models that had been Ford sporting flagships since 1981. The RS Cosworths had stopped in 1995 and the RS2000 was due to follow in 1996. In some ways the 1995 revisions improved a car that had been rather less than perfect in 1990; the ride was enhanced, the interior was classy, safety improvements such as twin airbags were included, and the entire range from 1.3i to Ghia, 3-door, 5-door, estate, and cabriolet was truly mature.

INTRODUCTION Jan 1995, produced until 1998.
BODY saloon; 3-doors, weight 1065kg (2348lb); 5-doors, weight 1085kg (2392lb), estate 1120kg (2469.2lb), cabriolet 1175kg (2590.4lb), 4/5-seats.
ENGINE 4-cylinders, in-line; front; transverse; 80.6mm x 88mm, 1796cc; compr 10:1; 77kW (103.3bhp) @ 5500rpm; 42.9kW (57.5bhp)/l; 156Nm (115 lbft) @ 4000rpm.
ENGINE STRUCTURE 2 belt-driven ohc, 4 valves per cylinder; aluminium cylinder head, iron block; electronic fuel injection and engine management; 5-bearing crankshaft.
TRANSMISSION front rear wheel drive; 5-speed manual synchromesh gearbox; final drive 3.82:1.
CHASSIS steel monocoque structure; ifs by struts, coil springs and anti-toll bar; rear suspension torsion beam axle and coil springs; telescopic dampers; hydraulic servo brakes, front 24cm (9.5in) dia ventilated disc, rear 18cm (7.1in) dia drums, ABS optional; rack and pinion PAS; 55l (12 gal) (14.5 US gal) fuel tank; 175/65HR14 tyres, 5J rims, various options.

DIMENSIONS wheelbase 252.5cm (99.4in); track 144cm (56.7in) front, 146cm (57.5in) rear; length 413.5cm (162.8in); width 169cm (66.5in); height 139.5cm (54.9in); ground clearance 12cm (4.7in); turning circle 10m (32.8ft).
EQUIPMENT driver's airbag, passenger airbag optional, electric front windows, central locking, electric mirrors £155.
PERFORMANCE maximum speed 187kph (116.5mph) *Ford*; 36.5kph (22.7mph) @ 1000rpm; 0-100kph (62mph) 10.7sec; 13.8kg/kW (10.3kg/bhp) 3-doors, 14.5kg/kW (10.8kg/bhp) estate; fuel consumption 7.1l/100km (40mpg).
PRICE £12,255.

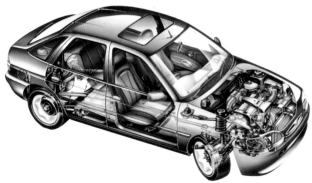

1995 Escort range

Engine	Max speed	0-96kph (60mph)	Weight	Trims	Body styles
1.3i 44kW (59bhp)	152.5kph (95mph)	16.4sec	1008kg (2222.2lb)	Encore	3-5-door, estate
1.4i 55.2kW (74bhp)	168.6kph (105mph)	13.5sec	1049kg (2312.6lb)	Encore L, LX	3-4-5door, estate
1.6i 16v 66.4kW (89bhp)	176.6kph (110mph)	11.5sec	1103kg (2431.7lb)	L, LX, Ghia, Si	3-4-5-door, estate
1.8i 16v 77.6kW(104bhp)	186.2kph (116mph)	10.0sec	1083kg (2387.6lb)	LX, Ghia, Si	3-4-5-door, estate
1.8i 16v 95.5kW (128bhp)	201kph (125.2mph)	9.1sec	1165kg (2568.4lb)	Ghia	Cabriolet
2.0i 16v 110.4kW (148bhp)	208kph (129.6mph)	8.7sec	1165kg (2568.4lb)	RS2000	3-door
1.8D 44kW (59bhp)	152.5kph (95mph)	16.7sec	1100kg (2425.1lb)	Encore, L, LX	3-4-5-door, estate
1.8TD 66.4kW (89bhp)	171.8kph (107mph)	10.8sec	1139kg (2511lb)	Encore, L, LX, Ghia	3-4-5-door, estate

Equipment	Encore	L	LX	Ghia	Si and RS
Driver's airbag	o	o	o	o	o
Passenger airbag	optn	optn	optn	optn	optn
Side-impact bars	o	o	o	o	o
Seatbelt pretensioners	o	o	o	o	o
Adjustable lumbar support	–	–	–	o	–
Electric front windows	–	–	o	o	o
Electric mirrors	o	o	o	o	o
Power steering	o 1.8TD	o 1.6,1.8	o	o	o
Central locking	–	–	o	o	o
Engine immobiliser	o	o	o	o	o (not diesel)
Alarm system	o	o	o	o	o
60/40 split rear seat	o	o	o	o	o
tinted windows	o	o	o	o	o
RDS radio-cassette	–	–	o	o	o
ABS	–	–	-	–	o RS only
o = standard equipment. optn = optional. – = not available					

Prices			
3-door		**5-door**	
1.3 CFi Encore	£ 9,495	1.3 CFi Encore	£ 9,915
1.4 EFi Encore	£ 9,760	1.4 EFi Encore	£10,180
1.8d Encore	£ 9,760	1.8d Encore	£10,180
1.4L EFi	£10,095	1.8 TD Encore	£11,155
1.8 LD	£10,095	1.6i 16v Si	£12,350
1.6i 16v	£10,630	1.8i 16v Si	£12,675
1.8TD Encore	£10,735		
1.8TD L	£11,070	**4-door/5-door**	
1.4 EFi LX	£11,320	1.4 EFi L	£10,515
1.8D LX	£11,320	1.8 LD	£10,515
1.6i 16v LX	£11,575	1.6i 16v L	£11,050
1.6i 16v Si	£11,930	1.8L TD	£11,490
1.8 TD LX	£12,015	1.4 EFi LX	£11,740
1.8i 16v Si	£12,255	1.8D LX	£11,740
2.0 EFi 16v RS 2000	£16,315	1.6i 16v LX	£11,995
2.0 EFi 16v RS 2000 4x4	£17,370	1.8i 16v LX	£12,320
2.0 16v RS Cosworth	£23,495	1.8TD LX	£12,435
2.0 16v RS Cosworth luxe	£26,925	1.6i 16v Ghia	£12,865
		1.8i 16v Ghia	£13,190
		1.8 Ghia TD	£13,305
Estates			
1.3 Cfi Encore	£10,670		
1.6i 16v L	£11,805		
1.8TD LX	£13,190	**Cabriolet**	
1.8Ghia TD	£14,060	1.8 16v Si	£16,995

Concept Fords like Probe III of 1981 invariably had a purpose. Probe's was to accustom public eyes to the lines of the Sierra, due the following year. It was radical but in the event it probably failed in its task. Confidence seemed to give out during Sierra's final phases, but there was no such faltering with the Ka. A prototype was shown at the 1994 Geneva Motor Show, ostensibly to gauge reaction, but really the decision to go ahead with a Sub-B class small car had already been made. The Geneva car used a shortened Fiesta platform, its overall length 335cm (131.9in), and it was designed by Ford Europe under Claude Lobo. The press speculated about it having the two-stroke engine that had just undergone field trials in 50 Fiestas, but there was scant chance. Concept Ka was reputed to be around 755kg (1664.5lb), or 75kg (165.3lb) lighter than a Fiesta (the production car was heavier) and according to Richard Parry-Jones, Ford of Europe head of product develoment, the production Ka would have strut front suspension, and confirmed the likelihood of a Peugeot-style torsion beam rear axle.

By the Turin Motor Show in May 1996 plans for Ka were well advanced. Ghia produced the Saetta, a roadster version of the Ka due to appear at the Paris Motor Show in the autumn.

The front was pure Ka, the rear modified and retro-like, in the vogue of the VW concept Beetle and the Renault Fiftie, with a spinal bar following the line of the Ka that probably provided some of the missing roof's structural integrity. Resplendent in blue and silver Saetta was inspirational, closely following the lines of the approaching production model. The interior was pure Ka, except for patent leather upholstery and silver console mouldings that were a pastiche of 1960s trendiness. Ghia added a tachometer to lend a sporty air, but Saetta was more of a fun roadster than a sports car.

Its real significance lay in the way it introduced so-called New Edge styling that was to play such an important role in shaping Fords of the 1990s and the 21st century. Camillo Pardo, the American who led the Saetta project at Ghia, said: "It is still edge design, but we are exploring surface development and using softer shapes and creases to get away from elliptical shapes."

Saetta created enormous interest at Turin because it represented a profound development in automotive style and above all demonstrated that Ford's hangover from Sierra and 1990 Escort was finally over. Saetta was proof that style and chic were going to be as important in future as technical prowess.

Ford was cautious about Saetta's implications, apart from its obvious relationship to Ka. As soon as the show was over, and Autocar's Peter Robinson had driven it cautiously on a special preview, it was crated up and flown to Detroit to be looked at carefully by senior management.

1996 Ka, Ka2

An important ingredient of the body style was the production technology that enabled it to be made. Chris Clements, head designer, said that 5 years earlier it would not have been contemplated because body-press techniques could not guarantee knife-edge fits and close-cut shut-lines. It was an ingenious mixture of fluid curves and near-flat panels, continuous lines between the practical polypropylene mouldings below the waistline and the sheet steel, providing exquisite balance. The proportions were exemplary, the wide-tracked and wheel-at-each-corner stance a masterpiece, the work of Chris Svensson, a former Royal College of Art student. Production Ka was crisper than the roly-poly prototype shown at Geneva in 1994, and had the further virtue of cutting 25% off a Fiesta's build time. It was as wide as the Fiesta, yet slightly taller, with more head room and shoulder room. There were two equipment levels, Ka and Ka2, only one engine option, the old pushrod Endura-E that was light and cheap to make. The interior was just as radical as the outside, the facia had sweeping curves and although in reality quite basic, looked stylish and well-resourced. Cars with power steering had 2.9 turns lock to lock instead of 4.2, different castor angles, fatter tyres and shorter gearing. PAS buyers would want different driving qualities.

INTRODUCTION 1996.
BODY saloon; 3-doors, 4-seats; weight 870kg (1918lb).
ENGINE 4-cylinders, in-line; front; transverse; 75mm x 75.5mm, 1299cc; compr 8.8:1; 44kW (59bhp) @ 5000rpm; 33.9kW (45.4bhp)/l; 103Nm (76 lbft) @ 2500rpm.
ENGINE STRUCTURE pushrod ohv; chain-driven camshaft, cast iron cylinder head and block; Ford EEC-V electronic sequential fuel injection and engine management; 5-bearing crankshaft.
TRANSMISSION front wheel drive; 5-speed synchromesh gearbox; final drive 4.06:1.
CHASSIS steel monocoque; ifs by MacPherson strut, offset coil springs, lower A-arms, anti-roll bar; rear suspension semi-independent twist beam with coil spring damper units; hydraulic servo brakes, front 24cm (9.5in) dia disc, rear drums, ABS optional; rack and pinion, optional PAS; 42l (9.2 gal) (11.1 US gal) fuel tank; 165/65R13 tyres, 5J rims.
DIMENSIONS wheelbase 245cm (96.5in); track 139.5cm (54.9in) front, 141cm (55.5in) rear; length 362cm (142.5in); width 164cm (64.6in); height 140cm (55.1in); ground clearance 14cm (5.5in); turning circle 10.3m (33.8ft).
EQUIPMENT Ka rear wash-wipe, driver's airbag, radio/cassette player standard, passenger airbag, air conditioning and alloy wheels opt. Ka2 PAS electric windows standard.
PERFORMANCE maximum speed 155kph (96.6mph); 32.4kph (20.2mph) @ 1000rpm; 0-100kph (62mph) 15.4sec; 19.8kg/kW (14.7kg/bhp); 6.7l/100km (42.2mpg).
PRICE £7350; Ka2 8195.

1996 Fiesta Classic

Old habits died hard at Ford, and just as the Populars of the 1950s and 1960s were born-again versions of superseded models, so in the 1990s the Fiesta of the 1980s carried on much as before. It was not called Popular. A new name was coined, implying continuity and good taste rather than bargain basement, so it was called Classic and came with 1.1, 1.3, and diesel engines. Different trim versions were distinguished as Quartz and Cabaret, 3- and 5-door prices were the same, and power steering was an option (at £430) only on the front-end heavy diesels. The 1.3 was a 152.5kph (95mph) car and reached 100kph (62mph) in 14.2sec; the more economical diesel, with much the same power to weight ratio, was only a shade slower at 150.9kph (94mph) and 15.4sec. Launched originally as the front-rank Fiesta in 1976, it was a lighter car than its successor, but the design of the all-iron pushrod crossflow 2-valve engine, now designated appropriately Endura-E, went back to the 1967 Cortina Mark II. Despite much modification over the years it was past its best although it had acquired fuel injection, necessary for stringent emission requirements of the 1990s, but not much more power. In 1976 the 74mm x 55.7mm 957cc had given 33.6kW (45bhp) @ 6000rpm, and the 74 x 65mm 1117cc 39.5kW (53bhp) @ 6000rpm.

INTRODUCTION 1976 as Fiesta II and 1989 as Fiesta III.
BODY saloon; 3 or 5-doors, 4-seats; weight 825kg (1818.8lb), diesel 875kg (1929lb).
ENGINE 4-cylinders, in-line; front; transverse; 1.1, 68.7 x 75.5; 1119cc; compr 8.8:1; 37kW (49.6bhp) @ 5200rpm; 33.1kW/l (44.3bhp/l); 83Nm (61 lbft) @ 3000rpm.
1.3: 74mm x 75.5mm, 1299cc; cr 8.8:1; 44kw (59bhp) @ 5000rpm; 33.9kW/l (45.4bhp/l); 103Nm (76 lbft) @ 2500rpm. Diesel 82.5 x 82mm; 1753cc; compr 21.5:1; 44kW (59bhp) @ 4800rpm; 25.1kW (33.7bhp)/l; 110Nm (81 lbft) @ 2500rpm.
ENGINE STRUCTURE pushrod ohv, chain-driven camshaft; cast iron cylinder head and block; electronic single point fuel injection; 5-bearing crankshaft.
TRANSMISSION front wheel drive; sdp clutch; gearbox 5-speed synchromesh; final drive 4.06:1, diesel 3.59:1.
CHASSIS steel monocoque structure; ifs by MacPherson struts, coil springs, anti-roll bar; rear suspension torsion beam axle; telescopic dampers;

telescopic dampers; hydraulic, vacuum servo 24cm (9.5in) front disc brakes; rear drums 19.1cm (7.5in); rack and pinion steering; 42l (9.2 gal) (11.1 US gal) fuel tank; 145R-13, 155/70R-13 or 165R-13 tyres, 4.5 or 5J rims.
DIMENSIONS wheelbase 244.5cm (96.3in); track 139cm (54.7in) front, 138.5cm (54.5in) rear; length 374.5cm (147.4in); width 160cm (63in); height 138cm (54.3in); ground clearance 14cm (5.5in); turning circle 10.3m (33.8ft).
PERFORMANCE maximum speed 153kph (95.3mph), 143kph (89.1mph) 1.1, 152kph (94.7mph) diesel); 33.5kph (20.9mph) @ 1000rpm; 0-100kph (62mph) 14.7sec, 18.1sec 1.1, 16sec diesel; 22.3kg/kW (16.6kg/bhp), 19.9kg/kW (14.8kg/bhp) diesel; fuel consumption 8.7-7.4l/100km (33-38mpg), diesel 5.3l/100km (53.3mpg).
PRICE 1997 1.1 £7615-£8015; 1.1 Quartz £8015-8445; 1.3 Cabaret £8415-£8845; 1.8D £8040-£8470; 1.8D Quartz £8440-£8870.

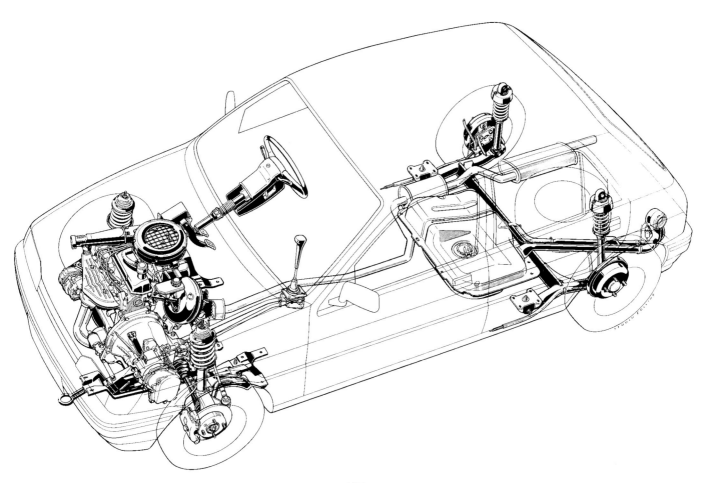

407

1996 Fiesta 1.25, 1.4, 1.6

BE91 was the codename for a complete reskin of the Fiesta round the 16-valve Zetec-SE engine. The platform was much the same as before but the body was extensively altered, not radically; it failed to gain the Ka's bold New Edge appearance, but with the corporate oval grille it looked sufficiently different to make sure customers knew they were buying the latest model.

The Zetec-SE was smoother and quieter than any previous Ford dohc 16-valve engine and not merely a redesign of the combustion process as with previous initiatives. It was all-aluminium instead of iron and aluminium, and cast-in ribs maintained the structural stiffness necessary for quietness and smooth running. The previous Zetec's hydraulic tappets reverted to ordinary mechanical means of operating the valves, yet the new engine was reckoned to be almost maintenance free with oil changes scheduled for 10,000 miles, new spark plugs at 30,000 miles, and routine valve clearance checks at 100,000 miles. Its greatest achievement lay in saving weight. At just 89kg (196.2lb) it weighed less than half its predecessor's 122kg (269lb), not only through the extensive use of aluminium, but also from making components such as the complex inlet valve tracts of plastic, and the cam cover from magnesium alloy.

INTRODUCTION January 1996.
BODY saloon; 3/5-doors, 4-seats; weight 940kg (2072.3lb).
ENGINE 4-cylinders, in-line; front; transverse; 71.9mm x 76.5mm, 1242cc; compr 10:1; 55kW (73.8bhp) @ 5200rpm; 44.3kW/l (59.4bhp/l); 110Nm (81 lbft) @ 4000rpm. 1.4: 76 x 76.5mm, 1388cc; 66kW (88.5bhp) @ 5500rpm; 47.6kW/l (63.8bhp/l); 122Nm (90 lbft) @ 4000rpm.
ENGINE STRUCTURE 2 belt-driven ohc; 4 valve; aluminium cylinder head and block; EEC-V multi-point sequential fuel injection, distributorless electronic ignition; 5-bearing crankshaft.
TRANSMISSION front wheel drive; gearbox 5-speed synchromesh; final drive 4.27:1. 1.4, 3.84:1.
CHASSIS steel monocoque structure; ifs by MacPherson struts, coil springs, anti-roll bar; rear suspension torsion beam axle; telescopic dampers; hydraulic, vacuum servo 24cm (9.45in) front ventilated disc brakes; rear drums 19.1cm (7.5in); rack and pinion PAS; 42l (9.2 gal)(11.1 US gal) fuel tank; 145R-13, 155/70R-13 or 165R-13 tyres, 4.5 or 5J rims.

DIMENSIONS wheelbase 244.5cm (96.3in); track 143cm (56.3in) front, 137.5cm (54.1in) rear; length 383cm (150.8in); width 163cm (64.2in); height 141cm (55.5in); ground clearance 14cm (5.5in); turning circle 10.3m (33.8ft).
EQUIPMENT ABS optional; driver's side airbag, Ford stereo, PAS, electric sunroof standard.
PERFORMANCE maximum speed 170kph (105.9mph), 1.4 171.8kph (107mph); 30.9kph (19.3mph) @ 1000rpm; 0-100kph (62mph) 12.7sec, 1.4 10.7sec; 17.1kg/kW (12.7kg/bhp); fuel con 6l/100km (47.08mpg), 1.4 6.2l/100km (45.6mpg).
PRICE 1.25 Cfi 3-door Encore £9965, 5-door Si £10335, Ghia £10630. 1.4Si £10,750, option packs £395 and £225, air conditioning £470. 1.6i Encore CTX £11,700; 1.6i L CTX £12,135.

409

1996 Fiesta 1.8 diesel

Among the new Fiesta's virtues was improved handling and road holding. The platform was reinforced to improve refinement, and stretched to include a crushable area at the front. The gearbox casing was webbed and ribbed to reduce noise.

Success in the roadworthiness of both Fiesta and Mondeo was the responsibility of Richard Parry-Jones, now accountable for all Ford's European small and medium cars. Together with consultant Jackie Stewart he had wrought a substantial improvement in the behaviour of the whole Ford range. Ironically it had been achieved when Ford's involvement in international motor racing was at its least, although a presence was retained in the world rally championship. Attention was concentrated instead on more practical, seemingly more mundane matters, such as the flourishing diesel market. This had been a neglected field because, owing to its dependence on volume production – economies of scale – Ford had yet to be wholly convinced the diesel market was going to be sustained. The Fiesta diesel was a development of the overhead cam 1.8-litre from the old CVH range, now known as Endura-D, although it was not yet turbocharged to give it a performance on par with its petrol counterparts.

INTRODUCTION January 1996.
BODY saloon; 3/5-doors, 4-seats; weight 1020kg (2248.7lb).
ENGINE 4-cylinders, in-line; front; transverse; 82.5mm x 82mm, 1753cc; compr 21.5:1; 44kW (59bhp) @ 4800rpm; 25.1kW (33.7bhp)/l; 105Nm (77 lbft) @ 2500rpm.
ENGINE STRUCTURE single gear and toothed belt driven ohc; 2 valve; iron cylinder head and block; fuel injection.
TRANSMISSION front wheel drive; gearbox 5-speed synchromesh; final drive 3.84:1.
CHASSIS steel monocoque structure; ifs by MacPherson struts, coil springs, anti-roll bar; rear suspension torsion beam axle; telescopic dampers; hydraulic, vacuum servo 24cm (9.5in) front ventilated disc brakes; rear drums 19.1cm (7.5in); rack and pinion PAS; 42l (9.2 gal) (11.1 US gal) fuel tank; 145R-13, 155/70R-13 or 165R-13 tyres, 4.5 or 5J rims.
DIMENSIONS wheelbase 244.5cm (96.3in); track 143cm (56.3in) front, 137.5cm (54.1in) rear; length 383cm (150.8in); width 163cm (64.2in); height 141cm (55.5in); ground clearance 14cm (5.5in); turning circle 10.3m (33.8ft).
EQUIPMENT ABS optional; driver's side airbag, Ford stereo, PAS, electric sunroof standard.
PERFORMANCE maximum speed 155kph (96.6mph); 34.3kph (21.4mph) @ 1000rpm; 0-100kph (62mph) 17.4sec; 23.2kg/kW (17.3kg/bhp); fuel consumption 5.8l/100km (48.7mpg).
PRICE 1.8D Encore £9195; Ghia £11,560.

Ford's European attitude to the development of diesel cars was not matched by the UK government's curious stance on keeping the price of diesel fuel high.

411

1996 Mondeo

Revisions three and a half years into Mondeo's term were carefully calculated. A tidier oval air intake, and wrap-around rear lights, detail changes to the facia and switchgear, new upholstery materials, and 4cm (1.6in) more knee-room in the back were among the visible items.

There was a new sporty V6, the ST-24, and an economy 1.6-litre Zetec; the gearshift was now cable-operated and more precise, and a weight-saving programme checked the customary trend for cars to put on unwanted kgs throughout their model cycles. In the interests of performance and economy the Mondeo lost 16-18kg (35.3-39.7lb). A gain in economy of 16 per cent was expected from taller gearing on the 1.6; 3.84:1 like the 1.8 provided four-gears-plus-overdrive fifth.

Safety was given a makeover with modifications aimed at improving crashworthiness, the airbags were brought up to date, side airbags were offered as an option, seat belts given pre-tensioners, and a 3-point belt introduced in the middle of the back seat. A brake light was positioned high in the tail and on GLX models 4-channel anti-lock brakes were standard. The ST-24 had a 2.5-litre 125.3kW (168bhp) V6, traction control, and specially sporty suspension.

Specification 2.0 16v.
INTRODUCTION September 1996.
BODY saloon; 4-doors, 5-seats; weight 1240kg (2733.7lb), 5-door estate 1300kg (2866lb).
ENGINE 4-cylinders, in-line; front; transverse 84.8mm x 88mm, 1988cc; compr 10:1; 96kW (128.7bhp) @ 5700rpm; 48.3kW (64.8bhp)/l; 176Nm (130 lbft) @ 3700rpm.
ENGINE STRUCTURE 2 belt-driven ohc; 4 valve; aluminium cyl head, iron block; sequential fuel inj, electronic engine management; 5-bearing crank.
TRANSMISSION front wheel drive; gearbox 5-speed synchromesh; automatic option £495; final drive 3.84:1; automatic 3.92:1; traction control option.
CHASSIS steel monocoque; ifs by MacPherson struts, coil springs, anti-roll bar; irs, multi-link coil springs, anti roll bar; telescopic dampers; hydraulic servo disc brakes, front 27.8cm (10.9in) dia ventilated, rear 25.2cm (10in) dia, ABS; rack and pinion PAS; 61.5l (13.5 gal) (16.3 US gal) fuel tank; 185/65HR14, 195/60HR15, 205/55HR15 tyres, 5.5, 6J rims.

DIMENSIONS wheelbase 270.5cm (106.5in); track front 150.5cm (59.25in), rear 148.5cm (58.5in); length 456cm (179.5in); width 175cm (68.9in); height 148cm (58.3in); ground clearance 12cm (4.7in); turning circle 10.9m (35.8ft).
EQUIPMENT automatic £925, metallic paint £230, passenger airbag £325, air conditioning £470.
PERFORMANCE maximum speed 200.7kph (125mph) *Autocar*; 32kph (19.9mph) @ 1000rpm; 0-100kph (62mph) 9.8sec; 12.9kg/kW (9.6kg/bhp), estate 13.5kg/kW (10.1kg/bhp); fuel consumption 10.5l/100km (26.8mpg).
PRICE 1.6 Aspen £12,395; 2.0LX £13,500; 2.0 Ghia £15,995; 2.5 24v V6 Ghia X £20,850; 2.0Si estate £15,950.

In the light of experience, ride and handling were improved throughout the range and engine management electronics recalibrated, completing a comprehensive package of changes that kept Mondeo ahead of the game.

1996 Scorpio 2.3 16v

Revisions to the Scorpio took place over 2 years. In 1994 the Ultima was introduced with the 24-valve Cosworth V6 and the old Cologne V6 phased out. This left a gap in the engine range between the economy 2.0 16-valve and the powerful Cosworth, with £10,000 between them. Accordingly in 1996 the 2.0 was dropped and a new 2.3 introduced with more power than the old V6, 111kW (149bhp) against 108kW (145bhp), but short of 2 cylinders. Accounting for something like half of Scorpio sales, its executive-class drivers had to be persuaded that it was as smooth running as a six, so the redoubtable Dr Frederick Lanchester (1868-1946) was called upon for a solution. His contra-rotating balancer shafts, with equal and opposite unbalanced weights to cancel engine imbalance, were invoked to secure a noise reduction of 6dB and minimise vibration. Despite the complications, the engine was actually 3.4kg (7.5lb) lighter than the old 2.0-litre and although it demanded over 3,000rpm to get the best out of it, served the Scorpio well in its declining years. Gearing was raised over the 2.0, making the 2.3 a relaxed motorway car, which the optional 4-speed automatic transmission with electronic control of shifting complemented in both its Sport and Economy modes. Ride and handling were improved with Mondeo-style revisions to the front suspension.

INTRODUCTION August 1996. BODY saloon; 4-doors, 5-seats; weight 1440kg (3174.6lb), estate 1495kg (3295.9lb). ENGINE 4-cylinders, in-line; front; 89.6mm x 91mm, 2295cc; compr 10:1; 108kW (144.8bhp) @ 5600rpm; 47.1kW (63.1bhp)/l; 202Nm (149 lbft) @ 4500rpm . ENGINE STRUCTURE 2 belt-driven ohc, 4-valve; aluminium cylinder head, iron block; EEC-V electronic fuel injection and engine management; 5-bearing crankshaft; 2 balancer shafts running x 2 engine speed. TRANSMISSION rear wheel drive; gearbox 5-speed synchromesh; 4-speed automatic option; final drive 3.91:1. CHASSIS steel monocoque structure; independent front suspension struts and lower wishbones, coil springs, anti-roll bar; independent rear suspension semi-trailing arms, coil springs, anti roll bar; telescopic dampers; hydraulic servo disc brakes, front 25cm (9.8in) dia ventilated, rear 25.3cm (10in) dia, ABS; rack and pinion PAS; 70l (15.4 gal) (18.5 US gal) fuel tank; 195/65HR15, 205/60VR15, 215/60VR15 tyres 6J, 6.5J rims. DIMENSIONS wheelbase 277cm (109in); track 148cm (58.3in) front, 149.5cm (58.9in) rear; length 482.5cm (190in); width 176cm (69.3in); height 140cm (55.1in); ground clearance 12cm (4.7in); turning circle 10.4m (34.1ft). EQUIPMENT Ghia: alloy wheels, stereo, all electric windows, central locking, electric mirrors, alarm. PERFORMANCE maximum speed 195.9kph (122mph) *Autocar*; 36kph (22.4mph) @ 1000rpm; 0-100kph (62mph) 10.3sec; 13.3kg/kW (9.9kg/bhp), estate 13.8kg/kW (10.3kg/bhp); fuel consumption 10.5l/100km (26.9mpg). PRICE £18,370.

1997 Puma 1.7

With the RS and XR models gone, new ways were found of making Fords glamorous. It remained important to get the most out of each platform and SE161 was a coupe based, like the Ka, on the much-improved Fiesta and introduced at the 1997 Geneva Motor Show. The Lynx concept at 1996 Geneva, like the Saetta, had curved roof hoops of carbon fibre, but extended rather than foreshortened the Fiesta framework by 25cm (9.8in) to 408cm (160.6in), 4cm (1.6in) longer than an Escort. The production Puma kept the Fiesta wheelbase and introduced Ka-style New Edge, rounded off to suit the sporty theme. Instead of the Ka's modest pushrods, it had the Yamaha-inspired 16-valve Zetec-SE with Variable Camshaft Timing (VCT) shifting the inlet valves' phasing, though not their lift or dwell, according to engine speed and load. A unique feature of VCT was continuous electronic operation rather than prompting by anything mechanical. A stiffer body shell than Fiesta, 1mm extra on the front anti-roll bar, 5 per cent up on spring rates, and 30 per cent on the rear suspension's twist beam made Puma a real driver's car. The 2000 limited edition Racing Puma had 114.1kW (153bhp), and extended aluminium wheel arches for £22,750, and last of all the 2000-off £13,995 Puma Thunder came in Magnum Grey, or Moondust with black leather trim.

INTRODUCTION Feb 1997, production to November 2001.
BODY coupe; 2-doors, 2+2-seats; weight 1039kg (2290.6lb).
ENGINE 4-cylinders, in-line; front; transverse; 80mm x 83.5mm, 1679cc; compr 10.3:1; 92kW (123.4bhp) @ 6300rpm; 54.8kW (73.5bhp)/l; 157Nm (116 lbft) @ 4500rpm.
ENGINE STRUCTURE Zetec-SE twin belt-driven ohc, 4-valve; variable camshaft timing; aluminium cylinder head, and block; Ford EEC-V multipoint fuel injection, electronic ignition; 5-bearing crankshaft.
TRANSMISSION front wheel drive; gearbox 5-speed synchromesh; final drive 3.82:1.
CHASSIS steel monocoque structure; independent front suspension by MacPherson strut, offset coil springs, lower A-arms, anti-roll bar; rear suspension semi-independent twist beam with coil spring damper units; hydraulic servo brakes, front 24cm (9.5in) dia disc, rear drums, ABS; rack and pinion variable PAS; 42l (9.2gal) (11.1 US gal) fuel tank; 195/50R15 tyres, 6J rims.

DIMENSIONS wheelbase 245cm (96.5in); track 145cm (57.1in) front, 141cm (55.5in) rear; length 398.5cm (156.9in); width 167.5cm (65.9in); height 134cm (52.8in); ground clearance 14cm (5.5in); turning circle 10.4m (34.1ft).
EQUIPMENT alloy wheels, metallic paint £240, passenger airbag £300, air conditioning £350.
PERFORMANCE maximum 197.5kph (123mph) *Autocar*, 31.4kph (19.6mph) @ 1000rpm; 0-100kph (62mph) 8.6sec; 11.3kg/kW (8.4kg/bhp); fuel consumption 7.4l/100km (38.2mpg).
PRICE £14,550.
PRODUCTION 45,000 UK sales.

1998 Puma 1.4i, 1999 ST160

In the summer of 1998 a 1.4-litre Puma was presented as an alternative to the 1.7. It cost some £1500 less, was 28kg (61.7lb) lighter, and took 2sec more to reach 100mph (62mph). It was 19.3kph (12mph) slower but had a fuel consumption advantage of some 15 per cent. The Zetec-SE engine, from the 1.4 Fiesta, was smoother running than the 1.7, the difference in performance was quite small, and the car ran on the same 15in alloy wheels and 195/50 tyres as the 1.7 so the handling was every bit as good. There was less likelihood of wheelspin in the wet or on loose surfaces, but as a stylish two-plus-two coupe it suffered from the same cramped rear seats and unevenly shaped boot. In 1999, encouraged by a 223.7kW (300bhp) concept Puma with stretched wheelbase and four wheel drive (it was an Escort Cosworth with longitudinal engine and steroid Puma bodywork) another concept car, the ST160 was shown at the Geneva Motor Show. This was developed by the Ford Racing Division at Boreham, based more on the production car, with 119.3kW (160bhp), front wheel drive, and imited slip differential. Brakes were bigger, with Alcon racing calipers, it did 225kph (140mph) and in the autumn the go-ahead was given for up to 1000 to be built for racing by Tickford at Daventry, Northamptonshire. It was priced at £23,000.

INTRODUCTION June 1998, production to November 2001.
BODY coupe; 2-doors, 2+2-seats; weight 1035kg (2281.8lb).
ENGINE 4-cylinders, in-line; front; transverse; 76mm x 76.5mm, 1388cc; compr 10.3:1; 66kW (88.5bhp) @ 5500rpm; 47.6kW (63.8bhp)/l; 123Nm (91 lbft) @ 4000rpm.
ENGINE STRUCTURE Zetec-SE twin belt-driven ohc, 4-valve; aluminium cylinder head, and block; Ford EEC-V multipoint fuel injection, electronic ignition; 5-bearing crankshaft.
TRANSMISSION front wheel drive; gearbox 5-speed synchromesh; final drive 4.19, 4.25:1.
CHASSIS steel monocoque structure; independent front suspension by MacPherson strut, offset coil springs, lower A-arms, anti-roll bar; rear suspension semi-independent twist beam with coil spring damper units; hydraulic servo brakes, front 24cm (9.5in) dia disc, rear drums, ABS optional; rack and pinion variable PAS; 42l (9.2gal) (11.1 USgal) fuel tank; 195/50R15 tyres, 6J rims.
DIMENSIONS wheelbase 245cm (96.5in); track 145cm (57.1in) front, 141cm (55.5in) rear; length 398.5cm (156.9in); width 167.5cm (65.9in); height 134cm (52.8in); ground clearance 14cm (5.5in); turning circle 10.4m (34.1ft).
EQUIPMENT alloy wheels, metallic paint £240, passenger airbag £300, air conditioning £350, ABS £390.
PERFORMANCE maximum 178.2kph (111mph) *Autocar*; 31.6kph (19.7mph) @ 1000rpm; 0-100kph (62mph) 10.6sec; 15.7kg/kW (11.7kg/bhp); fuel consumption 7.1l/100km (39.9mpg).
PRICE £13,200.
PRODUCTION 45,000 UK sales.

1998 Cougar

Announced at the Detroit Motor Show at the turn of the year, the Cougar was based on a Mondeo platform clad in a sleek coupe body with plenty of space for the 2 in the front, but not much headroom for the +2 in the back. A replacement for the Probe, or a successor to the Capri as Ford preferred, it was an American-inspired project although developed in Europe. Probe was a critical success but perhaps remained too Transatlantic. The suspension was ST24 with firmer springs, dampers, and anti-roll bars yet even with a body shell 20 per cent stiffer than a Mondeo the handling was touring rather than sporting. Luggage space was enormous and could be doubled by folding the split rear backrests flat.

The modified 2.0-litre Zetec engine came from Bridgend, the V6 Duratec was American. A 234.9kW (315bhp) V6 with a Jaguar 4x4 powertrain was floated at the 1999 Los Angeles Motor Show, but renamed ST200 at the Frankfurt Motor Show in September it remained front wheel drive only with the MTX-5 manual gearbox. Using the same ST200 engine as Mondeo, a Duratec V6 with dual-inlet air cleaner, revised camshafts, and free-flowing exhaust, it also had thicker anti-roll bars. Had it reached production it would have been one of the fastest-ever Fords sold in the UK.

INTRODUCTION January 1998, production to 2001.
BODY coupe; 3-doors, 2+2-seats; weight 1315kg (2900lb), V6 1390kg (3064.4lb).
ENGINE 4-cylinders, in-line; front; 84.8mm x 88mm, 1988cc; compr 10:1; 96kW (128.7bhp) @ 5600rpm; 48.3kW/l (64.7bhp/l); 178Nm (131 lbft) @ 4000rpm.
V6: 82.4x79.5mm; 2544cc; 9.7:1; 125kW (167.6bhp); 49.1kW/l (65.9bhp/l); 220Nm (162 lbft).
ENGINE STRUCTURE Zetec-E; 2 belt-driven ohc; 4-valves; aluminium cylinder head and block; fuel injection and EEC-V electronic engine management; 5-bearing crankshaft. Duratec V6, 2 chain-driven ohc per block, 4-valves; 4-bearing.
TRANSMISSION front wheel drive; gearbox 5-speed synchromesh; automatic option; final drive 3.82:1, automatic 3.92. V6 3.82/3.77.
CHASSIS steel monocoque structure; ifs MacPherson struts, anti-roll bar; Quadralink independent rear suspension; coil springs, anti roll bar; telescopic dampers; hydraulic servo disc brakes, front 260mm (10.3in) ventilated rear 252cm (9.9in) (V6 all ventilated), ABS; rack and pinion PAS; 60l (13.2 gal) (15.9 US gal) fuel tank; 205/60R15, 215/50R16 tyres, 6, 6.5Jrims.
DIMENSIONS wheelbase 270.5cm (106.5in); track front 150.5cm (59.25in); rear 149cm (58.7in); length 470cm; (185in); width 177cm (69.7in); height 132cm (52in); turning circle 11m (36.1ft).
EQUIPMENT airbags, alloy wheels, ABS, A/C, electric mirrors and windows, leather, CD player extra.
PERFORMANCE maximum speed 209kph (130.2mph), V6 225kph (140.2mph); 35.3kph (22mph) @ 1000rpm; 0-100kph (62mph) 9.6sec, V6 8.1sec; 13.7kg/kW (10.2kg/bhp); fuel consumption 8.3l/100km (34mpg).
PRICE £19,845, V6 £20,845, X-pack automatic £22,820.

421

1998 Focus 1.4/1.6/1.8

Replacing Escort after 30 years and 20m cars, the Focus was first shown at the Geneva Motor Show in March, and went on sale in the autumn of 1998. More sophisticated than its predecessor, and although only 1.1cm (.43in) longer and 1cm (.39in) wider, it was 8cm (3.15in) taller, so the occupants sat more upright within a wheelbase 7cm (2.76in) longer. The result was a substantial improvement in legroom and headroom and almost as much space inside as a Mondeo. The emphasis was less on speed than comfort, safety, and style. Refinement was improved by making the body 35 per cent stiffer, and reinforcing suspension attachment points to reduce their potential for generating resonance. The redesign of the front suspension offset the coil springs of the MacPherson struts to reduce the "stiction" so long a bugbear of the system. The rear suspension was entirely new, a double wishbone arrangement with coil springs that was just as effective as and a good deal cheaper than, a complex multi-link system. The Focus was 30kg-50kg (66.1lb-110.23lb) lighter than the Escort, which together with better aerodynamics made it 25 per cent more fuel-efficient. Power trains for the petrol-engined cars were familiar, the 1.4 Zetec-SE from the Fiesta, a new 1.6 version of the same engine, and a 1.8 and 2.0 as used in the Mondeo.

Specification 1.4i 3-door
INTRODUCTION autumn 1998.
BODY saloon; 3, 4 or 5-doors, estate car 5-doors; 5-seats; weight 1070kg (2358.9lb), 1.8 1125kg (2480.2lb).
ENGINE 4-cylinders, in-line; front; transverse; 76mm x 76.5mm, 1388cc; compr 11:1; 55kW (73.8bhp) @ 5000rpm; 39.6kW/l (53.1bhp/l); 123Nm (91 lbft) @ 3750rpm.
1.6: 76 x 81.4mm; 1596cc; 11:1; 74kW (99.2bhp); 46.4kW (62.2bhp)/l; 145Nm (107 lbft).
1.8: 80.6x88mm; 1796cc; 10:1; 85kW (114bhp); 47.3kW (63.5bhp)/l; 158Nm (117 lbft).
ENGINE STRUCTURE Zetec-SE or Zetec-E; 2 belt-driven ohc; 4-valves; aluminium cylinder head and block; fuel injection and electronic engine management; 5-bearing crankshaft.
TRANSMISSION front wheel drive; gearbox 5-speed synchromesh; final drive 4.06:1. 1.6 3.82; 1.8 4.06.
CHASSIS steel monocoque structure with sub-frames; ifs by MacPherson struts, angled coil spring damper units, and lower wishbones, anti-roll bar; independent rear suspension by control blade multi-link system, anti roll bar; telescopic dampers; hydraulic servo brakes, front 25.8cm (10.2in) dia ventilated discs; rear drums (1.6, 1.8 discs), dual circuit, ABS optional; rack and pinion PAS; 55l (12.1gal) (14.5 US gal) fuel tank; 175/70R14, 185/65R14, 195/55R15 tyres 5.5, 6J rims.
DIMENSIONS wheelbase 261.5cm (103in); track front 149.5cm (58.9in), rear 148.5cm (58.5in); length 415cm (163.4in); width 170cm (66.9in); height 143cm (56.3in); turning circle 10.9m (35.8ft).
EQUIPMENT various option packs, Climate, reflex, Styling, Luxury; CX, Zetec, LX and Ghia, CD upgrade, metallic paint.
PERFORMANCE maximum speed 171kph (106.5mph), 1.6 185kph (115.2mph), 1.8 198kph (123.3mph); 36.8kph (22.92mph) @ 1000rpm; 0-100kph (62mph) 14.1sec, 1.6 10.9sec, 1.8 10.2sec;19.5kg/kW (14.5kg/bhp), 1.8 13.2kg/kW (9.9kg/bhp); fuel consumption 6.4l/100km (44.1mpg).
PRICE 1.4CL 5-door £12,850; 1.6 Zetec £13,350; 1.8 Ghia £14,350.

Focus hatch back (above) and
Focus saloon with boot (right).

423

1998 Focus 2.0

The Focus name was used in 1992 for a concept roadster based on the Escort Cosworth, a voluptuous design shown at the Turin Motor Show as an experiment in exotic materials such as Kevlar and carbon fibre. A 3-piece fold away roof was tried but its market niche would have been small and nothing more was heard of it. The production Focus was made in Saarlouis and Valencia, capable of 450,000 a year, the rate at which Escort had been made, and a notchback saloon and estate car joined the model line-up. The 2.0-litre engine from the Mondeo was stiffened to reduce vibration so that it revved cheerfully to 6900rpm before the rev-limiter was invoked. Mondeos had been criticised for harshness at such speeds, but although power output was quite modest, its willingness to rev, and low gearing gave it a lively turn of speed. Anti-roll bars were increased from 20mm (.79in) to 21mm (.83in) and the wheel arches were flared to accommodate wider tyres, a modification that suited the Focus well. Interiors followed the Ka's curvaceous style and the 2.0 was given a mock titanium finish to match the modernist character. Accolades came thick and fast. An international panel of artists, designers, and architects elected it the world's most beautiful car, and automotive journalists voted it Car of the Year 1999.

INTRODUCTION autumn 1998.
BODY saloon; 3, 4 or 5-doors, estate car 5-doors, 5-seats; weight 1145kg (2524.3lb).
ENGINE 4-cylinders, in-line; front; transverse; 84.8mm x 88mm, 1988cc; compr 10:1; 96kW (128.7bhp) @ 5750rpm; 48.3kW (64.8bhp)/l; 174Nm (128 lbft) @ 3750rpm.
ENGINE STRUCTURE Zetec-E; 2 belt-driven ohc; 4-valves; aluminium cylinder head and block; fuel injection and EEC-V electronic engine management; 5-bearing crankshaft.
TRANSMISSION front wheel drive; gearbox 5-speed synchromesh; final drive 4.06:1.
CHASSIS steel monocoque structure with sub-frames; ifs by MacPherson struts, angled coil spring damper units, and lower wishbones, anti-roll bar; independent rear suspension by control blade multi-link system, anti roll bar; telescopic dampers; hydraulic servo brakes, front 25.8cm (10.16in) dia ventilated discs; rear 25.3cm (9.96in) discs, dual circuit, ABS optional; rack and pinion PAS; 55l (12.1gal) (14.5 US gal) fuel tank; 175/70R14, 185/65R14,

195/55R15 tyres 5.5, 6J rims.
DIMENSIONS 4-door wheelbase 261.5cm (103in); track front 149.5cm (58.9in), rear 148.5cm (58.5in); length 436.2cm (171.7in); width 170cm (66.9in); height 143cm (56.3in); turning circle 10.9m (35.78ft).
EQUIPMENT various option packs, Climate, reflex, Styling, Luxury; CX, Zetec, LX and Ghia, CD upgrade, metallic paint.
PERFORMANCE maximum speed 201kph (125.2mph); 36.1kph (22.5mph) @ 1000rpm; 0-100kph (62mph) 9.2sec; 11.9kg/kW (8.9kg/bhp); fuel consumption 8.9l/100km (31.7mpg).
PRICE 2.0 Ghia 5-door £15,350, estate £15,850.

The concept Focus roadster shown at Turin was sold at Christie's 2002 auction in Detroit for $1million.

1998 Focus turbodiesel

Diesel technology advanced a step with development of the ohc 2-valve 44kW (59bhp) engine of the 1996 Fiesta. Direct injection into the combustion chambers rather than the inlet tract, together with precise electronic metering, and turbocharger and intercooler added 23kW (30.8bhp) for the Focus. Emissions were reduced, and direct injection also raised the torque over an earlier version of the turbo by 11 per cent, so it pulled strongly between 1500 and 3600rpm until the fuel cutoff point at 4800rpm. It was also remarkably economical and more refined, once the turbocharger was integrated into the exhaust manifold. Among further enhancements were oil-filled engine mountings and fixings for the exhaust well outside the floor area of the cabin. In 2001 the diesel was brought completely up to date with the Duratorq TDCi common-rail version that averaged 4.4l/100km (65mpg) and was expected to save its owner £300 in fuel costs before its first service. Routine maintenance was claimed to cost 28 per cent less than the previous Fiesta, with service intervals increased to 20,000km (12,500miles). Bumpers were strengthened and bolt-on wings made repairs cheaper. A CO_2 rating of only 119g/km was significant for the UK's April 2002 tax structure that took account of vehicle emissions.

INTRODUCTION autumn 1998.
BODY saloon; 3, 4or 5-doors, estate car 5-doors, 5-seats; weight 1185kg (2612.5lb).
ENGINE 4-cylinders, in-line; front; transverse; 82.5mm x 82mm, 1753cc; compr 19.4:1; 67kW (89.9bhp) @ 5000rpm; 38.2kW (51.3bhp)/l; 200Nm (148 lbft) @ 2000rpm.
ENGINE STRUCTURE Endura Di; one chain and belt-driven ohc; 2-valves; aluminium cylinder head and block; fuel injection; 5-bearing crankshaft, turbocharger, intercooler.
TRANSMISSION front wheel drive; gearbox 5-speed synchromesh; final drive 3.56:1.
CHASSIS steel monocoque structure; ifs by MacPherson struts, angled coil spring damper units, and lower wishbones, anti-roll bar; independent rear suspension by control blade multi-link system, anti roll bar; telescopic dampers; hydraulic servo brakes, front 25.8cm (10.16in) dia ventilated discs; rear drums, dual circuit, ABS optional; rack and pinion PAS; 55l (12.1gal) (14.5 US gal) fuel tank; 185/65R14, 195/55R15 tyres 5.5, 6J rims.
DIMENSIONS estate wheelbase 261.5cm (103in); track 149.5cm (58.9in) front, 148.5cm (58.5in) rear; length 443.8cm (174.7in); width 170cm (66.9in); height 144.7cm (57in); turning circle 10.9m (35.8ft).
EQUIPMENT various option packs, Climate, reflex, Styling, Luxury; CX, Zetec, LX and Ghia, CD upgrade, metallic paint.
PERFORMANCE maximum speed 184kph (114.6mph); 45.8kph (28.5mph) @ 1000rpm; 0-100kph (62mph) 12.4sec; 17.7kg/kW (13.2kg/bhp); fuel consumption 4.9l/100km (57.6mpg).
PRICE: 5-door 1.8TDdi Ghia £14,850; estate 1.8TDdi LX £14,850.

1999 Fiesta range, Zetec-S

The 1996 changes transformed Fiesta from workmanlike into a best-selling class leader. For MY 2000 it was fine-tuned, Endura petrol and diesel editions chugged on in the bargain basement, 1.25 and 1.4 remaining mechanically unchanged, and all gaining a facelift with a lower bonnet line and trapezoidal headlights. Trying to disguise old presswork was not an unqualified success, showing that, provided basic ingredients of cost, economy, roadworthiness, and proportions were right, the rest could look after itself. Efforts at a flagship Fiesta had been sometimes undistinguished and it took 3 years to produce a new one after 1996. Key ingredients were the 1.6 Zetec-S engine and the transformation in handling. The sporty Fiesta took the Zetec-S's title, and wheels, tyres, gearbox, and interior changed. Suspension was lowered 13mm (.5in) in front and 10mm (.4in) at the back, the front anti-roll bar thickened by 2mm to 17mm (.7in) and the rear twist beam stiffened 42 per cent to ensure flat roll-free cornering. Importantly the steering gained a heavier rack to improve its feel and it reverted to 2.8 turns lock to lock. A fashion fad was a mesh grille over the oval air intake, imitating the wire screens that 1930s sports racing cars wore to protect headlamps and radiator cores from the flying stones with which racetracks, particularly Le Mans, abounded.

Specification Zetec-S
INTRODUCTION Oct 1999, production to 2002.
BODY saloon; 3-doors, 4-seats; weight 975kg (2149.5lb).
ENGINE 4-cylinders, in-line; front; transverse; 79mm x 81.4mm, 1596cc; compr 11:1; 76kW (101.9bhp) @ 6000rpm; 47.6kW/l (63.8bhp/l); 145Nm (107lbft) @ 4000rpm.
ENGINE STRUCTURE twin belt-driven ohc, 4-valve; aluminium cylinder head, and block; Siemens electronic fuel injection, electronic engine management; 5-bearing crankshaft.
TRANSMISSION front wheel drive gearbox 5-speed synchromesh; final drive 4.25:1; traction control.
CHASSIS steel monocoque structure; ifs by MacPherson struts, coil springs, anti-roll bar; rear suspension torsion beam axle; telescopic dampers anti-roll bar; hydraulic, vacuum servo 258mm (10.2in) front ventilated disc brakes; rear drums 190.5mm (7.5in); ABS; rack and pinion PAS; 42l (9.3 gal) (11.1 US gal) fuel tank; 195/55R15 tyres, 6J rims.

DIMENSIONS wheelbase 244.5cm (96.3in); track 143cm (56.3in) front, 137.5cm (54.1in) rear; length 383cm (150.8in); width 163cm (64.2in); height 141cm (55.5in); ground clearance 14cm (5.5in); turning circle 10.3m (33.8ft).
EQUIPMENT 15-spoke alloy wheels, CD player; electric front windows; 1.25-litre available with CVT optional £1000; Zetec-S 3-door only.
PERFORMANCE maximum speed 182kph (113.4mph); 33.7kph (21mph) @ 1000rpm; 0-100kph (62mph) 10.2sec; 12.8kg/kW (9.6kg/bhp); fuel consumption 6.9-6l/100km (40.9-47.1mpg).
PRICE 3-door 1.3 Encore £7750; 1.25LX £9750; 1.4 Zetec £9750; 4-door 1.4 Ghia £11,850.

1999 Focus WRC

The Focus was a winner almost from the start in the World Rally Championship (WRC). Colin McRae finished third in the Monte Carlo Rally, only to be excluded on a technicality, an oversized water pump resulting in a 2-week development programme reputedly costing £500,000 to make certain a standard water pump would work just as well. The turbocharged and intercooled engine was a close relative of the production Focus. It used a standard iron block, conformed strictly with the design criteria as rebuilt by Mountune, used design tolerances and electronics to eliminate turbo lag, and the drive was taken by a bevel gear from the tilted transverse engine to a longitudinal six-speed gearbox. It went to all 4 wheels by way of a central differential that split the torque 50:50, then to two more diffs front and rear. The front and central diffs had hydraulic locks controlled by microprocessor programs to deal with the broadside cornering required by loose-surface high speed driving. A regulation safety roll cage gave immense strength to a body shell that looked every inch a Focus, keeping many of the standard car's features, if not precisely at least in spirit. It had MacPherson struts front and rear, where it replaced Focus's own control blade system, and increased suspension travel to 20cm for gravel stages.

BODY saloon; 3-doors, 2-seats; weight 1230kg (2711.7lb).
ENGINE 4-cylinders, in-line; front; transverse, 1989cc; 223.7kW (300bhp) @ 6000rpm; 112.5kW (150.8bhp)/l; 551Nm (406 lbft) @ 4000rpm.
ENGINE STRUCTURE 2 belt-driven ohc; 4-valves; aluminium cylinder head, iron block; Garrett turbocharger, electronic engine management; 5-bearing crankshaft.
TRANSMISSION four-wheel drive; M-Sport X-Trac 240; gearbox 6-speed sequential; final drive to choice; electronic control of locking differentials.
CHASSIS steel monocoque structure supported by roll cage; reinforced chassis rails; independent suspension by MacPherson struts and adjustable links; adjustable telescopic dampers; hydraulic servo 300mm (11.8in) ventilated disc brakes; ABS; rack and pinion PAS; 120l (26.4 gal) (31.7 US gal) fuel tank; 7Jx15in wheels, choice of tyres.
DIMENSIONS wheelbase 263.5cm (103.7in); length 415.2cm (163.5in); width 177cm (69.7in); height 142cm (55.9in).
EQUIPMENT Sparco seats, safety harness, intercom, calculating and navigation equipment.
PERFORMANCE maximum speed approx 225 kph (140mph); 0-100kph (62mph) 4.3sec, 0-160kph (100mph) 10.0sec; 5.5kg/kW (4.1kg/bhp).

Third on its second WRC event in Sweden, it won on its third appearance, in Kenya. It won again in Portugal on its fourth and was in contention for the world title in only its second season.

1999 Fiesta diesel

Secure in the new improvements to ride, handling, comfort, equipment, and the refurbishment of the appearance, entry-level 1999 Fiestas carried on with much the same mechanicals as before, including the normally aspirated and rather noisy Endura D diesel. While it offered comparable power against rivals, it took half a second longer than the Volkswagen Polo to 100kph (62mph) and was around 6kph (4mph) down on top speed. Both used indirect injection, while many of their contemporaries were moving on to direct injection, and some even to common rail diesels. Even though it had power steering, sunroof, driver's airbag, and a radio that could be upgraded to Radio Data System (RDS) for £60, it had not kept pace with the improvements to the chassis. Fiesta diesel seemed well down the pecking order when it came to updating, until March 2000 when it inherited the turbocharged Focus TDdi, which also went into the small Fiesta and Courier panel vans. Performance was on a par with the 1.25 petrol Fiesta, it used less fuel (5.3l/100km (53.3mpg) against 6.1l/100km (46.3mpg)), but more importantly it was a match in smooth running and enjoyed a reduction in vibration. The price of the new generation diesel Fiesta was the same as the outgoing model, and it came in 5-door form. Option packs to upgrade the specification continued.

INTRODUCTION Oct 1999, production to 2002.

BODY saloon; 3-doors, 5-doors; weight 1015kg (2237.7lb); TD 1010kg (2226.7lb).

ENGINE 4-cylinders, in-line; front; transverse; 82.5mm x 82mm, 1753cc; compr 21.5:1; 44kW (59bhp) @ 4800rpm; 25kW (33.7bhp)/l; 105Nm (77 lbft) @ 2500rpm;. TD compr 19.4; 55kW (73.8bhp) @ 4000rpm; 31.3kW (41.1bhp)/l; 140Nm (103 lbft) @ 1900rpm.

ENGINE STRUCTURE Endura DE, 1 gear and belt driven ohc, 2-valve; iron head, and block; fuel injection; 5-bearing crankshaft. Endura DI-TD direct injection, turbocharger.

TRANSMISSION front wheel drive gearbox 5-speed synchromesh; final drive 3.84:1, TD3.61.

CHASSIS steel monocoque structure; ifs by MacPherson struts, coil springs, anti-roll bar; rear suspension torsion beam axle; telescopic dampers anti-roll bar; hydraulic, vacuum servo 240mm (9.45in) front disc brakes; rear drums 190.5mm (7.5in); ABS; rack and pinion PAS; 42l (9.2 gal) (11.1 US gal) fuel tank; 165/70R13, 185/55R14 tyres, 5.5, 6J rims.

DIMENSIONS wheelbase 244.5cm (96.3in); track 143cm (56.3in) front, 137.5cm (54.1in) rear; length 383cm (150.8in); width 163cm (64.2in); height 141cm (55.5in); ground clearance 14cm (5.5in); turning circle 10.3m (33.8ft).

PERFORMANCE maximum speed 155kph (96.6mph), TD168kph (104.7mph); 34.3kph (21.37mph) @ 1000rpm; 0-100kph (62mph) 17.2sec, TD14.3sec; 23.1kg/kW (17.2kg/bhp), TD 18.4kg/kW (13.7kg/bhp); fuel consumption 7.9-5l/100km (35.8-56.5mpg), TD 6.5-4.2l/100km (43.5-67.3mpg).

PRICE 1.8TDdi LX £10,850.

433

1999 Focus saloon and estate

By the beginning of 1999 the Focus range was being expanded, starting with a well proportioned saloon, which improved the appearance and enhanced its market prospects. Like the Orion (and the Escort saloon) before it, the Focus 4-door was aimed at a quite different sort of buyer from the hatchback. It was 21cm (8.3in) longer and 4cm (1.6in) taller, and the spring rates were softened, giving a more compliant ride. The absence of a large hatchback opening in the rear stiffened the bodyshell, enhancing roadworthiness, improving refinement, and making the car quieter. Rounding off the up-market presentation, the 4-door came only as a 1.6 or 2.0 Ghia, with air conditioning and CD prominent in a long list of standard equipment, topped off with timber-look trim round the facia, Ghia badges, and additional chrome. The Focus also lent itself well to an estate car configuration. The already low-line suspension was flattened further to reduce intrusions into the loading space, and triple-rate springs made allowance for heavy weights in the back. The roofline was made an extra 1.7cm (0.7in) taller, the modifications and the extra glassware increasing its weight by 41kg (90.4lb). Loadspace capacity was further improved by making the estate car's tailgate upright. Saloon Focus prices were the same as those for the 5-door hatchback, and the estate was only £500 more.

Specification 2.0.
INTRODUCTION January 1999.
BODY saloon; 4-doors, 5-seats; weight 1160kg (2557.3lb), estate 1197kg (2639lb).
ENGINE 4-cylinders, in-line; front; transverse; 84.8mm x 88mm, 1988cc; compr 10:1; 96kW (128.7bhp) @ 5500rpm; 48.3kW (64.8bhp)/l; 178Nm (131 lbft) @ 5500rpm.
ENGINE STRUCTURE Zetec-E; 2 belt-driven ohc, 4-valves; aluminium cylinder head and block; sequential fuel injection, EEC-V electronic engine management; 5-bearing crankshaft.
TRANSMISSION front wheel drive; gearbox 5-speed synchromesh; final drive 4.06:1.
CHASSIS steel monocoque structure; independent front suspension by MacPherson struts, coil springs, anti-roll bar; multi-link independent rear suspension; anti roll bar; telescopic dampers; hydraulic servo disc brakes, front 258mm (10.2in) ventilated, rear 253mm (10in) dia; ABS; rack and pinion PAS; 55l (12.1 gal) (14.5 US gal) fuel tank; 195/60R15 tyres 5J rims, alloy wheels.

DIMENSIONS wheelbase 261.5cm (103in); track 148.5cm (58.5in) front, 147.5cm (58.1in) rear; length 436.2cm (171.7in)/443.8cm (174.7in); width 169.9cm (66.9in); height 148cm (58.3in)/149.7cm (58.9in); turning circle 10.9m (35.8ft).
PERFORMANCE maximum speed 201kph (125.2mph); 36.1kph (22.5mph) @ 1000rpm;0-100kph (62mph) 9.2sec/ 9.6sec;12.1kg/kW (9kg/bhp); fuel consumption 9l/100km (31.4mpg).
PRICE 4-door £15,500, estate £16,000.

2000 Galaxy

A successful model required only a light touch. Tear-drop headlights and a narrow grille gave it a Ford family identity, while it gained new mechanical packages with 24-valve heads for the V6, and a new turbodiesel in addition to the existing 2.3 petrol. The V6 came with Electronic Stability Programme (ESP) as standard. ESP detected the onset of skidding by sensors measuring yaw, sideways acceleration, steering wheel angle, and road speed. The on-board computer worked out a combination of throttle responses, and judicious braking of individual wheels, to bring the vehicle back on course. Traction control was also optional with the 2.3. Further novelties included a 6-speed manual, and the option of 5-speed automatics with a capacity for push-pull manual sequential operation. The completely revised interior included so-called technical grain surface treatment for the facia, stemming from the texture of modern lightweight carbon fibre or bonded metallic materials. Optional satellite navigation, standard parking distance sensors, and a multi-media system providing screens on the backs of the front seats for videos or games, were among the high-tech features of this modern Ford. All Galaxy models had 7 seats as standard, with the option of 6 "captain's chairs" with integral armrests on the Ghia.

INTRODUCTION March 2000.
BODY minivan; 5-doors, 7-seats; weight 1650kg (3637.6lb); V6 1700kg (3748lb); turbodiesel 1666kg (3673lb).
ENGINE 4-cylinders, in-line; front; transverse; 89.6mm x 91mm, 2259cc; compr 10:1; 107kW (143.5bhp) @ 5500rpm; 47.36kW (63.5bhp)/l; 203Nm (150 lbft) @ 2500rpm. V6: 81x 90.3mm; 2792cc; 150kW (201.2bhp); 53.7kW (72bhp)/l; 264Nm (195 lbft). 1.9TDi: 1896cc; 66kW (88.5bhp) or 85kW (114bhp).
ENGINE STRUCTURE chain-driven 2 ohc; 4-valve; aluminium cylinder head, iron block; EEC-V engine management, and SEFI multi-point fuel injection; 5-bearing crankshaft. V6 2 chain ohc per bank; Bosch engine management; 4-bearing. Diesel, belt-driven sohc EDC16 management, turbocharged, intercooled.
TRANSMISSION front wheel drive; hydraulic clutch; gearbox 5-speed synchromesh; automatic optional; final drive 4.231:1, V6 and diesel 3.591, automatics 4.572, 3.684, 2.87.
CHASSIS steel monocoque; ifs by MacPherson struts, lower wishbones,

offset coil springs; irs by semi-trailing arms, coil springs; anti roll bars; gas-filled telescopic dampers; hydraulic servo disc brakes, 280mm (11in) dia front ventilated (V6 both ventilated), 313mm and 294mm; ABS; dual circuit; rack and pinion PAS; 70l (15.4 gal) (18.5 US gal) fuel tank; 195/65TR15; 205/60HR15, 215/55WR16.
DIMENSIONS wheelbase 283.5cm (111.6in); track front 152.6cm (60.1in), rear 151.2cm (59.5in); length 464.1cm (182.7in); width 181cm (71.3in) without mirrors; ht 173.2cm (68.2in) without roofrail; turning circle 11.1m (36.4ft).
EQUIPMENT optional xenon lights, air conditioning standard.
PERFORMANCE maximum 197kph (122.7mph), V6 217kph (135.2mph); 34kph (21.2mph), V6 41.5kph (25.9mph) @ 1000rpm; 0-100kph (62mph) 12.3sec, V6 9.9sec; 15.4kg/kW (11.5kg/bhp), V6 11.3kg/kW (8.4kg/bhp), TD 25.2 or 19.6kg/kW (18.8kg or 14.6kg/bhp); 10.1l/100km (28mpg), TDi 6.5l/100km (43.5mpg).
PRICE 2.3LX £18,245, 2.8 Ghia £24,245, 1.9TD Ghia automatic £23,740.

2000 Transit

It took the best part of 40 years for the Transit to embrace front wheel drive, but eventually for lighter loads the advantages of low floor and improved driving qualities won through. The transverse-engined front end was added to the long-standing range of ladder-frame rear-drive chassis. Both sorts shared 95 per cent of their components. Front wheel drive suited vans; chassis-cabs had a ladder-type frame with rear wheel drive and the option of twin wheels for extra traction. Front wheel drive enabled all the mechanical units to be packaged together, making it easy to ring changes in wheelbases, load lengths, roof heights, and body styles and, crucially with no propeller shaft, a low floor, low door openings, and more headroom in the back. It had more cube space, and the medium wheelbase model could take 4 Europallets, 1.2m (3.9ft) x 0.8m (2.6ft). The engineering challenge was providing for both longitudinal (rear drive) and transverse engines (front-drive). Cabs could have 3-abreast seats, separate chassis-cabs, or extended cabs with dual passenger and load-carrying roles. Manufactured in the former Spitfire factory at Southampton following a £600m investment, the Transit had a bewildering range of petrol and diesel engines. 4 valves per cylinder, once the prerogative of grand prix cars, and turbochargers made the Transit feel more like a car than ever.

INTRODUCTION January 2000. BODY cab, chassis-cab, various; SWB 260 2.0Di low roof van 2455kg (5412lb); LWB 350 med roof van 2.4Di 3500kg (7716lb).
ENGINES 4-cyls, in-line; front; transverse or longitudinal; diesel 2.0 DuraTorq Di: 55kw (73.8bhp) @ 3300rpm; 180Nm (133 lbft) @ 2250rpm; or 74kw (99.2bhp) @ 4000rpm; 230Nm (170 lbft) @ 2000rpm. 2.4: 55kw (73.8bhp) @ 3500rpm; 185Nm (137 lbft) @ 2000rpm; fuel injection direct Bosch VP30. 66kw (88.5bhp) @ 4000rpm; 200Nm (148 lbft) @ 1800rpm. 88kw (118bhp) @ 4000rpm; 240Nm (177 lbft) @ 2300rpm. Petrol 2.3dohc: 107kw (143.5bhp) @ 5700rpm; 200Nm (148 lbft) @ 2500rpm. 2.0 diesel: 86mm x 86mm; 1998cc; compr 19:1; chain-driven dohc; alumin 2-piece head, 4-valves; cast iron block with alumin ladder frame; cast iron exhaust manifold with integral turbocharger; Ford EEC-V engine management. 2.4 diesel: 89.9mm x 94.6mm; 2402cc; cr 19.0:1. 2.3L 16v petrol; 89.6mm x 91.0mm; 2295cc; compr 10:1; alumin head, iron block; chain-driven dohc; Ford EEC-V engine management; electronic fuel injection.
TRANSMISSION 2.0L DuraTorq Di, front wheel drive; Ford VXT75 transmission; hydraulic clutch; 5-speed synchro; final drive 4.23:1 or 4.54 for towing. 2.4L DurtaTorq Di and 2.3L petrol rear wheel drive Ford MT75 transmission, final drive 4.63:1 or 5.13 for towing.
CHASSIS steel monocoque cab or van; ifs by MacPherson struts; rear suspension dead beam; RWD live axle, leaf springs; gas-pressurised telescopic dampers; hydraulic servo brakes, front 276mm (10.9in) dia ventilated disc, rear 254mm (10in) dia drums, RWD 294mm (11.6in) and 280mm (11in); optional ABS, dual circuit; rack and pinion PAS; 80l (17.6 gal) (21.1 US gal) fuel tank; 195/70R x 15C tyres, RWD 215/75R x 16C.
DIMENSIONS wheelbase van 330cm (129.9in), 375cm (147.6in), chassis-cab 313.7cm (123.5in), 350.4cm (138in), 395.4cm (155.7in); length medium van 520.1cm (204.8in), long van 565.1cm (222.5in), medium chassis 545.2cm

(214.7in); width 1974cm (777.2in) excluding mirrors; height medium roof 235.3cm (92.6in), high roof 258.2cm (101.7in); turning circle 11.4m (37.4ft) SWB to 13.9m (45.6ft) LWB.
EQUIPMENT driver airbag, radio standard, passenger's airbag, perimeter alarm, metallic paint, electric mirrors, electric windows, heated windscreen, tow bar, CD player, parking sensor, tachograph, vinyl seat trim, air conditioning optional.
PRICE from £12,686.

Workhorse of the World. Five generations of Transit van. For the new millennium Transit service intervals Transit service intervals were extended to 25,000km (15,000miles) and warranty to 3 years or 160,000kms (100,000miles). The 3-piece easily repairable front bumper intended no reflection on van drivers' skill.

2000 Mondeo

In common with most of the British motor industry Ford prices edged downwards at the turn of the century, and Mondeo prices were reduced by 8.8 per cent. New equipment was added at an estimated value of £825, so, together with the price reduction, the customer gained 14 per cent more moneysworth. Three body styles, four engine options, and five levels of trim, LX, Zetec, Zetec-S, Ghia, and GhiaX, added up to 51 different Mondeos, all with ABS, airbags, electric windows, CD player, air conditioning, and heated windscreen. All Fords now had a three-year 60,000mile warranty.

The first European Ford to be created digitally, Mondeo showed close attention to detail. An increase in wheelbase of 5cm (2in) gave a disproportionate increase in rear seat room. Raising the seats by 1.5cm (0.6in) in front and 1.7cm (0.7in) in the back and enlarging the doors made access easier. An extra 15cm (5.9in) in length provided a full 500l of luggage capacity. A computer tool was used to analyse and simulate various luggage space designs, using a wide range of simulated real world cargos from suitcases to push chairs. The rear seat cushion folded forward allowing the seatbacks to be folded downward, providing a larger flat floor. First-aid kit and warning triangles were cleverly stowed to take up as little room as possible.

Spec 2-litre
INTRODUCTION October 2000.
BODY saloon; 4/5-doors, 5-seats; weight 1245kg (2744.7lb), estate 1300kg (2866lb).
ENGINE 4 cylinders, in-line; front; transverse; 84.8mm x 88mm, 1988cc; compr 10:1; 96kW (128.7bhp) @ 5600rpm; 48.3kW (64.8bhp)/l; 178Nm (131 lbft) @ 4000rpm.
ENGINE STRUCTURE Zetec-E; 2 belt-driven overhead camshafts; 4-valves; aluminium cylinder head, iron block; electronic fuel injection, EEC-V engine management; 5-bearing crankshaft.
TRANSMISSION front wheel drive; gearbox 5-speed synchromesh; automatic option; final drive 3.82:1; automatic3.92:1; traction control option £495.
CHASSIS steel monocoque structure; independent front suspension by MacPherson struts, coil springs, anti-roll bar; independent rear suspension, multi-link coil springs, anti roll bar; telescopic dampers; hydraulic servo ventilated disc brakes, front 260mm (10.2in) dia, rear 252mm (9.9in) dia, Teves ABS; rack and pinion PAS; 61.5l (13.5 gal) (16.3 US gal) fuel tank; 185/65HR14, 195/60HR15, 205/55HR15 tyres, 5.5J rims.
DIMENSIONS wheelbase 270.5cm (106.5in); track front 150.5cm (59.25in), rear 148.5cm (58.5in); length 456cm (179.5in), estate 467cm (183.9in); width 175cm (68.9in); height 142cm (55.9in), estate 151cm (59.5in); ground clearance 12cm (4.7in); turning circle 10.9m (35.7ft).
EQUIPMENT automatic option £1000.
PERFORMANCE maximum speed 206kph (128.3mph), estate 199kph (124mph); 32kph (19.9mph) @ 1000rpm; 0-100kph (62mph) 10sec, estate 10.2sec; 13kg/kW (9.7kg/bhp); fuel consumption 11.7-5.9l/100km (24.2-47.88mpg).
PRICE 2.0i £16,095, 2.0i Ghia X £19,395.

2001 Maverick

The Maverick developed with Nissan in the 1980s was built like the traditional 4x4, with a stout separate chassis and firm springing. The new Maverick was smaller, of unitary construction, and although its cross-country credentials were good, it rode and handled more like a car. In a reversal of its older namesake, it was front wheel drive until told otherwise; if the front wheels lost grip, Control Trac chipped in, diverting pull to the rear as well. A manual 4x4 override helped establish its towing capacity of 1700kg (3747.8lb), about the weight of a small boat. A versatile Sport Utility, it had plenty of space for 5 to sit in comfort with 92.5cm (36.4in) legroom in the rear. The rear seat back split 60:40 or could be folded away to provide 1830l of load space.

Displaying its environmental credentials, Ford studied a hybrid-electric Maverick. The Maverick HEV was to have regenerative braking, could be stopped and started almost instantaneously, yet was still capable of 6.01l/100km (47mpg). It could thus be driven 800km (around 500m) on a single tank with acceleration similar to a Maverick V6. Sophisticated motor generators saved fuel by shutting down the engine when coasting or stopped, restarting when the driver stepped on the accelerator.

INTRODUCTION April 2001.
BODY saloon SUV; 5-doors, 5-seats; weight 1470kg (3240.8lb).
ENGINE 4-cylinders, in-line; front; transverse; 84.8mm x 88mm, 1988cc; cr 9.6:1; 95kW (127.4bhp) @ 5400rpm; 48.8kW (65.4bhp)/l, 183Nm (135 lbft) @ 4500rpm. V6: 89 x 79.5mm; 2967cc; compr 10:1; 149kW (199.8bhp) @ 6000rpm; 50.2kW (67.3bhp)/l, 272Nm (201 lbft) @ 4750rpm.
ENGINE STRUCTURE 2 belt-driven ohcs; 4-valves; aluminium cyl head, iron block; sequential electronic fuel inj, EEC-V engine management, distributorless ign; 5-bearing crank. V6 60 deg; aluminium cyl heads and block; 2 chain-driven ohc per bank; 4-bearing crank, Ford coil-on-plug ignition.
TRANSMISSION front wheel drive; G5M 5-speed manual transaxle; final drive 4.588:1 Power Take Off (PTO) 2.928:1. Control Trac II 4wd full-time dual mode central viscous coupling, PTO for power transfer to rear axle, Rotary Blade Coupling (RBC) for front/rear proportioning. V6 CD4E 4-speed automatic transaxle final drive 3.770:1, PTO 2.927:1.

CHASSIS steel monocoque; ifs by MacPherson struts; independent multi-link rear susp; anti roll bars front & rear; telesc dampers; hydraulic servo brakes, front 278mm (10.9in) dia ventilated discs, rear 229mm (9in) dia drums, ABS with electronic brake-force distribution; rack and pinion PAS; 58l (12.8 gal) (15.3 US gal)) fuel tank; 225/70R15, V6, 235/70R16tyres, alloy wheels.
DIMENSIONS wheelbase 262cm (103.2in); track 155.5cm (61.2in) front, 155cm (61in) rear; length 439.5cm (173in); width 178cm (70.1in); height 170cm (66.9in); ground clearance 20cm (7.9in); turning circle 10.8m (35.4ft).
EQUIPMENT 1830l luggage space, 1700kg towing with V6, cruise control, CD player, leather trim standard on V6, ABS, EBD, air-con standard throughout range.
PERFORMANCE maximum 166kph (103.4mph), V6 190kph (118.4mph); 45kph (28mph) @ 1000rpm, V6 48.5kph (30.2mph); 0-100kph (62mph) 13.5sec, V6 10.5sec; 15.5kg/kW 911.5kg/bhp); 10.3l/100km (27.5mpg), V6 13.6l/100km (20.8mpg).
PRICE 2.0 £17,995. 3.0 £20,995.

First launched in the United States as the Ford Escape in August 2000, it collected media awards and sold 75,000 in its first 3 months.

2001 Fiesta 1.3 8v and 1.6 16v

Announced at the Frankfurt Motor Show on 11 September 2001, a completely new Fiesta entered an uncertain world. Production was not scheduled to start until the following spring, bringing Fiesta firmly into the 21st century with a stylish new body shell, more space inside, and engines promising fuel economy figures that only a few years previously would have been dismissed as freakish. Replacing Endura E, the petrol 1.3-litre Duratec's combined figure of 6.2l/100km (45.6mpg) was attainable in everyday driving, as was the 1.4 diesel Duratorq's 4.3l/100km (65.7mpg). The Fiesta's driving quality was well received and it was equipped with the IPS intelligent safety system with up to 6 airbags. The small Duratec 8-valve engine achieved economy by reducing internal friction. The camshaft drive was a roller chain instead of the usual toothed belt, the valve stems were reduced to 6mm (.24in) diameter, and the sophisticated electronic system kept the stoichiometric (petrol and air) mixture so consistent that emissions were controlled more than before and nearly 90 per cent of maximim torque was available between 1500rpm and 4500rpm. A compact engine 5.3cm (2.1in) less top to bottom, and 3mm (.12in) shorter end to end, it also featured a new Powertrain Control Module (PCM) electronic throttle control for the first time in a small Ford.

INTRODUCTION January 2002.
BODY saloon; 5-doors, 5-seats; weight 1045kg (2303.8lb), 1.6 1040kg (2292.8lb).
ENGINE 4-cylinders, in-line; front; transverse; 74mm x 75.5mm, 1299cc; compr 10.2:1; 50kW (67.1bhp) @ 5500rpm; 38.5kW (51.6bhp)/l; 106Nm (78 lbft) @ 2800rpm. 1.6: 79 x 81.4mm; 1596cc; compr 11:1; 76kW (101.9bhp) @ 6000rpm; 47.6kW (63.8bhp)/l; 145Nm (107 lbft) @ 4000rpm.
ENGINE STRUCTURE Duratec 8V; chain-driven ohc; 2-valves; aluminium cylinder head, iron block; sequential multipoint electronic fuel injection, Siemens integrated engine management, distributorless ignition; 5-bearing 4-counterweight crank. 1.6 Duratec 16V; 2 belt-driven camshafts; 4-valves; 8-counterweight crank.
TRANSMISSION front wheel drive; hydraulic single plate diaphragm spring clutch; gearbox 5-speed synchromesh; final drive 4.06:1, 1.6, 4.25:1.
CHASSIS steel monocoque; independent front suspension by MacPherson struts with offset spring-damper units, lower arms on separate cross-member; semi-independent rear suspension twist-beam, coil springs; telescopic dampers; hydraulic servo brakes dual circuit diagonally split, front 258mm (10.2in) dia discs, rear 203mm (8in) dia drums, optional 4-channel ABS; rack and pinion PAS; 45l (9.9 gal) (11.9 US gal) fuel tank; 175/65R14 tyres, 5.5J rims.
DIMENSIONS wheelbase 248.6cm (97.9in); track front 147.5cm (58.1in), rear 144.5cm (56.9in); length 391.7cm (154.2in); width 168.3cm (66.3in); height 146.3cm (57.6in); ground clearance 14cm (5.5in); turning circle 10.3m (33.8ft).
EQUIPMENT optional Blaupunkt satellite navigation.
PERFORMANCE maximum speed 158kph (98.4mph), 1.6, 185kph (115.2mph); 34.8kph (21.7mph) @ 1000rpm, 1.6 32.9kph (20.5mph); 0-100kph (62mph) 15.8sec, 1.6 10.6sec; 20.9kg/kW (20.3kg/bhp), 1.6 13.7kg/kW (10.2kg/bhp); fuel consumption 6.2l/100km (45.6mpg), 1.6, 6.6l/100km (42.8mpg).
PRICE 1.3 Finesse £8,495, 1.3LX £8995; 1.6 Ghia £11,195.

2001 RS Focus

It had been 5 years since RS (Rallye Sport) was featured as a premium sporting brand name. To motorsport purists it still meant a no-compromise road-going rally car, inspired by Ford's World Rally Championship (WRC) programme. Short of a works drive it was the closest most people would get to a WRC Focus, the ultimate road-going car with front wheel drive and a turbocharged 2.0-litre Duratec. On the outside it had the rally car's aerodynamics, inside it was functional with a racing appearance that included carbon-fibre-type panels, supportive bucket seats, and even a WRC-style engine start button. The Focus RS was a small-volume production car like its predecessors, with 70 per cent of the standard components re-engineered or replaced. These included the Quaife automatic torque-biassing differential that detected the output to each wheel and redistributed it to reduce wheelspin. Colin McRae helped to provide the rally-driver's eye ingredients essential to a true driver's car, even at the expense of ride and refinement. Along with the other works drivers Carlos Sainz and Pierro Latti, McRae drove prototypes on special stages to match chassis calibration to that of the works cars. Saarlouis-built RS Focus cars were sold through regular dealers although they could be collected from Ford's WRC headquarters in Cumbria.

INTRODUCTION October 2000, on sale spring 2001.
BODY saloon; 3-doors.
ENGINE 4-cylinders, in-line; front; transverse; 84.8mm x 88mm, 1988cc; compr 10:1; 158kW (211.9bhp) @ 5500rpm; 79.48kW (106.6bhp)/l; 310Nm (229lbft) @ 3500rpm.
ENGINE STRUCTURE Duratec RS; 2 belt-driven overhead camshafts; sodium-filled exhaust valves; 4-valves; aluminium cylinder head, iron block; sequential electronic fuel injection (SEFI); Ford EEC-V electronic engine management; electronic distributorless ignition; 5-bearing crankshaft; Garrett stainless steel water-cooled turbocharger, 1bar (14.5psi) max boost; water-cooled intercooler.
TRANSMISSION front wheel drive; heavy-duty AP racing clutch; gearbox 5-speed synchromesh; Quaife automatic torque biasing differential.
CHASSIS steel monocoque; ifs by MacPherson struts with uprated offset coil springs, Sachs racing dampers, 18mm (.71in) anti-roll bar; independent rear suspension by control blade multi-link, Sachs racing dampers with internal rebound spring; anti roll bar; hydraulic servo disc brakes, front Brembo 4-pot twin opposed piston callipers, 335mm (13.2in) dia ventilated front, rear 280mm (11in) dia discs and 2-pot calipers, Bosch MK25 ABS; rack and pinion PAS; 55l (12.1 gal) (14.5 US gal) fuel tank; Michelin Pilot Sport 225/40R18 tyres, 8in rims, OZ alloy wheels.
DIMENSIONS wheelbase 261.5cm (103in); track 148.5cm (58.5in) front, 147.5cm (58.1in) rear; length 429cm (168.9in); width 170cm (66.9in); height 148cm (58.3in); turning circle 10.9m (35.8ft).
EQUIPMENT Sparco race-style leather and Alcantara trimmed seats. Carbon-fibre console.
PERFORMANCE maximum speed 230kph (143.3mph); 36.9kph (23.1mph) @ 1000rpm; 0-100kph (62mph) 6.4sec; fuel consumption 10.1l/100km (27.9mpg).
PRICE £15,995.

447

2002 Mondeo ST220

Sport Technology (ST) was a new branding term for "Accessible and dependable performance derivatives, reflecting the character and extending the core strengths of their foundation models," according to Jost Capito, director of Special Vehicle Engineering Ford of Europe. Essentially they were what were once called Stage 1 performance conversions, less aggressive than Rallye Sport (RS), and in the case of the Mondeo ST220, introduced as what Ford liked to call a grand tourer version of the saloon. RS was for "performance purists", while ST was aimed at a broader group of enthusiasts who wanted a turn of speed without sacrificing practicality and dependability. Critics acclaimed the ST220 a resounding success. *Auto Express* rated it best against keen rivals the MG ZT+190, the Vauxhall Vectra GSi, and the Honda Accord Type R. The Ford's composure on twisty roads earned it praise, as did its luxurious interior and 500-litre boot. Subtly altered bumpers and grille, and 16-spoke alloy wheels gave it a purposeful appearance, along with being 15mm (.59in) lower. The stiffer springing affected the ride and compromised comfort and refinement, but it avoided the harshness associated with more extreme competition cars. More significantly the price of this executive express overlapped the bottom end of the associated Jaguar range.

INTRODUCTION March 2002.
BODY saloon; 4/5-doors, 5-seats; weight 1385kg, estate 1445kg (3185.7lb).
ENGINE Duratec ST 6-cylinders, 60 deg V; front; transverse; 89mm x 79.5mm, 2967cc; compr 10:1; 166kw (222.6bhp) @ 6150rpm; 55.9kw (75.1bhp)/l; 280Nm (207 lbft) @ 4900rpm.
ENGINE STRUCTURE 2 chain-driven overhead camshafts per bank; 4-valves; aluminium cylinder heads and block; sequential electronic fuel injection; Ford Black Oak engine management; electronic distributorless ignition; 4-bearing crankshaft.
TRANSMISSION front wheel drive; MTX75; hydraulic single plate 24cm (9.45in) diaphragm spring clutch with dual-mass flywheel; gearbox 5-speed synchromesh; final drive 3.56:1.
CHASSIS steel monocoque; independent front suspension by MacPherson struts with angled coil-spring units, lower control arms on subframe; anti roll bar; independent rear suspension by quadralink and struts; telescopic dampers; hydraulic servo disc brakes, front 240mm (9.5in) dia ventilated, rear 120mm (4.7in) dia, diagonally split dual circuit, ABS and Electronic Stability Programme (ESP) and emergency brake assist; rack and pinion PAS; 61l (13.4 gal) (16.1 US gal) fuel tank; 225/40R18tyres, 7J rims.
DIMENSIONS wheelbase 275.5cm (108.5in); track front 152cm (59.8in), rear 153.5cm (60.4in); length 473cm (186.2in), estate 480.5cm (189.2in); width 181cm (71.3in); height 144.5cm (56.9in), estate 145.5cm (57.3in); ground clearance 12cm (4.7in); turning circle 11.1m (36.4ft).
EQUIPMENT Recaro heated leather front seats, optional satellite navigation, telematics.
PERFORMANCE maximum speed 243kph (151mph); 0-100kph (62mph) 6.8sec; 8.3kg/kW (6.2kg/bhp); fuel consumption 10.2l/100km (27.7mpg).
PRICE £21,745.

2002 ST170 Focus

When ST (Sport Technology) was applied to the Focus the result, according to Andy Barratt, medium car brand manager, was refined performance, accessible value, and everyday practicality. A keen driver's car, it was a step back from a World Rally Championship contender, with a 2.0-litre Duratec engine and a notable Getrag close-ratio twin-layshaft 6-speed gearbox weighing only 46kg (101.4lb). Each layshaft had its own final-drive ratio; one of 2.88:1 contained first, second, third, and fifth gears, the second with 4.25:1 third, fourth, and reverse gears. One small family Ford in 4 sold through UK dealers was a performance or sporting derivative, so the ST170 with Duratec and variable valve timing (VVT) was important. The intake camshaft had an electro-mechanical and hydraulic control varying the valve opening through 60deg according to engine speed, load, and temperature. VVT calibrated combustion so precisely on cold start-ups that the exhaust catalyst worked straight away. The fuel injection was so exact that no return loop had to be plumbed into a system that met Euro Stage IV emissions requirements. The car was also swift as a result of VVT together with 33.5mm (1.3in) inlet valves and stiffer valve springs allowing it to rev to a red line at 7200rpm and electronic limiter at 7350rpm.

INTRODUCTION March 2002.
BODY saloon; 3-doors, 5-seats; weight 1208kg (2663lb), 5-door 1239kg (2731.5lb).
ENGINE 4-cyls, in-line; front; transverse; 84.8mm x 88mm, 1988cc; compr 10.2:1; 127kW (170.3bhp) @ 7000rpm; 63.9kW (85.7bhp)/l; 197Nm (145 lbft) @ 5500rpm.
ENGINE STRUCTURE 2 belt-driven ohcs with variable valve timing; 4-valves; aluminium cyl head, iron block; sequential multipoint fuel injection; Ford Black Oak electronic engine management; electronic distributorless ignition; 5-bearing crank.
TRANSMISSION front wheel drive; hydraulic 22.8cm (8.98in) clutch, dual-mass flywheel; Getrag twin layshaft gearbox 6-speed synchromesh; automatic; final drive see text.
CHASSIS steel monocoque; ifs by MacPherson struts with angled coil springs and A-arms on separate sub-frame; control blade multi-link rear suspension; 21mm (.83in) anti roll bars; telescopic dampers; hydraulic servo disc brakes, front 300mm (11.8in) dia ventilated, rear 280mm (11.1in)

dia, dual circuit diagonally split, ABS, optional Electronic Stability Programme (ESP); rack and pinion PAS; 50l (11 gal) (13.2 US gal) fuel tank; 215/45R17tyres, 7Jrims, 15-spoke alloy wheels.
DIMENSIONS wheelbase 261.5cm (103in); track front 148.5cm (58.5in), rear 147.5cm (58.1in); length 429cm (168.9in); width 170cm (66.9in); height 148cm (58.3in); turning circle 10.9m (35.8ft).
EQUIPMENT xenon self-levelling headlamps, arc-shaped tailgate spoiler, leather upholstery, Recaros optional; a/c, CD player, leather sports seats std.
PERFORMANCE maximum 210kph (131mph); 37kph (23.1mph) @ 1000rpm; 0-100kph (62mph) 7.9sec; 9.5kg/kW (7.1kg/bhp); 9.1l/100km (31mpg).
PRICE £15,995.

2002 3-door Fiesta 1.4 and diesel

The 3-door Fiesta was first shown at the Paris Motor Show in 2002, making its UK debut a month later at Birmingham in Finesse, LX and Zetec trim. To attract younger drivers it had a sportier sloping roofline, and angled tailgate glass, to create a coupe style against the more upright 5-door saloon. Identical below the body crease line, to achieve a separate identity the 3-door's roof was lowered from the top of the A-pillar towards the back and the C-pillar brought forward by 75mm (2.95in). It meant a loss of 8mm (.31in) in rear-seat headroom but by way of compensation there was more stowage in bigger front door bins and pockets beside the back seat. VDA boot volume was slightly smaller at 268 litres (9.5cuft) against 284 litres (10cuft) for the 5-door. There were 2 engine options, the diesel Duratorq TDCi 1.4-litre, first product of an agreement between Ford and PSA Peugeot Citroen, and the Focus's petrol Duratec 16v 1.4-litre, with electronic, drive-by-wire throttle control. The arrival of the 3-door coincided with Durashift EST (Electronic Shift Technology) an automatic-shift manual transmission providing the flexibility of manual shifting with the ease of an automatic. The driver could choose between fully automatic and a sequential manual shift actuated by three electric motors two for shifting the gears, one operating the clutch.

INTRODUCTION October 2002.
BODY saloon; 3-doors, 5-seats; weight 1035kg (2281.8lb), diesel 1065kg (2347.9lb).
ENGINE 4-cylinders, in-line; front; transverse; 76mm x 76.5mm, 1388cc; compr 11:1; 58kW (77.8bhp) @ 5700rpm; 41.8kW (56.1bhp)/l; 124Nm (92 lbft) @ 3500 rpm. TDCi: 73.7 x 82mm; 1399cc; compr 18:1; 50kW (67.1bhp) @ 4000rpm; 35.8kW (47.9bhp)/l; 160Nm (118 lbft) @ 2000rpm.
ENGINE STRUCTURE Duratec; 2 belt-driven ohcs; 4-valves; aluminium cyl head and block; Siemens electronic fuel inj, electronic EEC-V engine management, breakerless ignition; 5-bearing crankshaft. Duratorq TDCi 1 overhead camshaft; common rail direct inj with turbocharger.
TRANSMISSION front wheel drive; hydraulic 18cm (7.1in) clutch; gearbox 5-speed synchromesh; automatic; final drive 4.06:1. Diesel 21cm (8.27in) clutch, final drive 3.37:1.
CHASSIS steel monocoque; independent front suspension by MacPherson struts with offset coil spring, lower arms on subframe; rear suspension torsion beam axle; telescopic dampers anti-roll bar; hydraulic, vacuum servo, diagonally split dual circuit brakes 258mm (10.2in) front ventilated discs; rear drums 203mm (8in); ABS and 4-channel electronic brake force distribution; rack and pinion PAS; 45l (9.9 gal) (11.9 US gal) fuel tank; 175/65R14tyres, 5.5, 6J rims.
DIMENSIONS wheelbase 248.7cm (97.9in); track front 147.5cm (58.1in), rear 144.4cm (56.9in); length 391.7cm (154.2in); width 168cm (66.1in); height 141.7cm (55.8in); ground clearance 12cm (4.7in); turning circle 10.3m (33.8ft).
EQUIPENT passive anti-theft system D-PATS.
PERFORMANCE maximum speed 168kph (104.7mph), TDCi 164kph (102.2mph); 34.3kph (21.4mph) @ 1000rpm, TDCi 42.8kph (26.7mph); 0-100kph (62mph) 13.2sec, TDCi 14.9sec; 17.9kg/kW (13.3kg/bhp), TDCi 21.3kg/kW (15.9kg/bhp); fuel consumption 6.4l/100km (44.1mpg), TDCi 4.3l/100km (65.7mpg).
PRICE 1.6 Ghia 11,195, TDCi £10,965.

Durashift EST was tested to be maintenance-free for up to 145000miles (23,3350km). "Durashift EST adapts to changing driving conditions, like hills and curves, making it ideal for drivers who would prefer an automatic but don't want to pay a penalty in terms of performance feel or fuel economy."

Glen Goold, Chief Program Engineer, New Ford Fiesta

2002 Fusion

The Fusion concept at the 2001 Frankfurt Motor Show wore the customary aspect of an off-road adventure vehicle embarking on a safari. At Geneva 6 months later, in production form, it emerged as a practical highly adaptable mini-MPV, with 5 seats that could be folded flat to provide the load space of an estate car several sizes bigger. With ample compartments for maps, picnic items, and family paraphernalia, the Fusion was a versatile small car on the Fiesta platform, with all the Fiesta's roadworthiness and refinement. The obligation for a volume car manufacturer to produce as many variations on a platform as possible, brought Ford into a diverse flourishing market. But the Frankfurt Fusion's turbocharged direction-injection petrol engine with Variable Cam Timing (VCT), automated Durashift Electronic Select Transmission, navigation system with telematics, and integrated multi-media entertainment system, was not carried through to production. Instead, the Geneva car was an Urban Activity Vehicle (UAV) with a sensible choice of TDCi common rail turbodiesel, or 2 16-valve petrol engines. With its tall body easy to get in and out of, and clever detailing like a front passenger seat that folded into a table, Fusion provided taxi-like manoeuvrability and roominess for the urban dweller within the footprint of a compact car.

INTRODUCTION spring 2002. BODY saloon; 5-doors, 5-seats; 1070kg (2359lb), 1.6 1080kg (2381lb), TDCi 1102kg (2429.5lb). ENGINE 4-cyls, in-line; front; trans; 76mm x 76.5mm, 1388cc; cr 11:1; 58kW (77.8bhp) @ 5700rpm; 41.8kW (56bhp)/l; 124Nm (92 lbft) @ 3500 rpm. TDCi: 73.7 x 82mm; 1399cc; cr 18:1; 50kW (67.1bhp) @ 4000rpm; 35.8kW (47.9bhp)/l; 160Nm (118 lbft) @ 2000rpm. 1.6: 79 x 81.4mm; 1596cc; cr 11:1; 76kW (102bhp) @ 6000rpm; 47.6kW/l (64bhp/l); 145Nm (107 lbft) @ 4000rpm.
ENGINE STRUCTURE Duratec; 2 belt-driven ohcs; 4-valves; alumin cyl head and block; Siemens electronic fuel inj, electronic EEC-V engine management, breakerless ign; 5-bearing crank. Duratorq TDCi 1 ohc; common rail direct injection with turbocharger. TRANSMISSION front wheel drive; hydraulic 18cm (7.1in) clutch; 5-speed synchro; auto; 4.25:1. 1.6 and diesel 21cm (8.27in) clutch, diesel 3.37:1. CHASSIS steel monocoque; ifs by MacPherson struts, offset coil spring, lower arms on subframe; rear susp

torsion beam axle; telesc dampers anti-roll bar; hydraulic, vacuum servo, diag split dual circuit brakes 258mm (10.2in) front ventilated discs; rear drums 203mm (8in); ABS and 4-channel electronic brake force distribution; rack and pinion PAS; 45l (9.9 gal) (11.8 US gal) fuel tank; tyres 195/60R15 or 195/60R15 with alloy wheels, 5.5, 6J rims. DIMENSIONS wheelbase 248.5cm (97.8in); track 147.4cm (58in) front, 143.5cm (56.5in) rear; length 402cm (158.3in); width 172.1cm (67.8in); height 152.8cm (60.2in); clearance 12cm (4.7in); turning circle 9.9m (32.5ft). EQUIPMENT 60/40 split rear seat, dual-stage front airbags, Ambiente, Trend, and Elegance trims. PERFORMANCE max 1.4 163kph (102mph), 1.6 180kph (113mph), TDCi 159kph (99.4mph); 0-100kph (62mph) 1.4 13.7sec, 1.6 10.9sec, TDCi 15.5sec;18.4kg/kW (13.8kg/bhp), 1.6 14.2kg/kW (10.6kg/bhp), TDCi 22kg/kW (16.4kg/bhp); 6.5l/100km (43.5mpg), 1.6 6.6l/100km (42.8mpg), TDCi 4.4l/100km (64.2mpg). PRICE 1.4 £9995; 1.4TD £10,665; 1.6 £11,495.

2002 Transit Connect, Tourneo Connect

Light and sub one tonne vans at the Amsterdam RAI Commercial Vehicle Show in February 2002 incorporated the Transit name, which after 35 years meant almost as much as Ford did. Connect extended the Transit pedigree to the light commercial load-box market. Not a car-derived van, it had been designed, engineered, tested and constructed on commercial vehicle lines. The bodyshell was toughened with high-strength steel, double-skinned body sides, 2 side cross members and a boron steel front cross member. It was reinforced underneath and the suspension strengthened for off-road. Anti-roll bars gave car-like stability and handling. There was a high-roof long wheelbase derivative, and a short wheelbase light commercial, a choice of petrol, diesel and turbo diesel engines, and either a bulkhead or sliding side-load doors. The swb Transit Connect was the only vehicle in its class that could take 2 Europallets, 1.2m (3.9ft) x 0.8m (2.6ft), through the rear doors. Sloping body sides made best use of the load-box area and the folding passenger seat provided a long flat floor up to the footwell. An ingenious flexible load restraint system allowed customers to install their own racking. Tourneo offered van ability during the week, car qualities at the weekend, and warranty terms were 2 years with a 10 year anti-perforation body guarantee.

INTRODUCTION spring 2002. BODY saloon; 5-doors, 5-seats; weight swb Transit 1345kg (2965.2lb), lwb 1380kg (3042.4lb); Tourneo swb 1420kg (3130.5lb), lwb 1475kg (3251.8lb). ENGINE 4-cylinders, in-line; front; transverse; 80.6mm x 88mm, 1796cc; cr 10:1; 86kW (115.3bhp) @ 5750rpm; 47.9kW (64.2bhp)/l; 160Nm (118 lbft) @ 4400rpm. TDdi: 82.5 x 82mm; 1753cc; cr 19.4:1; 55kW (73.8bhp) @ 4000rpm; 31.4kW (42.1bhp)/l; 175Nm (129 lbft) @ 1800rpm. TDCi: 66kW (88.5bhp); 37.7kW (50.5bhp)/l; 220Nm (162 lbft) @ 1700rpm. ENGINE STRUCTURE Duratec; belt-driven two ohc; 4-valves; aluminium cyl head, iron block with aluminium ladder frame; Visteon Bosch sequential fuel inj; Visteon PCM engine management; breakerless ignition; 5-bearing crank. TDdi and TDCi all iron engine, 2-valves, single belt-driven ohc, turbocharged with intercooler, TDdi Visteon PCM management Bosch inj, TDCi Ford SMECU Delphi direct inj. TRANSMISSION front wheel drive; MTX75; hydraulic 22cm (8.7in) single plate clutch; 5-spd synchro; final drive 4.06:1. TDdi 23.8cm (9.4in) clutch, TDCi 22.8cm (9in). CHASSIS steel monocoque; ifs by MacPherson struts, gas pressurised dampers and anti-roll bar; rear susp dual rate multi-leaf springs, gas pressurised dampers; anti-roll bar; hydraulic servo brakes, front 278mm (10.9in) dia ventilated discs, rear 228cm (9in) dia drums, 278mm (10.9in) discs optional, ABS and Traction Assist opt with rear discs; rack and pinion PAS; 60l (13.2 gal) (15.8 US gal) fuel tank; 195/65R15 reinforced radial-ply tyres. DIMENSIONS wbase swb 266.4cm (105in), lwb 291.2cm (115in); track front 150.5cm (59.25in), rear 155.2cm (61.1in); length swb 427.8cm (168.4in), lwb 452.5cm (178in); width swb 179.5cm (70.7in); height swb 173.9cm (68.5in), lwb 190.6cm (75in); ground clearance 16.7cm (6.6in); turning circle swb 11m (36.1ft), lwb 11.9m (39ft).

Like the Transit, Transit
Connect had an engine
immobiliser, remote keyless
entry, and key locking bonnet.
Safety systems included
standard driver airbag.
ABS and passenger and side
airbags were optional.
Transit Connect was
assembled at the new Kocaeli
plant near Izmit, Turkey.

2002 Ford GT

In sporting terms the most famous car to carry the Ford blue oval, without qualification like Lotus or Cosworth, was the GT40. The series of sports-racing coupes culminated in the mighty J-car and Mark IV, but it was always known by its earliest title, signifying Grand Touring and the 40 inches (101.6cm) it stood from the ground to the top of the roof. Yet although the reproduction shared the mystique and the name and even a robust American V8 amidships, it shared not a single dimension. The new car was more than 45.7cm (18in) longer and at 111.8cm (44in) tall could well have been called the GT44. Its lines drew from, said Ford, and refined the best features of GT40 history, expressing the car's identity through modern proportion and surface development. The 5.4-litre engine looked the part, with a complex array of polished stainless-steel header pipes and braided stainless steel fuel lines with anodized aluminum fittings, but it now had a supercharger and an intercooler. Instead of the semi-monocoque hull of 23swg (.024in) sheet steel with square tube stiffening, here was an aluminium spaceframe. The interior, beneath doors cut away into the roof, was a more faithful reproduction, with ventilated seats, the same instrument layout with analogue gauges and big tachometer, and modern versions of traditional toggle switches

INTRODUCTION Detroit 2002.
BODY coupe; 2-doors, 2-seats; weight 1496.9kg (3300lb).
ENGINE 8-cylinders, 90deg V; mid; 90.2mm x 105.8mm, 5408cc; compr 8.5:1; 372.9kW (500bhp) @ 5250rpm; 68.9kW (92.5bhp)/l; 678Nm (500lbft) @ 3250rpm.
ENGINE STRUCTURE 2 chain-driven overhead camshafts per bank; 4-valves; aluminium cylinder heads and block; Bosch port fuel injection, 2 injectors/cylinder; electronic returnless fuel delivery; 5-bearing crankshaft; Eaton-Lysholm supercharger and intercooler; Ford EEC-V engine management
TRANSMISSION rear wheel drive; RBT transaxle; hydraulic twin plate 24cm (9.45in) clutch; gearbox 6-speed synchromesh; limited slip differential.
CHASSIS aluminium space frame, aluminium body shell, selected composite panels; front and rear independent suspension by unequal length control arm with coil-over spring-damper units; anti roll bars front and rear; 355.6mm (14in) hydraulic servo disc brakes, cross-drilled Brembo ventilated discs and 4-piston calipers;

rack and pinion hydraulic PAS; 71.9l (15.8 gal) (19 US gal) fuel tank; 235/45R18 and 315/40R19tyres, 18 x 8in x 10in wheels.
DIMENSIONS wheelbase 271cm (106.7in); track 159cm (62.6in) front, rear 160.8cm (63.3in); length 463.3cm (182.4in); width 194.4cm (76.5in); height 112cm (44.1in); ground clearance 14cm (5.5in); turning circle 12.2m (40ft).
PERFORMANCE maximum speed in excess of 305kph (190mph); 0-100kph (62mph) 4.0sec; 4kg/kW (3kg/bhp); fuel consumption 25.7-17.7l/100km (11-16mpg).

2002 StreetKa

The StreetKa roadster was a concept at the Turin Motor Show in 2000. Public and press reaction to it was good, and by Geneva the following spring Ford confirmed that it would go into production with the Duratec 1.6 8-valve engine. Designed by David Wilkie of the Turin Ghia Studio, it was turned into a production reality, ironically by Ghia's old rival Industrie Pininfarina SpA. Under Wilkie's supervision Pininfarina engineered it for volume production and launch in 2003.

"We drew crowds whenever we showed it," said Martin Leach, Ford of Europe's vice president of product development. Ford wanted to find a new way of reaching customers unconnected from motor sport, yet exemplifying the nature of the Ford range. StreetKa teamed up with Kylie Minogue as a sponsor of her 39-date 2002 European Fever Tour, from Cardiff to Barcelona. The production StreetKa featured in photographs with Kylie, providing a preview before it went on sale in 2003. "The partnership with Kylie was the perfect way to show off StreetKa ahead of its launch," said Peter Fleet, marketing director. "StreetKa and Kylie had a lot in common; they were both small, beautiful and stylish." The car was formally unveiled to the public at the Paris Motor Show in September 2002.

INTRODUCTION 2003.
BODY coupe; 2-doors, 4-seats; weight 1061kg (2339.1lb).
ENGINE 4-cylinders, in-line; front; transverse; 82.07 x 75.48mm; 1597cc; compr 9.5:1; 70kW (93.9bhp) @ 5500rpm; 43.8kW (58.8bhp)/l; 135Nm (100lbft) @ 4250rpm.
ENGINE STRUCTURE Duratec 8V; chain-driven overhead camshaft; 2-valves; aluminium cylinder head, iron block; sequential multipoint electronic fuel injection, Siemens integrated engine management, distributorless electronic ignition; 5-bearing 4-counterweight crankshaft.
TRANSMISSION front wheel drive; hydraulic single plate diaphragm spring clutch; gearbox 5-speed synchromesh; final drive 4.25:1
CHASSIS steel monocoque; independent front suspension by MacPherson struts with offset spring-damper units, lower arms on separate cross-member; anti-roll bar; semi-independent rear suspension twist-beam, coil springs; telescopic dampers; hydraulic servo brakes dual circuit diagonally split, front 25.8cm (10.16in)
dia ventilated discs, rear 20.3cm (8in) dia drums, 4-channel ABS optional on left hand drive; rack and pinion PAS; 42l (9.2gal) (11.1 US gal) fuel tank; 195/45R16tyres, 5J rims six-spoke alloy wheels.
DIMENSIONS wheelbase 244.8cm (96.4in); track front 141.7cm (55.8in), rear 145.2cm (57.2in); length 365cm (143.7in); width 169.5cm (66.7in); height 133.5cm (52.6in); ground clearance 14cm (5.5in); turning circle 11.1m (36.4ft).
EQUIPMENT Ford 6000 RDS/EON two-channel radio/CD player; air conditioning, leather upholstery optional.
PERFORMANCE maximum speed 173kph (108mph); 0-100kph (62mph) 12.1sec; 15.2kg/kW (11.3kg/bhp); fuel consumption 7.9l/100km (35.8mpg).

Chronology of Ford in Britain

1896 June: Henry Ford drives his first Quadricycle on the streets of Detroit.

1903 16 June: Henry Ford and eleven investors sign US incorporation papers.
July: First Ford car sold to Dr E Pfenning of Chicago.
Motor Car Act raises British speed limit to 20mph (32.1kph).

1904 Ford sales in Britain established by Central Motor Car Company London.
First showing of Ford cars outside US at the Agricultural Hall Exhibition London.

1906 Nov: Olympia. Model N Ford, £165 cheapest 4-cylinder on British market.

1907 Perry, Thornton & Schreiber take over Ford agency from Central Motor Car Co.

1908 1 Oct: Model T unveiled at Olympia Motor Show, London.

1910 Disproportionate Horse Power tax on large cars imposed in Lloyd George budget.

1911 Ford Motor Company (England) Ltd incorporated to handle Ford UK business.
Percival Perry heads new company, showroom at 55 Shaftesbury Ave, London.
May: Henry Alexander takes Model T to the top of Ben Nevis
23 Oct: Model T production at Trafford Park, first non US Ford assembly.

1912 Ford is Britain's biggest car manufacturer; annual production 3000.
Henry Ford watches Model Ts at Brooklands. Race won by dealer AE George.

1913 1 April: Detroit introduces moving assembly line.

1914 5 Jan: US Ford employees' pay rises to $5 per day.
Aug: Moving assembly line installed at Trafford Park.
By year's end 8300 Model Ts are made.

1915 War production of Model Ts increased to 100 a day.
McKenna Duties apply 33 per cent tax on imported cars and parts.

1915 Millionth Ford car produced.

1916 Model T Fords see war service with Lawrence of Arabia.

1917 July: Henry Ford & Son Inc registered; Ford family shareholders.
Fordson tractor production starts in Dearborn.
Percival Perry arranges Board of Agriculture & Fisheries to test Fordson tractors.
Government orders 6000 US tractors. *The Motor* complains on behalf of UK industry.
First Fordson tractor shipped from Detroit to Manchester.

1918 Percival LD Perry becomes Baron Perry.

1919 Sept, to end of 1920, Trafford Park builds 46,000 vehicles.
Tractor production starts in Cork.
Henry Ford buys Ford Motor Company stock held by outside shareholders.
Ford Motor Company and Fordson now personally owned
Jan: Edsel Ford succeeds Henry Ford as president of Ford Motor Company

1919 Mary Perry resigns from Ford Motor Company (England) Limited over policy.

1920 - to 1922 Trafford Park makes left hand drive cars for export.
UK Motor Car Act raises annual tax of Model T to £23.
Ford is making half the world's cars.

1922 Ford buys Lincoln for $8 million; Ford first to make 1million cars a year.
Research laboratory set up at Trafford Park with test microphotography.
Tractor production in Cork discontinued.
Dagenham (Essex) chosen as site of new Ford-Britain factory.

1924 Ford buys 295 acres at Dagenham. Williams' Docks Company paid £150,000.
McKenna Duties repealed, car imports 47,677, not matched until 1960.

1925 April: 250,000th Model T made at Trafford Park.
April: McKenna Duties reintroduced.
24 Nov: General Motors buys controlling interest in Vauxhall for £510,000.

1927 May: Model T production ends in USA at 16.5 million.
19 Aug: 11.58am Model T production at Trafford Park ends after 301,980.
2 Dec: Model A production starts; Model T

1927 production ends in Cork.

1928 April: Wall Street prices unsteady.
Henry Alexander takes Model A to the top of Ben Nevis.
Henry Ford visits UK; lunch with Lloyd George, tea with King and Queen.
7 Dec: Ford (England) Ltd floated as Ford Motor Company Ltd.
Ford Motor Company Ltd issues capital of £7million 40% UK 60% US.

1929 17 May: Edsel Ford inaugurates construction at Dagenham with silver spade.
Oct: Wall Street crashes.
Cork recommences tractor production with Model N serial no 757369.

1930 Britain abolishes 20mph speed limit, introduces compulsory car insurance.
Oct: Henry Ford visits part-completed Dagenham factory.

1931 First Ford made in Cologne; Morris introduces £100 Minor 2-seater
Friday 27 Sep: Trafford Park closes.
Tuesday 1 Oct: first vehicle made at Dagenham, a Model AA truck.
Perry asks Dearborn for small car; Model Y design starts.
Dec: Rowland Smith goes to America to monitor Model Y progress.

1932 A Standard 9, a Morris Minor, and an Austin 7 sent to Dearborn for evaluation.
Feb: Model Y design complete.
Feb: Irish tariffs compel transfer tractor production from Cork to Dagenham.
Cork makes last tractor Model N, serial no 779135.
9 March: Ford V8 launched in US.
Briggs Motor Bodies and Kelsey Hayes Wheel Company open Dagenham plants.
Model B production begins.
Aug: Dagenham production begins of Model Y, first Ford designed for Europe.
AA 1-ton truck with 3.3-litre 4-cylinder side-valve engine introduced.
Oct: first V8-18 on sale in Britain; Ford Motor Show, Royal Albert Hall.

1933 19 Feb: Model N tractor production starts at Dagenham with no 779154.
Model Y takes 19% of market against Austin 29% and Morris 27%.
Oct: V8-40 introduced in Britain; Ford Motor Show, Royal Albert Hall.
Model Y styling revised.
Fordson name applied to new 2-ton truck.
3.6-litre V8 available only 20-seat coach.
Dagenham makes 2,778 tractors in first year.

1934 Mar-May: Model A driven from India to London, 8075miles (12995km).
March: Road Traffic Act: driving tests, urban speed limits, pedestrian crossings.

1934 HRH Prince of Wales visits Dagenham; drives round plant in V8-40 Phaeton.
V8 in 2-ton truck, with half-elliptic springing, sliding roof in forward control cab.
Fordson truck payloads 5cwt to 2tons include 6x2 Surrey, 6x4 Sussex 2-tonner.
1 Oct: Model C 10HP production starts; Ford Motor Show, Royal Albert Hall.

1935 12 Mar: V8-48 on sale in Britain.
17 July: First Dagenham V8 engine: first V8 car 25 July.
1 Sep: V8-60 22HP introduced.
15 Oct: Model CX production starts; Ford Motor Show, Royal Albert Hall.
17 Oct: Perry announces the £100 Model Y; Fordson Tug 3-wheeled truck.
12 Nov: V8-68 on sale in Britain.

1936 Jan: PG Christea and I Zamfirescou win Monte Carlo Rally in Ford V8.
24 June: introduction of V8-62 22HP; discontinued 3 Feb 1940.
Oct: Ford Motor Show, Royal Albert Hall.
Dagenham makes 12,675 tractors. V8 engine standardised in trucks from 15cwt.

1937 25 Jan: V8-78 on sale in Britain. 25cwt truck with 2.2-litre V8 and forward cab.
22 Mar: Model 7W 10HP production starts.
1 Sep: Model 7Y 8HP production begins; V8-62 gets outside opening boot.
Oct: Ford Motor Show, Royal Albert Hall.

1937 Fordson tractors change from dark blue to orange.

1938 Jan: G Bakker Schut and K Ton win Monte Carlo Rally in Ford V8.
Jan: Sir Percival Perry becomes Lord Perry of Stock Harvard.
March: V8-78F on sale in Britain.
22 Apr: V8-81A on sale in Britain.
May: Sir Malcolm Campbell made director of Ford Motor Company Limited.
Car tax 15/- (75p) per horse power, petrol tax 9d (3.75p) per gallon.
Sep: 8hp Model 7Y goes into production at Dagenham.
3 Oct: Prefect 10HP E93A production starts, 10cwt van 30HP E83W.
13 Dec: V8-91A introduced in Britain; discontinued 16 Jan 1940.
Henry Ford and Harry Ferguson shake hands on joint tractor agreement.

1939 Feb: E93A Prefect coupe introduced.
16 Sep: petrol rationing introduced.
Oct: V8 30HP Model 91A introduced.
Oct: Air Ministry asks Ford-Britain make Rolls-Royce Merlin aero engines.
31 Oct: Anglia 8HP E04A production starts. Commercial Vehicle Division plans move to Manchester but remains in Essex.
Fordson tractors modified to run on Tractor Vaporising Oil (TVO).
Perry and Hennessy make wartime provision

1939 of 3000 tractors painted green.
Patrick Hennessy appointed general manager Dagenham.
Thames replaces Fordson name on medium and heavy duty trucks.
-1945: 262,007 V8 engines produced.

1940 Oct: 33% Purchase Tax on cars introduced. 5cwt van EO4C. 4-cylinder reinstated for trucks.
-1945 war casualties: Trafford Park 3 dead 8 injured. Dagenham 5 dead 24 injured.

1941 Rowland Smith made MD, Hennessy leaves for Ministry of Aircraft Production.
July: Patrick Hennessy knighted for work at the Ministry of Aircraft Production.
June: Specially equipped factory at Urmston Manchester makes Rolls-Royce Merlins.
-1945: 12,707 vehicles assembled from US and Canada components.
-1945: 184,579 2 and 4-wheel drive vehicles manufactured.
-1945 137,483 tractors manufactured.
-1945 15 and 30cwt 4x2s; 30cwt and 3-ton 4x4s; 3ton 6x4s made for military.
-1945 2ton fire engines made with Jensen bodywork for National Fire Service.

1942 3,637 vehicles boxed for North Africa.

1943 26 May: Death of Edsel Ford, aged 49.

1944 Rowland Smith knighted.

1945 June: car production recommences at Dagenham with 8HP Anglia.
Petrol is 2/- (10p) a gallon.
Sep: Henry Ford retires, 28-year old grandson Henry Ford II takes over.
19 March: Fordson Major E27N tractor goes into production at Dagenham.
Tractor colour changes from green to blue.
5 and 10cwt vans, forward control V8 trucks 2-5tons in production.
Mar: Sir Patrick Hennessy joins Ford-Britain board.

1946 Dagenham builds its millionth vehicle, a Prefect 10HP.
9N tractor introduced, Ferguson sues for $340million alleging patent infringement.

1947 7 Apr: death of Henry Ford aged 83.
Car Purchase Tax doubled to 66.6%.
16 July: V8 Pilot E71A introduced.
June: 25,000th tractor produced at Dagenham.

1948 1 Jan: Flat rate of car tax introduced at £10.
Feb: Henry Ford II drives 250,000th postwar Ford off Dagenham line.
27 Oct: Anglia 8HP E94A production begins.
Sir Patrick Hennessy appointed managing director; Lord Perry retires aged 70.

1948 27 Oct: First post-war Earls Court Motor Show.
21 Dec: Prefect 10HP E493A production starts.
Dagenham makes record 50,561 tractors, offers first Perkins P6 diesel for E27N.
First shipment of British Ford cars sent to the United States.

1949 Ken Wharton and Joy Cooke win Tulip Rally in Ford Anglia.
5cwt van E494C, E83W estate car.
Sep: Pound devalued against the US dollar by 30% from $4.03 to $2.80.
Briggs Motor Bodies acquires former Spitfire factory at Southampton.
Thames normal control 4x2s, 6x4s artic and PSV chassis introduced, 2-8tons.
Car and Truck Engineering Department installed at Rainham, Essex.
Perkins P6 diesel factory option on trucks.
Hydraulic servo brakes standard.

1950 Ken Wharton wins Tulip and Lisbon Rallies with Ford V8 Pilot.
Car Engineering and Truck Engineering divide. Staff Engineer for each.
Apr: petrol tax doubled to 1s 6d (7.5p). Gallon costs 3s 0d (15p).
Apr: Car Purchase Tax restored to 33.3%.
May: petrol rationing ends in Britain.
Oct: Consul and Zephyr announced at Earls Court Motor Show in London.

1950 Sir Rowland Smith appointed chairman.

1951 1 Jan: Consul EOTA production starts.
12 Feb: Zephyr Six EOTTA production starts. Consul, Zephyr Convertibles.
Government buys 5000 army 4x4s, 2E and 3E, Canadian V8 engine Commer cab.
Petrol Tax increased, reintroduction of double Purchase Tax on new cars.

1952 Jan: SH Allard wins Monte Carlo Rally in Allard P1 with Ford V8 engine.
Apr: Harry Ferguson settles for $9.25 million, pays $4million legal costs.
Petrol tax increased again.
British Motor Corporation formed.
Fordson New Major multi-fuel tractor launched at Smithfield Show.

1953 Jan: M Gatsonides and P Worledge win Monte Carlo Rally in Zephyr Six.
Jan: Ford-Britain builds its two millionth vehicle, a Zephyr Six.
Feb: Ford buys Briggs Motor Bodies and its five UK plants for £3.2m.
Apr: Car Purchase Tax now 50%.
7 Oct: Popular 10HP 103E production begins.
Southampton plant changes to commercial vehicles; production passes 50,000.
4-cylinder 5-bearing 3.6-litre 52.2kW (70bhp) ohv replaces V8 on Thames trucks.
Ken Wharton wins Tulip Rally in Consul.

1953 28 Oct: Anglia, Prefect 100E and Popular 103E production starts.
2 Nov: Zephyr Zodiac EOTTA introduced.
17 Dec: Prefect 100E production starts.

1954 Thames Trader 2-5 tons forward control, tipper, artic, first Ford diesel.

1955 Aug: new 250,000 sq ft paint, trim and assembly plant opens at Dagenham.
13 Sep: 100E Escort estate production starts.
23 Sep: 100E Squire estate production starts.
Car Purchase Tax rises to 60%. HP min deposit 15% repayment 24 months.

1956 Sir Patrick Hennessy appointed chairman, Sir Rowland Smith retires.
Feb: Mark II Consul, Zephyr, Zodiac production begins.
Apr: Government fixes car HP deposits at minimum 50%.
Death of Lord Perry.
Prefect wins Canadian Winter Rally.
Oct: Consul Mk II Estate production begins.
Oct: Suez Crisis; petrol rationing reintroduced until May 1957.

1957 2 pedal electric clutch option on Anglia and Prefect, only about 50 are made.
Ford Taunus 12M, 15M and 17M imported to UK.
Apr: official opening of Aveley, Essex parts centre.

1957 Consul Mark II De Luxe introduced.
10/15cwt unit construction Thames vans with ifs side loading replace E83W 10cwt.
Thames Trader forward control 4.9-litre petrol and 5.4-litre diesel 6cyl 1.5-7tons.

1958 Keith Duckworth and Mike Costin form Cosworth Engineering.
Ford first British motor company with computer system. It occupies entire room.
HP restrictions lifted.
Dec: First British motorway, 8.5 miles of Preston bypass opens.

1959 April: Car Purchase Tax reverts to 50%; reduces Zephyr from £916 to £865.
Ford analogue computer investigates suspension geometry and vibration.
5 May: Prefect 107E production starts.
25 Aug: Popular 100E production starts.
3 Sep: 997cc Anglia 105E and Popular 100E production starts.
Ford wins team prize in Safari Rally.
2 Nov: M1 opens, minister of transport Ernest Marples appalled at speeds.
Nov: G Burgess, S Croft-Pearson (Zephyr) win RAC Rally.
Dec: First race for Cosworth-modified 105E Anglia engine, Brands Hatch.

1960 Jan: Ford buys 346 acres near Liverpool for new factory.
Ford USA buys all shares of privately-held

1960 Ford of Britain .
19 March: Jim Clark wins Formula Junior Goodwood with Ford Cosworth engine.
May: Jaguar buys Daimler
Commercial vehicle assembly at Langley, former Hawker Hurricane factory, London.
Thames PSV double-deck special carries cyclists through Dartford-Purfleet tunnel.
Front wheel disc brakes optional on Consul, Zephyr, Zodiac.
Ford wins team prize in Safari Rally.
Aug: design and engineering staff move to Aveley, Essex.
Ford plans new tractor factory on 100-acre site at Basildon, Essex.

1961 April: Classic 109E, Anglia 5 and 7cwt van production starts.
July: Capri 109E production starts.
Ford wins team prize in Safari Rally.
Last Ford Prefect.
Oct: 3-door Anglia estate announced; disc brakes standard on Consul, Zephyr.
Dec: Mark III Zodiac production starts.

1962 Jan: Mark III Zephyr production starts.
Car Purchase Tax reduced from 55% to 45%, then in Nov to 25%.
28 July: Classic 1500, Capri 116E production starts.
Truck Engineering Division moves to Gants Hill, Ilford.
Normal control Traders have curved

1962 screens; options 5 gears and 2-speed axles.
Special Vehicle Operations tailors 7000
trucks, vans to customers' requirements.
1.6 Perkins diesel alternative to Consul 1.7-
litre in Thames van.
Sep: production Anglia 1200 and Super 123E
starts.
Sept: Cortina 1200 production starts; plan
for 2-seater Cortina abandoned.
Fordson tractors change from blue and
orange to blue and grey, new Dexta model.

1963 Jan: Cortina 1500 production starts, Lotus
Cortina (made by Lotus) introduced.
Ford bid for Ferrari fails; Ford Advanced
Vehicles, Slough set up.
Feb: Capri GT, March Cortina Estate; April
Cortina GT introduced.
8 Mar: first car produced from new
Halewood plant on Merseyside, an Anglia.
Production at former Briggs factory in
Doncaster transferred to Dagenham.
July: 4-door Corsair production starts.
Aug: GT production starts.
Sep: Corsair 2-door production starts.
Jack Sears (Cortina GT) wins British saloon
car championship.

1964 1 Apr: GT40 prototype announced;
Halewood transmission plant opens.
Peter Hughes (Cortina) wins Safari Rally.
17 Apr: Mustang announced.
100-acre tractor plant opens at Basildon,

1964 new 2000, 3000, 4000, and 5000 models.
June: Le Mans Ford team fails to finish.
Jim Clark (Lotus Cortina) wins British saloon
car championship.
Introduction Aeroflow ventilation system.

1965 Carroll Shelby takes over Ford racing team;
7.0-litre GT40 Mark II.
Executive Zodiac introduced.
Thames name dropped from commercials,
range discontinued except for K-series.
Ford makes 85,000 commercial vehicles,
launches D-series for heavy duty sector.
May: Jim Clark wins Indianapolis 500 in
Lotus-Ford 38.
Borg Warner Model 35 automatics optional
Cortina, Corsair.
Ford Germany introduces V4 and V6
engines.
Roger Clark (Cortina) wins Gulf London
and Scottish Rallies.
June: Le Mans, Ferrari 1-2-3, six Fords fail
to finish.
June: Lotus Cortina A frame discontinued,
leaf-spring suspension introduced.
9 Aug: first Transits out of Langley and
Germany, replace 10/15cwt Thames.
Sept: Corsair 2000 V4 GT production starts.
Oct: Transit goes on sale.
Sir John Whitmore (Lotus Cortina) wins
European saloon car championship.
Dec: production Mark IV Zephyr 4 and
Zodiac starts.

1965 Dec: 70mph (112.37kph) "temporary" speed
limit imposed in Britain.

1966 Apr: launch of MkIV Zephyr/Zodiac.
Ford wins team prize in Safari Rally.
Car Purchase Tax increased from 25% to
27.5%, petrol tax raised.
American-made J-cars not ready for Le
Mans.
June: 3 Mk II GT40s stage formation finish
1-2-3 at Le Mans.
Sep: Cortina Mark II production starts;
millionth Cortina made.
Oct: Cortina Mark II and Executive Zodiac
announced.
B Soderstrom, G Palm (Lotus Cortina) win
Acropolis and RAC Rallies.
John Fitzpatrick (Anglia) wins British Saloon
Car Championship.
US enacts safety and emission legislation for
cars.
After making 113,623 commercial vehicles
Ford is Britain's number one producer.
Cortina best-selling car in Britain; UK car
imports are 6 per cent.

1967 1 Jan: Slough factory taken over by JW
Automotive Engineering.
Jan: Corsair 2000E introduced.
Jan: approval given for Escort Twin-Cam,
project codename J25.
Feb: Cortina Mark II Estate launched.
Mar: Lotus-Cortina Mark II to be made at

1967 Dagenham.

Ford wins team prize in Safari Rally.

4 June: Jim Clark wins Dutch Grand Prix Zandvoort with Lotus-Ford 49.

June: Mark IV J-cars win Le Mans.

June: Comuta electric car announced.

June: creation of Ford of Europe, chairman John Andrews.

Transit automatic transmission optional.

B Soderstrom (Lotus Cortina) wins Swedish Rally.

Cortina 1600E introduced.

Sep: 1300 and 1600 crossflow Kent engines announced.

17 Nov: Escort, replacement for Anglia, begins production at Halewood.

Nov: Pound devalued against the US dollar from $2.80 to $2.40.

1968 17 Jan: Escort launched, Halewood makes 500 a day.

Sir Patrick Hennessy retires.

1 Mar: Group 3 homologation agreed for Escort with Type 49 strong bodyshell.

Mar: Car Purchase Tax, raised to 33.3%, then (Nov) 36.66% petrol tax up.

March: Road tax up from £17.10s (£17.50) to £25. Petrol 6s 0d (30p) a gallon.

Mar: Group 6 F3L sports prototype announced

Apr: Launch of Escort van.

1 May: Escort Group 2 homologated.

Sep: John Wyer Mirage Gulf GT40s win Le

1968 Mans.

Oct: Cortina 1600E launched.

Nov: HP deposit 40%; 1,144,770 cars sold in Britain 102,276 imported.

Harry Ferguson Research builds 20 Zephyr police cars with four wheel drive.

Graham Hill world champion with Ford-Cosworth engine.

1969 Jan: launch of 26 variants of Capri "the car you've always promised yourself".

Jan: Cosworth develops 16-valve twin cam version of Kent engine.

May: Escort Super Estate launched.

May: MOT Test introduced for cars over three years old.

June: John Wyer Mirage Gulf GT40s win Le Mans. P1075 first car to win twice.

June: GT40 Mark III announced.

Oct: 4-door Escort announced.

Jackie Stewart world champion with Ford-Cosworth engine.

1970 Jan: Halewood makes first RS1600 Escort; production to Aveley October.

Ford Advanced Vehicle Operations (AVO) established at Aveley.

Aug: Cortina Mark III production starts.

H Mikkola, G Palm (Escort) win World Cup Rally to Mexico.

BP explores Forties Field for oil.

Advanced Vehicles Operation (AVO) builds RS1600 and Escort Mexico.

1970 Jochen Rindt world champion with Ford-Cosworth engine.

1971 Jan: GT70 proposed rally car announced.

Easter Mon: Thruxton, Transit Supervan with Eagle V8 of 320.7kW (430bhp).

July: Car Purchase Tax reduced from 36.6% to 30%.

Perkins diesels discontinued in Transit, diesels now Ford-made.

Production of Transit transfers to Southampton.

Oct: Escort Sport launched; millionth Escort made for William Young, Wigan.

Ford production hit by nine-week strike. Market share falls to 16% in first half.

Oct: Escort Sport announced.

Nov: 2.0-litre Capri Special announced.

Dec: Granada production starts Dagenham.

Jackie Stewart world champion with Ford-Cosworth engine.

1972 Feb-June: Cortina Mk III range rationalised. Granada goes on sale.

Metropolitan Police vote Transit Britain's Most Wanted; a perfect getaway van.

H Mikkola, G Palm (Escort) first non-Africans to win Safari Rally.

Car Purchase Tax reduced to 25%; UK industry produces record 1,971,311 cars.

May: Capri S Special GT and XLR 1.6, 2.0, 3.0 announced.

Transit diesel, three world records Monza

1972 10,000km (6214mls)120.4kph (75mph). 2.5-litre V6 option for Transit, also light artic and high capacity parcels van.
Sep: Estate versions of Consul 2.5 and Granada.
Emerson Fittipaldi world champion with Ford-Cosworth engine.
Nov: R Clark, T Mason (Escort RS1600) win RAC Rally.

1973 Jan: Ford standardises radial-ply tyres for all but cheapest fleet Escorts.
8 Jan: Ford takes minority holding in Ghia of Turin.
Mar: Escort 1300E made at Aveley
A-series light/medium commercials fill gap between Transit and D-series.
Arab oil embargo; 50mph (80.3kph) UK speed limit; fuel ration cards printed.
April: Purchase Tax ends, VAT + 10% Special Car Tax (almost) keeps status quo.
July: RS2000 announced from AVO.
Sep: Halewood's millionth Escort. Production of 1300E transferred.
Ford factory planned in Spain to make new front wheel drive car.
Oct: Mark I Escorts made with Mark II Escort floorpan; RS 2000 launched.
Nov: RS3100 Capri production starts at Halewood.
Nov: T Makinen, H Liddon (Escort RS1600) win RAC Rally.
Nov: Capri RS3100 enters touring car racing.

1973 Dec: Capri Mark II production; national three-day week response to strikes.
Jackie Stewart world champion with Ford-Cosworth engine; DFVs win every race.

1974 16 Jan: Granada Ghia, first European Ghia-badged production model.
Jan: Capri Mark II launched; L, XL, GT and Sports Custom Pack.
Mar: VAT on petrol; price rises from 42p a gallon to 74p a gallon by year's end.
Apr: Capri II Ghia 2000, 3000; French-built C3 automatic replaces BorgWarner.
April: Escort 1300E 4-door made for export.
May: Economy 50mph (80.26kph) limit rescinded.
Safety belts compulsory fitment.
July: Granada Ghia 2-dr Coupe announced; Consul 2000V4 replaced by ohc.
Design Council Award for Cortina Mark III.
Sep: Cortina Mk III 2000E Estate launched; Consul name dropped.
Nov: T Makinen, H Liddon (Escort RS1600) win RAC Rally.
2 Dec: Mark II Escort production starts. Emerson Fittipaldi world champion with Ford-Cosworth engine.

1975 Jan: Mark II Escort launched
24 Jan: Ford Advanced Vehicles Aveley closes, a victim of the oil crisis.
Mar: Capri Mark II S shown at Geneva; John Player Special livery option.

1975 Mar: launch of Mark II Escort van.
Apr: launch of Transcontinental truck.
June: Escort RS 1800 launched.
CRS, French riot police, buys fleet of Transit buses with steel mesh screens.
July: Escort Popular announced.
H-series Transcontinental trucks and chassis cabs 16-19tons; Cummins diesels.
1.6-litre Crossflow 4-cylinder replaces V4 in Transit; production passes 1million.
Sep: Capri S replaces GT.
Oct: Cortina Mark III facelift with black radiator and central console.
21 Oct: millionth Cortina Mark III made at Dagenham
Nov: T Makinen, H Liddon (Escort RS1600) win RAC Rally.

1976 Jan: Mark II Escort Mexico and RS2000 on sale.
Fiesta in production; UK inflation 24%; British Leyland goes into state ownership.
Feb: 2.0-litre economy Granada launch.
Compulsory seat belt wearing introduced for 1977.
July: Granada production transferred to Germany.
Sep: Cortina Mark IV launched.
Oct: Capri production in Germany.
Nov: R Clark, S Pegg (Escort RS1600) win RAC Rally.
Escort Britain's top-selling car with 133,959.
Dec: all Granada production moved to

1976 Germany.
James Hunt world champion with Ford-Cosworth engine.

1977 –1981 Cortina Britain's best-selling car; Ford best-selling tractor and truck maker.

1977 UK car imports 52%.
Jan: Ford Bordeaux C3 automatic replaces Borg Warner in Transit.
Inflation still 16%; car prices go up every 90 days or so.
Feb: Fiesta launched in Britain (produced in Spain 1976).
Jody Scheckter scores Ford DFV's 100th grand prix win at Monaco in Wolf-Ford.
Aug: Granada Mark II launched.
OPEC raises oil prices 10% in January, 5% in July; UK petrol 86p a gallon.
Sep: 2.3-litre V6 for Cortina GL, Ghia, and S; 1298cc engine added to Fiesta.
Nov: B Waldegaard, H Thorzelius (Escort RS) win RAC Rally.
Fiesta 3rd in Car of the Year behind Rover 3500 and Audi 100.

1978 Mar: Capri Mark III production starts in Cologne.
9 Mar:Major changes to Transit, redesigned suspension, new ohc engines.
Mar: Fiesta van launched.
Bridgend £180million plant opens, capacity 500,000 engines per year.
June: 75 year anniversary of Ford Motor

1978 Company; special Fiesta launched.
Escort facelift, RS Mexico dropped.
Oct: first Motor Show at NEC; Ford stand empty due to 8-week strike.
Nov: H Mikkola, A Hertz (Escort RS) win RAC Rally.
Mario Andretti world champion with Ford-Cosworth engine.
Granada 3rd in Car of the Year behind Porsche 928 and BMW 7-series.

1979 Jan: Dagenham produces its millionth Dorset Diesel engine.
Mar: millionth Fiesta; special edition of 3100.
OPEC raises oil price 9%, petrol £1 then £1.22 a gallon, second oil crisis.
Aug: Cortina modifications "Mark IV$\frac{1}{2}$" Cortina 80.
Nov: H Mikkola, A Hertz (Escort RS) win RAC Rally.
Bjorn Waldegard wins world rally drivers' championship with Ford.
Ford wins world manufacturers' rally championship with Hannu Mikkola.
Oil price effectively doubles in year $12 to $26 a barrel.

1980 1980 February Capri GT announced
Feb: inauguration of Special Vehicle Engineering under Rod Mansfield.
Mar: Philip Caldwell succeeds Henry Ford II as chairman.

1980 July: rear wheel drive Escorts cease production including RS2000.
Aug: Escort Mark III production begins at Halewood, Saarlouis and Valencia.
Sep: XR designation makes debut on the XR3 Escort.
Oct: Sam Toy appointed chairman in succession to Sir Terence Beckett.
Alan Jones world champion with Ford-Cosworth engine.

1981 Mar: Death of Sir Patrick Hennessy.
Mar: Launch of Cargo truck.
July: Capri 2.8i on sale.
LPG option available for Transit.
Special Vehicle Engineering set up at R&D department, Dunton.
Dec: Fiesta XR2 launched.
Nelson Piquet world champion with Ford-Cosworth engine.
Ari Vatanen wins world rally drivers' championship with Ford.
Escort RS1600i shown; Granada gets mid-life facelift; Probe III shown.
Escort Car of the Year ahead of Fiat Panda and Austin Metro.

1982 Feb: Henry Ford II appointed Honorary Knight of the British Empire.
May: Cortina Crusader announced.
May: seat belt wearing compulsory for 1983.
Sep: last Cortina, the 4,279,079th, leaves Dagenham production line.

1982 Oct: Cortina's replacement, the Sierra, goes on sale.
13 Oct: 2 millionth Escort built at Halewood.
Oct: Fiesta XR3i replaces XR3.
Keke Rosberg world champion with Ford-Cosworth engine.
– 1989 Escort best selling car in Britain.

1983 Jan: 2.8i Capri introduced.
May: new diesel engine previewed.
June: Sierra XR4i with biplane spoiler introduced.
July: Orion and Escort Cabriolet launched.
Fiesta facelifted; Escort cabriolet made by Karmann.
Sept: three-door Sierra introduced.
Escort sells 174,190, third highest ever.
Sierra 2nd in Car of the Year poll behind Audi 100.
Ford and Cosworth Engineering form partnership for grand prix engine.

1984 Mar: E-Max 1.6 Sierra announced.
Apr: Launch of Transit with industry's first direct-injection diesel engine.
Petrol increases in price to £1 a gallon; lead-free fuel promised for 1989.
Diamond white XR3i is four millionth car built at Halewood.
Dagenham-made diesel engine installed in Fiesta/Escort/Orion.
Sep: 6-year anti corrosion guarantee.
Oct: repairs lifetime guarantee.

1984 Oct: RS Turbo Escort announced.

1985 Jan: launch of Escort RS Turbo.
Feb: Donald Petersen elected chairman.
Mar: Sierra RS Cosworth announced as basis for Group A racing car.
Apr: Vehicle Excise Duty rises again to £100, petrol passes through £2 a gallon.
New Granada/Scorpio range introduced.
25 July: two millionth Transit made.
Supervan II with Cosworth V8 does 279.3kph (174mph).
Sierra 4x4 announced with ABS.
23 Oct: Ford celebrates 75th anniversary of UK manufacture.

1986 Jan: New Transit range introduced.
M25 completed; Ford fails in bids to buy Austin-Rover and also Alfa Romeo.
Escort and Orion facelifted.
Sierra 4x4 Estate announced.
July: Launch of Sierra RS Cosworth.
Fiat and Ford of Europe's truck divisions merge to form Iveco.
Scorpio Car of the Year ahead of Lancia Y10 and Mercedes-Benz 200.
Last Capri made just before Christmas; 1.9million sold since 1969.
Nov: Dagenham engine plant wins British quality award.

1987 Jan: Sierra Sapphire goes on sale.
Ford has 29% of UK market with 178,000

Escort, 153,000 Fiesta, 140,000 Sierra.
CVT transmission optional on Fiesta.
Sierra Cosworth RS500 wins World Touring Car Championship.
Oct: Ford acquires 75% of Aston Martin.
Sierra Cosworth RS500 wins British Touring Car Championship.
Second highest total of Escorts at 178,001; Orion at 69,262 is seventh best.

1988 Jan: Sierra RS Cosworth II announced.
Feb: British Design Award for Sierra Cosworth.
May: changes to 1.8 Sierra.
Dagenham makes the 2 millionth Sierra.
MT75 5-speed gearbox fitted in Sierra, Granada, Scorpio.
Death of Sir Rowland Smith, aged 100.
Sierra Cosworth RS500 wins 1988 European Touring Car Championship.
Sierra Cosworth RS500 wins British Touring Car Championship.
Aug: Death of Enzo Ferrari aged 90.
Small Ford diesel enlarged from 1608cc to 1753cc.

1989 Fiesta II announced.
Ford Cosworth DFX scores 151 Indycar wins since 1976.
Record Escort sales, 181,218.
New 2.0-litre twin cam 8-valve engine for Sierra, Granada, Scorpio
Introduction of 1600E Orion.

1989 Sierra Cosworth RS500 wins British Touring Car Championship.
Nov: Ford buys Jaguar for £1.6billion.
Car market 2,373,391; 1,370,589 imported cars includes Fords and Vauxhalls.

1990 Car market drops by 300,000.
Bill Hayden replaces John Egan as MD of Jaguar.
Fastest Fiesta, RS Turbo, announced.
Sierra gets final facelift, 1.8 Ford turbodiesel replaces Peugeot-made engine.
Sierra XR4x4 launched.
Sierra Cosworth RS500 wins British Touring Car Championship.
New Escort and Orion range launched following £1billion investment.
Scorpio 24-valve launched; 4-door non-hatch Scorpio goes on sale.
Fiesta 3rd in Car of the Year behind Citroen XM and Mercedes-Benz SL.

1991 Dagenham becomes one-car plant to build Fiesta.
Rear seat belt wearing made compulsory.
Airbags begin to be fitted.
Oct: Zeta engine previewed; name changed to Zetec after Lancia objects.
Escort RS2000 goes on sale.
Walter Hayes succeeds Victor Gauntlett as chairman of Aston Martin.

1992 Jan: Fiesta RS1800 and XR2i16v introduced;

1992 sales start March.
Mar: Special Car Tax (extra rate of VAT on cars) reduced from 10% to 5%.
Escort RS Cosworth on sale; fuel injection standard throughout Ford.
Zetec 16-valve engine fitted to Fiesta, Escort, and Orion; PAS standard.
Fiesta 16-valve RS1800 replaces RS Turbo.
Nov: Special Car Tax abolished; makes mid-range Escort £400 cheaper.

1993 Jan: catalytic converters compulsory; airbags standard or optional equipment.
Mar: Annual Vehicle Excise Duty (VED) goes up to £125.
Mondeo replaces Sierra.
Maverick, joint venture with Nissan, announced.
Paul Radisch (Mondeo) wins FIA Touring Car World Cup.
Nigel Mansell wins Indycar championship in Lola-Ford T3.
Orion becomes Escort saloon; prototype RS2000 4x4 revealed.
Improvements for Granada/Scorpio; V6 Cosworth engined top model.
Ayrton Senna wins 5 grands prix for McLaren-Ford.
François Delecour (Escort) wins World Rally Championship in Portugal.
Driver airbags standard on all Fords.
Nov: Another £5 on VED.
Nov: Alex Trotman becomes first Ford

1993 chairman born outside USA.

1994 XR designations discontinued.
US-made Probe Coupe goes on sale.
Ford acquires remaining 25% of Aston Martin.
Fiesta and Escort Si models gain 16-valve Zetec engine.
François Delecour (Escort) wins Monte Carlo Rally.
Michael Schumacher world champion with Ford-Cosworth engine.
Mondeo wins World Touring Car Championship.
Escort RS2000 4x4 on limited sale.
Mondeo 24v V6 introduced.
Paris Motor Show, Scorpio reconfigured.
Galaxy previewed.
Mondeo named Car of the Year from Citroen Xantia and Mercedes-Benz C-class.

1995 Escort's last year as best-selling car in UK; over 4 million made at Halewood.
Feb: Galaxy goes on sale.
Supervan III has Cosworth F1 of 484.7kW (650bhp).
Sep: revised Fiesta on sale with new Zetec 16v.
Last Escort RS Cosworths and RS2000; Escort 4x4 revised.
Explorer replaces Maverick.
Dagenham builds its 28 millionth engine

1996 Saetta concept car at Geneva.
Ka announced.
Fiesta 1.3, 16v, and 1.8 diesel introduced.
Mondeo revised.
Scorpio 2.3 16v and diesel introduced.
Oct: 250 millionth Ford, a Fiesta, is
Dagenham's 10 millionth since 1931.
Jan: Ford and Jackie Stewart make five-year
agreement for grand prix team.

1997 Escort new engine programme
Ka 2nd in Car of the Year behind Renault
Megane.

1998 Puma 16v introduced.
Cougar introduced.
Focus range 1.4,1.6,1.8, 2.0 turbodiesel
launched.
All European Escort production moves to
Halewood.
Sep: Ford acquires Cosworth Racing; CR-2
for Jaguar F1, XF for CART.
Sep: Dagenham engine plant produces its
30 millionth engine
Nov: Ford Focus Car of the Year.

1999 Jan: Alex Trotman, chairman and CEO
retires.
William Clay Ford Jr is chairman, Jacques
Nasser president and CEO.
Jan: Ford buys Volvo for $6.45 billion.
Mar: Premier Automotive Group Jaguar,
Volvo, Aston Martin, Lincoln Mercury.

1999 Apr: Dagenham builds its 4 millionth 1.6/
1.8-litre diesel engine
Apr: Ford Motor Company buys Kwik-Fit
for $1.6 billion.
Fiesta Endura-E; Fiesta diesel introduced.
Johnny Herbert wins European Grand Prix
with Stewart Ford V10 CR-1.
Focus estate introduced.
Focus voted Car of the Year.
Dec: international motor journalist jury elects
Model T Car of the Century.

2000 Mar: Ford announces purchase of Land
Rover from BMW Group.
June: Ghia StreetKa Spider Concept at Turin
Motor Show.
21 July: Ford of Europe chairman Nick
Scheele drives last Escort off line.
Halewood made 5,202,412 Escorts, 1 million
Anglias, Capris, and Corsairs.
Halewood turned over to Jaguar production.
Galaxy revised.
New Transit launched.
Mondeo revised.
Sept: Transit range extended.
Oct: StreetKa Concept in UK
Ford Team Mondeo wins manufacturers'
British Touring Car Championship.
Alain Menu (Mondeo) wins driver's BTCC
from team-mates Reid and Rydell.
Ford's 500th BTCC win, Menu at Oulton
Park.

2001 Feb: Ford announces Pininfarina to produce
the Streetka.
Maverick introduced.
Ford 25 years Britain's best-selling make, 36
and 23 years best in commercials.

2002 Mar: Streetka sponsors Kylie Minogue's
European 'Fever' Tour.
Mar: Fiesta 5-door on sale.
RS Focus announced.
Fusion at Geneva Salon.
Transit Connect announced.
GT40 reintroduced.
Mondeo ST220 launched.
Sep: Streetka at Paris Motor Show.
Ian McAllister CBE retires as chairman and
managing director Ford of Britain.
Roger Putnam succeeds as chairman, Ford
of Britain.

2003 Streetka first small Ford roadster, first Ford
with Pininfarina, first Ford built in Italy.

Bibliography

The Motoring Encyclopedia and The New Motoring Encyclopedia, Amalgamated Press Fleetway, 1936 and 1938

Ford at War, Hilary St George Saunders, Ford Motor Co Ltd, 1947

The Lotus 49, David Hodges, Lionel Leventhal, 1970

The Ford GT40, David Hodges, Lionel Leventhal, 1970

The Encyclopaedia of Motor Sport, Rainbird, 1971

Military Wheeled Vehicles, Olyslager, Ward Lock 1972

British Cars series, Olyslager , Warne 1973

Let's Call it Fiesta, Edouard Seidler, Edita SA & Patrick Stephens 1976

V8, Michael Frostick, Dalton Watson 1979

Illustrated Encyclopedia of Military Vehicles, Ian Hogg, John Weeks, Hamlyn Quarto 1980

Capri, Jeremy Walton, Foulis 1981

A-Z of Cars 5 vols 1920s-1980s, Sedgwick, Gillies, Robson, Baldwin, Lewis, Bay View Books

Ford Popular, Dave Turner, Osprey 1984

Ford & Fordson Tractors, Michael Williams, Blandford Press 1985

British Family Cars of the Fifties, Michael Allen, Haynes, 1987

Ford, Robert Lacey, William Heinemann 1986

Ford File, Graham Robson, Temple Press 1987

Ford Vans, Trucks, and PSVs, Michael Allen, Les Geary, Foulis, 1988

British Family Cars of the Sixties, Michael Allen, Haynes, 1989

Henry, Walter Hayes, Weidenfeld & Nicholson 1990

Consul Zephyr Zodiac Executive Fords, Michael Allen, Motor Racing Publications 1990

Complete Catalogue of Ford Cars, David Burgess-Wise, Bay View Books 1991

Mondeo, World Publishing & Publicity SA 1992

World War Two Military Vehicles, G N Georgano, Osprey 1994

The Cosworth Fords, Jeremy Walton, PSL Haynes 1994

Ford Transit to 1986, Ed. Trevor Alder, Transport Source Books 1995

Ford's Kent Crossflow Engine, Peter & Valerie Wallage, Haynes 1995

Cars in the UK, Vols 1 & 2, Graham Robson, Motor Racing Publications 1997

Ford Chronicle, Flamming, Lewis, Consumer Guide 1997

A-Z of British Coachbuilders, Nick Walker, Bay View Books 1997

Cortina, The Story of Ford's Best-Seller, Graham Robson, Veloce 1998

Fordson Tractors, Robert N Pripps, Motorbooks International

Lotus 49, Michael Oliver Veloce 1999

Catalogue of British Cars, Culshaw & Horrobin, Veloce 1999

The Model T Ford, Jonathan Wood, Shire, 1999

The Beaulieu Encyclopædia of the Automobile, The Stationery Office 2000

Ford Model Y, Sam Roberts, Veloce 2001

Ford in Touring Car Racing, Graham Robson, Haynes, 2001.

Among the sources used in research were the author's archive collections of the annuals Automobil Revue/Revue Automobile published by BTM AG Bern, Automobile Year published by Editions J-R Piccard, Autocourse published by Hazleton, The Motor Year Books, Temple Press 1949-1957, Ford Motor Company press books, statements, reprints, and other material, and also of The Motor, The Autocar, Autosport, Automotive News Europe, Motor Sport, Classic Car, Classic Car Profiles, Classic & Sportscar, The Automobile, On Four Wheels, Automobile Quarterly, and Veteran & Vintage, to all of whose contributors and proprietors motoring historians owe continuing thanks.

Acknowledgments

The publishers thank Michael Callaghan and Daniel Ward, successive Executive Directors Communications and Public Affairs at Ford of Britain and their staff, in particular John Gardiner and Tom Malcolm for their help in making this book possible. Our thanks are also due to Ford Chairman Roger Putnam, a friend since his days at Lotus Cars, for his generous foreword. The author and publisher have many generations of public relations officials of Ford, including Syd Wheelhouse, Harry Calton, John Southgate and the late Walter Hayes, to thank for making available for test every Ford model since the 1950s. Our thanks also go to Alastair Smith AMA FSA Scot, formerly of the Museum of Transport, Glasgow, Trevor Cockburn, and Gordon Brennan for information on flathead V8s, Andy Anderson of Anderson Project Management Ltd for information on the GT70 restoration. Ford dealers down the years have had a great gift for public relations, from the late Jimmy Nicholson of Hamilton who entrusted the author with his spanking new Mark I Zodiac, to the late Morris Smellie of Braedale Garage, Motherwell whose 105E Anglias he drove in the 1950s, and Skelly's of Motherwell whose cars he drove in the 1960s. In the 21st century our local dealer Jim Duncan of Rothesay gave practical help with research into vintage tractors. Thanks also go to the library service in Rothesay for finding obscure books on Ford, including Hilary St George Saunders's invaluable Ford at War. As with other books in the File series, our thanks go to David Fletcher of the Tank Museum at Bovingdon for his prompt, courteous, and unfailingly accurate information on obscure military matters, and Caroline Johnson, library administrator at the National Motor Museum, Beaulieu, Hants.

Ford is well documented, yet the quest for accuracy remained challenging. Wide consultations were made to try and get things right, and the publisher is grateful to many people inside and outside Ford for help and encouragement to correct errors. In a work of some 120,000 words and countless items of information even 99.9% accuracy leaves room for 120 mistakes. Specialists in one make or model may spot them. To try and ensure that succeeding editions are as accurate as we can make them please let us know of any anomalies. This applies to facts, not matters of opinion, which remain our own. Fran Chamberlain and John Fowler of Ford Photographic were supportive in our quest for photographs. As with all Dove Publishing books, thanks are due to production consultant David Bann of Landmark, and Andrew Barron of Thextension, Little Critt, Benenden, Kent for the jacket design and patient support. Ashley Beeson BSc produced the computer program responsible for all the conversions in the specification tables. Book creation, typesetting, and production were by Ruth Dymock.

Index